The Sepulchre of Christ
and the
Medieval West

The Sepulchre of Christ and the Medieval West

From the Beginning to 1600

COLIN MORRIS

OXFORD
UNIVERSITY PRESS

OXFORD
UNIVERSITY PRESS

Great Clarendon Street, Oxford OX2 6DP

Oxford University Press is a department of the University of Oxford.
It furthers the University's objective of excellence in research, scholarship,
and education by publishing worldwide in

Oxford New York

Auckland Cape Town Dar es Salaam Hong Kong Karachi
Kuala Lumpur Madrid Melbourne Mexico City Nairobi
New Delhi Shanghai Taipei Toronto

With offices in

Argentina Austria Brazil Chile Czech Republic France Greece
Guatemala Hungary Italy Japan South Korea Poland Portugal
Singapore Switzerland Thailand Turkey Ukraine Vietnam

Oxford is a registered trade mark of Oxford University Press
in the UK and in certain other countries

Published in the United States
by Oxford University Press Inc., New York

First published 2005

British Library Cataloguing in Publication Data
Data available

Library of Congress Cataloging in Publication Data
Morris, Colin, 1928–
The sepulchre of Christ and the medieval West:
from the beginning to 1600 / Colin Morris.
p. cm.
Includes bibliographical references (p.   ) and index.
1. Holy Sepulcher—History.   2. Middle Ages—History.   I. Title.
BV196.H7M67 2005
232.96′4—dc22   2004027967
ISBN 0–19–826928–5 (alk. paper)
EAN 978 0–19–826928–1

1 3 5 7 9 10 8 6 4 2

Typeset by RefineCatch Limited, Bungay, Suffolk
Printed in Great Britain by
Biddles Ltd., King's Lynn

We shall enter into his sanctuary;
We shall worship in the place where his feet have stood.

> (Psalm 132: 7, Vulgate)

His sepulchre shall be glorious.

> (Isaiah 11: 10, Vulgate)

Jerusalem is to us as it is to you. It is even more important for us, since it is the site of our Prophet's night journey and the place where the people will gather on the day of judgment. Do not imagine therefore that we can waver in this regard.

> (Saladin to Richard I, 1192)

Christians, Jews and also heathen
Claim this heritage as theirs.
May God make the right to triumph
By the threefold name he bears.
All the world comes here to fight;
But to us belongs the right.
God defend us by his might!

> (Walther von der Vogelweide,
> *Palästinalied*, about 1228)

Preface

A GENERAL study of this kind depends on a huge amount of previous work, and the only means of expressing indebtedness is through a substantial bibliography. I owe many other debts of gratitude: to the Trustees of the Leverhulme Foundation for a generous grant for travel and research, and to the Roger Anstey Foundation at Canterbury University, Kent, for encouraging my research in the later Middle Ages. Similarly I am grateful to the staff of my favourite libraries, the Bodleian at Oxford and the Hartley at Southampton, for their expert and good-tempered advice in solving a variety of bibliographical problems. The Ecclesiastical History Society has often provided a lively forum for the exploration of the ideas expressed herein. I have benefited from discussions with many colleagues, including the late Professor Tim Reuter and Dr Ernest Blake (both outstanding and much-lamented representatives of Anglo-German scholarship), Professor Martin Biddle, Dr G. S. P. Freeman-Grenville, Dr Jonathan Phillips, Professor Norman Housley, Dr David Hunt, and Dr Simon Ditchfield. The subject has become something of a family enterprise: my wife, Dr Brenda Morris, supported the venture in innumerable ways, and my grandson, Marc Morris, has been active in finding imitations of the Holy Sepulchre on his holidays. To all these, and many others, I am much indebted. The infelicities are mine alone.

In the layout of this book, I have confined footnotes strictly to references to the source of statements or quotations in the text. Subjects that required specific examination, such as the character of some of the memorials of the Sepulchre, have been considered in separate insets, which also include mentions of the relevant literature.

C.M.

Southampton

Contents

List of Figures

List of Abbreviations

Crociate	M. Rey-Delqué (ed.), *Le Crociate: l'Oriente e l'Occidente da Urbano II a san Luigi* (Milan, 1997)
Crusade and Settlement	P. W. Edbury (ed.), *Crusade and Settlement: Papers . . . presented to R. C. Smail* (Cardiff, 1985)
Crusaders and Muslims	M. Shatzmiller (ed.), *Crusaders and Muslims in Twelfth-Century Syria* (Leiden, 1993)
Crusades and Sources	J. France and W. G. Zajac (eds.), *The Crusades and their Sources: Essays Presented to Bernard Hamilton* (Aldershot, 1998)
CSEL	Corpus Scriptorum Ecclesiasticorum Latinorum
Dei gesta per Francos	M. Balard and others (eds.), *Dei gesta per Francos: Études sur les croisades dédiées à Jean Richard* (Aldershot, 2001)
De Sion	Y. Hen (ed.), *De Sion exibit lex et verbum Domini de Hierusalem: Essays in Honour of Amnon Linder* (Turnhout, 2001)
DOP	*Dumbarton Oaks Papers*
EHR	*English Historical Review*
Felix Fabri	A. Stewart (tr.), *The Wanderings of Brother Felix Fabri*, PPTS 7–10 (London, 1887–97)
Francesco Suriano	T. Bellorini and E. Hoade (trs.), *Francesco Suriano, Treatise on the Holy Land* (Jerusalem, 1949)
Fremdheit und Reisen	I. Erfen and K.-H. Spiess (eds.), *Fremdheit und Reisen im Mittelalter* (Stuttgart, 1997)
Ganz-Blättler	U. Ganz-Blättler, *Andacht und Abenteuer: Berichte europäischer Jerusalem- und Santiago-Pilger, 1320–1520* (Tübingen, 1990)
Gauthier	M. M. Gauthier, *Highways of the Faith: Relics and Reliquaries from Jerusalem to Compostela* (Secaucus, NJ, 1983)

Gomez-Géraud	M.-C. Gomez-Géraud, *Le Crépuscule du Grand Voyage: les récits des pèlerins a Jérusalem, 1458–1612* (Paris, 1999)
Hans Roth	V. Honemann, 'Der Bericht des Hans Roth über seine Pilgerfahrt ins Heilige Land im Jahre 1440', D. Huschenbert and others (eds.), *Reisen und Welterfahrung in der deutschen Literatur des Mittelalters* (Würzburg, 1991), 306–26
Horns of Hattin	B. Z. Kedar (ed.), *The Horns of Hattin* (London, 1992)
Image of Christ	G. Finaldi, *The Image of Christ* (London, 2000)
Itineraria	*Itineraria et alia geographica*, ed. P. Geyer, R. Weber, and others, CCSL 175–6 (Turnhout, 1965)
Itinerarium Peregrinorum	H. J. Nicholson (tr.), *Chronicle of the Third Crusade: A Translation of the* Itinerarium Peregrinorum (Aldershot, 1997)
JEH	*Journal of Ecclesiastical History*
Jensen, *Early Art*	R. M. Jensen, *Understanding Early Christian Art* (London, 2000)
JerKonflikte	D. Bauer and others (eds.), *Jerusalem im Hoch- und Spät-mittelalter: Konflikte und Konfliktebewältigungen* (Frankfurt, 2000)
Jérusalem, Rome	*Jérusalem, Rome, Constantinople: l'image et le mythe de la ville au Moyen Âge* (Paris, 1986).
JMH	*Journal of Medieval History*
Journeys towards God	B. N. Sargent-Baur (ed.), *Journeys towards God* (Kalamazoo, 1992)
JWCI	*Journal of the Warburg and Courtauld Institutes*
Kreuzzugsbriefe	H. Hagenmeyer (ed.), *Epistulae et chartae ad historiam primi belli sacri spectantes: die Kreuzzugzbriefe aus den Jahren 1088–1100* (Innsbruck, 1901).
Levine	L. I. Levine (ed.), *Jerusalem: Its Sanctity*

	and Centrality to Judaism, Christianity and Islam (New York, 1999)
Mariano da Siena	P. Picirillo (ed.), *Mariano da Siena: Viaggio fatto al Santo Sepolcro* (Pisa, 1996)
Meeting of Two Worlds	V. P. Goss (ed.), *The Meeting of Two Worlds: Cultural Exchange between East and West during the Period of the Crusades* (Kalamazoo, 1986)
MGH	Monumenta Germaniae Historica
MGH SS	Monumenta Germaniae Historica Scriptores
Möbius, *Passion*	H. Möbius, *Passion und Auferstehung* (Vienna, 1978)
Montjoie	B. Z. Kedar (ed.), *Montjoie: Studies in Crusading History in Honour of H. E. Mayer* (Aldershot, 1997)
Neri	D. Neri, *Il Santo Sepolcro riprodotto in Occidente* (Jerusalem, 1971)
Niccolò of Poggibonsi	T. Bellorini and E. Hoade (trs.), *Fra Niccolò of Poggibonsi: A Voyage beyond the Seas* (Jerusalem, 1945)
Omnes Circumadstantes	C. Caspers and M. Schneiders (eds.), *Omnes Circumadstantes: Contributions towards a History of the Role of the People in the Liturgy Presented to Herman Wegman* (Kampen, 1990)
Ottoman Jerusalem	S. Auld and R. Hillenbrand (eds.), *Ottoman Jerusalem: The Living City, 1517–1917* (Jerusalem, 2000)
Outremer	B. Z. Kedar (ed.), *Outremer: Studies in the History of the Crusading Kingdom of Jerusalem Presented to Joshua Prawer* (Jerusalem, 1982)
Patterns of the Past	T. Hummel and others (eds.), *Patterns of the Past, Prospects for the Future: The Christian Heritage in the Holy Land* (London, 1999)
PEQ	*Palestine Exploration Quarterly*
Pero Tafur	M. Letts (tr.), *Pero Tafur: Travels and Adventures 1435–9* (London, 1926)

PG	Migne, *Patrologia Graeca*
Pietro Casola	M. M. Newett (tr.), *Canon Pietro Casola's Pilgrimage to Jerusalem in the Year 1494* (Manchester, 1907)
Pilgrimage Explored	J. Stopford (ed.), *Pilgrimage Explored* (Woodbridge, 1999)
Pilgrimage: The English Experience	C. Morris and P. Roberts (eds.), *Pilgrimage: The English Experience from Becket to Bunyan* (Cambridge, 2002)
PL	Migne, *Patrologia Latina*
PPTS	Palestine Pilgrims Text Society, 12 vols., repr. (New York, 1971)
Raymond, *Liber*	J. H. and L. L. Hill (eds.), *Le «Liber» de Raymond d'Aguilers* (Paris, 1969)
RB	*Revue Bénédictine*
Real and Ideal Jerusalem	*The Real and Ideal Jerusalem in Jewish, Christian and Islamic Art: Studies in Honor of B. Narkiss*, ed. B Kühnel, *Jewish Art*, 23/4 (1997/8)
RHC Occ.	Recueil des Historiens des Croisades, Historiens Occidentaux
ROL	*Revue de l'Orient Latin*
RS	Rolls Series
Santiago, Roma, Jerusalén	III Congreso Internacional de Estudios Jacobeos (Xunta de Galicia, 1999)
SC	Sources Chrétiennes (Paris)
SCH	Studies in Church History
Supplice	R. Favreau (ed.), *Le Supplice et la gloire: la croix en Poitou* (Poitiers, 2000)
Thiede	C. P. Thiede and M. D'Ancona, *The Quest for the True Cross* (London, 2000)
TRHS	*Transactions of the Royal Historical Society*
Tyerman, *England*	C. Tyerman, *England and the Crusades* (London, 1988)
VuF	Vorträge und Forschungen
Wallfahrt	L. Kriss-Rettenbach and G. Möhler (eds.), *Wallfahrt kennt keine Grenzen* (Munich, 1984)

Wilkinson/Hakluyt	J. Wilkinson and others (eds.), *Jerusalem Pilgrimage, 1099–1185*, Hakluyt Society, ser. 2. 167 (London, 1988)
Wilkinson, *Pilgrims*	J. Wilkinson, *Jerusalem Pilgrims before the Crusades*, 2nd edn. (Warminster, 2002)
Zs.	*Zeitschrift*

Introduction

THE original starting-point of my interest in this subject was the proclamation of the First Crusade at the Council of Clermont in 1095. While historians have disagreed about the intentions of Pope Urban II, it has been generally accepted that Westerners were deeply concerned with the fate of Jerusalem. To see its recovery for Christian rule as Urban's primary purpose is the simplest interpretation of the evidence, but other writers have concluded that the taking of Jerusalem was a distortion introduced by the imperative demands of Western opinion, which distorted a project originally designed for the protection of Constantinople. Such explanations take it as an axiom that Latin Christians were deeply concerned about the fate of the city in Palestine, but this concern itself requires explanation. There were good historical reasons why the faithful might have regarded the fate of the city with indifference. Palestine was a very little country and a long way away–a very long way indeed for medieval land travellers. In the long run it proved impossible to sustain a successful military effort in such a distant place. More profoundly, Christianity was a universal religion with at first a limited attachment to holy places, and the Jerusalem of the Old Testament had been completely destroyed and replaced by a Roman city. Christian propaganda saw this as a condemnation of its role in the crucifixion of the Saviour. It has been said by a recent scholar writing from a Protestant viewpoint that in the history of the church as a whole, interest in Jerusalem 'was the exception rather than the rule'. The Western concern for the Holy Sepulchre and its effect on European history and society alike require examination.

Historians of the church have not often investigated this subject: it is remarkable how little the tomb of Christ is mentioned in general histories. That is partly because it has largely disappeared from our contemporary culture. In spite of the importance of the historical Jerusalem in modern archaeology, tourism, and politics, there is not much awareness of it in Christian devotion. Westerners barely remember that there is a (diminishing) Christian community in Palestine. The hymn books contain plenty on the heavenly Jerusalem, on pilgrimage, and on spiritual warfare, but I have searched them in vain for material on the city in Palestine similar to that which fed the medieval imagination. The same is true in scholarly circles: commentaries on the Gospels rarely use the topography of Jerusalem to elucidate the events of the passion. Saint Paul may have proudly claimed that 'this thing was not done in a corner' (Acts 26: 26), but to judge by the way some people have written, one would think that it had happened on the moon.

Enthusiasts of pilgrimage literature may notice that I have made little use of concepts that are now common currency, such as the idea of 'sacred space' and the vocabulary that is sometimes associated with it ('liminality'). This is because they express our contemporary concerns rather than those of the past. They belong to a world which is interested in comparative religion and in ideas of holiness which are found in different cultures. They also reflect the prevailing modern scepticism about shrines. Modern Western people do not on the whole believe in the power of relics or the benefit to be derived from indulgences, and as a result our thinking about the subject is often concentrated on the nature of the pilgrimage journey itself and the self-awareness it induces. Undoubtedly past writers were interested in what it was like to travel, and we shall find many examples of that. But their primary concern was with the place or shrine to which they were travelling. There is nothing wrong with exploring wider boundaries of thought, but this book has a more limited goal: to understand the ideas of past generations, and the way they shaped the society of the time.

That still leaves us with more than enough to do. By its nature the Holy Sepulchre cannot be isolated from the rest of Christian culture. A few yards away, the place of the crucifixion was identified on the hill of Calvary and the relics of the cross were allegedly found. It is not possible to discuss the significance of the Sepulchre without including the cult of the cross and the veneration of its relics. In consequence, in order to avoid writing a total history of Christendom, I have exercised self-denial, although the reluctant reader might not suppose so. There is more to say about the extent to which the Holy Sepulchre was the target of the various crusades than is said here; and I have been selective in the choice of memorials of the Sepulchre, many of which present teasing problems of intention and dating. Palestinian and Egyptian monasticism were shaped by the proximity of the holy places, and their influence on religious life in the West was great, but this is a subject not pursued in this book. Nor have I considered in detail the impact on cartography of the idea that the Sepulchre was the *compas* or centre of the earth, nor yet the crucial position of the Jerusalem events in the development of drama in the late Middle Ages. There are problems, too, about writing in a post-Christian age. One is the recurrent question of authenticity: although I have briefly considered the credentials of the Holy Sepulchre itself, I have not challenged the reality of the numerous relics that will scatter the coming pages. From the point of view of the historian what matters is that contemporaries believed in most of them: critics and cynics existed, but they were not enough to prevent the emergence of numerous shrines and pilgrimage centres. It is difficult, too, to make allowance for writing in a multicultural society. With some exceptions the attitude of medieval Christendom to Muslims and Jews was intensely hostile. I have made some attempt to explain the importance of the Holy City, al-Quds, to the Muslims who were fighting to defend and recover it, but the total question of religious intolerance and misjudgement is far too large to approach here. Another major limitation of a different kind has been the decision to stop this history in the sixteenth century. There was a break at this time in the desire to visit and defend the Sepulchre. The holy places at Jerusalem, after an interval, were once again to become a major political and cultural influence on world history; but the circumstances are different, and one has to stop somewhere.

The shape of the discussion will inevitably follow the progress of scholarship. Archaeological work in the church of the Holy Sepulchre has now given us a much better idea of its history, culminating in Martin Biddle's essential work on the structure of the Sepulchre itself. There has been new thinking about the emergence of the reverence for holy places in the fourth-century church. The last generation has also seen an immense amount of work on the crusades, and on the development of the veneration of the cross and the form of the crucifix. Pilgrimage in general has been abundantly studied. The changing ways in which the Sepulchre was represented in Western art, on the other hand, have been given less attention, in spite of some normative articles, and so has the diminishing importance of the resurrection of Christ in the accepted pattern of devotion. Whatever the precise significance attached to them, memorials of the cross and Sepulchre can be found all over Europe. The traditional culture of the English church was disrupted at the Reformation, but in many medieval buildings one can trace signs of what was originally the Easter Sepulchre, and in almost all churches on Easter Sunday an Easter garden, with the hill of Golgotha, the three crosses and the empty tomb are depicted in a pleasing model.

The Golgotha events, the passion, entombment, and resurrection, left a mark on the buildings and social arrangements on communities far from Jerusalem. The small town of Rue in Picardy still preserves in its layout the recollection of its earlier importance. It was once a significant port, but its harbour disappeared with the silting of the coast. Memories of Jerusalem have marked this moderate-sized town at the opposite end of Europe. The connection was established at an early date when the parish priest, Wulphy, went on pilgrimage to the Sepulchre of Christ. On his return, he lived as a hermit until his death about 630, and the parish church is now dedicated to his memory. That was not all. In 1101, shortly after the crusaders' conquest of Jerusalem, a ruined boat was discovered in the harbour, containing a statue of Christ (or was it a complete crucifix? the accounts are uncertain). The find was later improved by the legend that the image had been placed in a boat without sail or rudder in Palestine, and had found its own way to Picardy. The story dictated the ecclesiastical architecture of the town. In the middle years of the fifteenth century a magnificent chapel of the Holy Spirit was built in flamboyant style on the north side of the parish church through the generosity of King Louis XI of France. It was designed to admit the streams of pilgrims to adore the miraculous crucifix, whose story was depicted on its doors. The parish church collapsed in 1798 and was rebuilt on a smaller scale, leaving a gap between the church and its former side-chapel, but the church still has a nineteenth-century Gothic reliquary containing fragments of the statue of Christ. There is also a large wooden cross beside the old harbour, commemorating the place where the boat was found, and marked on the town map as 'Croix de Jérusalem'. The Sepulchre and the cross shaped the history of this small port in Picardy.

We do not know for certain where the tomb of Christ was. We can be sure only that it was at Jerusalem, outside the wall which surrounded the city at the time when Pontius Pilate was governor. When, immediately after 325, excavations were undertaken at the command of the Emperor Constantine, a cave that they revealed in the outskirts of Jerusalem was at once identified as the tomb of Jesus of Nazareth. For more than 1600 years, this identification has been accepted by most Christians, and in this volume (although we shall take note of questions about authenticity) this tomb will simply be called the Holy Sepulchre.

The enormous influence of this place is to be explained by the Christian desire to remember the saving acts of God in Christ. Jacques Le Goff has even said that 'Christianity is memory'. Memory, *memoria*, could have a much more material form than it has for us: objectively the Sepulchre at Jerusalem, or a relic from it, or a picture or copy of it, was a 'memory' that people could visit on pilgrimage or carry with them on their persons. For Muslims to have possession of the Sepulchre of Christ was in itself a defilement in Christian eyes, which carried with it the danger that the church would lose its 'memory'. These attitudes do not form a necessary part of Christian belief: they were seriously different in the Greek churches, and perhaps at no time were they universally held. They were, however, dominant in the medieval West, which was to play such a large part in the future shaping of the world. The purpose of this book is to examine how this attitude to the Holy Sepulchre arose, and what its cultural and historical consequences have been.

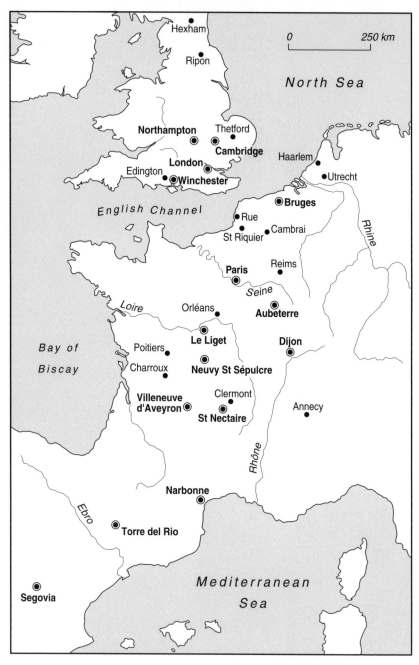

Western Europe, with important centres of Holy Sepulchre devotion.
Places in bold still have surviving remains of the cult.

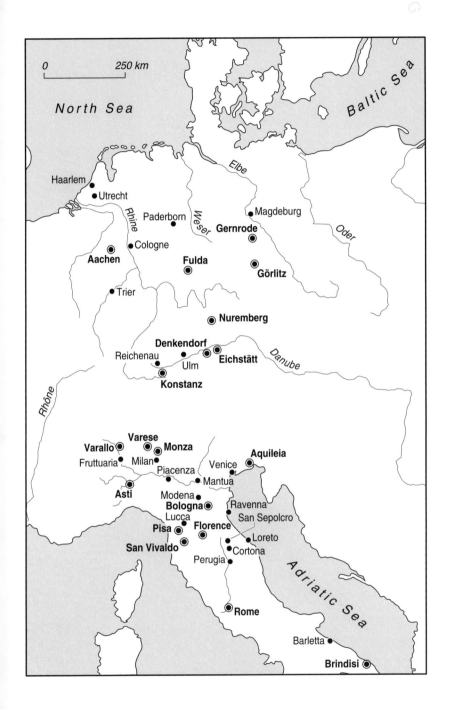

North Sea

Baltic Sea

0   250 km

Haarlem
● Utrecht
Paderborn
Weser
Elbe
● Magdeburg
Gernrode
◉
Rhine
● Cologne
Aachen
◉
Fulda
◉
Görlitz
◉
Oder
● Trier

◉ **Nuremberg**

Denkendorf
Reichenau ●
Ulm
◉ **Eichstätt**
Danube
◉
Konstanz

Rhône

Varese
◉
Varallo ◉
◉ **Monza**
Aquileia
◉
Fruttuaria ● Milan ●
Venice
●
Piacenza ●
● Mantua
Asti
◉
Modena ●
Bologna ◉
Ravenna ●
San Sepolcro
Lucca ●
Pisa ◉
Florence ◉
● Loreto
San Vivaldo ◉
● Cortona
Perugia ●

Adriatic Sea

◉ **Rome**

Barletta ●

Brindisi ◉

I

Beginnings, to 325

THE MINISTRY AND DEATH OF CHRIST

The Gospels leave us with a disputed picture of the presence in Jerusalem of Jesus of Nazareth. Mark, Matthew, and Luke do not define the length of his public preaching ministry: the three years traditionally assigned to it rest on a precarious deduction from the text of John. The natural meaning of the text of the first three Gospels is that the ceremonial entry by Jesus into the city a few days before the crucifixion was his first public appearance there. Luke in particular presented the decision to go to Jerusalem as a major turning-point in the life of Jesus: 'when the days drew near for him to be received up, he set his face to go to Jerusalem' (Luke 9: 51). In John's Gospel, several earlier visits are mentioned, and a more careful examination of the other Gospels tends to confirm the presence of Jesus in Jerusalem on a number of occasions. The repeated disputes with scribes, lawyers, and Pharisees can be located more naturally there than in Jesus' homeland of Galilee, and the anxiety of the authorities about his preaching is easier to understand if he already had a following that welcomed him when he made his solemn entry. The writers of the Gospels were not inclined to make much of the Jerusalem ministry of Jesus, but stress the importance of the period of a few days during which he entered the city, engaged in controversy in the Temple, was arrested, tried, executed, and buried. They saw the tomb as the memorial of a short visit and brutal reaction by the authorities.[1]

The earliest description which we have of the tomb of Jesus is that by St Mark, written probably about AD, 70 some forty years after the events that it describes:

[1] The evidence is succinctly set out by J. M. O'Connor, 'Pre-Constantinian Christian Jerusalem', A. O'Mahony (ed.), *The Christian Heritage in the Holy Land* (London, 1995), 13–21.

And when evening had come, since it was the day of the preparation, that is the day before the sabbath, Joseph of Arimathea, a respected member of the council ... took courage and went to Pilate, and asked for the body of Jesus ... And when he learned from the centurion that he was dead, he granted the body to Joseph. And he bought a linen shroud ... and laid him in a tomb which had been hewn out of the rock; and he rolled a stone against the door of the tomb. Mary Magdalene and Mary the mother of Joses saw where he was laid. And when the sabbath was past, Mary Magdalene, and Mary the mother of James, and Salome, bought spices, so that they might go and anoint him. And very early on the first day of the week they went to the tomb when the sun had risen. And they were saying to one another, 'Who will roll away the stone for us from the door of the tomb?' And looking up, they saw that the stone was rolled back—it was very large. And entering the tomb, they saw a young man sitting on the right side, dressed in a white robe; and they were amazed. And he said to them, 'do not be amazed; you seek Jesus of Nazareth, who was crucified. He has risen, he is not here; see the place where they laid him.'   (Mark 15: 42–16: 6)

Mark was writing in Greek for a church that had many contacts with the Gentile world, but his description fits closely into the tomb-culture of Judaea. As Martin Biddle has emphasized, 'the kind of tomb suggested by the Gospel accounts is consistent with what is now known of contemporary practice in the Jerusalem area'. It appears that the tomb used for the body of Jesus was a new one (Matthew 27: 60; Luke 23: 53; John 19: 41), and we can safely imagine a cave entrance, protected by a rough stone. The interior would have some sort of antechamber, and the tomb proper have a burial bench (or benches?). Such a layout would fit Mark's report that the women were invited to look into the tomb to see the empty burial-place. His is not an imaginary reconstruction created in a foreign context. Nor is there any reason to suppose that the penalty of crucifixion would exclude a solemn burial afterwards: we know of the ossuary of a certain Yehohanan, whose remains show clear signs of death by crucifixion some time in the first century.[2]

Nobody tells us where the tomb was. It must have been outside the city wall. Burial inside a classical or Jewish city was inconceivable: Cicero had recalled the legal prohibition, 'do not bury or cremate a dead man in a city'. If the first Christian writers did not usually say that it was outside the wall, that was because no other possibility would have occurred to them. There is a confirmatory hint in the

---

[2] J. Zias and E. Sekeles, 'The Crucified Man from Giv'at ha-Mivtar: A Reappraisal', *Israel Exploration Journal*, 35 (1985), 22–7.

Palestinian Tomb Culture

Very large numbers of tombs survive at Jerusalem and in the highlands of Judaea. They are difficult to date, but they give us a clear picture of the prevailing customs of burial. Ordinary people received simple burials. At Beit Safafa, outside Jerusalem, bodies were placed at the bottom of shafts, and elsewhere they were laid in an excavation in the bedrock, a foot or so beneath the surface. Richer families would have more elaborate rock-cut graves. Inside there would be enough space to admit a small burial party, and benches were provided on which a body could be placed. Further chambers might be cut into the rock to provide for family burials. There is just such a complex, now rather perversely ascribed to Joseph of Arimathea, at the western end of the church of the Holy Sepulchre. The entrance to a tomb would be provided with a large stone, which could give protection but also allow access. Flattened stones (rather like later millstones) which would run easily along a rock-formed channel did exist, but only in elaborate tombs. Usually the bench area was simply cut out of the wall, and the chamber had a flat ceiling extending over it, but a substantial minority had a bench cut beneath an arch or arcosolium. Subsequently the body, which had been prepared and left on the bench, would be disarticulated. Shortly before the birth of Jesus, it became customary to place the bones in a bone-box or ossuary. The custom was widespread in Jewish society, especially in the area of Jerusalem, and prevailed until the fall of the Temple in 70, and in some cases a good deal longer.

E. Bloch-Smith, *Judahite Burial Practices and Beliefs about the Dead* (Sheffield, 1992); Biddle, *Tomb*, 116–18; E. Regev, 'The Individualistic Meaning of Jewish Ossuaries', *PEQ* 133 (2001), 39–49.

statements that Jesus 'went out . . . to the place called the place of a skull' (John 19:17), and that Simon of Cyrene was recruited to carry the cross 'as they went out' (Matthew 27: 32). It seems to have become an established tradition in the church that 'Jesus suffered outside the gate' (Hebrews 13: 12). The only additional evidence comes from the statement by John, and John only, that the tomb was close to the place of crucifixion: 'in the place where he was crucified there was a garden, and in the garden a new tomb where no one had ever been laid . . . The tomb was close at hand' (John 19: 41–2). The evangelists do give us the name of the place of the crucifixion. All of them agree that it was called Golgotha, the Hebrew or Aramaic word for skull, and all provide the Greek translation *kranion* ('cranium') (Mark 15: 22; Matthew 27: 33; John 19: 17; and Luke 23: 33— although Luke, mindful of the sensitivities of his Greek readers, spares them the barbarous Hebrew word). It is not surprising that such a sinister place-name caught the attention of these writers, but its use implies that they expected readers to know where it was. Unfortunately, no other contemporary source mentions Golgotha. As it stands in the text it sounds as if it were the name of a small district, but no early evidence enables us to identify it. Speculation about the origins of the name are, I think, pointless. In relatively recent periods efforts have been made to search for a place which would have once looked like a skull. Apart from the impossibility of reconstructing in detail the scenery two thousand years ago, there is no reason to suppose that this was the derivation of the name.

FROM JERUSALEM TO AELIA

During the century after the death of Jesus, the city near which his body had been buried was utterly transformed. The first change was the extension of the walled area of the city on its north-eastern side. We do not know the precise position of the city wall at the time of Christ, but we do know that Herod Agrippa, between AD 40 and 44, built a new one further out. Unfortunately, the description Josephus gives us of the position of the walls of Jerusalem cannot easily be made to tally with its topography or the results of archaeological investigation. Herod Agrippa's extension of the city area has a special importance from our point of view. It is probable that the wall of Jesus' time (what Josephus described as the 'second wall') excluded from the city the important site where subsequently Constantine was to build the church of the Holy Sepulchre. This had certainly been included in the city area by AD 44. We shall be revisiting this site, and assessing the information it offers, in a later chapter.[3] Given the aversion to the presence of bodies of the dead among the living,

---

[3] The evidence is briefly summarized in Biddle, *Tomb*, 56–64, and J. Wilkinson, *The Jerusalem Jesus Knew* (London, 1978), 63–5.

the extension presumably involved emptying the tombs in the enlarged area.

The next disturbance was on a cataclysmic scale. Tension had been mounting for some years between the Roman authorities and Jewish nationalists, and a complete split between them in AD 66 led to a long civil war. In 70 the legions of Titus broke into Jerusalem, and in the course of the assault the Temple caught fire and was wholly destroyed. That was far from being the end of the transformation of the city. Some 60 years later the Emperor Hadrian, a liberal Hellenist who had no sympathy for the obscurantist practices of narrow religions, decided on a total rebuilding. It is not clear whether this radical plan was the reason for another major Jewish revolt, or the response to it. Whichever is the correct explanation, the Bar Kokhba rebellion had been suppressed by 135 and the great rebuilding could be put into action. The city became a Hellenistic *polis*, and received the name Aelia or Aelia Capitolina, after the emperor's own name, Publius Aelius Hadrianus.[4] Jerusalem no longer existed. The attempt to obliterate the name was probably deliberate, and is paralleled by the renaming of the province of Judaea as Syria-Palaestina. It was successful for a long time. In the fourth century, the church historian Eusebius called the modern city Aelia, and it seems that the very name Jerusalem was forgotten in government circles. The Byzantines dropped the 'Capitolina', perhaps because of its implications of pagan worship, but the name Aelia was still sufficiently established in the seventh century for the city to be called 'Iliya' in Arabic.[5]

Unfortunately, there is no surviving account from Hadrian's time describing the works he undertook. The written evidence comes from the fourth century, when Christian writers, notably Eusebius and Jerome, reflected on what had happened. Apart from the classical layout of the main streets, Hadrian apparently created pagan shrines on two major sites: the old Temple ruins and a quarry on the western edge of the city, where the tomb of Christ was later identified. They must both have been attractive propositions for building development. The Temple platform in all probability still offered a solid foundation for major building, and the quarry site was close to the new main street or *cardo*. Eusebius' assumption that Hadrian intended to

[4] Michael Grant, *The Jews in the Roman World* (London, 1973), 242 ff.; D. Golan, 'Hadrian's Decision to Supplant "Jerusalem" by "Aelia Capitolina" ', *Historia*, 35 (1986), 226–39.
[5] Eusebius, *Martyrs of Palestine* 11. 4 (PG 20. 1503–6), and Y. Tsafrir, 'Byzantine Jerusalem: The Configuration of a Christian City', in Levine, 133–50.

desecrate a known Christian site was natural, but rested on no solid information:

> Certain ungodly and impious persons had determined to hide this cave of salvation from the eyes of men . . . Having expended much labour in bringing in earth from outside, they covered up the whole place. Then, when they had raised this to a moderate height and paved it with stone, they entirely concealed the divine cave within a great mound. Next . . . they prepared above ground a . . . building to the impure demon called Aphrodite.[6]

Whatever Hadrian's intentions, archaeological investigation confirms that there was indeed a major Roman construction on the site, but unfortunately it cannot be conclusively shown that (as Eusebius apparently indicates) it stood on a landfill and raised podium. Nor is there agreement among the later descriptions of the site about the location of the various places of pagan worship. It may well be that there was a temple of Venus/Aphrodite on the site of the quarry, and another temple to Jupiter (or more strictly to the Capitoline triad of Jupiter, Minerva, and Juno) within the limits of the Temple Mount, where a statue of Hadrian himself was also erected.[7] In any event, from 135 for two centuries the area that the church of the Holy Sepulchre was later to occupy had become inaccessible, buried beneath buildings designed by Hadrian's town planners for pagan cults. Hadrian's buildings may have had the paradoxical effect of marking it strongly upon the memory of the local community: if they could no longer visit it, the temple made sure that it would not be forgotten.

The physical transformation of Jerusalem between 70 and 135 had been so enormous that it refashioned not only the appearance of the city, but its very identity, and consequently the thinking of the communities that reverenced it. The Jews were now excluded from their former holy places. Even in the fourth century, they were allowed access for only one day of the year, to lament the fall of their Temple on its anniversary. This obviously had a profound impact on the character of Judaism, but the effect upon Christians was scarcely

[6] Eusebius, *Life of Constantine* 3. 26 (PPTS 1. 2).
[7] On this conflict of evidence, see S. Gibson and J. E. Taylor, *Beneath the Church of the Holy Sepulchre Jerusalem* (London, 1994), ch. 4. Virgilio Corbo attempted an ambitious reconstruction of the details of the Hadrianic temple on the quarry site, *Il santo sepolcro di Gerusalemme*, 3 vols. (Jerusalem, 1981–2); but see R. Ousterhout in *Journal of the Society of Architectural Historians*, 43 (1984), 266–7, and D. Bahat, 'Does the Holy Sepulchre Church Mark the Burial of Jesus?', *Biblical Archaeology Review*, 12 (1986), esp. 35.

less. The church at Jerusalem was, in the time of the apostles, a largely Jewish body, and it is clear from the Acts of the Apostles that it was influential in the affairs of the international church. The cataclysmic events of the first and second centuries left a powerful mark on the Jewish Christian community. It may be that shortly before the destruction of AD 70 many of them left the city and moved to the distant town of Pella, although the historicity of this move is uncertain; nor is it clear whether they returned.[8] After 135, with the end of the Second Jewish War, the remaining Christians in Aelia were a largely or wholly Gentile community. The Judaeo-Christian tradition was weakened by these events, and much of the early Christian literature in Hebrew or Aramaic disappeared; the new Scriptures accepted as authoritative have been entirely in Greek, and addressed largely to Gentile readership. It may well be that the widespread preaching in Mediterranean cities would in any case have created this shift towards a predominantly Greek religion, but the events of AD 70 and 135 accelerated it in a dramatic fashion.

WAS THERE A CULT OF THE TOMB OF JESUS IN THE FIRST CENTURIES?

The continuous, observable, history of the Holy Sepulchre begins just after 324. Until that time, the experiences of the Christian community at Jerusalem/Aelia had been traumatic, and were divided by the chasm in 135. A largely Jewish church had become a Gentile one, and if there had been any Christian sacred sites where Hadrian chose to build, they were no longer available for Christian reverence. This raises the important question whether the church in the centuries before Constantine knew or cared where the tomb of Jesus was. There are reasons to suppose that they did so. There was in Judaism a strong popular interest in the tombs of the patriarchs, prophets, and martyrs. It was an ancient tradition: Nehemiah could see Jerusalem as 'the city of my ancestors' graves' (Nehemiah 2: 5). Holy men and women were believed to work wonders from their tombs and to intercede effectively with God, and in the generation before Christ a series of splendid memorials had been built to the illustrious departed. Some of the contemporary structures, such as the tombs attributed to Absalom and Zacharias in the Kidron valley, can still be seen near

---

[8] M. Simon, 'La Migration à Pella, légende ou réalité?', in *Judéo-Christianisme: recherches historiques et théologiques offertes au homage au cardinal Jean Daniélou* (Paris, 1972), 37–54, and O'Connor, 'Pre-Constantinian Christian Jerusalem'.

Jerusalem. Even apart from such commemorations of the great and
good, concern for burial in the family grave was widespread. It is
hard to think that the burial place of Jesus would be regarded with
indifference by his followers, especially when the head of the church
at Jerusalem was his own brother, James. For that matter, the location of the tomb of James himself, who was executed in 62, was still
known when Hegesippus wrote over a century later. The strength of
the argument for commemoration is increased by the fact that the
tomb of Jesus, as it is described in the Gospels, was in some sense an
honorific one. It was certainly not on the same level as the more
elaborate memorials in the Kidron valley, but nor was it an anonymous shaft or surface burial. Memory, in various senses of the word,
will be a central theme of this book, and in the early centuries it was
fundamental as providing a framework for thinking and locations:
'diligent memorialisation of important sayings and locations was a
sacred task, as well as a social duty'.[9] This would be a knockdown
argument in favour of continued veneration, were it not for the
unique character of the tomb of Jesus. All other graves were venerated because of the presence of the holy remains; but that of Jesus
was important precisely because his body was believed not to be
there. There seems to be no way of deciding whether, in these
very special circumstances, the normal arguments for expecting a
veneration of the tomb retain their force.

There is, however, another line of argument that may strengthen
the case for thinking that there was early reverence for the
Sepulchre. As devout Jews, the early Christians kept the passover (or,
to use the contemporary name, Pascha) as the centre of their annual
calendar, and since their Lord had died then for their salvation, the
events of the crucifixion and resurrection were remembered as part
of the deliverance of Israel. The reality of this observance can be
seen in the treatise *On Pascha* written by Melito of Sardis in the
160s.[10] The importance of *Pascha* may provide a basis for a more
speculative suggestion, that the passion narrative in the Gospels
incorporates reminiscences of liturgical observances from the
earliest days, and a record of the places where events took place,
including those which happened at the tomb.

During the two centuries between Hadrian and Constantine, from
135 to 324, the material is thin, but there are a few pieces of evidence

    [9] Thiede, 50–1.
    [10] S. G. Hall (ed. and tr.), *Melito of Sardis, On Pascha* (Oxford, 1979).

The Passion Story and the Tomb

The passion story is distinctive within the Gospel narrative. While most of the records of Christ's life were preserved in brief snippets, the record of the crucifixion and resurrection displays an unusual continuity, within which time and place are carefully preserved. The narrative does not distinguish sharply (as modern devotion tends to do) between the death of Jesus and the visit to the tomb, but reflects the spirit of the early paschal festival by keeping both within one continuous whole. Its function was to provide a standardized record of these crucial events, at a time when the first apostles were no longer alive to act as witnesses; but how it was constructed is one of the mysteries of early Christian literature. There are indications that in the process of composition use was made of reminiscences from worship. It begins and ends with striking ritual actions, the anointing of Christ at Bethany and in the tomb (Mark 14: 3–9 and 16: 1), and the account of the Paschal meal has a crucial place within it. There are acclamations that suggest quotations from worship: 'Hosanna! Blessed is he who comes in the name of the Lord!' (Mark 11: 9). It is full of teaching, both by Jesus and the evangelists, which is addressed to the whole Christian community and is not simply required by the flow of the narrative: 'wherever the Gospel is preached in the whole world, what she has done will be told in memory of her' (Mark 14: 9). There are also some verses that would gain enormously in power if they were designed to be read or acclaimed in the place to which they refer. The words 'he is not here; see the place where they laid him' (Mark 16: 6) almost demand to be said at the Sepulchre. For all the attractions of this theory, it has its problems. While some elements of the passion story sound like prescriptions for worship, others do not, and advocates have had to suppose that there was an earlier form, which was rewritten for inclusion in the Gospels, but which has left no other trace. Even some who believe in the existence of an original passion liturgy are not convinced that it was connected with the Holy Sepulchre as it subsequently emerged. Trocmé, while affirming the early community's awareness of the topography, holds that 'there is no continuity whatever between the concrete localizations of the years 30–70 and the arbitrary designations attempted 300 years later'. One basic certainty does remain amid the doubts: the location of the events is an essential part of the record. Mark had given us very few references to places throughout most of his Gospel, but in the last few days he introduced us to Bethphage and Bethany, the Mount of Olives, the Temple and its treasury, the upper room, the courtyard of the high priest, and finally Golgotha and the tomb of Joseph of Arimathea. This makes sense only on the assumption that the hearers knew where these places were, however uncertain we may be about the devotions by which they were honoured.

G. Schille, 'Das Leiden des Herrn: die evangelische Passionstradition und ihr Sitz im Leben', *Zs. für Theologie und Kirche*, 52 (1955), 161–205, and E. Trocmé, *The Passion as Liturgy: A Study in the Origin of the Passion Narrative in the Four Gospels* (London, 1983).

that tend to suggest that the location of the Holy Sepulchre was still known to the church. Just after 160, Melito of Sardis wrote in his treatise *On Pascha* that Christ had been put to death 'in the middle of Jerusalem . . . in the middle of the square and the middle of the city and the middle of the day, for all to see'.

Shortly after 244 the great theologian Origen, who had resided in Palestine for some time, reported a tradition that Adam was buried at Golgotha, a statement that strongly suggests that the church in Palestine knew where it was.[11] What is more, Eusebius, in his treatise on the place-names of Palestine, the *Onomasticon*, mentioned that Golgotha 'is shown' at Aelia, north of Sion.[12] While this leaves open the question of what he meant by 'north of Sion', he plainly had a specific location in mind. We shall also have to notice later the important evidence of a letter from the Emperor Constantine to Bishop Macarius of Aelia. In this, he spoke of his desire to free from 'the heavy weight of idol worship a spot which has been accounted holy from the beginning in God's judgement'. Clearly, people regarded it as a holy place. There is also a teasing modern discovery

---

[11] Origen, *Commentary on Matthew* 27: 32–3 (PG 13. 1777c).
[12] Eusebius, *Onomasticon* 74, 19–21. The book was written before the work of Constantine at Jerusalem, perhaps as early as the 290s.

Melito in the Middle of the Square

The evidence of Melito is important, because it is the first reference to the location of the crucifixion and the first record of a
Christian visitor to the Holy Land (outside the New Testament,
that is), and because it appears to contradict the tradition that
Jesus suffered outside the city wall. Melito went to Palestine,
but we do not know that he actually visited Aelia or that he had
made his visit by the time he wrote *On the Pasch*. Perhaps he
was merely using theological symbolism based on a text such
as 'working salvation in the midst of the earth' (Psalm 74: 12)
or 'the street of the great city . . . where their Lord was crucified' (Revelation II: 8). It may be the earliest instance of the
Christian appropriation of the Jewish belief that the Temple
was the centre of the world. But his words do sound like a piece
of town mapping, and it may be that Christians from Aelia
pointed out to him the site on the main street, with its new
imperial temple, where they had once visited the tomb of the
Lord. If so, it is the first reference to the place where later the
Holy Sepulchre was identified. But, obviously, we cannot be
sure.

A. E. Harvey, 'Melito and Jerusalem', *Journal of Theological Studies*,
NS 17 (1966), 401–4; S. G. Hall (ed. and tr.), *Melito of Sardis, On the
Pasch* (Oxford, 1979), 53, 23, and 39; and Biddle, *Tomb*, 58–62.

of an impressive votive panel of a ship, difficult to date and unexpect-
edly found under the Constantinian basilica. It is clear evidence of
pilgrimage, but it was an odd site for a pilgrim to be visiting, and
unfortunately appears to have been damaged during its discovery
and restoration. It has generated a large amount of discussion, but
it seems most probably to be a pagan offering that antedated the
work of Constantine, and may conceivably be a stone reused from
some other site.[13] The likelihood that there was some continuing
knowledge of the site of the Holy Sepulchre is supported by the

---

[13] Gibson and Taylor, *Beneath the Holy Sepulchre* chs. 1–2, conclude that 'we believe
with some degree of confidence that the ship drawing was made during the second
century A.D., and that it is not the work of a Christian pilgrim of the early fourth
century'. See also J. Wilkinson, 'The Inscription on the Jerusalem Ship Drawing', *PEQ*
127 (1995), 159–60.

undoubted fact that the site of the birth at Bethlehem was known: Justin Martyr implied its existence in about 153, and in 248 Origen unambiguously wrote that 'in Bethlehem you are shown the cave where he was born'.[14] The evidence for Christians visiting the Holy Land in the period before Constantine is limited, but the weight of probability seems to me to be in favour of a real interest in the sites there.

Whether the travellers of the centuries before Constantine should be regarded as pilgrims in the later sense is not entirely clear. They are rather differently described. Melito's purpose in coming to Palestine was said to be 'to know the accurate facts about the ancient writings, how many they are and in what order', while Clement of Alexandria, Origen, and Alexander, who later became bishop of Aelia, are said to have come for reasons connected with ecclesiastical politics or teaching.[15] As major figures they were more likely than others to have some obligation to public service to cause them to travel. They also said that they had come 'to see the traces of Jesus, of his disciples and of the prophets', as Origen remarked in his commentary on John 1: 28. Learned curiosity or *historia* for a long time was a major theme in tourism. Jerome observed later that a Christian scholar would be interested to visit Palestine in the same way that classical students would want to see Athens, and Melito and Origen do not seem to be far from that position. 'Pilgrims' in the later sense is our word, and not theirs, and the decision whether to describe them as such is therefore in the end almost a matter of taste.

A small number of statements have sometimes been taken as demonstrating that the location of the tomb was not known in the third century, but they do not carry the weight of doubt that has been placed upon them. When Eusebius said that the discovery of the cave 'transcends all marvel', he need not have meant that they had no idea that this was the site of the Holy Sepulchre; only that contemporaries did not imagine that it could have survived the massive works of Hadrian.[16] Several writers commented that 'the

[14] For references, and further evidence, see G. S. P. Freeman-Grenville, *The Basilica of the Nativity in Bethlehem* (Jerusalem, 1998), 9–11; and P. W. L. Walker, *The Weekend that Changed the World: The Mystery of Jerusalem's Empty Tomb* (London, 1999), 4, 10, and 84.

[15] S. Hall (ed. and tr.), *Melito of Sardis*, 67, fragment 3, taken from Eusebius, *Ecclesiastical History* 26. 12–14; and Jerome, ep. 46. 9.

[16] Eusebius, *Life of Constantine* 3. 30 (PPTS, 1. 30).

place was hard to find, the persecutors of old having placed a statue of Venus on it, so that, if any Christian should presume to worship Christ in that place, he would seem to worship Venus. Thus, the place had fallen into oblivion.' This suggests that there was still a tradition of where Golgotha was, however difficult it was of access.[17] The balance of probability is that the site of Golgotha, like certain other Biblical sites, remained known to the Palestinian Christians during the first three centuries. It is another question, to which we must return, whether the place of Constantine's excavations was the same as the Golgotha of Origen and the *Onomasticon*.

JERUSALEM LOST

Christians had quite quickly lost the holy places which they had originally reverenced: first the Temple, and subsequently (on the assumption that it indeed been a place of reverence) the tomb. One early reaction to the destruction of the historical Jerusalem was the belief that it would be replaced by a new and perfected city. The author of the Apocalypse saw 'the new Jerusalem': it was 'coming down out of heaven from God, having the glory of God, its radiance like a most rare jewel' (Revelation 21: 2 and 10–11). This passage spoke clearly of the descent of Jerusalem to earth, even if later ages understood it as the heaven to which they hoped to ascend. The obvious meaning of the text is that the city ruined by the Roman armies would be replaced by a new one, the eschatological Jerusalem where the saints will dwell in triumph. Justin Martyr, in the middle of the second century, professed complete confidence that Jerusalem would be rebuilt.[18]

There was, however, another strand in the thought of the early church. The worship of God, no longer bound to the historical Jerusalem, was perceived as being henceforth universal, to be found wherever the faithful are assembled. Even before the destruction of the Temple by Titus, St Paul had dismissed Jerusalem from its preeminent place: 'the present Jerusalem', he wrote, 'is in slavery with her children; but the Jerusalem above is free, and she is our mother'

---

[17] This observation seems to come from the *Ecclesiastical History* of Gelasius (Borgehammar, 54), and is likely to preserve a genuine local recollection from the middle of the fourth century.

[18] Justin, *Dialogues* 80 (The Ante-Nicene Fathers, I (Buffalo, 1885), 239).

(Galatians 4: 25–6).[19] This sense of freedom from geographical limits marked Christian thinking in the first few centuries. God is to be worshipped wherever his faithful servants are. The point was already clearly expressed in the words in which Jesus criticized at once the Jewish and the Samaritan idea of the necessity of worship at a holy place: 'the hour is coming, and now is, when the true worshippers will worship the Father in spirit and truth, for such the Father seeks to worship him. God is spirit, and those who worship him must worship in spirit and truth' (John 4: 23–4). There is a good deal in the early Fathers in line with this thinking: 'The Jerusalem below was precious, but is worthless now because of the Jerusalem above . . . For it is not in one place, nor in a little plot that the glory of God is established, but on all the ends of the inhabited earth his bounty overflows.'[20] The Fathers were happy enough to perceive Jerusalem as a symbol: Tertullian saw it as representing faith as against Athens, and Cyprian recollected the authoritative model that it provided for Christian living in Acts 4: 32.[21] Josef Engemann stated the implications of this early Christian universalism: 'Pilgrimage originally was not a Christian devotional practice. Visiting a particular place, which was connected with the earthly life of Christ, or with the life and death of martyrs and saints, essentially contradicts the intentions of Christianity.'[22]

In the first decades of the fourth century, Eusebius of Caesarea was to be the principal chronicler of Constantine's work at the Holy Sepulchre. Nevertheless, in most of his voluminous work, Eusebius dismissed the claim of Jerusalem to be the city of God. His study of Palestinian place-names, the *Onomasticon*, normally refers to the city by its pagan name of Aelia, and uses 'Jerusalem' only in a historical sense. Eusebius could be scathing about any attempt to claim spiritual status for Jerusalem. Commenting on the text, 'Glorious things are spoken of you, O city of God' (Psalm 87: 3), he wrote acidly:

[19] E. P. Sanders, 'Jerusalem and its Temple in Early Christian Thought and Practice', in Levine, 90–103. Paula Fredriksen sees the Gospels as the point at which the rejection of the Temple was incorporated into Christian thinking: 'The Holy City in Christian Thought', N. Rosovsky (ed.), *The City of the Great King* (Cambridge, Mass., 1996), 74–92.

[20] Hall, *Melito of Sardis*, 23.

[21] See L. Perrone, ' "The Mystery of Judaea" (Jerome, ep. 46): The Holy City of Jerusalem in Early Christian Thought', in Levine, 221–39.

[22] J. Engemann, 'Das Jerusalem der Pilger: Kreuzauffindung und Wallfahrt', *Akten XII*.

To think that the formerly established metropolis of the Jews in Palestine is the city of God is not only base, but even impious, the mark of exceedingly base and petty thinking . . . Its gates are now deserted and destroyed . . . The city of God is clearly . . . the godly polity throughout the world. It is the church of God which is the greatest city fit for God.[23]

In the second and third centuries, therefore, the earthly city of Jerusalem and its Temple no longer existed. The church proclaimed a God who was worshipped wherever believers lifted up their hearts to him or the community broke bread in his presence, a presence which was not located in certain sanctuaries. Such reflections do not necessarily exclude the existence of holy places; nor do they mean that the location of the Holy Sepulchre was unknown or of no interest. In the first centuries, however, there was, as far as we can trace it, no sense that such holy places had replaced the Temple in God's plan of salvation. They might be seen as evidences of Biblical truth, but the heart of the matter was that the sacred city and places had been swept away, and a new religion of open accessibility had arisen instead. Thinking of that sort provides an unpromising beginning to a study of Christianity's greatest holy place. It is incompatible with any idea that the Holy Sepulchre is central in the purposes of God.

[23] For a full discussion, see P. W. L. Walker, *Holy City, Holy Places?* (Oxford, 1990), with the reference on p. 371.

2

Consequences of Constantine, 325–50

DISCOVERIES: THE HOLY SEPULCHRE

In the course of 324, Constantine defeated the Eastern Emperor Licinius at Chrysopolis, and thus united the Roman Empire under his sole rule. Within a few months, he had given instructions for extensive work to be undertaken on the site on the eastern side of the city where Hadrian's buildings stood. There are three major sources that describe these works, and that go back to Constantine's own times. The earliest is a letter of Constantine to Bishop Macarius of Jerusalem, quoted by Eusebius in his *Life of Constantine* and datable apparently to 325–6.[1] The second source is provided by the same Eusebius of Caesarea, and in particular by his *Life of Constantine*, which was composed towards the end of the 330s, with further information in his sermon at the dedication of the church on 13 September 335 and in a formal oration in praise of Constantine.

The third source is of a different kind: during the past 30 years, it has for the first time been possible to carry out serious excavations in the church, whereas until that time all attempts to reconstruct the Constantinian plan had to depend almost entirely on literary sources. The site is an ancient and complicated one, and its continued use imposes severe limitations on the area that can be explored. Moreover, a good deal of the research has been carried out without expert archaeological supervision, and much of it has not been properly published.[2] Nevertheless, a great deal of new information has come to light about the design of the fourth-century buildings.

---

[1] Eusebius, *Life of Constantine* 3. 30 (PPTS 1. 4–5). On the probable authenticity of the letter, H. A. Drake, 'What Eusebius Knew: The Genesis of the *Vita Constantini*', *Classical Philology*, 83 (1988), 20–38.

[2] See the remarks throughout S. Gibson and J. E. Taylor, *Beneath the Church of the Holy Sepulchre Jerusalem* (London, 1994).

The Authority of Eusebius of Caesarea

Eusebius, who died as a very old man about 339, is a figure of
enormous importance. As bishop of Caesarea, he had oversight
throughout the Palestinian church. Aelia/Jerusalem did not
obtain the independent status of a patriarchate until long after
his time. When Jacob Burkhardt described his work as 'dishon-
est from beginning to end', he was thinking primarily of the
Ecclesiastical History, but Eusebius' accounts of the emperor's
work at Jerusalem have also been subjected to severe criticism.
He lived throughout the building of the new church of the
Resurrection (Holy Sepulchre), and must have been familiar
with its site. His standing as a source for what happened
should, on the face of it, be excellent, but there are problems.
His earlier theological position had been universalist, in the
sense that he believed in the presence of God to all believers,
and rejected the claim of Jerusalem to be a holy city. The subsequent tension between his admiration of the first Christian
emperor and unease at the great Jerusalem shrine that Constantine was developing makes it difficult to evaluate his
account. The question is asked in its sharpest form by the discovery of the cross. Most evidence suggests that its remains had
been found during the lifetime of Constantine, who died in 337.
Its omission from such an important source is staggering, and
raises the question of what has been described as 'the deviousness of Eusebius' or his 'silence and evasion'. If the cross had
really been found in the course of the excavation of Hadrian's
site, Eusebius' suppression of it must have been due to ecclesiastical politics (the rivalry between Aelia and Caesarea) or to
his theology: it has been argued that he was unhappy about the
cult of the cross, just as he was originally about the veneration
of Jerusalem as a holy place. Neither of these explanations is
completely convincing, but undoubtedly there is a serious question mark over Eusebius' standing as an historian of Constantine's policy at Jerusalem.

T. D. Barnes, *Constantine and Eusebius* (Cambridge, Mass., 1981); H. A.
Drake, *In Praise of Constantine: A Historical Study and New Translation
of Eusebius' Tricennial Orations* (London, 1975); Borgehammar,
104–13; and Z. Rubin, 'The Cult of the Holy Places and Christian

Politics in Byzantine Jerusalem', Levine, 151–62. Eusebius' skill as a spin-doctor has been evaluated in a lively book by D. Mendels, *The Media Revolution of Early Christianity: An Essay on Eusebius' Ecclesiastical History* (Grand Rapids, Mich., 2000).

This area had originally been a quarry, which produced a limestone with red or pinkish streaks within it. The quarry was extensive, at least 200 × 150 metres. Centuries of quarrying had cut deeply into the original bedrock, and created a number of caves. It had also produced an artificial spur or hillock on the southern edge, with a top some 11 metres above base level to the north. The rock here was split by a number of natural cavities, and presumably for this reason it had been left untouched by the quarriers, who would have found it unsatisfactory as a building material.

It is not clear when the quarry went out of use. Parts of it may have become a garden, but the archaeological support for this is not compelling and may well reflect a reading back of the description in John 19: 41. Like so many of the rocky places around Jerusalem, it was used for burials, and four or five tombs can be identified within the bounds of the disused quarry.[3] This was the site chosen for Hadrian's pagan temple or shrines adjoining the main thoroughfare of his new city of Aelia.

If we are to trust the account in Eusebius' *Life of Constantine*, the emperor committed himself to a general restoration of prosperity among the churches after the persecution to which they had been subjected during the previous generation. This involved major building work at Bethlehem and at Mamre, where the angels had revealed the nature of God to Abraham, and (most important of all) at Aelia. Eusebius' account, and the dating of the emperor's letter to Bishop Macarius of Aelia, indicate that the policy was undertaken with little delay after Constantine's assumption of power in the East.

It would be interesting to know who inspired this overall encouragement of the churches in the East, and in particular the removal of Hadrian's shrines at Golgotha. Constantine's policy in 325 was more aggressively pro-Christian than his cautious approach at Rome when he took power there in 312. Christian writers were tempted to exaggerate the emperor's personal involvement in church

[3] Ibid. 52, 63.

affairs. He was a valuable trump to use against pagan resistance, and Cyril Mango has warned us that we should be 'a little reluctant to attribute to Constantine's fertile brain so many innovations in Christian devotion—the origin of the basilica, the cult of relics, the institution of pilgrimage'.[4] It is unlikely that Eusebius himself was the main inspiration for the emperor's approach. Apart from his probable reservations noted in the inset above, he may never have had much influence at court, at least until the mid-330s. Nor, indeed, did he claim to be the adviser behind the policy, which he specifically ascribed to the personal decision of the emperor, 'impelled to it in his spirit by the Saviour himself'.[5] It is now more usual to suggest that Bishop Macarius of Aelia/Jerusalem had begun the pressure for clearing the holy sites: he would know the local traditions, would gain from the glorification of Golgotha, and was at the Council of Nicaea. It must be said, though, that Constantine's letter to him does not suggest that his role was more than that of the responsible bishop of the see, and he was hardly in a position to shape the wider policy of advancement for the churches within which the work at Aelia took place.

The timing suggests that the project had been discussed even before 324, and it is worth remembering that Constantine's government was a strongly Latin one. After the first year or two of his dominance in the East (when his decrees were bilingual) his laws were issued in Latin, and throughout the fourth century his new city of Constantinople was a centre of Latin government. The emperors, although they mostly knew Greek as well, were predominantly Latin-speaking, and their administrators were trained in Latin, to the indignation of Hellenistic traditionalists.[6] The history of the Council of Nicaea in 325 suggests that Western advisers were influential. Yet, tempting though it would be to argue that the cult of the holy places had a Western origin, there is no proof of a distinct Western interest in them, or of any Latin visitor before Constantine's work there. The influences under which he took so rapid a decision after the defeat of Licinius remain unclear.

Whatever the reasons for the emperor's policy in the East as a whole, the choice of location must have been made by the leaders of the local church in Palestine or at Aelia. The site would have been

---

[4] C. Mango, 'The Pilgrim's Motivation', *Akten XII*, 4.
[5] *Life of Constantine* 3. 25 (PPTS I. 3).
[6] G. Dagron, 'Aux origines de la civilisation byzantine', *Revue Historique*, 241 (1969), 23–56.

attractive because of its central position in the city, but Constantine's letter did not mention this, but described it as a special place of Christian remembrance. Since 290, as we know, Golgotha 'was shown' at Aelia north of Sion. If this was not the quarry site, we must accept the remarkable conclusion that in 325 the church of Aelia recommended a place that they believed was not Golgotha, an unconvincing assumption in the absence of further evidence. In his summary of the events, Eusebius reports that after the Council of Nicaea Constantine resolved to clear of defilement the place of the resurrection: he 'judged it incumbent on him to render the blessed locality of our Saviour's resurrection an object of attraction and veneration to all'.[7] The emperor's letter to Macarius, which Eusebius quotes, places the stress on decontamination, referring to 'the sacred spot, which under divine direction I have disencumbered as it were of the heavy weight of foul idol worship'. In the course of these works, a significant discovery was made, which the emperor describes as 'the trophy (*gnōrisma*) of the most holy passion, so long ago buried beneath the ground' and as 'a clear assurance of our Saviour's passion'. As a result, Constantine resolved to create a magnificent place of worship: 'I have no greater care than how I may best adorn with a splendid structure that sacred spot.' The sequence here is the cleansing of a Christian holy place from pagan defilement, followed by the exciting discovery of the 'trophy of the passion'.

The main line of Eusebius' narrative echoes the summary of events in the emperor's letter. The removal of the pagan temples, designed to restore the holiness of the site, was transformed into something much bigger by the unexpected discovery made in the course of the work. Eusebius is very clear what it was:

As soon as the original surface of the ground, beneath the covering of earth, appeared, immediately and contrary to all expectation, the venerable and hallowed monument of our Saviour's resurrection was discovered. Then indeed did this most holy cave present a faithful similitude of his return to life, in that after being buried in darkness, it again emerged to light, and afforded to all who came to witness the sight a testimony to the resurrection of the Saviour clearer than any voice could give.[8]

They had found the Holy Sepulchre. As told by Eusebius, it all makes good sense. The first stage of clearance had been undertaken because of the sacred associations of Golgotha. When they began to

---

[7] *Life of Constantine* 3. 25 (PPTS I. I).
[8] Ibid. 3. 30, 28 (PPTS I. 3–5).

dig, they found a tomb (to their astonishment, because they had no idea it had survived) and identified it as the Holy Sepulchre itself. Eusebius did not, in the *Life of Constantine*, explain how it was recognized, but he gave us the clue in the *Theophany*, a work almost exactly contemporary with the excavations: 'It is marvellous to see even this rock, standing out erect and alone in a level land, and having only one cavern in it; lest, had there been many, the miracle of him who overcame death should be obscured.'[9] In other words, they found a single tomb. Given that they were clearing the site traditionally known as Golgotha, the only conclusion could be that this was the Holy Sepulchre. There is, it must be confessed, a problem. The two multi-celled tombs that stand immediately to the west must have been revealed in the same campaign of excavation. It does not follow that Eusebius was being economical with the truth. The single-chamber tomb may have been the first to be found, and in any case the other tombs did not fit the description in the Gospels. Eusebius' explanation is the only one we are given for the identification of the tomb; unlike the finding of the wood of the cross, no miraculous proof is offered of its authenticity.

DISCOVERIES: THE WOOD OF THE CROSS

One of the most remarkable texts surviving from fourth-century Aelia is the series of lectures given to candidates for baptism by Cyril. There are doubts about the date and authorship of some of these *Catechetical Lectures*, but general agreement that most of them were delivered just before 350. Cyril was speaking within the walls of Constantine's new church, and several times indicated the presence there of the true cross. Cyril was already able to claim that 'the holy wood of the cross gives witness: it is here to be seen in this very day, and through those who take pieces from it, it has from here already filled almost the whole world'.[10] This statement is no doubt an exaggeration, but there is confirmatory evidence for the spread of fragments of the cross shortly after the middle of the fourth century, and by the 380s the veneration of the cross had become a central feature in the observance of Good Friday at Jerusalem.

---

[9] Cited P. W. L. Walker, *Holy City, Holy Places?* (Oxford, 1990), 100–6; see further his discussion on the date and character of the *Theophany*.

[10] Cyril, *Catechetical Lectures* 4. 10, 10. 19, and 13.4 (*PG* 33. 468B, 685–8, 776–7; also PPTS 11. 13).

When Was the Cross Found?

Cyril's account establishes that relics of the cross were present in the church of the Resurrection by 350, and that they had been there for some time. It may have been found under Constantine, before his death in 337; in fact, a letter from Cyril to Emperor Constantius II about 350 said that it had been. If the letter is authentic, it would be good evidence, but in that case it is surprising that the Bordeaux pilgrim in 333 did not mention the presence of the cross. More serious still is the silence of Eusebius, the major source for events at Aelia; but Eusebius is a dubious witness in this matter of the cross. It can be said with confidence that the cross (or what purported to be its remains) was on display in the church of the Resurrection by 350, and that it may very well have been discovered in the time of Constantine himself.

From the 390s, the discovery was almost universally attributed to a deliberate search by Helena, the mother of Constantine. The earliest reference is in the *Ecclesiastical History* of Gelasius of Caesarea, which does not survive as an independent work but was extensively used by historians in the next generation. The discovery of the cross, and of two nails from it, was also mentioned by Bishop Ambrose of Milan, in his funeral oration on the death of Emperor Theodosius I in 395. From that time onwards, the attribution to Helena is almost universal. Nevertheless, a gap of over sixty years in the recording of the evidence is almost disastrous to its credibility, especially as Gelasius' account came replete with miracles that rapidly became more florid in subsequent writers. It is not surprising that most historians have come to the conclusion that the finding by Helena 'must be regarded as historical fiction'.

Maybe it cannot be dismissed completely. There is no doubt of Helena's major importance in Constantine's court. She had been raised to the imperial rank of *Augusta*, and some time about 326, in her old age, she visited Aelia. Eusebius gives a considerable amount of detail about this visit, even though he wholly omits the finding of the cross. Moreover, the story clearly originated before the 390s. Ambrose was preaching in the presence of the imperial court, and his statements, made on a solemn occasion, must have reflected what the court believed. Gelasius was the nephew of Cyril, and therefore a representative of Jerusalem tradition. A century later, it was affirmed at Rome that there were relics of the cross in the chapel that had originally belonged to the palace of Helena, and which she had placed there. The Helena stories thus circulated also at Rome and in the imperial court well before the end of the fourth century. Stephan Borgehammar and Peter Thiede have accordingly argued for 'a strong presumption in favour of the traditional account being true'.

J. W. Drijvers, *Helena Augusta* (Leiden, 1992); Borgehammar, where the reconstructed text of Gelasius of Caesarea may be found; and Thiede. Also R. Klein, 'Helena II (Kaiserin)', *Reallexikon für Antike und Christentum*, 14 (1988), 355–75; S. Heid, 'Die Ursprung der Helenalegende im Pilgerbetrieb Jerusalems', *Jahrbuch für Antike und Christentum*, 32 (1989), 41–71; and J. Engemann, 'Das Jerusalem der Pilger: Kreuzauffindung und Wallfahrt', *Akten XII*, 24–35. For Cyril's letter see H. Grégoire and P. Orgels, 'Saint Gallicanus . . . et la "vision constantinienne" du crucifié', *Byzantion*, 24 (1954), 579–601. On the encaenia, L. van Tongeren, 'Vom Kreuzritus zur Kreuzestheologie: die Entstehungsgeschichte der Kreuzerhöhung und seine erste Ausbreitung im Westen', *Ephemerides Liturgica*, 112 (1998), 216–45.

Some historians have argued that Eusebius' misinterpretations extended to the total distortion of Constantine's work. On this theory, the dramatic discovery that changed the subsequent planning of the site would not be the Sepulchre but the cross, and the great church buildings would have essentially been designed as a memorial to the cross. The letter to Macarius can be cited as key evidence for this reinterpretation: the emperor spoke there of 'the trophy of the most holy passion, so long ago buried beneath the ground', and that sounds to modern ears very like a reference to the cross. The account of the finding of the tomb in the *Life of Constantine* would then have to be accepted as essentially a fabrication, which substituted the tomb for the cross; with the emperor's letter misused, whether intentionally or inadvertently, to support Eusebius' stress on the Sepulchre. This theory, however, lacks supporting proof from elsewhere, and one must remember that Eusebius' writing and speeches would be known to his fellow-bishops and to the court. The idea that they contain such a serious fabrication of the events is implausible. It is, moreover, by no means certain that 'the trophy of the most holy passion' of the emperor's letter must have been the cross rather than the Sepulchre. There could, after all, scarcely be better evidence of a death than the identification of a tomb. On any showing, the sacred site, as it was eventually recognized, involved not one discovery, the Sepulchre, but a second also, the cross.

DISCOVERIES: CALVARY

There was in a sense a third discovery also. The column of rock that had survived from the quarrying on the southern edge came, for Latin writers, to be called Calvary and to be identified as the precise place where the cross of Jesus was raised.

A visitor to the present church of the Holy Sepulchre will now find the Calvary chapel, covering the original top of the rock spur, up a flight of stairs to the right of the main entrance. The distinction between the two holy sites, the Sepulchre and the place of the cruci-fixion, is made clear in Jerome's account of the triumphal visit of Epiphanius of Salamis for the Encaenia celebration in 393. He went first to the Anastasis or Sepulchre, where he preached against Origen's theology, and then proceeded 'to the cross', where 'a crowd of every age and sex flowed to him'.[11]

Nobody at the time told us why the top of the rock was identified as the place of the crucifixion. This usage did not develop in response to the Gospels, which nowhere indicate that Jesus was crucified on a hill. The large number of Western pictures of the passion, which so often show the mount of crucifixion, reflect the layout in the Church of the Holy Sepulchre. A number of allusions, stretching from the late third century to the fifth, indicate the reasons which may have encouraged this identification.[12] One was the fact that the rock column was a natural recognition point for Golgotha as a whole. When about 290 Eusebius reported in the *Onomasticon* that Golgotha 'was shown', he may have had the rock in mind: certainly, nothing else would have been visible at that time alongside the shrines erected in Hadrian's time. In 333 the Bordeaux pilgrim, looking at the site

---

[11] Jerome, *Contra Johannem Hierosol.* 11 (PL 23. 264B).

[12] The following section draws heavily upon J. Jeremias, *Golgotha* (Leipzig, 1926). Joan Taylor, *Christians and the Holy Places* (Oxford, 1993), ch. 6, thinks that the transfer of traditions from the Temple to the Constantinian sites began only in the fourth century. She sees the earlier evidence as inconclusive, or as referring to a different site.

Calvary/Golgotha

The name 'Calvary' presents no problem: it is merely the Latin equivalent of the Hebrew 'Golgotha'. *Golgotha* in Hebrew, *kranion* in Greek, and *calvaria* in Latin all mean 'a skull'. Saint Jerome himself bluntly defined *Golgotha* as *Calvaria*, while noting that is was a 'Syrian', not a Hebrew, word. The Latin Vulgate accordingly retains the name 'Golgotha', adding the Latin rendering *locus calvariae* in place of the original Greek *kranion*. Greek writers normally continued to use Golgotha, Latin writers Golgotha or Calvary. *Kranion* did not become a place-name. The wider meaning of Golgotha as a district was still apparent when Egeria in the 380s described Constantine's extensive church as being 'on Golgotha'. Place-names, however, are in their nature ambiguous, and may slide from one usage to another. Increasingly, Calvary/Golgotha came to be used for the rock, now understood to be the precise spot of Jesus' crucifixion. In about 570, the Piacenza pilgrim could specify that it was about 80 paces from the tomb to Golgotha. By then, evidently, the name was already being used in the narrow definition, as it is today. The meaning of Golgotha became still narrower in the later Middle Ages, when it was used for the area under the rock, which was accessible because of the existence of a huge split. Readers could then be told, 'Golgotha is the place under Mount Calvary, as it were concave', or 'going out on the left hand of the choir is Mount Calvary, where God was placed on the Cross, and beneath it is Golgotha, where the precious blood of our Saviour fell on the head of Adam. There Abraham sacrificed to our Lord'.

The reference to Jerome is in his *Liber interpretationis Hebraicorum nominum*, CCSL 72. 136; late-medieval examples can be found in *Anonymous Pilgrim*, 5. 1. 22; *The Condition of the City of Jerusalem*, 2. 2; and *Guidebook to Palestine 1350*, chs. 24, 39 (PPTS 6. 22, 34, 5, 8).

from Mount Sion to its south, noted that 'on your left is the hillock Golgotha where the Lord was crucified, and about a stone's throw from it the vault where they laid his body'. The obvious meaning of this description is that Golgotha is a small hill, distinct from the

Sepulchre, and in that case the assumption that the Lord was crucified on the hill had already been made. Eusebius does not mention
the site of the crucifixion: its absence from his account has been
treated by David Hunt as one more sign of Eusebius' famous
deviousness, and he has argued that Constantine's letter shows that
Calvary was part of the design from the beginning.[13] Bishop Cyril,
who knew the place well, mentioned Golgotha on a number of occasions in the middle years of the fourth century, but his evidence is
inconclusive. It is not always clear whether he meant the rock or the
whole site, and he may not have been consistent in his usage.[14]

The character of the rock as a mini-mountain tempted Christian
writers to transfer to it mysteries that had formerly been attributed to
the Temple mount. This process had certainly begun before Constantine. It has sometimes been supposed that the identification of the
Temple mount with the centre of the world was an age-old conception, although Philip Alexander has argued for a relatively recent
origin of the idea, in the polemic against Hellenism in the second
century BC.[15] Whatever its origin, the transfer of the idea to Golgotha
may, as we have seen, be found in Melito of Sardis as early as 160. It
was present in Bishop Victorinus of Pettau before 300:

> It is the place where we acclaim
> The world's central location.
> Golgotha is its Hebrew name
> In native conversation.[16]

The tradition of the centrality of Golgotha was seemingly not to the
taste of Eusebius. When he quoted the text of Psalm 74: 12, 'working
salvation in the midst of the earth', he meant that it was not limited
to any one place, but available throughout the world. By about 350,
its centrality seems to have been widely accepted by Western writers:
Hilary of Poitiers taught that 'the place of the cross is in the midst of
the earth and the summit of the universe, so that all peoples can
equally obtain the knowledge of God'. The developing theology of
Jerusalem had almost reversed the interpretation of Eusebius, by
understanding the psalm as declaring that the holy place was central

[13] E. D. Hunt, 'Constantine and Jerusalem', *JEH* 48 (1997), esp. 413.
[14] For the contrary view, that it was a considerable time before the rock was
identified as the place of the crucifixion, see Gibson and Taylor, *Beneath the Holy
Sepulchre*, 79 ff.
[15] P. S. Alexander, 'Jerusalem as the *Omphalos* of the World: On the History of a
Geographical Concept', in Levine, 104–19.
[16] Jeremias, *Golgotha*, 40 n.

to the whole world.[17] However, the centre or 'navel' of the world was eventually located within the whole complex of the church buildings, and not on the rock itself.

Another borrowing from Temple symbolism, which had certainly appeared before the time of Eusebius and was more specifically linked with the rock, was the belief reported by Origen that Golgotha was the burial-place of Adam. He associated the legend with the name: it was 'the place of a skull' or 'the place of a head' because Adam, the first head of the human race, was buried there. Adam's skull became established in the tradition of Jerusalem, and was eventually marked by the presence of a chapel within the rock. Before the end of the fourth century, Golgotha had thus already acquired the status of the place where the crucifixion took place, where the skull of Adam was to be found, and where the centre of the world lay. In this thinking Golgotha the rock and Golgotha the district seem to coexist. The skull of Adam was seemingly buried in the rock, but Jerome's 'Calvary of the beheaded' must have been a wider area. It is interesting that this ambiguity in usage did not escape the more intelligent medieval pilgrims. In his account of his pilgrimage in 1483, Felix Fabri noted that Calvary is 'not called a mount in Scripture, but it is only common talk which speaks of it as a mount, since in truth it is not a mount, but a rock or crag . . . The place Calvary means the entire site of the church, the rock of Calvary supports the cross alone.'[18]

There were other reasons for supposing that the cross had stood exactly on the rock: pinkish stains could be seen in the underlying stone, reminding observers of the Lord's blood, and the crevasses within the rock raised memories of the earthquake at the Lord's death. Although fourth-century observers do not mention these, they could be observed, and may well have already influenced their imagination. It is striking that, by the time of Egeria's visit in the 380s, the surface of the rock still remained visible, bare of any chapel, but in all probability already marked by a great cross. The creation of a building on Calvary, and still more the enclosure of the natural rock, belongs to a later period.[19]

---

[17] Cyril applied to Golgotha the text, 'working salvation in the midst of the earth' in *Cat.* 13. 28: see also 14. 16 and 17. 22, and Hilary, *De Trinitate* 1. 15 (PG 39. 324). For the contrast between the assumptions of Eusebius and Cyril, see Walker, *Holy City, Holy Places?*, 126.

[18] *Felix Fabri*, PPTS 7–8. 366–7.

[19] The relationship between the archaeological and literary evidence is explored in Gibson and Taylor, *Beneath the Holy Sepulchre*, 56–60, 78–9.

The Burial of Adam in Western Tradition

Over the course of many centuries, Western writers and pilgrims eventually accepted the idea that Adam had been buried on Calvary, but its reception had a chequered history in the West. Jerome, who originally accepted its truth, later was critical, probably because he was aware of the Jewish tradition that the burial place of Adam was at Hebron:

I have heard somebody expound how the place of Calvary is where Adam was buried, and that it was so called because the head of the first man was located there . . . It is a nice story and ordinary people like it, but it is not true. For outside the city and the gate were the places in which the heads of criminals were struck off, and they took the name of Calvary, that is of the beheaded.

At much the same time, Ambrose did accept that Adam was buried at Golgotha, and in the early sixth century Cesarius of Arles wrote that 'it is called the place of a skull (*calvariae*) because the first head of the human race is said to have been buried there'. All the same, the powerful influence of Jerome ensured that the Adam legend did not appear much in Latin literature before the time of the crusades. Paschasius Radbertus in the ninth century followed Jerome's derivation of the name Calvary from the fact that it was 'the place of the beheaded', and denied the story of Adam's burial there.

Jerome, *Commentary on Matthew* 27: 33 (SC 259, 288); Cesarius, Ps-Augustine, sermo 6: 5 (PL 39. 1751); Paschasius, *Expositio in Matthaeum* 27: 33 (CCCM 56B. 1366).

AUTHENTICITY

From the 320s onwards, the site of the ancient quarry on the western side of the old city became the site of the church of the Holy Sepulchre, and was venerated by most generations of Christians as the place where Jesus had been crucified and buried. It is not crucial to this inquiry whether this really was the same place as the Golgotha mentioned in the Gospels, but it is not possible to resist the temptation of speculating about its authenticity. The difficulty is obvious: in spite of the occurrence of the name in all the Gospels, none of them actually says where it was. The name was mentioned again in the third century by Origen and Eusebius, once again without any firm geographical description. The attribution to a specific site begins clearly only after 324. That is a very long tunnel period, in which we have no secure identification. One thing that is clear is that the quarry site was lost altogether for almost two hundred years, if not from the memory of mankind, at least from the surface of the earth, for it had been covered by Hadrian's builders.

On reflection, the tunnel period diminishes. The care with which the places associated with the passion story were recorded in the Gospels seemingly indicates that people did know at the time where Golgotha was. At the other end of the tunnel, we find that Constantine's letter of 325–6 indicates that the former quarry was regarded as a place of special holiness. It had certainly not been selected for its inherent probability: being inside the existing wall, which had been rebuilt in 44, it was not a plausible site for something that had happened 'outside the gate'. The emperor's letter on the holiness of this place was extremely emphatic, and was a long way from the universalist tendency in third-century Christian thinking. He described it as 'a spot which has been accounted holy from the beginning in God's judgement, but now appears holier still'.[20] Since there are no other traditions, it seems to me perverse to assign to some other, unknown, place the references to Golgotha by Origen and Eusebius. It is, I think, likely that Constantine was in truth carrying out his work at the Biblical Golgotha.

If this was the correct place, was it also the right tomb? The evidence comes from Eusebius, and from him alone, and his argument is that the excavations led to the discovery of a tomb, 'standing out erect and alone in a level land'. Of course, if this account by Eusebius is largely fiction, his evidence disappears; but we have already found reasons for trusting him on this point. If his report is correct, it does not for the modern reader establish certainty. There were several other tombs in the quarry area, and for that matter the original could have been destroyed in excavations following 135. Yet the tomb highlighted by Eusebius does seem to be the only one that fitted the Gospel account. The so-called tomb of Joseph of Arimathea and Nicodemus, for instance, is plainly a long-established family sepulchre. At least there is no obvious discrepancy between what the evangelists tell us and what Constantine's workers discovered. They

---

[20] *Life of Constantine* 3. 30 (PPTS, I. 5).

were probably working in the right place, Golgotha, where the tomb of Christ had originally stood. For purposes of convenience, we shall in this book have to call the tomb they discovered 'the Holy Sepulchre'. That may well, in fact, be the truth.

The location of the crucifixion is less plausible. Calvary, understood as the rock summit, appears an improbable site for an execution. The historical accounts do not mention that it took place on a hill. The surface area at the top is narrow, almost too small for the erection of one cross, let alone two more for the execution of the thieves. Hard rock, with many fissures, would make the place almost unmanageable for embedding the crosses required for the savage rites of crucifixion. This may well have taken place somewhere within the bounds of the larger Golgotha, but the place which is now marked by the elaborate Calvary chapel is unlikely to be original. To this, however, one must add a rider. The removal of the stone pavement, which had been laid in the Calvary chapel during the reconstruction after 1808, laid bare the natural rock. Among the features were the great chasm in the rock, which had not been visible since the reconstruction, and, behind the altar, a socket where evidently a cross had stood. These simply confirm what we already know, that the rock had long been identified as the crucifixion site. More remarkable was the discovery that on the left side of the altar there is an area of softer rock, on which a number of crude crosses have been incised. It has been suggested that they are closely similar to inscriptions that elsewhere in Palestine have been dated between the first and third centuries. If that is right, it would provide archaeological confirmation of the possibility that the 'mount' was already identified before Constantine as the site of the crucifixion, and that it had been accessible to pilgrims even when the adjoining site was occupied by an imperial temple.

Fourth-century accounts suggest that the remains that were discovered, and were claimed to be fragments from the crucifixion, consisted of a wooden beam, some nails, and the surviving title that had been pinned on the cross. They are unlikely to be the real thing. If the first disciples were not interested in preserving them, or if they were unable to preserve them, or if they regarded them with horror, then the likelihood of their rediscovery would be virtually zero, while the chances of finding promising-looking wood and nails on a huge building site would be only too large. If we make the assumption that the first disciples saw these things as relics, to be preserved as part of the memory of the saving death, then some possibility of authenticity remains. They would presumably have been kept at or near the tomb. When the site was bulldozed under Hadrian, they could have survived (as it was believed that the Sepulchre did) as an identifiable trove under the ground. It must be said that fourth-century accounts do not much support such a supposition. They speak of the finding of three crosses: but the idea that the disciples preserved the cross-beams of the thieves seems to be a further improbability. No historical reason for the identification, such as can be alleged for the Sepulchre, is provided for the cross. The original place was said to have been revealed either by a heavenly message or by a rather strange tradition among the Jews of Jerusalem. The cross itself was identified by healing miracles, which differ greatly in the various stories. The one element that offers some solid evidence is the puzzling indication of the survival of the title describing Jesus as 'king of the Jews': the significance of which is difficult to assess.

THE BUILDINGS

The Golgotha where Constantine built was a unique site, and as a result we have a volume of material on the buildings without parallel elsewhere in this period. In addition to the evidence already mentioned there are several eyewitness descriptions, from Latins as well as Greeks. We have already mentioned the very brief account of the anonymous visitor from Bordeaux; Bishop Cyril of Jerusalem delivered his *Catechetical Lectures* there about 348, and repeatedly referred to the buildings, although he did not describe them; another Western pilgrim, Egeria, was in Jerusalem in the years after 382, and provided a detailed account of the ceremonies there; and Jerome and his companions were resident in Palestine during the later years of the fourth century. Within their descriptions, their terminology differs a good deal.

The description by the Bordeaux pilgrim in 333, brief as it is, establishes the main outline of the buildings that then existed. At this point in his account, he is on his way from the hill of Sion in the south of the city to the present Damascus gate, and thus outside the site altogether, and he writes, as was mentioned above:

On your left is the hillock Golgotha, where the Lord was crucified, and about a stone's throw from it the vault where they laid the body, and he rose again the third day. By order of the emperor there has now been built a basilica, I

The Title on the Cross

The evidence is teasing. Ambrose's statement that the title had been found had been confirmed in advance by Egeria, who said it was preserved with the cross itself in the church of the Resurrection, and exposed with the holy wood for devotion each year. All that now remains is a fragment in the church of Santa Croce at Rome, the former chapel of Helena's palace. (That would be a natural place for it to survive, but also a tempting site for a forgery to be installed.) It is only a small piece. If it is authentic, someone, most obviously Helena, broke it from the Jerusalem title, leaving the greater part for devotion there in its place of origin. Whatever that was, it has long ago disappeared. The fragmentary title in Santa Croce was placed in a new box, with the title TITULUS CRUCIS, some time before 1144, and then rediscovered in the course of restoration work on the mosaics of the chapel in 1492. There appears to be little doubt that it was very ancient. It preserves, in a very damaged Hebrew line, in Greek and Latin, the inscription NAZARINUS R., or 'Nazareth K(ing)'. It was clearly intended to be part of a full inscription, 'Jesus the Nazarene, King of the Jews'. The relic has not been subjected to scientific testing, but if it is a forgery, it is an odd one. The Greek and Latin inscriptions are written backwards, in the same style as Hebrew. Some of the features correspond with known Roman practice: for example, it seems to have been originally whitewashed to make it plainer to read. Circumstances make it difficult to accept as authentic, but its features cannot easily be written off as a forgery.

Thiede, 59–106; M. Hesemann, *Die Jesus-Tafel* (Freiburg, 1999). Borgehammar, 129–30, is dismissive, and most scholars ignore it altogether.

mean a *dominicum*, which has beside it cisterns of remarkable beauty, and beside them a bath where children are baptized.[21]

By the end of the fourth century, the buildings formed an articulated set of structures. They were surrounded by an enclosing wall, with a

[21] *Egeria's Travels*, 158. This passage seems to me to distinguish clearly between the top of the rock of the crucifixion and the tomb, but this is not accepted by everybody.

The Church of the Holy Sepulchre and Its Names

To the Greeks, over long centuries, the whole complex has been called the church of the Anastasis or Resurrection, and Arab Christians gave it the equivalent name, *Qiyyaama*. Already, however, in the fourth century, we begin to find Jerome using the term, 'the Lord's Sepulchre', which, along with 'the Holy Sepulchre', was to become the standard Latin usage (Jerome *Contra Johannem Hierosol.* II (*PL* 23. 380B)). From the beginning, the great church was described as a 'basilica', in Constantine's letter to Macarius, by Eusebius, and by the Bordeaux pilgrim. This would be a natural name. A basilica was an imperial hall, and came to be used for the great hall-churches sponsored by Constantine. More surprisingly, the bishops assembled for the consecration in 335 called it the *martyrium*: 'Having come together . . . to a great gathering we have held for the consecration of our Saviour's *martyrium*, which has been established to the service of God the king of all and of Christ, by the zeal of our Emperor Constantine, most beloved of God . . .' (Athanasius, *De Synodis*, 21. 3). *Martyrium* was the standard word for a martyr's shrine, and would more naturally have been used to describe the tomb or the rotunda around it. The use of the term does confirm the speculation that the rotunda around that Tomb had not been built at first, so that it was natural to see the basilica as the *martyrium* or shrine-church. Later writers used a variety of terms, with a preference for 'the church (or basilica) of Constantine'. The Bordeaux pilgrim in 333 called the church a *dominicum* built by order of the emperor. This was presumably a Latin version of the regular Greek word for a church, *kyriakon*. In the 380s, Egeria several times used phrases such as 'in the great church which Constantine built behind the cross' (25: 1 and elsewhere). Surprisingly, as well as calling the rotunda the Anastasis, she called it a 'basilica', although it was not in the least like the halls from which great churches were being developed. Clearly, the vocabulary was still very fluid. Just before 700 Adomnan spoke of 'the basilica built with great magnificence by King Constantine', adding 'it is also called the *martyrium*'—so the name had stuck for a long time. It should be remembered that Anastasis is simply the Greek word for 'resurrection', and it became the standard word for pictorial depictions of it, and in particular for icons of what in the West would be called 'the descent into hell', a very popular theme of Eastern art.

G. Kretschmar, 'Festkalender und Memorialstätten Jerusalems in altkirchlicher Zeit', in H. Busse and G. Kretschmar (eds.), *Jerusalemer Heiligtumstradition in altkirchlicher und frühislamischer Zeit* (Wiesbaden, 1987); and, on the whole subject, R. Ousterhout, 'The Temple, the Sepulchre and the Martyrion of the Saviour', *Gesta*, 29 (1990), 44–53. Further uses of the term *martyrium* are noted in Borgehammar, 103–4. The names for Christian cult buildings in general are discussed by F. J. Dölger, 'Kirche als Name . . .', *Antike und Christentum*, 6 (1940), 161–95; and C. Mohrmann, "Les Dénominations de l'église . . .', *Études sur le latin des chrétiens*, 4 (1977), 211–30.

splendid doorway on the main road in Aelia, the Cardo Maximus. The visitor would enter into the large court which stood at the east end of the site. Beyond it stood the great basilica, sometimes called, as we have seen, the *martyrium*. Continuing westward, there was another colonnaded court, which gave pilgrims access to the most holy places. To the south side it had the hill of the cross, and to its west the Sepulchre.

The size of the basilica, and of the court at the east end, strongly suggests that it was intended from the beginning to make provision for large numbers of pilgrims. The great church was demolished in the eleventh century, and nothing can now be seen of it except a few foundations; but we do know that Constantine insisted that 'the most marvellous place in the world' must be fittingly adorned. Eusebius mentioned its 'boundless' height, which was in fact 22 metres. The congregation was intended to face westwards, that is the opposite direction from the one we now take as normal, and at the west end was an apse, or 'hemisphere' as Eusebius calls it, with a ring of twelve columns. This was later thought to be the place where the cross was found.[22] Recent excavation has given us a good deal of information about the positioning of the basilica. It was not, as we would rather expect, laid out in a straight line with the tomb precisely to the west. Presumably because of the obstruction offered by

---

[22] See the evidence in Gibson and Taylor, *Beneath the Holy Sepulchre*, 83–5.

the rock spur ('Calvary') on the south side, the apse or hemisphere was not aligned perfectly with the tomb further west, but was offset to the south. It may also be that this slightly crooked design was the result of reusing the Hadrianic foundations, but they also might have been shaped by the same rock feature.

At the westernmost end was the place which, in the accounts of Eusebius and Egeria, gave significance to the whole: the Sepulchre or cave where the Lord was buried, and had been raised from the dead. By 380, it was surrounded by a mighty building, which accounts for Egeria's description of it as the 'basilica of the Resurrection', *basilica Anastasis*. This consisted of a great rotunda, which provided a semi-circle 12 metres in diameter, with apses to the west, north, and south. There were twelve magnificent columns, with six pilasters between them. Their massive masonry, in its lower parts at least, resisted the attempts of Caliph al-Hakim's officers to demolish it in the early eleventh century, so that the existing ground-plan of the rotunda corresponds with the original one. It is effectively the only part of the

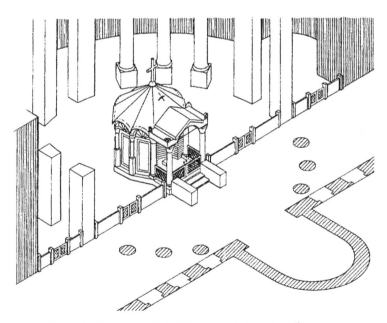

FIG 2.1 The edicule, or tomb building, set below the great rotunda or Anastasis, as it was from the late fourth century, reconstructed by John Wilkinson.

fourth-century building that now survives. The upper part was over-thrown, and its original design is uncertain, and the columns are now as a whole enclosed in later fabric. The date of the construction of the rotunda is also unclear. It has been argued that Cyril referred to the rotunda, but the meaning of his words is ambiguous. The first certain mention is in Egeria, and that would suggest that it had not been built before the consecration of 335, although it might have been part of the original design.[23]

At the centre of the rotunda was the Sepulchre. Eusebius calls it a cave, and it was apparently a grave cut into a rock wall, surviving from the original quarry. The Garden Tomb beloved by English nineteenth-century visitors, while it is certainly not the correct site, gives some impression of what the Holy Sepulchre was originally like. Constantine's architects decided to turn it into a formal memorial. Their intention seems to have been, not to preserve the sacred fabric intact, but to recast it into a memorial worthy of the Saviour. They handled it brutally. Felix Fabri once again comments accurately: 'A man who sees the ancient tombs in the holy land easily understands what the Lord's Sepulchre must have been like; but it cannot possibly now be like what it then was, because of the church which has been built above it and because of its decorations . . . No part of the shape of the ground has remained like that described by the evangelists.'[24] The cliff behind it was cut away, leaving the grave-chamber with its bench, still in the natural rock. The ante-room or vestibule was cut away in the process of clearing the rock, but the stone that had originally closed the entrance had been found in the course of the excavations, and was preserved in front of the entrance.[25] The cave was enclosed in a little building or 'edicule', as it has come to be known, faced in marble, and provided with columns and rich ornament. 'Edicule' is a word mainly characteristic of modern discussions. The Vulgate translation referred to the tomb as *monumentum* (for Greek *mnēmeion*) and *sepulcrum* (for *taphos*) in Matthew 27: 60 and 28: 1. These became the two standard words in Latin authors throughout the Middle Ages. A monument, in classical usage, was

---

[23] Ibid. 77; W. E. Kleinbauer, 'The Anastasis Rotunda and Christian Architectural Invention', *Real and Ideal Jerusalem*, 140–6.

[24] *Felix Fabri*, PPTS 7–8. 400.

[25] For references, see V. C. Corbo, *Il santo sepolcro di Gerusalemme*, 3 vols. (Jerusalem, 1981–2), i. 70 ff., and in particular Cyril, *Cat.* 14. 9; Jerome, ep. 108. 9 (Wilkinson, *Pilgrims*, 83). Cyril is our sole evidence for the original 'vestibule', but as a local man his evidence deserves full weight.

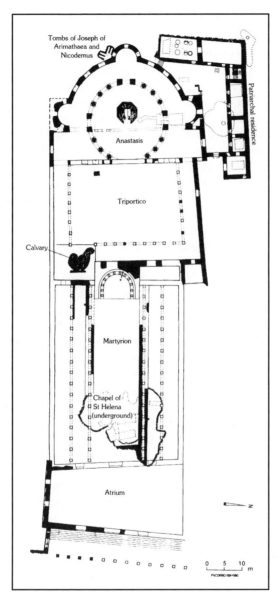

Tombs of Joseph of
Arimathaea and
Nicodemus

Patriarchal residence

Anastasis

Triportico

Calvary

Martyrion

Chapel of
St Helena
(underground)

Atrium

0   5   10
        m

N

P.CORBO 199-1980

FIG 2.2 Plan of the church of the Resurrection or Holy Sepulchre as completed before 400. The main street of Aelia is at the bottom, and the west at the top of the plan. The rotunda around the tomb was probably added well after the consecration in 335. The rock of Calvary was left without buildings, but by 380 may well have acquired a monumental cross.

essentially a memorial. As Cicero remarked, 'a monument should be addressed more to the memory of posterity than the beautification of the present'. The word means, in fact, simply 'that which preserves the memory of anything'. It recalled the essential function of the Holy Sepulchre as addressing the memory of the church.

It is unlikely that Christians had built basilicas, or great churches, before the time of Constantine.[26] He sponsored churches of the basilican type, among many variations of detail, in Rome at St John Lateran and St Peter Vatican, and at Jerusalem, Bethlehem, and Constantinople. Equally distinctive of the imperial building programme was the rotunda. This recalled the circular or polygonal mausoleum built in commemoration of past emperors. The demands of Christian worship were, however, distinctive, and as a result Constantine's projects combined a mausoleum with a basilica for the eucharist and with transepts to allow for the circulation of pilgrims to pay their devotions at the shrine. Probably the first experiment in this direction was the mausoleum of Helena at Rome, which may originally have been intended for Constantine himself. The plan was subsequently adopted for a series of holy places and tombs: St Peter Vatican, St Paul *fuori le mura*, both at Rome, the Holy Sepulchre at Jerusalem, and the Church of the Nativity at Bethlehem.[27] Constantine's building campaigns saw the emergence for the first time of a distinctive Christian pilgrimage architecture, although it is impossible to be sure whether the emperor himself participated in the design. At the Holy Sepulchre, it provided the memorial to Christ, the greatest emperor of all. If the completion of the rotunda over the Sepulchre cannot be demonstrated before 380, the design fits closely with the approach adopted elsewhere. The Anastasis rotunda was to be one of the features regularly invoked by builders when they sought to provide architectural memorials of the Holy Sepulchre in the West.

VISITORS TO THE HOLY SEPULCHRE

Constantine's new church was dedicated on 13 September 335 in the presence of an assembly of bishops who had come from the Council

---

[26] J. B. Ward-Perkins, 'Constantine and the Origins of the Christian Basilica', *Papers of the British School at Rome*, 22 (1954), 69–90; but also Gregory Dix, *The Shape of the Liturgy* (Westminster, 1945), ch. 11.

[27] F. Tolotti, 'Il S. Sepolcro di Gerusalemme e le coeve basiliche di Roma', *Mitteilungen des Deutschen Archäologischen Instituts*, Römische Abteilung, 93 (1986), 471–512.

of Tyre.[28] By then pilgrims had begun to arrive. In this period, and for long afterwards, the word *peregrinus*, the origin of our 'pilgrim', was not specific to a visitor to a shrine. It meant a foreigner or an alien, and *peregrinatio* in late classical usage implied having foreign customs or accent, or an unfavourable legal status in contrast with that of a citizen. *Peregrinus* could mean a traveller, but only in the sense that long-distance travellers are by definition foreigners. When, in the Vulgate translation of the Bible, God promised to Abraham that the *terra peregrinationis tuae* would be given to his descendants (Genesis 17: 8), the meaning was precisely that of the old English translation, 'the land wherein thou art a stranger'. It is rare for a traveller to Palestine to be described as a 'pilgrim' until many centuries later, and if the word *peregrinus* were used it would only mean that he or she was a stranger there. There was, moreover, no alternative word. The 'pilgrim' has to be identified by the context, or by an explanation of purpose: 'to pray' (the most common of all), 'to worship', 'to visit', or 'to see' were among the expressions used. Greek *xenos* was the equivalent of *peregrinus*, but never acquired a specialized sense. In the twelfth century the Palestine pilgrim John Phocas was still using a clumsy periphrasis, 'people who travel abroad for Christ'. For most travellers the goal was the point, and the character of the experience was defined by that rather than by the experience of travel.

In Ch. 1 some examples were given of Christian visitors to Palestine, but we have no secure idea of the volume of visits from outside or the provision that was made for them at any shrines that may have existed. The long period of freedom from persecution in the second half of the third century, between Decius and Diocletian, would have given opportunity for devout travel, which presumably increased after Constantine's edict of toleration in the Western Empire in 313. Eusebius does indeed provide us with some indications that there was already an increase in the number of visitors to Biblical sites before Constantine's victory in the East. In his *Proof of the Gospels* (*Demonstratio Evangelica*), probably written between 314 and 320, he spoke of those who came to worship at the Mount of Olives and to say their prayers at Bethlehem. None of the travellers known to us before 324 was a Westerner.

Helena's tour of the Eastern provinces as *augusta* or empress,

[28] M. Black, 'The Festival of *encaenia ecclesiae* in the Ancient Church', *JEH* 5 (1954), 78–85, and Borgehammar, 99–103.

probably in 326, was an imperial visitation. Eusebius indicated that care for the churches was an essential part of her mission, and credited her, not necessarily correctly, with the building of the basilica at Bethlehem, and emphasized her 'pious devotion to God, the king of kings'. The next recorded visitor was the anonymous traveller from Bordeaux, who left behind a record of a journey in AD 333: the first Western arrival of whom we know. Whatever the level of travel to the Holy Land up to the time of Constantine, there is not much sign of a marked change while Constantine himself was emperor. In particular, the Bordeaux traveller remains unique, as far as we know, as a Western pilgrim. We shall therefore return to this subject in the next chapter.

Among the many uncertainties about what happened at Jerusalem in the time of Constantine, there are some things that can be said with confidence. Immediately after he came to power in the East, Constantine, whose policy was becoming much more assertively pro-Christian, authorized the removal of the buildings for pagan worship on what were reputed to be holy places at Jerusalem. By 335 a great basilica had been provided there, and the Sepulchre had been excavated and provided with a stone dressing or edicule. By 380 it had also been surrounded by the mighty rotunda of the Anastasis. The holy cross (or what was believed to be the cross) had been found in the course of the works, and the rocky knoll to the south of the site had perhaps already been provided with a monumental cross, appropriate to its status as the location of the crucifixion. These places, moreover, were the centre of a new Christian Jerusalem, in which basilicas marked some of the most vital places in the Christian story, and which provided the scenario for a new pattern of worship. Its influence was already beginning to be disseminated throughout East and West—a process we must study in the next chapter.

3

Dissemination: The Spread of Interest in the Holy Sepulchre in Western Europe, 350–600

PILGRIMAGE TO THE HOLY SEPULCHRE UNDER THE CHRISTIAN EMPIRE

It is a curious fact that we hear far more about visitors from the West than from the East. This can hardly be because people were not coming from other regions. We know of pilgrims from Egypt and Cappadocia, and Jerome reported their arrival even from India, Persia, and Ethiopia; John Chrysostom reported that 'all the world comes to see the Sepulchre which has no body: some power draws those who live in the distant parts of the earth, to see where he was born, where he was buried, where he was crucified'.[1] Nevertheless reports from Western visitors testify to Latin interest in the Holy Land, and are more abundant than anything similar from Eastern sources. It is clear, too, that for more than two generations after 380 the city was an international cultural centre with links with most parts of the Christian world. Although the liturgy was in Greek, Syriac and Latin were widely used there.

It is tempting to think of pilgrimage as impelled by personal devotion, which leads individuals to leave their homeland and go to worship at distant shrines. This was always an element in its history, but the movement was shaped at least as much by patronage and politics. Pilgrimage to the Holy Sepulchre was a public and political act, dimensions that were evident from the beginning: 'Constantine's policy for Jerusalem . . . was aimed at expressing the Christian victory. But the fact that this policy came from the Roman emperor himself, and was to signalise a victory which affected all Christians in his dominions, meant that Jerusalem was once again to assume an international role, this time as a place of pilgrimage for Christians

---

[1] Jerome, ep. 107. 2. 3; Chrysostom, *Commentary on Ps. 109* (PG 55. 274).

Travel Narratives to the Holy Land

The three best early eyewitness accounts of travel to Jerusalem
are those of the anonymous Bordeaux pilgrim, Egeria, and the
anonymous Piacenza pilgrim. We have already had occasion to
use the information provided by the Bordeaux anonymous and
Egeria, as they are prime evidence for fourth-century Aelia. It
is not clear whether the Bordeaux pilgrim was a man or a
woman. The account of the journey in 333 is similar to other
contemporary itineraries in being a list of place-names that
record a journey along the great imperial roads. The one exception to this extreme brevity is the description of Judaea, where
the holy places are described, although still very succinctly. The
writer's interest is in the Biblical events that had taken place
there, some of them already identified with specific sites. It is
possible that some of them were served by communities of
monks, as they certainly were fifty years later during Egeria's
visit.

The name 'Egeria' is not clearly established, but is now generally preferred to the older Silvia (which is certainly wrong)
and Etheria. The evidence suggests that she had Spanish connections. The date of her travels, usually given as 382–5, rests
on a precarious deduction, but she would fit naturally into the
Spanish culture of the imperial court at Constantinople in the
time of Theodosius I. She apparently belonged to one of
the devout circles of Western ladies, whose most outstanding
representatives were prominent at Rome and Jerusalem.
Unfortunately, although her text is extensive, it is not complete.
In particular, the address to her Western correspondents is
missing, and with it we have lost any clear explanation of why
she wrote such a full account of her travels. The character of
what she wrote suggests that she had in mind the evidence for
the Gospel, whose truth was authenticated by the places where
events had happened. It was authenticated, too, by the liturgy
and devotion of the communities that had grown up around
the Biblical sites. Egeria's contacts wanted to know about the
special features of Eastern worship, which was much richer
than that in the West. Egeria is our evidence for the existence of
the complex liturgy based at the church of the Holy Sepulchre,

and accordingly for the adoration of the cross on the rock of Golgotha, and arguably for the monumental cross there.

The Piacenza pilgrim named one Antoninus as his saintly protector on his journey. All we know about his date is that he mentions the severe damage 'recently' done to Berytus (Beirut) by an earthquake. There was a quake there in 554, but there were others, and there is no proper indication of the time that had elapsed. The accepted date, 570, is thus approximate. In addition, there are guides to Western pilgrims called the *Handbook* (*Breviarius*), and a compilation by a certain Theodosius. Both perhaps originated around 500, and exist in various forms.

For dates and identities, see the literature cited in the main Bibliography.

throughout the world.'[2] The elite had always travelled widely, and ostentation was implicit in the life of the upper classes in the city or *polis*. With the acceptance of Christianity by the senatorial classes at Rome, it became conventional to express personal devotion more publicly than ever before. There is a good deal of force in the view that 'people went on pilgrimage in the early Christian period because it had become the thing to do'.[3] The predominantly Latin court at Constantinople provided an important connection between the Holy Sepulchre and circles in the West. The Bordeaux anonymous of 333 travelled through Constantinople. Bordeaux was a university centre, from which Constantine had invited Aemilius Magnus Arborius to Constantinople as professor of rhetoric and tutor to his family. The anonymous may not have been a resident of Bordeaux (the return journey terminated at Milan), but clearly had connections with the city. The next generation saw the development of personal links of a different kind, with the exile from the West of Latin dissentients from imperial church policy. Bishop Eusebius of Vercelli spent six years in the East from 355 to 361, some of it at least in Palestine.[4]

[2] J. Wilkinson, 'Christian Pilgrims in Jerusalem during the Byzantine Period', *PEQ* 118 (1976), 82; E. Wipszyca, 'Les Pèlerinages chrétiens dans l'antiquité tardive', *Byzantinoslavica*, 56 (1995), 429–38.
[3] C. Mango, 'The Pilgrim's Motivation', *Akten XII*, 9.
[4] J. Matthews, *Western Aristocracies and Imperial Court 364–425* (Oxford, 1975), 82–5; on the career of Eusebius, Dal Covolo and others (eds.), *Eusebio di Vercelli e il suo tempo* (Rome, 1997).

Relations between the imperial court and the West became especially close under the Emperor Theodosius I (379–95). Theodosius
was a Spaniard and a devout Christian. Most of the influential members of his administration were Westerners, in several cases com-
patriots of his from Spain, and they championed an aggressively
Christian policy. It was at Constantinople that Egeria wrote up the
reports on her travels for her circle in the West. Other pilgrims at the
time of Theodosius were Bishop Gaudentius of Brescia in the decade
after 385, and a wealthy lady from Aquitaine, Silvia. David Hunt has
observed that 'the early Christian pilgrim, in taking the decisive step
of journeying to the Holy Land, destined himself for a major role in
the life of the church, not only at the scene of the holy places but no
less in the community to which he returned . . . Pilgrimage was a
qualification for influence.'[5] The imperial capital was Constantinople,
and almost no emperor visited Jerusalem, but there were prominent
patrons from the imperial family, among them Helena, Pulcheria,
and Eudochia. Egeria's journals draw our attention to another
important aspect of Western interest in Jerusalem. She included in
her journey visits to the holy men in the monasteries of the East:
Latin religious communities in the city, which were to be founded
shortly after her visit, were to have close links with Egyptian and
Syrian monasticism, and helped to form a bridge that brought its
ideals to the West.

The senatorial families at Rome had remained immensely wealthy,
even when political power had moved from them to the imperial
administration. From the 370s onwards they recovered a good deal of
their political influence, especially within Italy itself, and sections
of this group emerged as devout catholics with an ascetic way of
life. Two of the outstanding Latin scholars of the age, Jerome and
Rufinus, wielded influence over the senatorial ladies at Rome, and
with them they created two major centres near Jerusalem. The elder
Melania came to Palestine around 372/4, and founded a double
monastery on the Mount of Olives with Rufinus. Meanwhile at Bethlehem were Jerome and his protégée Paula and her relatives who
came to Jerusalem about 385, together with a stream of visiting
scholars from Egypt and the West. Jerusalem became a centre of
Latin and Greek theology, while the communities kept in touch with
sympathizers in Italy, and welcomed them on visits to the Holy Land.

[5] E. D. Hunt, 'St Silvia of Aquitaine', *Journal of Theological Studies*, NS 23 (1972),
372–3.

With their links with senatorial circles in Rome and the imperial court at Constantinople, and with the ascetic movement in both East and West, these Latin settlements at Jerusalem were major religious influences in the contemporary church. During the century after the dedication of Constantine's basilica Jerusalem, Bethlehem, and the other holy places became the goal of many travellers. Only the wealthy and their servants could undertake the expensive journey from the West, but numbers were large. Jerome commented that 'here people come together from the whole world. The city is full of people of every kind, and there is a great tumult of men and women'.[6]

The collapse of the frontiers in the West in 406 and the barbarian invasions that followed, including the sack of Rome by the Goths under Alaric in 410, transformed the situation. Its first effect was to increase the flow of Westerners to Palestine, and to bring people who no longer arrived as great patrons, but were destitute: 'holy Bethlehem, to which noble men and women once came in streams with their riches, receives beggars every day'.[7] The elder Melania, who had returned to Italy, finally came back to Palestine around the time of the sack of Rome by the Goths. Her granddaughter the younger Melania, who was even richer and has been called 'the great heiress of the Roman world', moved first to Africa and then subsequently to Jerusalem. Her career provides us with a dramatic illustration of the significance of the Holy Sepulchre. She resided at first within the church in premises put aside for poor pilgrims. Yet even after her retirement to the Mount of Olives, Melania's contact with the imperial court continued: she travelled to Constantinople in 437 to meet, and convert, her uncle who was on an embassy from Rome, and she influenced the Empress Eudochia, another devotee of the Holy Land. The liturgy of the Jerusalem church was always important to her: in the days before her death in 439 she travelled to Bethlehem to celebrate the nativity (the first indication, by the way, that the Western Christmas of 25 December had reached Jerusalem), and then to the basilica of Saint Stephen, the supreme Jerusalem martyr. Although a pure Roman by birth, Melania was absorbed into the memory of the Greek churches: because of the monasteries she founded, she was commemorated in all the Orthodox calendars, but remained virtually unknown in Western churches. Meanwhile in the

---

[6] Jerome, ep. 58.4 to Paulinus (*Lettres*, ed. J. Labourt (Paris, 1953), iii. 78.
[7] Jerome, *Commentary on Ezekiel* chs. 3 and 7 (CCSL 75 (1964), 9, 277).

first half of the fifth century, scholars such as Orosius and Pelagius went to Jerusalem partly as refugees, but also because of the sanctity of the holy places and the role of the church there in the current theological debates.

In the longer run the influence of the Latin settlement at Jerusalem could not survive the increasing isolation of large parts of the West. Hydatius, a native of Galicia in northern Spain, illustrates what happened. At the age of 10, he had been to Jerusalem and even met Jerome, but by the time he wrote a chronicle in 455 he had lost touch with Palestine. Dwelling as he did 'at the edge of the entire world', he encountered few travellers from the Holy Land, and none of them knew when Jerome had died.[8] On the other hand, the existence of handbooks, such as the various editions of *Breviarius* and Theodosius in the early sixth century, indicate a considerable pilgrim traffic. Given the uncertainty of the date of the Piacenza pilgrim, his journey may be a testimony to Justinian's renewal of the unity of the empire—a renaissance that had so little future; but there are other possibilities. The Piacenza narrative was interested in the 'blessings', flasks brought back from Palestine containing such relics as oil that had been in contact with the wood of the cross. A fine collection of these was presented about AD 600 by the Roman Church to the Lombard Queen Theodelinda, and by her to the basilica of San Giovanni, Monza, where they are still preserved. This certainly suggests the existence of a steady flow of visitors to the holy places in Palestine during the second half of the sixth century, and associates the Roman church and the new Lombard rulers, along with the anonymous Piacenza pilgrim, in interest in the Palestinian sites. Other new kingdoms in the West similarly maintained an interest in Jerusalem. We shall look further on at Queen Radegund's acquisition of a portion of the wood of the cross; and a later legend told how the Burgundian King Guntram (died 593) discovered a treasure, shown to him by a dragon in a dream. He intended to send it to Jerusalem, but eventually used it to provide a great ciborium for the Church of St Marcel at Châlon.[9]

The one large surviving collection of papal correspondence from this period, the register of Gregory I, contains evidence of a regular connection with Jerusalem in the first decade of the seventh century.

[8] P. Brown, *The Rise of Western Christendom* (Oxford, 1996), 56.
[9] Paul the Deacon, *Historia Langobardorum*, ed. G. Waitz (MGH SRG in usum scholarum, ii. 34). Paul was writing in the second half of the eighth century, and there is no way of knowing when the legend arose.

The pope was concerned about quarrels within the church there, and mentioned a number of indications of pilgrimage: the journey seems to have been so routine that a group of monks could escape from Rome on the pretence that they were going to Jerusalem. The development of pilgrimage sites carried with it a progressive christianization of the journeys. The first travellers were using the imperial road network and its supporting facilities, but both Egeria and the elder Melania seem to have been regularly greeted by bishops during their travels. Charitable patrons established hostels (*xenodochia*) to assist travellers. The provision of hospitality at Jerusalem was apparently on a vast scale. When the Piacenza pilgrim visited St Mary's, the 'New Church' magnificently built by the Emperor Justinian, he commented on 'its guest houses for men and women. In catering for travellers they have a vast number of tables, and more than 3000 beds for the sick.'[10] How many Latins used the facilities is another matter, but a generation later, we hear of money left by the Roman Abbot Probus to create a hostel at Jerusalem.[11] By this time, the cult of the holy places had long been established within Christian practice.

HOLY PLACES IN CHRISTIAN THINKING

In the course of the fourth century, the church qualified its earlier universalism and moved towards the reverence for holy places that was to shape Christian culture in subsequent centuries. The change was of profound importance for the future history of Europe and the Middle East: 'To this period can be attributed the origins of those traditional Christian notions, concerning the holiness of Jerusalem and of particular places, which now in the light of the crusades, of church history, of Zionism and Middle East politics need to be reassessed.'[12] The contrast was not absolute, and it would be better to speak of the 'large development' rather than the 'origins' of these ideas. Reverence for the relics and tombs of the martyrs can be traced back into the second century: the cemeteries of Rome had almost

---

[10] Piacenza pilgrim, 23 (Wilkinson, *Pilgrims*, 141).

[11] *pro faciendo xenodochio*: Gregory I, letter xiii. 28 (ed. L. M. Hartmann, MGH Ep. II (Berlin, 1957), 393). It is often said that the pope himself was the founder of this hostel: this is the view of P. Maraval, 'Grégoire le Grand et les lieux saints d'Orient', *Gregorio Magno e il suo tempo* (Rome, 1991), 68. In the letter, however, the pope does not seem to be claiming responsibility for the undertaking.

[12] P. W. L. Walker, 'Eusebius, Cyril and the Holy Places', *Studia Patristica*, 20 (1989), 306–14.

certainly come to contain holy places by this time. Nor did the cult of
holy places come to dominate without reservation. From the beginning, Western writers expressed reservations about the pilgrimage to
Palestine. Jerome himself provided some of the classic texts for and
against sacred places. On the one hand, he insisted that Jerusalem
does still retain a significance for the believer: 'if after the Lord's
passion, as is wickedly said, this is an accursed place, why did Paul
want to hasten to Jerusalem to keep Pentecost there?'[13] Conversely
he wrote, most notably in his letter to Paulinus, some of the most
persuasive texts against pilgrimage. It contains the magnificent
assertion that 'the heavenly court stands open, alike from Jerusalem
and from Britain; for the spirit of God is within us', and some famous
words that were never forgotten in medieval theology, that 'it is not to
have been at Jerusalem, but to have lived well at Jerusalem, that
is worthy of praise'.[14] Eastern visitors shared similar reservations.
Gregory of Nyssa at times spoke approvingly of holy places, but he
reverenced the graves of the martyrs of Cappadocia more than the
sacred sites of Palestine, about which he could be remarkably negative: 'We knew about the incarnation through the Virgin before we
saw Bethlehem; we believed in the resurrection before we saw the
tomb; we believed in the truth of the ascension without seeing
the Mount of Olives.' He observed, correctly enough, that the Lord
in the Beatitudes did not count the journey to Jerusalem among the
good deeds—a remark that, long afterwards, was to secure favourable comment from Protestant scholars.[15] In the early fifth-century
West, the great theologian Augustine was unimpressed by the claims
of the holy places of Palestine. He accepted that it was useful to go
there for a reason well recognized by tradition, namely to determine
the precise meaning of Biblical passages, but he was also insistent on
the universalist tradition. Psalm 132: 7, 'let us worship at his foot-
stool' (Vulgate version, 'where his feet have stood'), a central text for
pilgrim enthusiasts, was taken by Augustine to mean that, for all
believers, our feet stand in Christ. Even when faced by the text of

---

[13] Jerome, ep. 46 (PPTS I. 9). The reference is to Acts 20: 16: 'he was hastening to be
at Jerusalem, if possible, on the day of Pentecost'. Jerome disregards the fact that this
was before the destruction of the Temple in AD 70.

[14] Jerome, ep. 58. 3, 2 (nn. 77, 75). The quotation in the first text is of Luke 17: 21,
which in modern exegesis is often seen as referring to the sudden appearance of the
kingdom among the hearers, rather than to its inward nature, which is how Jerome
understood it.

[15] Gregory, *Letters* (PG 46. 1010C, 1011BC, and 1014C).

Psalm 76: 1, 'in Judah God is known', he emphasized that God is not to be found in one place more than another.[16] In spite of the contacts between East and West a century later in the time of Pope Gregory I, Gregory's theological works attached no particular importance to the historical reality of Biblical sites, whose names were almost invariably glossed with spiritual interpretations, and he commented that 'God lives wherever we seek true peace, where we love the glory of inward contemplation'.[17]

Jerusalem was not a simple concept. It consisted of four hills: Golgotha or Calvary, Sion, the Mount of Olives, and the Temple Mount. Of these, the fourth was regarded as cursed by God from the time of the destruction of the Temple in AD 70. No attempt was made to christianize it until the crusader period, and Jerome nastily called it a *sterquilinium* or dung-pit. Sion, the hill that was truly within the old city, contained one of the oldest churches and was thought to be the place where the Last Supper was celebrated, where the disciples met after the resurrection, and where the Spirit was given at the first Pentecost. Golgotha was the place of the crucifixion, in the vicinity of the empty tomb. The Mount of Olives had little basis for its sanctity in the Hebrew Scriptures, but was heavily marked out by Christian holy places. It was thought to be the site of the resurrection of Lazarus, of the starting-place of Jesus' triumphal entry, of the temptation at Gethsemane, and of the ascension. Its special status was acknowledged by Constantine's foundation of the church of the Eleona (or Olives). The one Old Testament reference, Zechariah 14: 4, gave it a place in the coming end of the world: 'On that day (the Lord's) feet shall stand on the Mount of Olives before Jerusalem on the east.' These eschatological references were strengthened by the vision of Joel 3: 1–2, in which the judgement of the nations was seen as taking place in the Valley of Jehoshaphat. From the time of Eusebius' *Onomasticon*, at least, this was identified with the valley 'between Jerusalem and the Mount of Olives'. In Christian tradition, and in the eyes of pilgrims, the Mount and its surroundings became the preferred site of the events of the last day.[18]

Such ideas enhanced the wide appeal of Palestine in the fourth

[16] B. Bitton-Ashkelony, 'The Attitudes of Church Fathers to Jerusalem in the Fourth and Fifth Centuries', in Levine, 188–203.

[17] Gregory I, eps xi. 26, 52, xiii. 28; cf. viii. 6, vii. 29 (ed. L. M. Hartmann, MGH Ep. 11 (Berlin, 1957), 289, 325, 393; I. 475–6); Maraval, 'Grégoire le Grand', 65–76.

[18] O. Limor, 'The Place of the End of Days: Eschatological Geography in Jerusalem', *Real and Ideal Jerusalem*, 13–22.

century: 'a Christian Palestine, or at least a Christian Jerusalem . . .
fitted the mood of the moment perfectly'.[19] The Sepulchre of Christ
was a holy place of unique significance, one newly brought to light
by the work authorized by Constantine. The terminology 'holy
places' had not occurred in Christian literature before Constantine's
letter to Bishop Macarius, which referred to the 'sacred spot . . . holy
indeed from the beginning in God's judgement'.[20] Eusebius himself
echoed this language in referring to 'the blessed place of the
Saviour's resurrection' and 'the venerable and hallowed monument'.[21] In his later works he was adjusting his theology to the new
circumstances. To clarify the journeys of the Empress Helena he cited
Psalm 132: 7, 'we shall worship in the place where his feet have
stood'.[22] Within ten years Bishop Cyril, teaching in Constantine's
basilica, repeatedly described the sites around him as holy, even as
all-holy (*panagios*) and blessed (*makarios*), and before the end of the
century 'holy places' was a standard expression in the works of Jerome, as it was in the *Life* of the younger Melania, written by her
disciple Gerontius shortly after her death in 439. She, too, was concerned to build a small *martyrium* on the Mount of Olives in the
'place where the Lord's feet have stood'.[23] The term 'Holy Land' also
became current. It occurs only once in the Old Testament: 'The
Lord will inherit Judah as his portion in the Holy Land, and will
again choose Jerusalem' (Zechariah 2: 12), and it had been used by
Origen. By the middle of the fifth century it was a generally
accepted way of referring to Palestine. The precise meaning of Holy
Land, holy places, and Holy City was varied in different writers, but
their use was certainly encouraged by the prayer of Solomon at the
foundation of the Temple, where he spoke of the people of Israel
when they address God and 'pray toward their land, which you
gave to their ancestors, the city that you have chosen, and the
house that I have built for your name' (2 Chronicles 6: 38). Some
writers have seen this new attachment to holy places as part of a
larger shift in the theology of the church, from eschatology to what
is sometimes called historicism, away from its earlier hope and

---

[19] P. W. L. Walker, *Holy City, Holy Places?* (Oxford, 1990), 16.
[20] Eusebius, *Life of Constantine* iii. 30 (PPTS 1. 5). When Origen used the term in his
Commentary on John 4: 19–20 (SC 222. (1975), 74–6), he was referring to the ideas of
Jews and Samaritans.
[21] Eusebius, *Life of Constantine*, 3. 25, 28 (PPTS 1. 3).
[22] Ibid. 3. 42 (1. 42).
[23] *Life of Melania* c. 57 (ed. D. Gorce, SC 90 (1962), 240).

towards an acceptance of its historical place in the world. Joan Taylor presents the change as an extreme and dramatic one: 'suddenly, with Constantine, the church began to focus on earth: the divine substance intermixed with certain material sites and resided in things which could be carried about'.[24] We must return to this issue shortly.

The reverence for the holy places of Palestine was the motor that drove the huge development of monasticism there, whose origins can be traced almost precisely to the time when Constantine began to create a Christian Jerusalem. At the beginning of the fourth century Chariton made a pilgrimage to Jerusalem, and by the time of his death in about 350 he had founded three monasteries. Most of the monks who settled in Judaea had come as pilgrims from provinces of the Eastern Empire: they were primarily non-Palestinians by origin, and kept links with the pilgrims, for whom some of the largest monasteries ran hospices in the holy city itself. The monasteries formed the basis for a society of increasing prosperity, within which the overwhelming proportion of the population were Christians, and which secured Palestine for Byzantine culture until the political collapse of the seventh century. The growth of the monasteries was encouraged by spiritual, political, and economic considerations—a distinction that it is more natural to make now than it was under the Christian Empire:

The modern concept of spirituality needs reinterpretation in order to be applied to the lives of the Byzantine saints. It is not a personal and interior dimension which can be contrasted to the hard world of the material order. Instead it describes the means by which the saint expressed the purposes of God in the midst of the society of the time.[25]

Accordingly, the monastic activity of St Sabas was described by the word *polisai*, to build or colonize. A splendid mosaic map, which has been unearthed in the church at Madaba, near Amann, seems to be a celebration of the populous society of Christian Palestine, gathered around the mother church of Jerusalem, which was conceived as the centre of orthodoxy in the current theological disputes. The proportion of Latin monks was small, and tended to be confined to a few special establishments like those of Jerome and Melania in Jerusalem itself.

[24] J. E. Taylor, *Christians and the Holy Places* (Oxford, 1993), 314.
[25] J. Binns, *Ascetics and Ambassadors of Christ: The Monasteries of Palestine 314–631* (Oxford, 1994), 221.

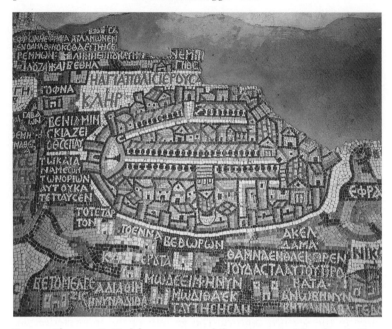

FIG 3.1 The mosaic Madaba map covered the pavement of the church there with an illustration of Christian Palestine. It was a theologically controlled rendering. Jerusalem (illustrated here) was at the centre of the whole pavement, in front of the eastern apse. Madaba itself was shown on the same axis: the claim was being made of a special association between the two. The Temple mount was omitted, and the city depicted so as to bring the church of the Holy Sepulchre to the centre, here shown below, that is to the west of, the main street. Nevertheless, the design rests on cartographic reality, and many of the actual features of the contemporary city can be identified in it. The date may be around 600.

This Christian Palestine naturally became a powerhouse for the insistence on the special character of sanctity of Jerusalem. The visual effect of the city upon pilgrims was dramatically declared in the *Life of Peter of Iberia*: 'they saw, shining like the sunrise, the lofty roofs of the holy and venerable churches, those of the saving and adored cross, the holy resurrection (Anastasis) and also of the ascension, worthy of adoration, on the mountain opposite'.[26] This was declared

---

[26] Peter of Iberia (in Georgia) visited the city about 430; his *Life* was written around 500. See B. Flusin, 'Les Lieux Saints de Jérusalem', *Lieux sacrés*, esp. 120–34.

in a remarkable letter from the monks of Jerusalem to the Emperor Anastasius (491–518) in defence of the theological position of the Council of Chalcedon. It was his task, they said, to work for the defence of all the churches,

> but especially for the mother of churches, Sion, where was revealed and accomplished for the salvation of the world, the great mystery of piety . . . From that precious and supernatural mystery of Christ, through the victorious and precious cross and the life-giving Anastasis, indeed all the holy and adored places, receiving by tradition from above and from the beginning through the blessed and holy apostles, the true confession . . . we, the dwellers of this Holy Land, have kept it invulnerable and inviolable in Christ.[27]

Confidence of this sort lay behind the tremendous affirmation of Leontius of Byzantium, writing about 640, of the value of images and of holy places:

> All we, the faithful, worship the cross of Christ as his staff; his all-holy tomb as his throne and couch; the manger and Bethlehem, and the holy places where he lived as his house; the apostles, the holy martyrs and other saints as his friends; we reverence Sion as his city; we embrace Nazareth as his country; we embrace the Jordan as his divine bath . . . Not honouring the place, nor the house, nor the country, nor the city, nor the stones, but him who dwelt and appeared and was made manifest in the flesh in them.[28]

There is no parallel in the West for so ecstatic a proclamation of the supreme significance of the holy places, but the developing spirituality of Latin monks owed a great deal to ideas imported from the East. One of the essential aims of monastic leaders was to reproduce the fervour of the apostolic community that had originated at Jerusalem. The descriptions of its life in Acts 2: 42 and 4: 32–5 were ceaselessly quoted as a sort of foundation charter of the monastic life.

The new Christian Jerusalem was centred on Constantine's church, but it included other ancient sites, all of which were marked by large memorial churches and linked by processions. Shortly after 415, a great basilica was added to mark the discovery of the body of St Stephen, the first martyr. This was a spectacular development in less than a hundred years, and it continued subsequently. Under

---

[27] R. L. Wilken, 'Loving the Jerusalem Below: The Monks of Palestine', in Levine, 240–50.

[28] C. Barber, 'The Truth in Painting: Iconoclasm and Identity in Early Medieval Art', *Speculum*, 74 (1997), 1031.

Justinian in the sixth century, there was still further expansion with the provision on the south side of the city of the 'New' church, the Nea, in honour of the Virgin Mary. As Jerome had already put it, 'the city is moved on its foundations'.[29] There were two important gaps in the structure of pilgrim Jerusalem. In spite of the many processions that marked the liturgy at the church of Jerusalem, there was nothing faintly like the way of the cross, the *via dolorosa* that led the Saviour to his suffering on Calvary, and to which we must return, because long afterwards it was to become the centre of the Jerusalem experience.

More immediately significant was the fact that the site of the Temple remained in ruins, as a perpetual reminder of God's destruction of the worship of the old Israel. The site was not sanctified, but was to be for ever unsanctified. It had been replaced. By the 330s, Eusebius was proudly announcing that 'built on the very spot which witnessed the Saviour's sufferings, a new Jerusalem was constructed, over against the one so celebrated of old'. He had persistently asserted that the Temple had lost its God-given standing, and in his early work, the *Onomasticon*, he had claimed that the Christians worshipping on the Mount of Olives were a replacement of the devastated Temple. His new thinking now was that God had replaced the Temple with the Holy Sepulchre: 'the monument of salvation itself was the new Jerusalem built over against the old.'[30] This was certainly the thinking of Jerome: 'Formerly the Jews venerated the holy of holies, because there were the cherubim and the place of atonement and the ark of the covenant and the manna and the rod of Aaron and the altar of gold. Does not the Lord's Sepulchre seem to you more worthy of honour?'[31] The Sepulchre, Jerome argued, brings us back to the essential truths of our faith: 'As often as we enter it we see the Lord lying there . . . and the angel sitting at his feet.' Jerome noticed that the Vulgate version of Isaiah 11: 10 expressed this new centrality of the Holy Sepulchre: 'In that day the root of Jesse shall stand as an ensign to the peoples; him shall the nations worship, and his Sepulchre will be glorious.'[32]

Themes that had been associated with the Temple began to be appropriated for Golgotha, and the accumulation of relics and

[29] *urbs movetur sedibus suis*: Jerome, ep. 107 to Laeta (ed. J. Labourt (Paris, 1955), v. 145).

[30] Eusebius, *Life of Constantine* 3. 37 (PPTS 1. 6–7).

[31] Jerome, ep. 46. 5 (PPTS 1).

[32] Commentary on Isaiah 11: 10 (CCSL 73 (1963), 153).

legends continued apace. Shortly after 500, the *Breviarius* was promising pilgrims an impressive set of treasures, some of which were
relics of the passion and others linked with the Temple. Thus, the
cross was kept in a chamber at the entrance to the basilica whose
apse marked the place where the three crosses had been found. The
plate that had carried the head of John the Baptist was on display
there, and the horn with which David and Solomon were anointed,
along with the ring with which Solomon sealed the demons. 'There
(i.e. on the mount of Calvary) Adam was formed. There Abraham
offered his son Isaac as a sacrifice in the very place where the Lord
was crucified.' Within the rotunda of the Anastasis was to be seen
the stone that was rolled away, and the tomb itself was covered with
a roof of silver and gold. In front of it 'is the altar where holy Zacharias was killed, and his blood dried there'. The treasury of the basilica contained the reed and the sponge, and the cup used at the Last
Supper.[33] Late in the sixth century, the Piacenza pilgrim noted that
the colour of blood could still be seen on the mound, but it was now
attributed to Christ himself; in all probability it was a patch of the
pink that occurs within the natural rock.[34] Many of the items in this
museum of devotion really belonged to the Temple, where the Lord
had driven out the sellers of doves, and where Zacharias had been
killed (Matthew 23: 35, Luke 11: 51). Christian tradition had stolen
the stories and relics that once belonged to the Temple and attached
them to the Holy Sepulchre complex. Late in the fourth century,
Egeria thought that the *encaenia* or dedication festival had been fixed
on 13 September because it replaced Solomon's dedication of Israel's
Temple. The Sepulchre, martyrium, and Calvary were thus displayed
to pilgrims as the centre of the new Jerusalem in place of the Temple,
which now stood in ruins.

The fourth and fifth centuries saw a profound reordering of the
topography of the increasingly Christian empire. Constantine had
made New Rome (Constantinople) the capital and Jerusalem the
great religious centre—two cities that, in their former incarnation as
Byzantium and Aelia, had not even ranked as centres of provinces.
The two were linked by imperial patronage of the churches at Jerusalem and by the transfer of relics to Constantinople, beginning with
fragments of the cross immediately after its discovery. The great city
was becoming a second Jerusalem as well as a second Rome. The

---

[33] *Breviarius* A 3 (Wilkinson, *Pilgrims*, 118–19).
[34] Piacenza 19 (Wilkinson, *Pilgrims*, 139).

reverence for holy places echoed the spirit of the age all over the
Christian world. Access to holy places came to dominate Christian
culture. In city after city the centre of gravity moved to the tombs of
the martyrs, in the same way as it had moved in Jerusalem/Aelia.
The structure of government within the church was reshaped to
correspond with the new devotion. Jerusalem, when Constantine
came to the East, was only the bishopric of Aelia, under the control of Caesarea as archbishop or metropolitan. In 451 its bishop,
Juvenal, was elevated to the supreme rank of patriarch, in accordance with its devotional significance. In the same way in the West
places such as Compostela and Durham, which in the late Roman
period did not exist, eventually became major ecclesiastical centres
because they sheltered the relics of James and Cuthbert. Historians
have often, reasonably enough, seen the conversion of Europe as a
turning-point in its history. Almost equally important was the
exorcism of Europe, the removal of the spirits who resided in
innumerable glades, springs, and woods. In the church's observation
of place, holiness was determined by what had happened there, by
sacred history. Aelia/Jerusalem and Bethlehem, and soon Nazareth
and Sinai, became centres of pilgrim imagination, ecclesiastical
government, and monastic establishment.

It was a change that was to determine the subsequent character of
Christianity. We have already noted that Christian religion is a
religion of memory, rooted in the recollection of a sacrifice made and
a victory won, and in ritual obedience to the command, 'Do this in
remembrance of me'. As Jacques Le Goff has said, 'Christian teaching
is memory, Christian cult is commemoration.'[35] Memory was focused
on location. Jerusalem was seen as a specially suitable model for
meditation. The meaning assigned to the name was constant. Its
distant origin was probably as *uru* + shalem, the city of [the god]
Shalem'. In the Hebrew Scriptures it had already been theologized
into the 'city of peace', as in Psalm 122: 6, 'pray for the peace of
Jerusalem'.[36]

Those who went to Jerusalem were looking for a variety of satisfac-
tions. In the early days, there was a strong insistence on the eviden-
tial value of the sites, in continuity with the tradition of learned
tourism or *historia*. Paulinus of Nola remarked that 'no other feeling

[35] J. Le Goff, *History and Memory* (New York, 1992), 70.
[36] S. Talmon, 'The Significance of Jerusalem in Biblical Thought', *Real and Ideal Jerusalem*, 1–12.

draws men to Jerusalem, save to see and touch the places in which
Christ was bodily present, and as a consequence to recite, "We will
worship at the places where his feet have stood" '. For Pope Leo I they
gave unassailable evidence of the reality of Christ's humanity. In 453
he pointed out to the Empress Eudochia, who had become a resident
of the Holy Land, that she was living 'where the signs of his miracles
and the proofs of his sufferings proclaim that Jesus Christ is true God
and true man in one person'. The holy places asserted the necessity
of a theology that acknowledged that Christ was truly man.[37]

Western visitors under the later empire were not primarily interested in telling readers about their personal feelings. The Bordeaux
pilgrim provided a brief factual record of the sites that he (or she)
visited and the Biblical memories they contained. Egeria's interest
was in the Biblical texts that underlay the sacred sites and the liturgies in use there. A different impression, however, comes from two
letters in that Jerome described the pilgrimage that Paula undertook
under his direction about 385: one to Marcella in about 392, and a
fuller account written in 404 as Paula's obituary. He described not
only her external acts at the holy places, but the imaginative reliving
of the events that had happened there—what long afterwards would
have been called a 'composition of place':

She fell down and worshipped before the cross as if she saw the Lord hanging
on it. On entering the tomb of the resurrection she kissed the stone which
the angel removed from the Sepulchre door; then like a thirsty man who has
waited long, and at last comes to water, she faithfully kissed the very shelf on
which the Lord's body had lain. Her tears and lamentation there are known
to all Jerusalem.[38]

We should understand this, not as a description of a single visit by a
disciple of Jerome twenty years before, but as an expression of his
own ideas of devotion at the Sepulchre. His description reflects a type
of piety found elsewhere in his works. Inspired by Ezekiel's vision of
the Temple, in which the prophet was told to 'set your mind upon all
that I shall show you', he spoke of the need to 'paint in our heart' the
images we find in the Bible.[39] Paula's visit was reported as combining
'seeing with the eye of faith' with a powerful desire to touch, to
handle, and to kiss. Two centuries later, we meet in the Piacenza

---

[37] Paulinus, ep. 49. 14 (CSEL 29 (1999), 402); Leo, ep. 123. 1.
[38] Jerome, ep. 108. 9, obituary of Paula (ed. J. Labourt (Paris 1955), v. 167). Similar
account of the tomb in ep. 46. 5 (Wilkinson, *Pilgrims*, 83–4).
[39] Carruthers, *The Craft of Thought* (Cambridge, 1998), 133–5.

pilgrim a man with a tremendous desire to handle holy things: 'In the courtyard of the basilica there is a small room where they keep the wood of the cross. We venerated it with a kiss. The title [i.e. the inscription] is also there . . . This I have seen, and had it in my hand and kissed it.'[40] He was the first writer to record the actual measurements of the holy places as themselves possessing mystical value—a strong feature of medieval piety—and he provided a good description of the collection of relics and the wonders that attended it:

At the moment when the cross is brought out . . . for veneration, and arrives in the court to be venerated, a star appears in the sky, and comes over the places where they lay the cross. It stays overhead whilst they are venerating the cross, and they offer oil to be blessed in little flasks. When the mouth of one of the little flasks touches the wood of the cross, the oil instantly bubbles over, and unless it is closed very quickly it all spills out.

The Piacenza account tells us of the Jerusalem origins of two different types of relics, or blessings (*eulogiae*) as contemporaries called them. Fragments of the cross and flasks of relics conveyed to Latin churches the mysterious graces that flowed so abundantly in the Holy Land. Touch and sight were closely associated in invoking memory, which was the point of a visit to a shrine. They had both been linked in I John I: I as means of access to the Christian revelation: 'We declare to you what was from the beginning, what we have heard, what we have seen with our eyes, what we have looked at and touched with our hands, concerning the word of life.' For the pilgrim who had heard the Scriptures, seen the events with the eye of faith, and touched the 'monuments' that served as memorials, this experience had been fulfilled in the holy places.

BRINGING THE HOLY SEPULCHRE TO THE WEST

Obviously, most people in the Western empire were unable to travel to the Holy Land, and it was important to bring the presence of the Sepulchre to Western churches. Gregory of Tours regarded as sacred anything that had been in contact with the Holy Sepulchre: 'faith should accept that everything which has touched the holy body is sacred.' Contact relics, sanctified by touching sacred things, were esteemed as much as the bodies of the saints themselves. They need

---

[40] Piacenza 20 (Wilkinson, *Pilgrims*, 139).

not necessarily carry an image of the holy things: Gregory told how water would be mixed with the dust of the Holy Sepulchre and counters or tokens made of the clay 'and are sent through various parts of the world. From these, many sick have drawn healing.'[41] The collection of relics and treasures in a great church, such as the important collection given to Monza in Lombardy about 600, formed its 'memory' and defined the history of its foundation, and were perceived as containing the grace and power of the holy places themselves and as providing a strong sense of community with what would otherwise have been distant places and events.

It is often supposed by modern writers that the Christian past believed in a three-decker universe, in a God who was 'up there' or 'out there', and that the task of the church was to make heaven accessible to humanity. The devotion of believers aspired to the Jerusalem above or to the heavenly places, while the accepted cosmology, in large part inherited from the classical past, envisaged the earth as the centre, surrounded by the circles of the heavens. Yet equal importance must be given to the conviction that salvation is from the East. As with the desire for heaven, the devotion to the Holy Land, while spiritual at root, was also given cosmological expression, with Golgotha at the centre of the world. Guy Stromsa has argued that the idea of a heavenly Jerusalem and the reproductions of Jerusalem on earth complemented one another: 'The way to heavenly Jerusalem does not pass as much through earthly Jerusalem as it does through the multiple Jerusalems disseminated throughout Western Europe.' This is an important truth, although it has to be qualified by an awareness that the 'multiple Jerusalems' were inspired by visits to the historical Holy Sepulchre in Palestine.[42] In this respect the West was different from the East. There, Constantinople became a second Jerusalem, containing many of the relics that had once been there. In spite of the importance of Rome for Western pilgrims, it did not become in the same sense a replacement for Jerusalem, at least until the closing centuries of the Middle Ages.

The most powerful way of making present the Holy Sepulchre was by relics. To have a fragment of the wood of the cross, or dust from the Holy Sepulchre, or oil from its lamps, brought blessing and protection from the misfortunes of this life. The idea of a relic could be

---

[41] Gregory, *Liber de gloria martyrum* 6 (MGH SRM I. 492); Piacenza 20 (Wilkinson, *Pilgrims*, 139).
[42] G. G. Stromsa, 'Mystical Jerusalems', Levine, 352.

extended. It was a source of power to contain in one's shrine the true measure of the body of Christ or of some aspect of the Holy Sepulchre: as we have noticed, the Piacenza pilgrim in 570 was already interested in recording these. You could go even further, and incorporate a representation of the Sepulchre or of Calvary on the flasks or in the mosaic of your church, until—the most elaborate recollection of all—the building itself could be given the circular form that recalled the great rotunda of the Anastasis. Alongside relics was worship. In illiterate societies history has been kept alive in dance and ceremonial, and for much of the history of the church liturgy performed the same function. It was not a simple visit to the holy places that brought the pilgrim close to the saving events, but participation in processions, liturgy, and prayers.

If you brought the worship of Jerusalem to your home church it would be natural to incorporate some visible reminiscences of Jerusalem. At Santa Maria Maggiore, the triumphal arch was decorated with named representations of Jerusalem and Bethlehem: the motif for Jerusalem included a circular building, presumably a reference to the church of the Holy Sepulchre. The same theme appeared in Ravenna in the seventh century. The representations were not exact but evocative. Bianca Kühnel has remarked that 'early Christian Jerusalem is an ambiguous visual creature: neither earthly nor heavenly, still bound to the formulas proper to any city but endowed with some unique features'.[43]

The ambition to reproduce the layout of the holy places themselves seems to have been born relatively late, and in the early centuries it was manifested only rarely. For a long time their image was evoked more by relics than by architectural imitation. Yet the mystique of the copy is a natural expression, and has never ceased to be. In 1948 the *Rheinische Merkur* informed its readers that 'in every capital of the world President Truman intends to ensure that the American embassy will be built as an exact copy of the White House. When an American citizen visits his embassy, he will feel himself transported to the house of the president.'[44] Whether Truman did entertain this striking project is doubtful, but it illustrates the continued power in the twentieth century of the cult of the copy. Western architects began, rarely and hesitantly at first, to reproduce the Sepulchre in the

---

[43] B. Kühnel, 'Geography and Geometry of Jerusalem', in N. Rosovsky (ed.), *City of the Great King: Jerusalem from David to the Present* (Cambridge, Mass., 1996), 291.

[44] Cited P. Crossley, 'Medieval Architecture and its Meaning: The Limits of Iconography', *Burlington Magazine*, 130 (1988), 116.

Copies of the Holy Sepulchre

On the whole, people before the modern period did not speak precisely in terms of copies. The nearest words available in medieval Latin were *exemplar* and *forma*. In the thirteenth century the English schoolman Robert Grosseteste defined *forma* as 'the name given to the pattern from which the artist works, in order by imitation to shape his work in its likeness'. We have only a limited number of statements of what patrons thought they were doing, and they usually employed less precise terms such as *in honore sancti sepulchri*, or *in similitudine/ad similitudinem*, or *in modum*. There were formidable difficulties in producing a copy of the buildings on Golgotha. The rotunda was vast, and almost no one could afford to reproduce it in the West. A miniature was possible, but that then produced a confusion with the more human proportions of the tomb chamber itself. Architects often could not have known what the original was like, and mechanisms for precise reproduction did not exist until late in the Middle Ages. In a fundamental article, Richard Krautheimer long ago established that the problems were not merely technical. Master masons and their patrons had a cavalier attitude to the idea of copies: 'indifference towards precise indications of given architectural shapes', he wrote, 'prevails throughout these "copies" of the Holy Sepulchre'. An exact reproduction was not necessary, either for personal devotion or for liturgical commemoration. Meditation could be based upon a purely imaginary scheme of Jerusalem or on an abstract plan of a monastery. It is true that throughout the centuries, there are mentions of care taken to measure Christ's grave-slab, but such measurements were designed to provide a 'presence' of Jerusalem, in the same way as earth from the Sepulchre might be preserved in a chapel. They were not intended to form the basis of an accurate copy. Even at the end of the Middle Ages, when accurate drawings of the Sepulchre were being printed, there were some astonishing instances of indifference to literal representation: Hartmann Schedel's *Nuremberg Chronicle* could use the same woodcut for the cities of Ferrara, Milan, Mantua, and, amazingly, Damascus. What was wanted was remembrance of the Holy Sepulchre, not copies. A chapel on a small

hill just outside the city centre could represent Golgotha, and
an ambo or pulpit was sometimes designed as a recollection of
the Sepulchre. The remarkable *pontile* carved at Modena just
after 1200 contains a magnificent illustration of the passion
story. The fact is that a whole series of ideals overlapped with
each other and shaped the depictions: 'a tightly linked chain
binds together the earthly Jerusalem through its buildings,
which recall the death and resurrection of Christ; the heavenly
Jerusalem of the Apocalypse (the triumph of the Lamb);
and lastly sacred building construction in the West, whose
architecture is influenced by the liturgy itself, in the yearning
to anticipate here on earth the heavenly Jerusalem.' Adolf
Reinle has put it incisively: 'they thought in terms of salvation
history, not archaeology', *man dachte heilsgeschichtlich, nicht
archäologisch.*

R. Krautheimer, 'Introduction to an Iconography of Medieval
Architecture', *JWCI* (1942), 1–33, esp. 6; E. H. Gombrich, *Art and
Illusion* (5th edn. London, 1977), 59–60; C. Valenziano, '*Mimesis
anamnesis*: spazio-temporale per il triduo pasquale', *Studia Anselmiana*,
102 (1990), 13–54; C. Frugoni, *A Distant City: Images of Urban
Experience in the Mediterranean World* (Princeton, 1991), 19–20; R. W.
Scheller, *Exemplum: Model-Book Drawings and the Practice of Artistic
Transmission in the Middle Ages* (Amsterdam, 1995), 9–12; A. Reinle,
'Das Nachleben Solomons und seines Tempels', *Neue Zürcher Zeitung*,
18/19 (Dec. 1976), 45; A. Arnulf, 'Mittelalterliche Beschreibungen
der Grabeskirche in Jerusalem (Mainz, 1997), 7–43; H. J. Böker,
'The Bishop's Chapel of Hereford Cathedral and the Question of
Architectural Copies in the Middle Ages', *Gesta*, 37 (1998), 44–54.

West. It is almost impossible now to discuss such a representation
without talking about a 'copy', but the concept is primarily a modern
one, belonging to the period after the dawn of printing, and it must
be used with great care when applied to former periods.

   From the patristic period onwards, certain privileged places were
given the name 'Jerusalem'. This had certainly happened by 500 at the
latest to the chapel of Helena's palace at Rome, now the church of
Santa Croce in Gerusalemme. It has sometimes been supposed that the
whole layout of the churches of Rome was planned as a reminiscence
of Jerusalem: Damiano Neri argued that 'it was necessary to copy the

The Narbonne Model

A small stone model, with a base measuring 1.12 metres × 0.90 metres, was found in the course of demolitions at Narbonne, in the south of France, in 1636. Enough survives to make it almost certain that this is a copy of the tomb monument or edicule, in the form that it took before its demolition by al-Hakim in the eleventh century. While it is damaged, it does seem to have been an unusually accurate depiction of the interior of the tomb. It was found with some early sarcophagi and an inscription dating from about 500, all used as infill for new fortifications, and this gives some indication of its date. Probably it was designed as a type of votive offering, and belongs to a tradition that has left few remains. There is a model of a theatre stage, also in marble, which survived at Rome and was apparently an offering to Dionysius. The accuracy of the piece tempts one to think it was carved at Jerusalem, but its marble appears to be from the Pyrenees. It is therefore likely that Jean Porcher is right to associate it with the elegant sculptural work centred on Arles in the fifth century.

J. Hubert and others, *Europe in the Dark Ages* (London, 1969), fig.17; A. Bonnéry, 'L'Édicule du S-Sépulcre de Narbonne', *Les Cahiers de S-Michel de Cuxa*, 22 (1991), 7–42; L. Kötsche, 'Das Heilige Grab in Jerusalem und seine Nachfolge', *Akten XII*, 276–80; and Biddle, *Tomb*, 22 and fig. 16.

sanctuaries, not only in the form of those imitated, but also (as far as possible) at the same distance and with the same orientation as they had between them'.[45] But there is no real evidence of a systematic scheme of the sort. The very fact that Santa Croce was christened 'Jerusalem' is difficult to reconcile with the view that the churches of Rome as a whole were designed to reproduce the holy city. There seems to be more substance in the contrary view that 'the attempt to make present all the holy places of Jerusalem in multiple architectural quotations was first undertaken in the later medieval and post-medieval period'.[46] We should, though, notice one instance of what does seem to be a model on a small scale: the Narbonne Model (see inset).

[45] Neri, 43–4. The basic theory was set out in H. Grisar, *Antiche basiliche di Roma imitanti i santuari di Gerusalemme e Betlemme* (Analecta Romana, 1899).
[46] M. Untermann, *Der Zentralbau im Mittelalter* (Darmstadt, 1989), 53.

The Buckle of Cesarius

This is now in Arles museum, but was originally part of the treasure of the cathedral. Its genuine connection with St Cesarius, who died in 542, is supported by the fact that in his will he left his liturgical garments to the cathedral. There is nothing implausible in this dating. There are some similarities with Eastern designs, which may be explained by cultural links, or even by the possibility that this treasure was a gift from the Holy Land. The details are curious: two guards sleep beside the tomb, which is still closed, and which consists of a block or cube surmounted by a rotunda. The comment of Carol Heitz that it is 'astonishingly accurate' seems very wide of the mark. Since the rotunda has an *oculus* or hole at the top, it is presumably meant as a reference to the Anastasis, but it has only four columns. Unsurprisingly, the proportions of guards, tomb, and Anastasis are wildly unrealistic. Why does this scene (exceptionally) show us the tomb before the arrival of the women? Were they shown on some other part of the vestments?

Another small example of a representation of the Holy Sepulchre is provided by the buckle attributed to St Cesarius of Arles. A relatively large number of pagan buckles remain from Gaul in the fifth and sixth centuries, but the fact that grave goods were not deposited in Christian burials means that portions of liturgical dress are extremely rare. There is a reasonable chance that the Narbonne votive model and the Cesarius buckle represent art forms that were once widely spread.

As well as the votive model and buckle, which may represent numerous portrayals that have been lost, another possible form of imitation was the round church. It has been said that 'early Christian architecture had in the Anastasis [rotunda] a fundamental reference point for its extraordinary symbolic richness'.[47] This is a large claim,

---

[47] M. Rossi and A. Rovetto, 'Indagini sullo spazio ecclesiale: immagine dello Gerusalemme celeste', M. L. Gatti Perer (ed.), *La dimora di Dio con gli uomini: immagini della Gerusalemme celeste dal III al XIV secolo* (Milan, 1983), 81.

FIG 3.2 This buckle, supposedly from the vestments of St. Cesarius of Arles, provides a powerful, if in accurate representation of the guards at the Holy Sepulchre.

which would place the Holy Sepulchre at the very heart of the tradition of church building, and it requires careful examination. 'Round' is an approximate term: designers seem to have been insensitive to the distinction between a round and a polygonal building, and we have therefore to keep in mind any centrally planned church. It is far from the truth that all such churches were designed as a representation of the rotunda at the Anastasis. Round churches do not necessarily require a special explanation. From the fourth century onwards, all major churches had separate baptisteries, for which a circular form was specially suitable. There may have been, in the minds of the builders, a connection with the Holy Sepulchre, because baptism was associated with the idea of resurrection and was at the centre of the Easter liturgy. An eighth-century inscription in St Thecla, Milan, commemorated 'the light of the resurgent Christ, who scatters the cloister of death and lifts from the grave those who have breathed their last breath'. On the other hand, specific architectural reminiscences of the rotunda in baptisteries are hard to trace; nor do inscriptions, which survive quite commonly, refer directly to the Holy Sepulchre. The only unambiguous case is the baptistery at Pisa, which was designed as late as the twelfth century by Diotisalvi. There were other reasons, both practical and theoretical, for centrally planned churches. It was a convenient way of giving access to relics: circular crypts, or others developed in a ring pattern, surrounded the place where the relics were housed. There was also an influential tradition of round churches dedicated to the Blessed Virgin, originating perhaps with the Pantheon at Rome, which was dedicated to the Virgin on 10 May 610. It is not safe to treat a centrally planned church as a commemoration of the Sepulchre unless (and this is rare) there are other reasons for accepting the attribution.[48]

The one early Roman church that does look like an architectural commemoration of the church of the Holy Sepulchre is Santo Stefano. This was the largest round church in the West, a brick-built structure dedicated to the first Christian martyr, whose relics had been brought from Jerusalem to the West. It was completed under Pope Simplicius (468–83) and was undoubtedly a piece of prestige architecture. It is not obvious why the Sepulchre buildings should have formed the model for this particular church, but it was a rotunda, its dimensions were quite close to those of the Anastasis, and excavations in 1987 have indicated that it was provided with a cross-axis formed by side rooms in the same way as the buildings at Jerusalem. The most natural assumption is that the Roman church was consciously creating a mausoleum for the great martyr, and that the similarity to the Anastasis rotunda was produced by the fact that they were both adaptations to Christian use of classical mausolea. The two buildings, nevertheless, are close in design, and the reproduction may be deliberate.[49]

[48] M. Unterman, *Der Zentralbau im Mittelalter* (Darmstadt, 1989); A. Grabar, *The Beginnings of Christian Art, 200–395* (London, 1967), 165–9; J. Hubert and others, *Europe in the Dark Ages* (London, 1969), 1–4; M. Gervers, *Rotundae Anglicanae, Actes du XXIIe Congrès International d'Histoire et d'Art* (Budapest 1972), 359–76; R. Krautheimer, 'Santa Maria Rotunda', *Arte nel primo millennio* (Turin [1954]), 21–7; P. Cramer, *Baptism and Change in the Early Middle Ages, c. 200–1150* (Cambridge, 1993), 270; J. Hubert, 'Les Églises à rotonde orientale', in *Frühmittelalterliche Kunst in den Alpenländen: Actes du IIIe Congrès international pour l'étude du haut Moyen Age* (Lausanne, 1954), 308–20; and S. Casarti-Novelli, 'L'Église du S. Sépulcre ou le baptistère S.-Pierre-Consavia [Asti]', *Congrès Archéologique*, 129 (1977), 358–63.
[49] A. Frazer in K. Weitzmann (ed.), *Age of Spirituality: Late Antique and Early Christian Art* (New York, 1979); and H. Brandenburg, 'La chiesa di Santo Stefano Rotondo a Roma', *Rivista di Archeologia Cristiana*, 68 (1992), 201–32.

Conscious reproductions of the Holy Sepulchre are equally difficult to find outside Rome. The claim has been made for Bologna under Bishop Petronius shortly before 450, but there is no real evidence for 'Jerusalem at Bologna' as early as the fifth century—an issue discussed in a later inset. The attempt to identify a likeness of the Sepulchre at Trier seems to rest on even more insecure speculation. Trier is indeed a remarkable site, but at the most it provides another example of the early deposit of relics from Palestine (and probably not even that). In the late empire Golgotha was being commemorated in the West through relics, liturgy, and pictorial art. Architectural imitation of it, at this relatively early stage, is doubtful and extremely hard to establish.

THE HOLY SEPULCHRE AND CHRISTIAN SYMBOLISM

But if there were still few attempts to build the Holy Sepulchre in the West, people were certainly interested in portraying it, and this interest was of great importance in the development of Christian art. In the first centuries, there had been no intention to give pictorial expression to the biblical narrative. Indeed, there may have been no distinctively Christian art at all. Even in the early third century, Clement of Alexandria was advising his Christian readers to choose, among the traditional symbols decorating seals and finger rings, ones that were consonant with their faith.[50] About 200 the catacombs began to be decorated with specifically Christian motifs, but they used thematic symbols: the good shepherd, a vine, a fish, birds of paradise, doves, and *orantes* (figures with hands raised in prayer). Even in the fourth century, when artistic themes such as Daniel and Jonah occurred frequently, portraits of Christ were uncommon. Eusebius of Caesarea seemingly regarded them as a concession to pagan taste, and disapproved of them: 'I have examined images of the apostles Peter and Paul and indeed of Christ himself preserved in painting: presumably, men of olden times were heedlessly wont to honour them in their houses, as the pagan custom is with regard to saviours.'[51] The remarkable survival of early church decorations at Duro Europos in Mesopotamia (about 240) introduces us to the first

[50] A. Grabar, *The Beginnings of Christian Art, 200–395* (London, 1967), 287. For the view of early Christian art adopted here, see in particular P. C. Finney, *The Invisible God: The Earliest Christians on Art* (Oxford, 1994).
[51] Eusebius, *Historia Ecclesiastica* 7. 18. 4. On his attitude, and fourth-century Christian themes in general, see Jensen, *Early Art*, 103–6.

known representation of the women at the tomb. This stands in a tradition different from the one that emerged after the creation of the Sepulchre complex under Constantine: there were perhaps originally five women in this composition, carrying ointments and torches; stars were designed to indicate the presence of the angels. A fine expression of the tradition that centred on themes and abstract designs is to be found in the so-called mausoleum of Galla Placidia at Ravenna, which is to be dated about 425 and is the earliest complete scheme of accomplished decoration surviving. The old tradition was still alive.

'The visual arts hold a privileged position in defining Jerusalem'.[52] A mosaic or painting could incorporate references to biblical events, to the existing holy places, to relics brought to the West and to the expectation of a heavenly Jerusalem at the end of time. It is often difficult to establish which of these references would be most prominent in the minds of contemporary worshippers. Our first major artwork (the term is unavoidable, but of course these were designed to shape the pattern of worship) illustrates the ambiguity nicely. It has been suggested that the changeover point in the decoration of major buildings at Rome is represented by an apse mosaic at Sta Pudenziana, which has been called 'the first, or at any rate the first surviving, of a new type: its designs are planned to be something far more than symbolic decoration'. Walter Oakeshott believed that 'the mosaic as a whole marks the beginning of a new era in Christian art'. As far as we know, the Santa Pudenziana apse is the first attempt to represent the Sepulchre and other holy places of Jerusalem in the West, and it is a singularly important and original composition.

The rich senatorial classes at Rome began to adopt Christianity in the course of the fourth century, and their ivory carvings and sarcophagi from about 350 onwards introduce us to the first elaborate and luxurious Christian art. At first, there is not much sign of influences from the holy places, and sarcophagi told the passion story without a reference to the visit of the women to the tomb. This artistic theme seemingly had not yet penetrated Italian spirituality. Perhaps its earliest representation appears in an ivory now in the Sforza Castle museum at Milan, showing the tomb as a cube with a door and a cylindrical tower above, datable perhaps to 380/400. Here we see two women kneeling before a young man with a halo, and it may be a reference to the post-resurrection appearances of Jesus. At

---

[52] B. Kühnel, 'The Use and Abuse of Jerusalem', *Real and Ideal Jerusalem*, pp. xix–xxxviii.

FIG 3.3 The mosaic at Santa Pudenziana, Rome.

The Apse Mosaic of Santa Pudenziana, Rome

This mosaic is a remarkably early survival. Inscriptions suggest a dating to 401–17. The composition is not now intact, but the overall impact is of early fifth-century work. The mosaic represents the presence of Christ and his apostles at the eucharistic liturgy. The first viewers would have seen them sitting behind the bishop and his clergy. Beyond the screen or wall appears to be a memorial of Jerusalem. The hill of Calvary, surmounted by the glorious cross, is unmistakable. Other elements are more uncertain. It has been suggested that to the right of Golgotha is the rotunda of the Anastasis, which would thus be in its correct position topographically if viewed from outside the city wall. The buildings on the left may be those on Mount Sion, after their reconstruction in the later fourth century. In line with the thinking of the early centuries, Jerusalem is made present in the eucharistic assembly. The reference to Golgotha may recall the cross that stood on Cavalry: but was there one by this time?

W. Oakeshott, *The Mosaics of Rome* (London, 1967), 25–6, 65–7; R. Beny and P. Gunn, *The Churches of Rome* (London, 1981), 30–1; G. Hellemo, *Adventus Domini: Eschatological Thought in Fourth-Century Apses and Catacheses* (Leiden, 1989); C. P. Thiede, *Heritage of the First Christians* (Oxford, 1992), 151–7; F. W. Schlatter, 'Interpreting the Mosaic of Santa Pudenziana', *Vigiliae Christianae*, 46 (1992), 276–95; W. Pullan, 'Jerusalem from Alpha to Omega in the Santa Pudenziana Mosaic', *Real and Ideal Jerusalem*, 405–17; J. M. Spieser, 'The Representation of Christ in the Apses of Early Christian Churches', *Gesta*, 37 (1998), 63–73; and Jensen, *Early Art*, 108–9. See also the insert, 'The Cross on Calvary', below.

all events, it does not take the form of the meeting of the women and the angel that was to become standard. By this time the wealthy Roman patrons of Jerome and Rufinus had close links with the holy places at Jerusalem, and fine carving of scenes from the Gospels, related to what they could see at Jerusalem, emerged in such compositions as the British Museum passion plaque and the Munich ascension plaque. These were relatively small compositions, not large enough for liturgical use, and were probably intended for the private devotion of wealthy Christians, or for their palace chapels. They may well have originally formed part of reliquary boxes.

The existence of such ivories raises the question whether there was already a 'pilgrim art' on flasks or *ampullae* brought back from Palestine, but this cannot be demonstrated before the sixth century. If the ivories were the first expression of Gospel scenes in high-quality products, they were followed by similar scenes in the churches, such as the sequence of mosaic panels illustrating the passion and resurrection scene on the nave wall of S. Apollinare Nuovo at Ravenna, decorated under Theodoric between 493 and 526. The resurrection panel there is based on the visit of the women to the tomb, but is clearly not a representation of the form of the Holy Sepulchre as described in the Gospels.

FIG 3.4 The women at the tomb, S. Apollinare Nuovo, Ravenna, sixth century (detail). The women approach a circular building with elegant columns and a tomb-slab. The angel (not shown here) is opposite them on the other side; the women extend their hands in witness. The picture apparently recalls the rotunda of the Anastasis, which in reality was immensely bigger than the worshippers or the tomb.

Western representational art did not have a strong tradition independent of the holy places in Palestine For many centuries, no attempt was made to present the moment of Christ's resurrection, and the depiction of the Sepulchre virtually always involved the visit of the women to the tomb, whose form echoed either the edicule or the rotunda in the church of the Holy Sepulchre. The artist might sometimes provide a gloss on the meaning of the empty tomb by linking it with some other central mystery, but essentially resurrection art was the visit of the women to the tomb. The British Museum ivory, which contains the earliest known Christian representation of the crucifixion, has in a separate panel two women with guards at the empty tomb. This may conceivably embody a recollection of the edicule at Jerusalem, although if so it is far from exact. The ivory is normally dated about 420.

Such narrative art was an act of worship, provided for the liturgy or for personal devotion. Major importance was attached to the visualizing of the events by the faithful. Leo I (440–61) urged his hearers to enter imaginatively into the events, 'so that the Lord's pasch should not be remembered in the past but honoured in the present'. He commanded that they should 'hold the sequence of events so plainly in mind as if you had reached them all in bodily sight and touch'. In other words, Leo wanted worshippers in Rome to 'see' the events in the same way as pilgrims could literally do in Palestine.[53]

The centrality of the visit of the women in the thought of the church was evident, not only in art, but also in the spiritual theology of the Fathers. In the mid-fifth century Peter Chrysologus, the bishop of Ravenna, endeavoured to bring his hearers closer to the resurrection by comparing the women entering and leaving the sepulchre with burial and rising again with Christ. The visit to the tomb also left its impression on the early commentaries on the Gospels, whose writers spent a good deal of ink on the apparent inconsistencies of the recorded journeys of the women. The methods of Biblical commentators contrasted with those of the artists. They did not use the newly revealed Holy Sepulchre as a way of elucidating the details of the resurrection narrative, but worked directly from the Gospel text without reference to what was on the ground at Jerusalem. This was true even of Jerome, who knew the sites very well and was an enthusiastic advocate of the holy places. Visitors seem to

---

[53] W. Loerke, ' "Real Presence" in Early Christian Art', in T. G. Verdon (ed.), *Monasticism and the Arts* (Syracuse, 1984), 40–1.

FIG 3.5 Ivory relief now at the Bayerisches Nationalmuseum at Munich, about 400. The visit of the three women to the tomb is here associated with the ascension of Christ. The representation of the Sepulchre as a cube surmounted by a domed building is found in a number of the early examples. There are weeping figures at the tomb (Peter and John?), and a young man rather than an angel.

FIG 3.6 Four panels survive from an ivory casket probably designed as a reliquary, about 420. The tomb in this panel is depicted in much the same way as on the Munich ivory, but here there is an open door, and the guards are represented with the women.

have accepted the sites at Golgotha as corresponding with what the evangelists described, without any attempt at criticism.[54]

We have already noticed the existence of representation of the holy places in major monumental contexts, at Sta Pudenziana, Rome, and at Ravenna. Kurt Weitzmann has traced similar thematic elements through many different art forms. From our present knowledge, the most important route of transfer to the West from the sixth century onwards was through the flasks or *ampullae* that contained consecrated oil, or earth from the Holy Land, some of which were decorated with the saving events. The iconography appears on the painted lid of a relic box preserved in the Sancta Sanctorum at Rome, and now in the Vatican museum, and on a number of early icons. They shared the function of initiating the beholder into the mysteries that had been enacted in the holy places and were materialized in the relics which they contained.

---

[54] Jerome, *Commentary on Matthew* 27: 33 (CCSL 77 (1969), 270; Hilary of Poitiers (SC 258 (1979)), 252–3; and Ambrose on Luke, ed. G. Tissot (SC 52 (1958)), 205.

FIG 3.7 This ampulla, or bottle for holy oil, has been flattened, and gives only an approximate sense of the original vessel: but it does make it possible to see clearly the scene of the women approaching the tomb. The great rotunda around the tomb appears to be shown. On the other side is an abstract representation of the crucifixion.

Pictures at the Holy Places?

There has been a good deal of discussion as to whether the representations that began to appear in the West in the fifth century were copies of pictures that pilgrims had seen on their visits to the holy places. Some scholars have supposed that on the walls of the major churches there would be mosaics of the nativity, the crucifixion, and the visit to the tomb. The case for the existence of pictures 'which are in effect the origin of archetypes which were reproduced by the media of the time' is argued among others by P. Maraval and W. C. Loerke. Occasionally, this can be established: the shrine of St Menas in Egypt had a representation of the saint between two camels which appears repeatedly in the miniature arts of the period. One of the Monza flasks of about 600 commemorates the holy place at Bethlehem and figures a 'majesty' of Mary and the child seated on a throne, in a way which strongly suggests a copy of a large-scale original. It is, however, difficult to find solid evidence of pictures in the church of the Holy Sepulchre, and it is more likely that it was the tomb itself, rather than a wall mosaic, that provided the pattern. Undoubtedly, the complex had mosaic decorations, but it is probable that at first these were abstract or symbolic. There is no evidence of true pictures there before 570, when they are mentioned by the pilgrim from Piacenza (*c*.20, 23). Even these pictures, which included one of Christ 'painted while he was still alive', were in the courtyard. What is more, Kurt Weitzmann argues that it is possible to trace the existence of two quite different traditions of depiction of the crucifixion, and this is hard to account for if they were an imitation of a mosaic. Most images on the flasks or *ampullae* are amply explained by attempts to represent the edicule, with or without the rotunda above it, while representations of Golgotha are seemingly either a 'spiritual' tradition to depict the presence of the relics of the cross, or alternatively a copy of a monumental cross present there. They do not look like a version, however simplified, of a mosaic.

P. Maraval, *Lieux saints et pèlerinages d'Orient* (Paris, 1985), 201; W. C. Loerke, 'The Miniatures of the Trial in the Rossano Gospels', *Art Bulletin*, 43 (1961), 171–95; K. Weitzmann, '*Loca Sancta* and the Representational Arts of Palestine', *DOP* 28 (1971), 40, 49; K. Weitzmann (ed.), *The Age of Spirituality* (New York, 1979), 565 fig. 78; G. Vikan, 'Early Byzantine Pilgrimage *Devotionalia* as Evidence of the Appearance of Pilgrimage Shrines', *Akten XII*, 377–88; and G. Kühnel, 'Kreuzfahrerideologie und Herrscherikonographie: der Kaiserpaar Helena und Heraklius in der Grabeskirche', *Byzantinische Zs.*, 90 (1997), 396–404.

By the late sixth century, metal flasks and glass bottles were being manufactured on a large scale at Jerusalem for sale to pilgrims. The flasks were made of a tin-lead alloy, and must have been relatively cheap to purchase; approaching forty survive, in whole or in part.[55] The glass bottles and pilgrim badges were presumably even more available to the general mass of visitors, and the most accessible objects of all were the baked clay disks, stamped with a pattern, that were formed out of soil from the holy places. These must have been very numerous indeed; one collection of ninety-three has been found in Syria. Gregory, who was bishop of Tours from 573 to 594, was familiar with such 'tablets'. He said that they could be worn to

---

[55] J. Engemann, 'Palästinensische Pilgerampullen', *Jahrbuch für Antike und Christentum*, 16 (1973), 5–27. For the dates and the nature of the representations, see the articles by Dan Barag and John Wilkinson listed in the Bibliography.

provide protection, and also that earth from the tomb of Christ healed diseases and protected from snakebite. It is difficult to date this whole range of 'blessings'. The only secure evidence is the mention of flasks by the Piacenza pilgrim and the arrival of a group at Monza just after 600. It may be that their manufacture continued after the Islamic conquest in the seventh century. The flasks in many cases were inscribed with pictures of the cave at Bethlehem, the cross, and the Anastasis, and their decorations, though small, were often of good quality. The 'blessings' they contained were intended to bring back with the returning pilgrims the power of the sacred sites. Flasks might be inscribed, '*eulogiae* of the holy places of the Lord Christ', or 'oil of the wood of life of the holy places of Christ'. The glass bottles had more simplified symbols of the holy places. There are some twelve representations of the Sepulchre. They give a basic picture of what it looked like around 600, with entrance screens, a pointed roof and a cross surmounting it. There remain uncertainties. It is difficult to interpret the second layer of roofs which sometimes appear, above the edicule: is this the rotunda high above it, or was there, above the edicule, a further stone canopy? The clearest representation of the rotunda itself seems to be on the Vatican reliquary lid, mentioned above, where it stands above the scene of the visit to the tomb, with its dome and row of windows. The women in such resurrection scenes may be shown as carrying censers rather than spices: the aim is to crystallize a pilgrim experience, and contemporaries were apparently unaware of the gap that had opened between this and the historical events. Calvary is normally represented by a cross upon a mound, with the thieves being crucified on right and left. The monumental cross there does duty for a picture of the crucifixion, which people were hesitant to reproduce. The nearest they came was to place a bust of Christ above the cross. The one surviving flask which shows the lance and the sponge at the crucifixion, presents them as raised to the cross, not to the figure of Christ. The cross acted for the crucifixion as the visit of the women did for the resurrection.

THE WOOD OF THE CROSS COMES TO THE WEST

The cross has, throughout most of the history of the church, been the pre-eminent Christian symbol. The Gospels showed no inclination towards a cult of the cross, which appeared there as the instrument of Christ's execution. It may indeed carry a metaphorical meaning, as in the phrase, 'anyone who does not take his cross and follow in my footsteps is not worthy of me' (Matthew 10: 38), but even here it expresses obedience or suffering. When John wanted to announce the victory of Christ, he employed a periphrasis for the cross: 'When I am lifted up from the earth, I shall draw all men to myself' (John 12: 32). Only in the epistles of Paul do we find the foundation of a theme that was later to be so dominant: 'far be it from me to glory except in the cross of our Lord Jesus Christ, by which the world had been crucified to me, and I to the world' (Galatians 6: 14). There has been a running controversy whether the early church used the cross as a symbol. Certainly, there were no elaborate representations, but then at first there was no elaborate Christian art at all. The weight of opinion among scholars now is that the cross sign can be found quite frequently, in simple inscriptions and also concealed under the depiction of anchors, ships' masts, ploughs or the Hebrew letter *tau*.[56] The depiction of the crucifix was unknown before the fifth century. Constantine's use of the symbol probably took the form of the *chi-ro* sign, combining the initials of Christ with a sign for the cross. Certainly this sign, surrounded by a crown of laurels, did service as a symbol of the passion on the splendid Roman sarcophagi of the fourth century.[57] Whatever may be the truth behind these suggestions of earlier beginnings, it was the discovery of the wood of the cross at Jerusalem that released the cult of the cross in a flood throughout the church as a whole.

The cross was the most potent of the relics that brought to the West the grace of the holy places. By 385, the church of Jerusalem was observing on Friday of Great Week (Good Friday, as we would call it) the solemn veneration of the cross. Egeria gave a full account of it to her friends in the West:

Then the bishop speaks a word of encouragement to the people . . . 'Now off you go home until the next service, and sit down for a bit. Then all be back here at about eight o'clock so that till midday you can see the holy wood of the cross, that, as every one of us believes, helps us to attain salvation' . . . It is not long before everyone is assembled for the next service. The bishop's chair is placed on Golgotha behind the cross, and he takes his seat. A table is placed before him with a cloth on it, the deacons stand round, and there is brought to him a gold and silver box containing the holy wood of the cross. It is opened, and the wood of the cross and the title are taken out and placed on the table. As long as the holy wood is on the table, the bishop sits with his

---

[56] Jensen, *Early Art*, 137–41.
[57] Thiede, 123–48; K. G. Holum, 'Pulcheria's Crusade A. D. 421–2 and the Ideology of Christian Victory', *Greek, Roman and Byzantine Studies*, 18 (1977), esp. 166.

hands resting on either end of it and holds it down, and the deacons round him keep watch over it . . . Thus all the people go past one by one. They stoop down, touch the holy wood first with their forehead and then with their eyes, and then kiss it, but no one puts out his hand to touch it.[58]

This ceremony, which took most of the morning, was followed by readings of the passion. This is the first description we have of the veneration of the cross, and the fact that Egeria recorded it so carefully indicates that it was not familiar to her in her home church in the West. She speaks of the 'wood of the cross', thus stressing devotion to the actual material. Much later, usage came to prefer 'the true cross' or 'the holy cross'.

Even thirty years earlier, Cyril had spoken of 'the holy wood of the cross . . . which is seen among us to this day, and which because of those who have in faith taken thereof, has from this place now almost filled the whole world'.[59] The first example of such a transfer may plausibly be ascribed to a gift by Constantine himself at Rome: 'The Emperor Constantine created a basilica in the Sessorian palace, where he also enclosed a fragment of the wood of the holy cross of our Lord Jesus Christ in gold and gems; and where he dedicated the name of the church, which is still to our own day called "Jerusalem".'

There are other instances of the early dispersal of fragments of the cross described by Cyril, sometimes in churches that otherwise were little known. In Mauretania about 359 there was some holy soil from Bethlehem and a portion *de lignu crucis* [*sic*]; before 371, also in North Africa, we hear of a basilica which was built 'after the bringing of the holy wood of the cross of the Saviour Christ'.[60] One of the best documented early transfers of a fragment to the West was in 402, when the elder Melania returned to Italy and gave a relic to Bishop Paulinus of Nola, who in turn sent some to his old friend Sulpicius Severus in Gaul, together with one of the earliest accounts of the finding of the cross.[61]

During the fifth century, the dissemination of relics of the cross in the West continued. Pope Leo I in 454 acknowledged the gift of a

---

[58] *Egeria's Travels* 36. 5–37. 3 (136–7).
[59] *Catechetical Lectures* 10. 19 (PPTS 11. 13).
[60] W. H. C. Frend, *The Archaeology of Early Christianity* (London, 1996), 114–15.
[61] Paulinus, ep. 31 (CSEL 29 (1999), 267–75); H. Brandenburg, 'Altar und Grab: zu einem Problem des Märtyrerkultes im 4 und 5 Jahrhundert', M. Lamberigts and P. van Deun (eds.), *Martyrium in Multidisciplinary Perspective: Memorial L. Reekmans* (Louvain, 1995), 71–98.

Santa Croce in Gerusalemme

Santa Croce in Gerusalemme at Rome contains a collection of relics in the modern chapel devoted to the purpose: a fragment of the cross, thorns and a nail from the crucifixion, a portion from the cross of one of the thieves who were crucified with Jesus, and the title bar, 'Jesus of Nazareth, King of the Jews'. In addition the church possesses an inscription recording that 'here holy earth from Calvary is preserved, solemnly deposited by Saint Helena in the lower vault, and thus the name Jerusalem was ascribed to the chapel'. The continuity of the name Jerusalem is well established from about 500, when the *Life of Sylvester I*, quoted in the text above, was composed. Its evidence is confirmed by the further mention in the *Liber Pontificalis* of a council held then 'in Jerusalem, the basilica of the Sessorian palace'; and we hear in about 700 of a procession on Good Friday from the Lateran, carrying a cross-relic, to keep a station at 'Jerusalem'. When Archbishop Sigeric of Canterbury visited Rome in about 993, his tour of the shrines was still said to include 'Jerusalem'. The present name of Santa Croce, *ad sanctam crucem in Hierusalem*, appeared as late as the eleventh century.

Whether the *Life of Sylvester* was right in supposing that the name and the relic dated back to Constantine is another matter. It is true that the building would be a natural place to begin the story of the wood of the cross in the West: the Sessorian palace was owned by Helena after Constantine's occupation of Rome in 312, and the church probably originated as the empress's chapel. Whatever their origin, the Sta Croce relics were apparently incorporated within a mosaic about 1144, and were subsequently found in concealment during building works in 1492.

For the history of Santa Croce, see *Liber Pontificalis* (ed. L. Duchesne), i. 179, 196; D. B. Bedini, *Le reliquie della Passione del Signore*, 3rd edn. (Rome, 1987), 30; P. Jounel, 'Le Culte de la croix dans la liturgie romaine', *La Maison-Dieu*, 75 (1963), 68–91; J. Vogt, 'Helena Augusta, the Cross and the Jews', *Classical Folia*, 31 (1977), 135–51; G. Goldberg, '"Peregrinatio, quam vocant Romana"', *Wallfahrt kennt keine Grenzen*, 348; R. Klein, 'Helena II (Kaiserin), *Reallexikon für Antike und*

Christentum 14 (1988), 355–75; Webb, *Pilgrimage*, 33 (doc. 5); and S. de Blaauw, 'Jerusalem in Rome and the Cult of the Cross', *Pratum Romanum: R. Krautheimer zum 100 Geburtstag* (Wiesbaden, 1997), 55–73. One of the best surveys of the Santa Croce relics themselves is still that of H. Thurston, 'Relics, Authentic and Spurious', *The Month*, 155 (1930), 420–9. See also the inset on The Title on the Cross in Ch. 2.

fragment by Bishop Juvenal of Jerusalem.[62] This may well have been the relic used by Pope Hilary (461–8) when he added three chapels to the baptistery at the Lateran, dedicating one of them to the holy cross, providing there 'a confession [shrine] where he placed the wood of the Lord'.[63] By this time, the story of Helena's finding of the cross had become known in the West. The account had probably begun in Jerusalem, to explain to pilgrims the presence of the cross there, and by 450 an elaborate set of stories explained the circumstances. The date for the feast of the cross was fixed at Rome on 3 May, in conformity with the date of the finding by Helena in the legend. The date of the feast at Jerusalem, 14 September, is only found a little later in the Latin churches.[64]

In Gaul, too, the continued links with the East during the times when politically the empire was collapsing opened the way for the arrival of relics of the cross. Avitus, metropolitan of Vienne, sent a mission to secure a fragment, and towards the end of the sixth century Gregory of Tours was offered an old silk robe in which, the owner claimed, the cross had been wrapped. Gregory was dubious, because he knew that the relic was well protected, and that suspicious-looking characters were driven away from it by whips. He was convinced of the authenticity of the cloth by the miracles it worked.[65] The most important arrival of the cross in the West, however, was its coming to Poitiers.

[62] Leo I, ep. 139 (*PL* 54. 1108).
[63] L. Duchesne (ed.), *Liber Pontificalis* (Paris, 1955), i. 242, 261; M. Romano, 'L'oratorio della Santa Croce al Laterano', *Zs. für Kunstgeschichte* 59 (1996), 337–59; and P. Jounel, 'Le Culte de la croix dans la liturgie romaine', *La Maison-Dieu*, 75 (1963), 80.
[64] Borgehammar, ch. 9.
[65] E. Salin, *La Civilisation mérovingien* (Paris, 1949), 151 ff., and E. James, 'A Sense of Wonder: Gregory of Tours, Medicine and Science', in M. A. Meyer (ed.), *The Culture of Christendom: Essays in Medieval History in Commemoration of Denis L. T. Bethell* (London, 1993), 45–60.

The Wood of the Cross at Poitiers

The acquisition of this major relic was masterminded by Radegund, the wife of the Frankish ruler Chlothar I, and shortly after 550 the founder of a major house of nuns at Poitiers. It arrived in a superb reliquary in the course of 569. A portion of this reliquary survives, but we can envisage it better from that presented by Justin to the pope at much the same time, and which is housed at the Vatican. The region became an important centre for the growth of devotion to the cross and the carving of early crucifixes. Two great hymns, and a series of poems, were produced for the occasion by Venantius Fortunatus, the Ravenna poet who had settled in Gaul: *Pange lingua* and *Vexilla regis* were probably designed to be sung in procession as the cross was brought into the city. Originally, processions had been accompanied by antiphons and psalms, whereas processional hymns were rare or unknown. Those of Venantius Fortunatus were a major influence on the development of this enrichment of the Catholic liturgy. The underlying philosophy of this transfer was that it brought to the West the salvation which, through the work of Helena, had already come to the East. Venantius saw the donors, Justin and Sophia, as embodying the virtues of their great predecessors:

> A second Constantine, another Helena,
> Like them in honour and the cross's love;
> She found, and you distribute, its salvation.
> What first came from the East now fills the West.

In the *Vita Radegundis* it was Radegund who continued the work of Helena: 'What she did in the Eastern lands, St Radegund did in Gaul.'

I. Moreira, '*Provisator optima*: St Radegund of Poitiers' Relic Petitions to the East', *JMH* 19 (1993), 285–306; P. Lasko, *The Kingdom of the Franks* (London, 1971), fig. 58, and D. Redig de Campos (ed.), *Art Treasures of the Vatican* (London, 1974), fig. 410, where, however, there is a confusion with Justinian; C. Heitz, '*Adoratio crucis*: remarques sur quelques crucifixions préromanes en Poitou', in *Études de civilisation médiévale: Mélanges offerts à E.-R. Labande* (Poitiers, 1975), 395–405;

Venantius, 'Ad Iustinum et Sophiam Augustos', MGH Auct. Ant. IV. I (Berlin, 1881), 275–8; *Vita Sanctae Radegundis* 2 c.16 (MGH SRM 11 (1888), 388; D. Kleinmann, *Radegunde: eine europäische Heilige* (Graz, 1998); and R. Favreau (ed.), *Le Supplice et la gloire: la croix en Poitou* (Poitiers, 2000). On the education and career of Venantius, *Venanzio Fortunato tra Italia e Francia* (Treviso, 1993).

This widespread devotion to the cross did not normally carry with it a desire for direct representation of the crucifixion. On the contrary, one of the most powerful influences on Western artistic themes was the floreated or jewelled or triumphal cross, which perhaps originated in a cross actually located at Golgotha. In 420, under the impact of an outbreak of persecution in Persia, the Empress Pulcheria urged her brother, Theodosius II, to embark on a war of vengeance. The project was an example of the development of the traditional ideology which saw the emperor as the embodiment of the spirit of victory into a war undertaken for the defence of the church. It may (but the matter is problematic) have provided the origin of the Western jewelled cross.

Fourth-century Lateran sarcophagi carved at Rome represented the crucifixion with a cross surmounted by the *chi-ro* monogram of Christ and a laurel wreath of triumph sometimes surrounded by historical episodes of the passion. The concern to symbolize the passion and resurrection, and not to portray them, was dominant.[66] As well as the depiction of the crucifixion on the British Museum ivory, apparently of Italian origin from the 420s, there is a powerful representation of Christ on the cross on the wooden doors of Santa Sabina on the Aventine at Rome, which may be confidently dated about 432.[67] In the patristic period, we are a very long way indeed from the great crucifixion images that were to dominate churches in the high Middle Ages and afterwards.

Gifts of the relics from the Sepulchre or the cross were not of purely religious significance; their devotional meaning was dovetailed into the social structure of the period. International gift-giving and exchange of letters helped to create the network of holy places

---

[66] An example is F. W. Deichmann (ed.), *Repertorium der christlich-antiken Sarkophage* (vols. 2 Wiesbaden, 1967), no. 208.
[67] G. Jeremias, *Die Holztüre der Basilika S. Sabina in Rom* (Tübingen, 1980), 60–4.

The Cross on Calvary

There are problems about this cross. Eusebius made no mention of the hill, and the Bordeaux pilgrim in 333 did not mention a cross there. Egeria's account about 382 paid a lot of attention to the rock, and she repeatedly distinguished ceremonies which took place 'at the cross', 'before the cross', or 'behind the cross'. She must be distinguishing the great basilica, the rock, and the western courtyard, which contained the Sepulchre. Her reference is primarily to the relic of the wood of the cross, which was preserved there, but there may also have been a standing cross. The story was later told that Theodosius II, in order to secure divine protection in the war of 420, not only sent a donation to the poor of Jerusalem, but presented a magnificent cross, gold and studded with stones, for the hill of the cross. A new design of coinage, in the name of Pulcheria, displayed the statue of victory with the cross, but it is doubtful whether this can refer to the cross of Calvary. The glorious cross of Calvary may have been the inspiration behind the simple illustrations of a cross on the *ampullae* coming from the holy places. However, the jewelled cross shown in the apse mosaic of Santa Pudenziana at Rome almost certainly predates 420, and can therefore not have been inspired by a cross given by Theodosius. The radical solution of Christine Milner is to point out that it is only with Adomnan about 700 that we have certainty about the presence of a monumental cross on Calvary, and she thinks that all previous references and depictions refer to the relic alone. An opposite view, which is also sustainable, is that it was the early erection of the cross there which provided the basis for the identification of the rock as Golgotha, which is otherwise unexplained.

K. G. Holum, 'Pulcheria's Crusade A. D. 421–2 and the Ideology of Imperial Victory', *Greek, Roman and Byzantine Studies*, 18 (1977), 153–72; C. Milner, 'Lignum Vitae or Crux Gemmata? The Cross of Golgotha in the Early Byzantine Period', *Byzantine and Modern Greek Studies*, 20 (1996), 77–99; and P. Braun, 'The Victorious Signs of Constantine: A Reappraisal', *The Numismatic Chronicle*, 157 (1997), 41–59. S. Gibson and J. E. Taylor, *Beneath the Church of the Holy Sepulchre* (London, 1994) hold that Calvary was not identified as the site of the crucifixion until later.

that we have already observed as characteristic of the new Christendom. The authority of the first Christian emperors was commended to the elites of the provinces by the traditional culture which they had in common: rituals, court ceremonial, mosaics, and rhetoric, although of course no longer by sacrifice at the ancient shrines. The demand was growing, however, for a specifically Christian definition of the sources of authority. The development of the legends of Helena's discovery of the cross can be understood in this light. In his funeral oration for Theodosius I in 395, Ambrose reported that Helena had also found the nails used on the cross and had sent two to her son, Constantine, to be incorporated into a bit for his horse and a diadem. Ambrose greeted these gifts as the fulfilment of the prophecy of Zechariah 14: 20, 'On that day there shall be inscribed on the bit of the horses, "holy to the Lord the Almighty" '(Vulgate). Thus Helena 'wisely placed the cross upon the head of kings, that the cross of Christ might be adored in kings'.[68] A century and a half later, the coming of the holy cross to Poitiers sanctified the new royal powers of the West: it was obtained, wrote Radegund's biographer, 'for the safety of the whole fatherland and stability of the kingdom'. The public importance of such a relic explains the character with which its arrival was vested: it was seen as a solemn entry, an *adventus*, in a ceremony that ultimately went back to the welcome of an emperor on a civic visit, and which recalled also the procession of the Saviour into Jerusalem.

THE INFLUENCE OF LITURGY

Relics, the symbol of the cross, and artistic motifs could evoke the presence of the Holy Sepulchre and Golgotha. So could the pattern of worship. Several historians of Christian worship have made the large claim that in the fourth and fifth centuries its character in East and West was essentially determined by the liturgy of Jerusalem.[69] The view rests on some solid foundations. Jerusalem was a centre much visited by pilgrims, one of whom, Egeria, indicates the strong interest of other churches in the forms of worship in use around the Holy

---

[68] Ambrose, *De Obitu Theodosii* 40 ff. (CSEL 73 (1955), 369–401). Jerome, on the other hand, thought the interpretation of the Zechariah text ridiculous: *In Zach.* 14 (PL 25. 1540A). For comments on these political ideas, see J. W. Drijvers, *Helena Augusta* (Leiden, 1992), 95–113; Borgehammar, 60–6; and M. Sordi, 'La tradizione dell'*Inventio Crucis* in Ambrogio e in Rufino', *Rivista della Storia della Chiesa Italiana*, 44 (1990), 1–9.

[69] This is a central theme of A. Baumstark, *Comparative Liturgy* (London, 1958).

Sepulchre. Her book reads like a research report designed to satisfy the interest of her home church in what was happening at Jerusalem: 'Loving sisters, I am sure it will interest you to know about the daily services they have in the holy places, and I must tell you about them.' She did not report customs that were familiar in her home church, but in such cases recorded that 'they do what is everywhere the custom on the Lord's Day'.

But there are problems. The most intractable one is our sheer ignorance of the liturgies followed in most Western churches until the advent of liturgical reform in the Carolingian period, beginning in the eighth century. The appearance at that time of ceremonies ultimately derived from Jerusalem leaves us in doubt by what route, and when, they arrived. Egeria's description is virtually unique as a record of the liturgy of a great church in the patristic period. The question of the influence of the Holy Sepulchre liturgy turns upon the emergence of the distinctive Jerusalem processional or 'stational' liturgy, so called because the formal acts of worship took place at the stopping-places or 'stations' along the way. On special occasions the location of worship moved between several different sites at Golgotha: the basilica, the Sepulchre, Calvary, and others. Originally, the two major centres were Golgotha and the Mount of Olives: several of the major events, such as the Last Supper and the descent of the Spirit at Pentecost were still 'unearthed' and without a home. The new basilica on Mount Sion was probably consecrated just after 392, and soon afterwards, or perhaps even by that time, it provided the location for these events. The most distinctive ceremonies of all were those for Great Week, or Holy Week as we call it. During this period, the normal worship in the basilica of Constantine in the morning and evening had been supplemented by a series of striking ceremonies. On the preceding Saturday, an assembly at the Lazarium at biblical Bethany celebrated the raising of Lazarus, and on the next day there was an elaborate evening procession from the Mount of Olives, with a series of stational readings, and with everyone carrying branches of palm and olives and singing, 'Blessed is he that comes in the name of the Lord'; the first description anywhere of the now familiar Palm Sunday procession. The Friday of the paschal vigil ('Good Friday') was marked by a long devotion in which all the faithful came to kiss the wood of the cross, followed by readings and hymns about the passion. As we have already seen, this is another 'first'; nowhere earlier do we have a description of the ceremony of the adoration of the cross. Egeria was hugely impressed by the thematic character of this worship, and repeatedly recorded that 'they have hymns and antiphons which—like all the readings— are suitable to the days and the place', and 'they have hymns and antiphons suitable to the place and the day'.[70]

The wide adoption in the church as a whole of ceremonies commemorating the historical events of the last week of the Lord's life can be ascribed to Jerusalem, but the circumstances of their emergence are unclear. Since their distinctive features were not mentioned in the *Catechetical Lectures* of Cyril of Jerusalem about 348, it has often been ascribed to Cyril's period as bishop, which lasted for almost forty years after 349. But his episcopate was a troubled one, and little suited to a radical reorientation of the worship of his church. It may be that (in spite of the argument from silence presented by the *Catechetical Lectures*) we should look to the 330s and the time of the consecration of Constantine's great church for the new liturgical order. There was clearly huge popular participation, and it may also be that the new ceremonial ordering emerged in response to the demands of pilgrims and of the monastic communities that were gathering around the city, and not as a piece of systematic planning by a bishop. At least, whatever the origins, we can be in no doubt about the special character of worship in the holy city in the fourth century. Stational liturgy seems to have been common to most large cities: the link with the holy places must be accepted as peculiar to Jerusalem.

This specific development there has to be seen in the light of the transformation in Christian worship generally which was in progress in the fourth century. Just as the church was refashioning the geography of the empire into a Christian topography, marked by the Biblical events and by the tombs of saints and martyrs, so the year was being subdivided into festivals commemorating individual mysteries of redemption. Before 300, the pasch was incomparably the most important feast, and it contained within itself the commemoration of both the passion and resurrection. There was no separate Palm Sunday or Good Friday, no Lent or Christmas or Ascension Day; the whole pattern of salvation was rolled up in the pasch. From the fourth century onwards, we can trace a general tendency which has been called differentiation or historicization. The attachment to a single great feast was being replaced by a series of days, each expressive of one of the New Testament events, timed to correspond with

---

[70] *Egeria's Travels* 31: 1 (p. 132), 32: 1 (133), 37: 6 (138), 29: 5 (132), and 35. 4 (135).

the historical record in so far as that could be determined. In the fourth century we find for the first time the keeping of Christmas, Holy Week, and the Ascension. Some historians of liturgy have seen this process as part of the incorporation of the church into public life in the new Christian empire. Gregory Dix argued that 'as the church came to feel at home in the world, so she became reconciled to time. The eschatological emphasis in the eucharist inevitably faded . . . The eucharist came to be thought of primarily as the representation, the enactment before God, of the historical process of redemption.' In his view, the fourth century was 'the formative age of historic Christian worship, which brought changes the effects of which were never undone in the East or catholic West at all'. In the same way, Anton Baumstark called the feasts of the early church 'feasts of idea', and argued that they were 'not historical commemorations of such and such an episode in the sacred history but were instituted rather to give expression to great religious ideas'. For him, the change came out of Jerusalem: 'It is in Palestine that they became increasingly closely linked with the New Testament history because . . . the remembrance of the earthly life of Jesus was still very vivid there.'

These two main developments are not in doubt: the fourth century was the time when Jerusalem developed a liturgy centred on the Sepulchre and the other holy places, and when the worship of the church as a whole was placed on a more historical basis. It is, however, difficult to assess with confidence the scale of the movement towards historicization. It was real, but there are questions about its abruptness. We must not assume that the church of Jerusalem was observing a detailed re-enactment of the historical events, particularly during the night of Thursday of Great Week, since the location (whether real or imaginary) of these events had in most cases not been identified. The Anastasis rotunda and the hill of the cross were so close together that they necessarily appeared as part of a common mystery. Egeria mentioned how, when the Gospel of the resurrection was read each Sunday at the Anastasis, the people wept at the sufferings of Christ: the bishop must have been reading the whole passion story, and not splitting it into two separate actions.

What is more, the abundant stream of visitors meant that currents of influence flowed both into and out of Jerusalem. Some historians have argued that important elements in the ceremonies of Great Week, including even the Palm Sunday procession, had been imported from other churches. There are certainly instances where historicization proceeded in spite of Jerusalem, not because of it.

Christmas first appeared at Rome in the 330s, and then later in the century entered the Greek churches, perhaps under the Westernizing influence of the Emperor Theodosius I. It was adopted late at Jerusalem. In face of the indications that influences were flowing in both directions, some modern scholarship has tended to move away from the close linkage between Jerusalem and historicization: 'Rich documentation has frequently seduced scholars into assigning to Jerusalem a larger and more innovative role in liturgical development than can be supported.'[71]

In the end, we are left in doubt. The level of pilgrim interest, the importance of monastic contacts, the research of Egeria into the liturgical customs of the East, all suggest a high level of influence from the ceremonies surrounding the Holy Sepulchre upon churches in the West. The adoption of artistic themes, which were so closely linked with worship, also suggests strong influences travelling from the holy places. We know also that other Jerusalemite customs, including the Palm Sunday procession, the adoration of the cross, and the Easter stations, were widespread in the Western church in the ninth and tenth centuries; and this is a phenomenon we shall explore later. But it does not prove early influence, because we do not know how these ceremonies had arrived. Moreover, while the Arab conquest of Palestine and the Germanic invasions in the West may briefly have produced migrations that made contact closer, in the long run they were bound to disrupt liturgical exchanges between East and West. It was only with the emergence of stable political units in the West that a new chapter in the adoption of Jerusalem worship could begin.

[71] G. Dix, *The Shape of the Liturgy* (London, 1945), 303, 305; A. Baumstark, *Comparative Liturgy* (London, 1958), 157; T. J. Talley, *The Origins of the Liturgical Year*, 2nd edn. (Collegeville, 1991), 38–9; J. G. Davies, *Holy Week: A Short History* (London, 1963), 35 ff.; and *Egeria's Travels* 24. 1 and 25.

4

The Frankish Kingdoms and the Carolingians, 600–1000

Early in the seventh century, Byzantine Jerusalem came to an end. Its death began with the Persian conquest of the eastern provinces of the Christian Empire. Jerusalem itself was besieged, and fell about 5 May 614. The immediate impact upon the city was devastating: contemporaries recorded large numbers of casualties in the massacre, and many inhabitants were taken away as captives. The wood of the cross was captured and removed to Persia. Strategios' *Fall of Jerusalem* makes it clear that much damage was done to the churches there, including the church of the Holy Sepulchre, and contemporaries blamed the Jews for encouraging the Persians in their work of destruction. After the first devastation, King Chosroes allowed rebuilding to take place, and Modestus (who was subsequently to become patriarch) raised funds for restoration. He probably aimed at preserving the existing buildings as far as possible, although there may have been some changes in the form of the edicule. The gold cross attributed to Theodosius II disappeared from Calvary and a chapel was erected upon the rock, which previously had remained uncovered.

The Emperor Heraclius, from 622 onwards, planned and executed a massive military revival. Heraclius' use of crosses and icons in his army was much greater than ever before, and he has accordingly been seen by some historians as the first crusader.[1] The campaign ended with the collapse of the Persian empire, and its withdrawal from the conquered territories. On 21 March 630 Heraclius triumphantly brought back the holy cross to Jerusalem, although there is a

---

[1] 'The first of the crusaders', N. H. Baynes, *Cambridge Medieval History* (Cambridge, 1913), ii. 301; 'making this reconquest a sort of "crusade" ', G. Dagron, *Histoire du Christianisme* (Paris, 1993), iv. 24, 86–7.

good deal of doubt about the authenticity of what he brought back. The triumph was short-lived. While the great war was in progress between Byzantium and Persia, Mahomet had been preaching in Arabia, and in the 630s the Arabs began a dramatic expansion, in the course of which they overran Syria, Egypt, and much of the Middle East. In 638 Jerusalem surrendered to them. Heraclius had already retreated to Constantinople, taking the cross, or most of it, with him. This time, there was to be no Byzantine revival. Western response was muted. Communication problems were by now real, and the complicated religious situation in the East made it difficult for Westerners to be sure what was happening. It was not clear that Muslims should be seen as unbelievers, adherents of an alternative and dangerous religion. In the long run the struggle with the Persians left behind it more themes for Western imagination to dwell on than did the Arab conquest. Heraclius as a hero of the holy war and champion of the cross, and the Jews as specially guilty for the desecration of the holy sites, stirred the imagination of later generations in the West, even if their effect was not immediate.

The Arab conquest had deprived the church of Jerusalem of its natural protection from the emperors of Byzantium. The extent to which the churches suffered under Muslim rule is a matter of dispute. Islam does not require the persecution of Christian subjects, who along with Jews are recognized as 'people of the Book', sharing in part the same Scriptures, and distinct from the idolaters who are condemned in the Koran. At the same time, their role must be subordinate, their buildings more humble than those of the mosques, and they were required to pay a tribute from which Muslims were exempt. Jerusalem for a long time remained a predominantly Christian city, but its buildings decayed: Justinian's great church, the Nea, was damaged in an earthquake and never restored. It was difficult to maintain the churches without the financial patronage of a Christian government, and it was difficult to secure the agreement of the authorities to the building of new churches, or even to their repair.

There is clear evidence of the decay of the Christian hierarchy during the centuries after 638: throughout Palestine, the number of bishoprics fell disastrously. It is more difficult to say how many direct attacks were made upon the Christian community and its buildings. The theory of the benevolent Muslims is most persuasively stated by Steven Runciman, who assembles evidence to show that Nestorians, Jacobites, and other dissenting groups, who would have suffered from

The Covenant of ʿUmar

It has often been claimed that at the Arab conquest Patriarch
Sophronius secured unusually favourable surrender terms from
Caliph ʿUmar, preserving some of the special privileges of the
church at Jerusalem, but it is not clear that these were different
from the standard treaties of surrender to the Muslim expansion. In any case, the monopoly enjoyed by Christians was
bound to suffer from the new order. In particular, the former
Temple area, which had remained in ruins in the Byzantine
period, was developed as a Muslim sacred centre, the Haram
al-Sharif or noble sanctuary. The Dome of the Rock of 692 is
one of the most beautiful buildings in the world: a later Muslim
historian, Muqadassi, said it was built by Caliph ʿAbd-al-Malik
'noting the greatness of the dome of the Holy Sepulchre'. With
it, the splendid al-Aqsa mosque was also built at the edge of the
Temple enclosure.

M. Gil, *A History of Palestine, 634–1099* (Cambridge, 1992), 51–5, and
M. Borgolte, *Der Gesandtenaustauch der Karolinger mit den Abbasiden und
mit Jerusalem* (Munich, 1976), 20 ff., and literature discussed there. For
the text of the 'covenant with ʿUmar', see Palmer, *The Seventh Century
in West Syrian Chronicles* (Liverpool, 1993), 161–2.

Byzantine government policy, were content with Muslim rule. He
says more controversially of the Muslim rulers that 'their justice and
restraint was often remarkable'.[2] It is true that Christian society continued to flourish for a considerable time. Some new mosaics were
still being laid down in the eighth century. Yet it is hard to accept
Runciman's optimistic estimate of the attitude of the new rulers.
Even the church of the Holy Sepulchre was not exempt from the
danger of destruction. We are told that Caliph al-Walid (705–15)
demanded a master builder from Constantinople to work on the
mosques of Damascus, threatening to destroy all the churches of the
land if one were not sent. In 787 Patriarch Elias II wrote of the plight

    [2] S. Runciman, *A History of the Crusades* (Cambridge, 1951), i. ch. 2. More balanced
statements in M. Gil, *A History of Palestine, 634–1099* (Cambridge 1992), 461–76; R.
Schick, *The Christian Communities of Palestine, from Byzantine to Islamic Rule* (Princeton, 1995), 68 ff.; and W. H. C. Frend, *The Archaeology of Early Christianity* (London,
1996), 367–8.

of Christians who 'sit in darkness and in the fear of death, among Arabs who have no reverence of the Lord'. It seems justified to say that 'a picture of maltreatment and varying degrees of persecution emerges from the sources'. In 966 rioters murdered the patriarch and set fire to the church, badly damaging the roofs of the basilica and the rotunda. The eventual destruction of the church of the Holy Sepulchre in the early eleventh century has the air of a disaster that was waiting to happen.[3]

The Byzantine emperors commanded the nearest, indeed for a time the only, great Christian power, but their patronage was not welcomed by Muslim authorities, and there were serious religious divisions between Constantinople and Jerusalem. The Greek patriarchs there were in frequent contention with the official policy: they championed the opposition to the monothelite doctrine which the emperors, in an ill-judged attempt to advance unity among Christians, were pressing. Then from the middle of the eighth century John of Damascus, a monk of St Sabas, and the church of Jerusalem as a whole, led the opposition to the iconoclastic movement. In the circumstances, the Latins were more congenial allies and correspondents than the Greeks. Political difficulties weakened the links between the West and Palestine in the seventh century, but some contact remained. Merchants and monks from Syria made the journey to France and Italy. Gregory I's interest in the East at the beginning of the century was not lost. Papal concern with the Holy Land was kept alive by theological controversies in the Greek East, and subsequently by the growing influence of Easterners within the Roman church itself. Martin I (649–53) was accused by Constantinople of plotting an alliance with the Muslims, but defended himself on the grounds that he was merely trying to send assistance to the churches at Jerusalem.[4] From the end of the seventh century, and throughout the first half of the eighth, the popes had a strongly Greek, sometimes even Syrian, background. Between 687 and 752, of the thirteen popes only two were Romans: all the rest were Greek-speaking, and included two Sicilians, four Syrians, and five Greeks. Refugees from Islamic conquests, including Greek monastic communities that had settled at Rome, were influential within the church. Still earlier, Pope Theodore I (642–9) was a native of Jerusalem, the

---

[3] R. Ousterhout, 'Rebuilding the Temple: Constantine Monomachus and the Holy Sepulchre', *Journal of the Society of Architectural Historians*, 48 (1989), esp. 69–70.

[4] Martin I, ep. 14 (*PL* 87. 199–200).

son of a Palestinian bishop. Sergius I (687–701), one of the most influential pastors of the Roman church in the period, had been born at Palermo, but he came of a Syrian family from Antioch, and his father had probably come to the West to escape Islamic rule. Sergius introduced at Rome a number of Eastern liturgical customs, including the singing of the *Agnus Dei* at mass, and probably the celebration of the Jerusalem feast of the Exaltation of the cross on 14 September, which was a combination of two Jerusalem traditions: the return of the cross there by the Emperor Heraclius, and the Invention by Helena.[5] The conclusion seems to be that the seventh and eighth centuries were characterized by a weakening of Latin links with Jerusalem, but not by a dramatic change in the way the West thought about the holy places.

However this may be, the advent of Charlemagne opened a new era. The decade following 797 saw the first sustained involvement of a Western government in the affairs of the church of the Holy Sepulchre. We know that Charlemagne, around the time he was crowned as Roman emperor in the West, exchanged a series of embassies with Caliph Harun ar-Raschid at Baghdad and with the patriarch of Jerusalem. Our sources are confined to mentions by Einhard and other court writers. We know as much about the elephant that the caliph sent to Aachen as a present as we do about the content of the negotiations. Nevertheless, the appearance on the international stage of this first Western *Überseepolitik*, as it has been called, is significant. The most probable interpretation is that Charlemagne was anxious about the problems the church at Jerusalem was facing, and that his 'concern was to negotiate with Harun over the situation of the Christians in the Holy Land'.[6] Sources close to the Frankish court reported that in 799 a monk from Jerusalem brought 'blessing and relics from the Sepulchre of the Lord, which the patriarch of Jerusalem had sent to the lord king', and recorded the arrival in 800 of two monks 'who for the sake of blessing brought the keys of the Sepulchre of the Lord and of the place of Calvary, also the keys of the city and of the mount, with a banner'. We can only guess at the intentions of the caliph and the patriarch, but it is reasonable to suggest that they were willing to recognize Charlemagne's right to protect Christians and to provide for their needs. This would be

---

[5] Borgehammar, 188 ff.; J. Richards, *The Popes and the Papacy in the Early Middle Ages* (London, 1979), 270: 'a dramatic change came over the papacy'.

[6] M. Borgolte, *Der Gesandtenaustauch der Karolinger mit den Abbasiden und mit den Patriarchen von Jerusalem* (Munich, 1976), 112.

comprehensible from the standpoint of Harun ar-Raschid, who by transferring responsibility for the well-being of the Christians would protect himself from possible claims by the Byzantine emperors to extend their protection over Jerusalem. Harun could hardly have imagined that three centuries later the Franks would come in the guise of crusaders to turn their brotherly protection into military occupation.

Charlemagne's Protectorate at the Holy Places

On first reading, the transfer of the keys of the city and of a banner appear to have political overtones; but the phrase 'for the sake of blessing' probably means that they were brought as *eulogiae* or sacred memorials from the holy places. The mind boggles at the idea that the Holy Sepulchre really had a banner in 800: such military symbolism would be rare or non-existent even in Western churches at the time. It is more probable that this was a relic from the cross, in the familiar liturgical phrase the *vexillum crucis*. Einhard further reported that a later mission from the West carried with them 'gifts for the most Holy Sepulchre of the Lord our Saviour, and for the place of the resurrection'. Harun, he claimed, 'not only allowed what they asked, but even conceded that sacred and saving place should be assigned to his power'. This last phrase is the one evident basis for the interpretation, championed by Louis Bréhier, that Charlemagne was granted a protectorate over Jerusalem: the theory attracted some French historians between the wars because it gave historical support to French ambitions in Syria. Modern historians, on the whole, have found the 'protectorate' theory implausibly political.

See Borgolte, *Gesandtenaustauch*.

Whatever the precise status indicated by the concession of keys and by the assigning of the sacred place to Charlemagne's power, the question remains why the Frankish emperor should have wanted to involve himself in such an expensive and distant responsibility. If we are to believe Einhard, he saw himself as having a general charge for the support of needy Christians 'not only in his own homeland and realm, but across the sea in Syria and Egypt and Africa, at Jerusalem and Alexandria and Carthage, wherever he had discovered that Christians were living in poverty'.[7] Within this context a concern for Jerusalem would have a good Biblical basis: Saint Paul had been eager about 'going to Jerusalem with aid for the saints' (Romans 15: 25). We have only partial knowledge of the ways in which Charlemagne's revenues were allocated at Jerusalem, but the evidence points to the foundation of a hostel 'in which were received all speakers of the Roman tongue who went to that place for the sake of devotion'. Charlemagne was also probably the founder of a community of Latin nuns at the Holy Sepulchre and monks on the Mount of Olives.

The repeated exchange of ambassadors took place largely between 797 and 807, and was a unique episode in the history of Western concern for the Holy Sepulchre. It did, however, leave an inheritance. For a considerable time afterwards there was a substantial Latin presence at Jerusalem, and a continued correspondence between the patriarchs and the West. Latin monks, buoyed up by support from outside, began to take an aggressive line on the use of the *filioque* clause in the creed, that perpetual sore point in Latin–Greek relations. The dispute led to an unseemly fight in the church of the Nativity at Bethlehem, and to the sending of a deputation to Pope Leo III by Patriarch Thomas in 809. The discussion of the issue at the Council of Aachen confirms that Charlemagne was taking seriously issues raised by the church of Jerusalem.[8] It was probably during this period of relatively close links between the Franks and Jerusalem that the church there adopted a Western ceremony, the lighting of holy fire on Easter eve, or rather gave a remarkable gloss to a traditional practice of the Eastern church.

Most of the records of dealings with the patriarchs at Jerusalem, however, concerned their appeals for help in the face of Muslim oppression, and the Western response to them. After the death of Caliph Harun ar-Rashid in 809, a war of succession provided the occasion for a series of attacks on the churches at Jerusalem, and apparently inflicted serious damage on the Anastasis itself. The decision in a capitulary of Aachen in 810 to send alms to Jerusalem 'for the restoration of the churches of God' presumably reflected this

---

[7] Einhard, *Life of Charlemagne*, c. 27, L. Thorpe (tr.), *Two Lives of Charlemagne* (Harmondsworth, 1969), 80.

[8] Gil, *A History of Palestine*, 452–3, and Borgolte, *Gesandtenaustauch*, 99–103.

crisis. The new Emperor Louis the Pious is said to have imposed a tax on royal estates in Germany 'for the relief (*redemptionem*) of Christians dwelling in the land of promise', who had pleaded for help from both Louis and his father Charlemagne.[9]

With the progressive disintegration of the Carolingian empire, evidence becomes less frequent, although we may guess that the thin trickle of references represents only a small part of the exchanges that actually took place. Thus in 881 Pope John VIII explained to the Patriarch Theodosius that he was sending only modest gifts 'because of the great oppression of the pagans'.[10] Help was requested from Rome and from distant England. Even in the chaos produced by the Danish invasions, Archbishop Ethelred of Canterbury was still sending alms in 890. From 984 there is an important letter written by Gerbert, later Pope Sylvester II, when he was secretary of the church of Reims. It was addressed 'to the universal church in the name of the devastated church of Jerusalem'. In it, Gerbert lamented a 'well-known disaster' that had overtaken it: 'while the prophet says, his Sepulchre will be glorious, the devil endeavours to make it inglorious, with pagans overthrowing it.' Gerbert appealed for funds: 'Shine forth, therefore, soldier of Christ, be a standard-bearer and a fellow warrior, and what you cannot do in arms, assist by advice and the help of riches.' The oblique reference to warfare, if unexpected, is not without parallel. In the East, the Byzantine Emperor John Tzimisces had been campaigning against the Muslims, and a letter to the ruler of Armenia boasted in 975 that he was intending to liberate the Holy Sepulchre. If it is authentic, this is an important 'first', but the letter survives only in the twelfth-century chronicle by Matthew of Edessa, and it may be a later forgery composed in the light of the First Crusade.[11]

By 993 at least Abbot Guarin, the emissary to Jerusalem, was back in Italy, where he induced Margrave Hugh of Tuscany to donate land for the support of the Holy Sepulchre, and King Stephen of Hungary is said to have founded a community in Jerusalem in 1002 for the

---

[9] Gil, *A History of Palestine*, 474–5, and Borgolte, 94, 99–103; *Gesta Karoli*, ii. 9 (MGH SS 11. 753).

[10] John VIII, ep. 213 (*PL* 126. 829–30), where the pope was clearly referring to Saracen threats to Rome, not to the situation in the Holy Land, and A. Graboïs, 'Anglo-Norman England and the Holy Land', *Anglo-Norman Studies*, 7 (1984), 133 n.

[11] P. J. Walker, 'The "Crusade" of John Tzimisces in the Light of New Arabic Evidence', *Byzantion*, 47 (1977), 301–27, and T. Bianquis, *Damas et la Syrie sous la domination Fatimide* (vols. 2) Damascus, 1986).

Gerbert's Appeal for Jerusalem

There are puzzles here, which have occupied the attention of many commentators. It is startling to find a reference to armed force a whole century before the First Crusade, even if Gerbert rejects warfare as impractical. A variety of explanations and dates have been given to this letter, but the most probable context is the defeat of Otto II by the Sicilian Muslims in Calabria in July 982. There is no other record of a disaster to the church of Jerusalem at this time, and it seems likely that Gerbert was combining a general reference to the supposed servitude of the Christians there with a specific allusion to Otto II's defeat. The letter was probably designed as an appeal in support of Abbot Guarin of Cuxa, who was on his way to spend several years in the East, apparently on some sort of formal mission. The Biblical references in Gerbert's letter are to Isaiah 11: 10 (Vulgate) and 2 Timothy 2: 3–4.

P. Ponsich, 'S.-Michel de Cuxa au siècle de l'An Mil (950–1050)', *Les Cahiers de S.-Michel de Cuxa*, 19 (1988), 7–32, and C. G. Mor, 'Silvestro II e Gerusalemme', in *Studi ... in onore di C. Manaresi* (Milan, 1953), 219–23; H. P. Lattin (tr.), *The Letters of Gerbert* (New York, 1961), letter 36, pp. 73–5; F. Weigle (ed.), *Die Briefsammlung Gerberts von Reims* (MGH Ep. ii. 2 (Berlin, 1966), letter 28, pp. 50–2); and P. Riché and J.-P. Callu (eds.), *Gerbert d'Aurillac, Correspondence*, letter 28, vol. i. p. 59.

care of Latin pilgrims.[12] This was a time, too, when dedications to the Holy Sepulchre began to be found among abbeys, and Gerbert as Pope Sylvester II (999–1003) may conceivably have been connected with them. San Sepolcro in Tuscany had been founded by two hermits, Arcanus and Giles, returning from the Holy Land, and appears with this dedication shortly after his time, as does Acquapendente. But here we are on the edge of a double change: the destruction of the Holy Sepulchre in the East, and an explosion of pilgrimage from the West. To this new period we must return later.

---

[12] P. Riant, *Mémoires, Acad. des Inscriptions et Belles-Lettres*, 31 (1884), 158–62; *Vita Stephani* (MGH SS xi. 227–35).

EXPECTATION

It was the view of Joshua Prawer that the Arab conquest was decisive in shaping the Latin attitude to Jerusalem. Its effect, he thought, was to make it much less a holy place, the centre of pilgrimage, and more a symbol of heaven: 'All of a sudden there is a marked change, one may almost say a *volte-face*, in the attitude of Christendom . . . New winds were definitely blowing. Heavenly Jerusalem was gaining ground, relegating earthly Jerusalem to a subservient position.'[13] The fact is, though, that the most obvious effect of the loss of Jerusalem to Christian rule was to produce a new type of political prophecy, the story of Antichrist and the last emperor.

This took its distant origin from the picture given by Saint Paul in 2 Thessalonians 2: 4, according to which the end must be preceded by the appearance of 'the man of lawlessness . . . the son of perdition', who 'takes his seat in the temple of God, proclaiming himself to be God'. From this beginning, Greek and Latin apocalypses evolved that made the expectations turn on the holy places at Jerusalem and gave a crucial role in the drama to a last world emperor. This literature was being persistently rewritten, and many stages in its evolution have disappeared; but it is likely that the theme originated in the East in the seventh century, when the Byzantine emperors were resisting the expansion of Islam. The eighth-century prophecies of Pseudo-Methodius represented the first appearance of the last emperor theme in Latin literature, and were hugely influential in subsequent centuries. They prophesied the restoration of Christians by the 'king of the Greeks, that is the Romans', to the lands they had lost. Then subsequently

when the Son of Perdition has arisen, the king of the Romans will ascend Golgotha, upon which the wood of the cross is fixed, in the place where the Lord underwent death for us. The king will take the crown from his head and place it on the cross, and stretching out his hands to heaven will hand over the kingdom of the Christians to God the Father. The cross and the crown of the kingdom will be taken up together to heaven . . . When the cross has been lifted up on high to heaven, the king of the Romans will directly give up his spirit.[14]

---

[13] J. Prawer, 'Christian Attitudes towards Jerusalem', in his *History of Jerusalem* (New York, 1996), 311–48.

[14] Pseudo-Methodius, cc. 13–14 (B. McGinn, *Visions of the End: Apocalyptic Traditions in the Middle Ages* (New York, 1979), 75–6).

Golgotha had now become central to the eschatological drama. Here, the 'king of the Romans' was presumably still the Byzantine emperor. We do not have evidence that Charlemagne appropriated his functions in this prophetic literature. The first ascription to Western rulers of the leadership was in Abbot Adso of Montier-en-Der's book, *On the Origin and Time of Antichrist*, written about 949 at the request of Gerberga, the sister of Otto I and wife of Louis IV of France. He assigned the crucial role to the king of the Franks:

Some of our learned men say that one of the kings of the Franks who will come in the last time will possess anew the Roman empire. He will come at the last time and will be the last and greatest of all rulers. After he has successfully governed the empire, at last he will come to Jerusalem and will put off his sceptre and crown on the Mount of Olives.[15]

Adso's personal commitment to the Holy Sepulchre was to be shown by his death on pilgrimage to Jerusalem. The significance of these political apocalypses is that by the middle of the tenth century, at the latest, a Latin was being seen as the world ruler who would offer up his kingdom at Jerusalem and thus unloose the drama of the last days. Eschatological concern can be traced in many other aspects of Carolingian and post-Carolingian culture, including commentaries on *The Book of Revelation*, the anxiety for reform, and the identification of the cross as the 'sign of the Son of Man' (Matthew 24: 30), which linked eschatology with cross-devotion.[16]

   Alongside the works that attempted to establish the ruling dynasty as the agent for the deliverance of the Holy Land and consequently as the key to the final drama of redemption, was another tradition that served a quite separate purpose. Joshua Prawer derived its influence from the fall of Jerusalem to the Arabs, but it was already flourishing before then. This was the search for the spiritual meaning of Jerusalem, which would enable the many biblical references to the city to be understood. It was basically a monastic tradition, and virtually every monk would know its classic expression in the *Collations* of Cassian (about 400). He defined Jerusalem 'historically as the city of the Jews; allegorically as the church of Christ; anagogically as that heavenly city of God, which is the mother of us all; tropologically as the soul of man'.[17] Three centuries later, Isidore recorded two

---

[15] Adso, *De ortu et tempore Antichristi* (McGinn, *Visions of the End*, 86).

[16] J. Fried, 'Endzeiterwartung um das Jahrtausendwende', *Deutsches Archiv für Erforschung des Mittelalters*, 45 (1988), 381–473.

[17] John Cassian, *Collations*, 14. 8 (CSEL 13. 404); Isidore, *Etymologies*, 15. 1. 5.

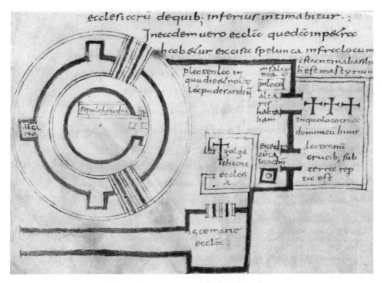

FIG 4.1 Plan of the church of the Holy Sepulchre, known widely in the Carolingian churches from the Arculf–Adomnan–Bede tradition. The Sepulchre is shown in the centre: the rotunda of the Anastasis (tugurium rotundum), the church of Golgotha (i.e. Calvary), and the basilica of Constantine, much reduced in size to show the place where the cross was found.

definitions of major importance: Sion, he said, meant 'sight' (*speculatio*), and Jerusalem meant 'vision of peace'. 'The church', he observed, 'is called Sion for its present pilgrimage': Jerusalem as a pilgrim goal had worked itself into the very definition of the name. The texts of Cassian and Isidore provided an outline within which a variety of discussion could take place. Carolingian scholars revived the older emphasis that the Temple, and the city of the Jews, had been destroyed by Titus and Vespasian because God had rejected them. This theme was powerfully explored in Walafrid Strabo's tract, *De subversione Ierusalem*: 'rightly and deservedly, those who denied God the Father and the Son were slain by father and son'. Strabo's thought stood in an older tradition, but it did not express a dominant element in contemporary thinking: people were more concerned, if not about the contemporary city of Jerusalem, then about the holy places and the monastic communities that survived around them. This was the interest that sustained pilgrimage through centuries in which travel to the East had become much more difficult.

Throughout these centuries educated people knew a fair amount about the Holy Sepulchre. Adomnan, abbot of Iona, produced an account of the holy places between 679 and 688, which he claimed was based on the reminiscences of Bishop Arculf from Gaul, who had spent some nine months at Jerusalem, but it also incorporated other material. The Holy Sepulchre itself was central to the interest of the account: Adomnan reported how he had 'carefully questioned holy Arculf, especially about the Lord's Sepulchre and the church built over it, and Arculf drew its shape for me on a wax tablet'.[18] The manuscript contained plans of four of the edifices at Jerusalem, including the rotunda at the Sepulchre itself, whose basically circular design thus became widely known to Western builders. The account included an extremely detailed description of the tomb and of the grave-slab on which the Lord's body had been placed, with some measurements taken by Arculf. There was an entire chapter on the *sudarium*, or 'cloth which was placed over the Lord's head when he lay buried', which had recently been rediscovered, and which Arculf had seen. Adomnan wrote in the hope of disseminating knowledge of the Holy Sepulchre. His patron, King Aldfrith of Northumbria, was anxious to make the book available to others, and Bede remarked that it was 'useful to many people, especially those who live far away from the places where the patriarchs and apostles used to be, and can know the holy places only through what they learn from books'.[19] It was, in other words, the opposite of a guidebook, or rather it was a guide for those who could not go in person. In 702–3 Bede himself incorporated information from Adomnan and from other sources into a book on the holy places which became the one best known throughout the early Middle Ages, and he also quoted the description in his Biblical commentaries. Over twenty manuscripts of Adomnan's book survive, and forty-seven of Bede's, located in most Western countries; nine of these preserve Arculf's plans. Such numbers suggest that originally most important churches had a copy. Paschasius Radbertus and Hrabanus Maurus both drew on the Adomnan–Bede tradition for their Biblical commentaries. The descriptions had an impact on Carolingian art: the prominence of the *sudarium* in

---

[18] Adomnan I. 2 (Wilkinson, *Pilgrims*, 171).
[19] Bede, *Ecclesiastical History* 5. 15 (tr. L. Sherley-Price (Harmondsworth 1990), 294–5); *In Marci evangelium* iv. 15 (CCSL 120 (1960), 238), and *Homiliarum Evangelii Libri* II ii., hom. 10 (CCSL 122 (1955), 247–8).

Carolingian Knowledge of the Holy Sepulchre

There is no doubt about the interest of Carolingian scholars in exact descriptions of the tomb, which can be found in several areas of scholarship, including biblical commentaries. Hrabanus Maurus was precise about it in his Commentary on Matthew:

About the Lord's tomb (*monumentum*) people who have been to Jerusalem in our days say that it was a round building cut out of the underlying rock. Its height was such that a man standing inside could just touch the roof with his arm outstretched. It had its entrance from the east, where that great stone had been rolled and located. On the northern side of the tomb the Sepulchre proper, that is the place of the Lord's body, was formed out of the same rock. It was seven feet long and stood three palms above the floor. This place did not stand open from above, but from the southern side, from which the body had been placed. The colour of the tomb and the area is said to be a mixture of red and white.

Paschasius Radbertus made use of his detailed knowledge of the layout of the Sepulchre to explain the apparent disagreements in the Gospel narratives: 'It is quite essential to know the layout of the Lord's Sepulchre if we are fully to understand the visions of the angels, and also truly to bring into common agreement the divergences of the evangelists.'

Liturgical orders, too, show a genuine knowledge of the Sepulchre; in one of about 800 it was observed that the vessels for the bread at the eucharist are called towers (*turres*) 'because the Lord's Sepulchre (*monumentum*) was cut out of the rock like a tower, with a bed inside where the Lord's body rested'. Walafrid Strabo knew that the high altar at the Holy Sepulchre church, like that in two major churches in Rome, was not at the east end. He said that he had the information 'from a most reliable report'.

Hrabanus Maurus, *Commentarium in Matthaeum* 8 (PL 107. 1146c): Hrabanus was largely following Bede's description of the appearance of the Holy Sepulchre in his own Biblical commentaries. Also Paschasius Radbertus, *Commentary on Matthew* (CCCM 56B), 1406–11; *Ordo Romanus* xv; Walafrid Strabo, *Libellus de exordiis et incrementis* (MGH Legum ii, cap. ii. 3–4 (1897), 477–8).

Adomnan must account for its frequent appearance in Carolingian drawings of the visit of the women to the Sepulchre. People went on using the Arculf–Adomnan–Bede information for centuries. About 870 Bernard the Monk, describing his visit to Jerusalem, commented that 'it is unnecessary to write a great deal about this Sepulchre because Bede says quite enough about it in his history', and even in the twelfth century Bede still provided a major source for Peter the Deacon's book on the holy places, and the basis for William of Malmesbury's description of Jerusalem. This body of learning about distant travel and foreign places was significant for the shape of Western culture, as it 'enlarged for the West geographical and historical perspectives which were tending to become narrower with the rupture of the great Roman unity'.[20]

The existence of some knowledge of the layout of the holy places does not mean that much was known about what was going on there. Up-to-date information was confined to a few places and periods, such as Rome in the early seventh century or the court of Charlemagne. Nor does it tell us anything about the prevalence of pilgrimage to the East. The predominant view is that there was a long interruption of the pilgrim route, which was resumed only sometime around 900. Steven Runciman held that 'the great age of pilgrimage begins with the tenth century', and Jean Chélini stressed in particular the small number of ninth-century participants.[21] Conditions of travel must have been difficult throughout, and for the whole period 600–1000 we have only three major pilgrim narratives: Arculf, Willibald, and Bernard. Sometimes the problems of pilgrims to the East suggest that they were very rare birds. When Fructuosus in Spain had 'an immense ardour of holy desire' to go on pilgrimage shortly after 650, he had to prepare a ship specially and he was forbidden to travel by the king.[22] It is particularly striking that, even in circles close to the court of Charlemagne, when Jerome's words about pilgrimage to Jerusalem were quoted, they were applied to Rome, as if travel to the East was no longer an issue. Thus Theodulph of Orléans wrote

> *Non tantum isse iuvat Romam, bene vivere quantum,*
> *Vel Romae, vel ubi vita agitur hominis.*

[20] Bernard the Monk c.11 (Wilkinson, *Pilgrimage*, 266); P. de Labriolle, *Histoire de l'église* (Paris, 1936), iii. 369).

[21] Runciman, *Crusades*, i. 43; J. Chélini, *L'Aube du Moyen Age* (Paris, 1991), 338.

[22] M. C. Diaz y Diaz (ed.), *La vida de San Fructuoso de Braga* (Braga, 1974), ch. 17, p. 110.

It does not help as much to go to Rome
As to live well, at Rome or else at home
In any place where human life is lived.[23]

It may be significant, too, that when Angilbert, the founder of the great abbey of Centula or Saint-Riquier, was collecting relics from all over, including Rome and Jerusalem, he relied on the official contacts of the imperial court: the relics from Constantinople and Jerusalem were 'sent to us by legates despatched thither by my lord'.[24]

Yet there are indications of continued pilgrimage, which suggest that the accidents of evidence may be producing an optical illusion. The very success of the Arculf–Adomnan–Bede information would dissuade later travellers from composing an account of their own. The relative abundance of mentions of journeys from 950 onwards may be the result of the survival of more lives of bishops and monks, and then of the profuse works of two chroniclers, Adhemar of Chabannes and Raoul Glaber, both of whom were very interested in Jerusalem. Willibald's reminiscences of his visit to the holy places in the 720s were taken down by the nun Hugeburc when she wrote the life of the great man around 780. A good deal of his narrative suggests that it was a dangerous and unusual enterprise: he was harassed by the authorities and arrested as a spy. On the other hand, he was rescued by a rich old man who said that he had 'many times' seen such visitors, and he apparently found it possible to go to Jerusalem on four separate occasions during his stay in the East.[25] We have already noticed Charlemagne's provisions for pilgrims and Latins at Jerusalem around the year 800.

There is a good picture of the travelling conditions for pilgrims about 870 in the narrative of Bernard the Monk. He was himself French, and travelled with two monks, one of them from Benevento in Italy and the other a Spaniard. He went via Bari and Taranto, both then in Arab control in southern Italy, and thence to Alexandria and Jerusalem. Bernard gives a generally favourable impression of the possibilities of travel. He mentions the need to pay landing fees in Egypt and the need for permits (failing which, one is likely to be arrested as a spy), but he is impressed by the facilities for hospitality that exist at Jerusalem as a result of Charlemagne's benefactions.

---

[23] *Theodulfi Carmina*, no. 67 (MGH Poetae I. 557). The Council of Châlons in 813 quoted Jerome in the context of a warning against the misuse of pilgrimages, detailing Rome and Tours: canon 45 (MGH Legum III Concilia II. I. 282).

[24] MGH SS xv. ii. 175.

[25] Willibald, c. 12 (Wilkinson, *Pilgrims*, 236).

'Relations between pagans and Christians are excellent.' Bernard's picture of pilgrimage can be filled out by brief records of other travellers at various times throughout this long period. Madelveus, bishop of Verdun, travelled to Jerusalem in the middle years of the eighth century because his church, as a result of the sins of its members, had been burned. We are told that 'for that reason he travelled through Gaul and Italy, and then through Greece and Joppa, and came to Jerusalem with great trials on the roads. He received the relics of many saints from the patriarch of that place, and brought them to Verdun with a crystal chalice, carved with marvellous skill.'[26] If, as it appears, the bishop's journey was designed as penance for the sins of his church, it was a very early instance of penitential pilgrimage. The first example usually quoted is that of a Frankish noble, Frotmund, who had killed a priest and was ordered by a synod to go on a series of visits to holy places. He spent many days in Rome, and then obtained a letter from Pope Benedict III (855–8) and crossed the sea to Jerusalem.

In the tenth century the evidence of pilgrimage becomes more abundant, and although the mentions are still only brief we are able to form a rather broader impression of the scene. The Ottonian court in Germany, which continued many of the Carolingian ideals, had a keen interest in Jerusalem and the Holy Sepulchre. Nobles related to the emperors went to Palestine, including Countess Hilda of Suabia, who died on the journey in 969, and Duchess Judith of Bavaria, the sister-in-law of Emperor Otto I. Judith travelled in 970. Bishop Conrad of Konstanz, a favourite of the Ottonian court, went to Jerusalem on several occasions: 'he risked the dangers of the sea three times, that he should thus often see at least the earthly Jerusalem', and in his cathedral church he founded 'the Sepulchre of the Lord in the likeness of that of Jerusalem'. French nobles and bishops, although without the same royal leadership, were no less assiduous than their German counterparts. Hilduin, count of Arcy in Champagne, set off in 992. He had 'committed many cruel offences out of military enterprise'. He was persuaded 'to undertake the labour of the Jerusalem journey' along with Abbot Adso of Montier-en-Der. They were accompanied to embarkation by some of the monks of the abbey, and Adso wrote back to say that they were sailing directly to Egypt. In

[26] Wilkinson, *Pilgrims*, 261–9; *Gesta episcoporum Virdunensium* 12 (MGH SS IV. 44). For Frotmund, see *Gesta Conwoionis abbatis Rotonensis* (Redon), c. 8 (MGH SS XV. i. 458).

fact, however, the abbot died at sea on the way. The monk Eminard, from the abbey of Anzy-le-Duc in France, spent almost seven years in the East 'for love of the Sepulchre of our Lord and Saviour'. Such a desire was often linked with the wish to make the Sepulchre present at home through the bringing back of relics: Abbot Fulcher of Flavigny went in 944 'and endowed his church with precious relics which he had brought back'. Other monks were more concerned to spend time in the East learning from the famous monasteries of the Greek church. We hear, for example, of a certain John who 'obtained licence from his abbot, and went to Jerusalem and spent six whole years in the service of God on Mount Sinai'. He subsequently went on to Mount Athos.[27] These tenth-century journeys point us forward to the apparently great explosion in the eleventh century, to which we must turn in a later section.

JERUSALEM AND THE CAROLINGIAN LITURGY

One special feature of the Carolingian church was the greatly enhanced richness of its worship, the 'swell of liturgical elaboration' of which Henry Mayr-Harting has written. It is not easy to trace the sources of their new ideas. Carol Heitz has written that 'Jerusalem, the Holy Sepulchre and the liturgy of the resurrection appear to be the origin of the whole [Carolingian liturgy]', and in one sense the comment is self-evidently true: crucifixion and resurrection are bound to be the starting-point of Christian worship.[28] Yet when contemporaries approached the Biblical events, it is hard to be sure whether they were focusing solely upon the historical happenings, or whether they were trying to recreate the Jerusalem that had been their setting. The Carolingian liturgists were by and large good scholars, but even when it seems obvious that they are borrowing ceremonies from worship at Jerusalem the evidence does not usually allow us to trace the route by which such loans arrived in the West. It may have come from reports by Charlemagne's representatives in

---

[27] Runciman, *Crusades*, i. 45; *Life* of Conrad by Udalscalc, MGH SS IV. 433 (written about 1120, but on the basis of reliable material); Hilduin, *Miracula S. Bercharii* (*AASS*, 16 Oct., VII. 1022); Eminard, *AASS*, 20 April, II. 770); Fulcher, *Chronicle of Verdun*, Recueil des Historiens des Gaules et de la France, 8. 291; and (for the monk John) Desiderius, *Dialogus de miraculis S. Benedicti* ii. 2 (MGH SS XXX. 2), 1128, written about 1078 using older materials.

[28] C. Heitz, *Recherches sur les rapports entre architecture et liturgie à l'époque carolingienne* (Paris, 1963), 246. Similarly, 'Jerusalem is at the root of everything', (101).

contemporary Palestine. More probably some of it came through Constantinople, whose liturgy was largely derived from Syria. On the other hand, a custom might have been adopted long before by one of the Latin liturgies (Rome, Spain, Milan), and borrowed by one of the Carolingian liturgical experts. Our view of the relationship between Carolingian liturgy and that of Jerusalem needs to be diluted by a great deal of speculation.

The Carolingian liturgy was dominated by Holy Week. It thus echoed the character of Egeria's account so many centuries before, which had given prominence to the observance of 'Great Week'. The Carolingians fashioned Holy Week as it has subsequently been observed in Catholic tradition. In some ways they were simply reflecting the universal practice of the church: Easter continued, in spite of the growing unfamiliarity of adult baptism, to be the major baptismal occasion, as it had been since the early centuries. Perhaps for the first time, Rome was an important liturgical influence. It was the specific policy of Pepin and Charlemagne to unify their dominions on the basis of the acceptance of Roman customs. However, the Holy Week programme as a whole was not a pure imitation of Rome. Its first day was marked by the procession on Palm Sunday, which first appears in a fully developed form in the West in the *Institutes*, composed shortly after 800, which describe the rituals followed at Saint-Riquier or Centula, in Picardy near the modern Abbeville. This was an abbey founded in the seventh century, which under Abbot Angilbert came to be closely associated with the imperial family. He undoubtedly developed the relics and liturgy there, but it may well be that some of the ceremonies in the *Institutes* predated his time. This may include the Palm Sunday procession. Whenever this arrived in the Carolingian lands, it almost certainly did not travel through Rome.[29] There is ample evidence for the Palm Sunday procession from this time onwards. In about 820, Amalarius noted that 'in memory of this event we are accustomed to carry branches before our churches and to shout "Jerusalem" ', and Carolingian liturgists composed processional hymns and antiphons, the most famous of them Theodulph's hymn known to English worshippers as 'All glory, laud, and honour':

---

[29] H. J. Graef, *Palmenweihe und Palmenprocession* (Steyl, 1959); C. Wright, 'The Palm Sunday Procession in Medieval Chartres', M. E. Fassler and R. A. Balzer (eds.), *The Divine Office in the Latin Middle Ages* (Oxford, 2000), 344–71; and M. Spurrell, 'The Procession of Palms and West-front Galleries', *Downside Review*, 119 (2001), 125–44.

Gloria, laus et honor tibi sit, rex Christe, redemptor,
cui puerile decus prompsit hosanna pium.[30]

The full version of Theodulph's hymn refers clearly to the stages of the Palm Sunday procession at Angers. The inclusion of the procession in the Romano-German Pontifical suggests that it was in general use by the 960s at the latest.

The veneration of the cross on Good Friday was established at Rome by the eighth century, but in detail the ceremony followed at Saint-Riquier does not look like an imitation of Roman practice. It is likely to have travelled from Jerusalem along with relics of the cross: one Carolingian scholar still remembered that the devotion should ideally be addressed to a genuine relic, and remarked consolingly: 'Although every church cannot possess it, yet the virtue of the holy cross is not wanting to them in those crosses which are made after the likeness of the Lord's cross.'[31] The distinctive Easter ceremony of the lighting of the new fire seemingly offers a different pattern of transmission: if its foundation was of Jerusalem origin, the peculiar role it assumed in the history of the church of the Holy Sepulchre may be the result of Western expectations. The finished Carolingian recipe for Holy Week contained a rich flavour of Jerusalem, however varied the influences that provided ingredients for the cooking.

One prominent feature of Frankish worship was its 'stational' character. Outside the standard daily or weekly worship, processions on major occasions would circulate to a variety of churches and holy places. At each there would be a stop or station for worship by the clergy and people. Their origin was within the great cities of the Roman world (the note in the Roman Missal, *station at St Pancras*, has sometimes provided mild amusement to the modern English reader). The adoption of such forms also enriched the liturgy in the different circumstances of Carolingian Europe. Their aim was to associate the people with the performance of worship, in spite of the barrier presented by a Latin liturgy; 'to keep the participants in liturgical ceremonies in continual movement, so that they could feel themselves to be not merely simple spectators, but active participants'.[32] Monastic worship was marked by elaborate processions both inside and outside the main church. Contemporaries were impressed by the similarity

---

[30] F. J. E. Raby (ed.), *The Oxford Book of Medieval Latin Verse* (Oxford, 1959), no. 81.
[31] Amalarius, *De ecclesiasticis ordinibus* i. 14; N. Bux, 'Le liturgie pasquali della croce e del fuoco da Gerusalemme a Roma', *Nicolaus*, 21 (1994), 5–12.
[32] Möbius, *Passion*, 23.

Easter Fire

One of the most evocative of the holy Week ceremonies, the kindling of new fire on Easter eve, has specially strong connections with Jerusalem. Its remote origins must be the ceremony of lamp-lighting, which was a standard evening observance in the early church. Egeria fails to give details, because the Jerusalem Paschal vigil was like the one she knew at home, and she therefore did not record it. We know that the ceremony of lighting a Paschal Candle was being observed, along with a song of praise like the present *Exultet*, in northern Italy around the year 400. None of this indicates that any particular importance was attached to the moment of the kindling of the fire, but by the time Bernard visited Jerusalem in 870, the new fire for Easter was being kindled inside the Holy Sepulchre itself, and moreover was believed to be a miraculous gift of God. Bernard himself reported that it was brought by an angel. There is no previous mention of the emergence of the fire, but there are further references during the following century, including a quite detailed report to the Byzantine Emperor Constantine VII in 947. It is plausible to suggest that the new understanding of the practice was brought from West to East— not, indeed, from Rome, where the Easter fire was simply preserved from Maundy Thursday, but from the newly converted Germanic peoples (who were familiar with ceremonies of 'spring fire'), through the Frankish church. If that is right, one of the most striking features of the Paschal ceremonies was not derived from the Holy Sepulchre, but taken there by Latin visitors. Its appearance in the years before 870 corresponds with the period of Carolingian influence in Palestine.

G. Fuchs and H. M. Weikmann, *Das Exsultet* (Ratisbon, 1992); D. R. Dendy, *The Use of Lights in Christian Worship* (London, 1959); M. Canard, 'La Destruction de l'église de la résurrection par le calife Hakim et l'histoire de la descente du feu sacré', *Byzantion*, 35 (1965), 16–43; A. Franz, 'Die Feuerweihe', *Die kirchliche Benediktionen im Mittelalter* (Freiburg, 1909), ii. 507 ff.; and P. Sartori, 'Osterfeuer' (H. Bächtold-Stäubli (ed.), *Handwörterbuch des deutschen Aberglaubens*, 6 (1987), 1333–6).

between cities and abbeys, which necessarily seem so different to us. A great part of the population of a city would consist of clergy and their dependants, and the place would be full of shrines; while a great monastery would be surrounded by workshops and craftsmen. The general 'feel' of Tours or Metz would be that of a holy city, not unlike the impression that would once have been given by Jerusalem. A stational liturgy would be appropriate for both types of social organisms. While on the whole we are not well informed about the liturgy of the cathedrals at this time, there are good reasons for thinking that many of them, like Metz and Autun, had developed stational liturgies by 700 or soon afterwards. The stational worship of Jerusalem certainly influenced the practice of the West in the patristic period, and perhaps helped to shape the ideas of the Carolingian reformers, but the practice was widespread, indeed universal in any community that was large enough to support it.

The imaginative power of worship had therefore been developed beyond anything known in the past, but in most instances it did not involve the precise enactment of biblical episodes. Some of the most important elements in the Holy Week ceremonial, such as the adoration of the cross or Angilbert's great Easter Day procession, were celebrations of redemption in Christ, but not representations of what had happened. True, there were some rehearsals of New Testament events, but the stress was not on the historical content. Theodulph's Palm Sunday hymn has surprisingly little reference to the passion, but is a celebration of the cosmic kingship of Christ:

> *coetus in excelsis te laudat caelicus omni*
> *set mortalis homo et cuncta creata simul.*

'the heavenly host all praise you in glory supernal, and mortal mankind and all creatures on earth do the same'. The evidence points to a strong interest in the liturgical inheritance of the Holy Sepulchre at Jerusalem: to the centrality of Holy Week and Easter and to a pattern of processions and ceremonial, which consciously as well as historically incorporated a range of references to the holy places. Processions and ceremonial alluded to the solemn entry, just as, we shall shortly see, they commemorated the cross and the empty tomb; but they did not seek to re-enact the events or reproduce the buildings. The picture of Carolingian worship for which Carol Heitz has argued was one of grand ceremonial, in which the Easter liturgy was celebrated in a dedicated space at the west end of the newly designed great churches, to which we must turn in a moment.

Yet we do find elements of realism. Perhaps they began with preaching. It has been said that the homilies of Paul the Deacon, in the years before 800, told the Gospel stories 'as if they had happened in the Frankish people's own day to people they could have known' and that, in general, 'the instruction of the people in matters of faith was undertaken on the basis of an identification of the Frankish people with the first hearers of Christ's teaching in Judaea'.[33] In the early ninth century, Amalarius of Metz took a considerable step forward in the imaginative re-enactment of the Gospel history. His commentary on the mass treated the various liturgical actions as descriptive of the historical events of the passion, so that the whole became in a sense the story of the life and death of Jesus. He observed that 'with the cross of Christ placed before me I hold Christ in my mind as if he were actually hanging upon it'. This seems to be the period when the reproaches or *improperia* were introduced into the veneration of the cross, expressing a sense of being actually addressed by the dying Christ: 'my people, what have I done to you?' Amalarius, writing of this ceremony, cited Paula's devotion in the fourth century: 'She fell down and worshipped before the cross as if she could see the Lord hanging on it.'[34] The fact that he could quote from Jerome indicates that this approach was not without precedent, but it is difficult to find this sort of devotional expression in the centuries before him. Amalarius appears to represent the beginning of a new realism, but in his writing the events of the Gospel history were being discovered symbolically within the liturgy. Many of his interpretations of the mass were so highly imaginative, not to say far-fetched, that only a scholar educated in the tradition could hope to discover them. The fact that his approach raised angry protests indicates that the main weight of most liturgists' objectives still lay elsewhere. With the tenth century, however, the desire for a more detailed and dramatic style became more general.

This approach was primarily intended to bring the Gospel history to those who could not understanding the readings nor follow an elaborate allegory of the actions of the mass. In that sense, it stood in line with the Carolingian concern for the christianization of the population, but this time in a more intimate and direct way.

[33] R. McKitterick, *The Frankish Church and the Carolingian Reforms, 789–895* (London, 1977), 103–4, 141.
[34] Amalarius, *Liber officialis* i. 14. 7–8 (J. M. Hanssens (ed.), *Opera liturgica omnia* 2, Studi e Testi 139 (Vatican, 1948), 101), citing Jerome, ep. 108. 9; B. C. Raw, *Anglo-Saxon Crucifixion Iconography* (Cambridge, 1990), 55.

Realism was advancing on a broad front, and came to include a vivid presentation of Easter morning. The first surviving description of the new Easter ceremonies occurs in the *Regularis Concordia*, approved in England in 970 as a guide to monastic reform under Dunstan and Ethelwold, where two associated ceremonies are recommended to be used 'if anyone should care or think it fit to follow in a becoming manner religious men in a practice worthy to be imitated for the strengthening of the faith of unlearned common persons and neophytes'. On Good Friday, on a suitable part of the altar, 'there shall be a representation, as it were, of a sepulchre, hung about with a curtain, in which the holy cross, when it has been venerated, shall be placed'.[35] This enacted burial is to be followed on Easter Day by a visit to the tomb by three monks, representing the three women. They are to be questioned by an angel, sitting beside the tomb, who will ask them *Quem queritis*, whom are you seeking? As in the Gospels, the angel then announces to them the resurrection.

We soon find in various churches a series of ceremonies involving a representation of the sepulchre: *depositio* (the placing on Good Friday of a symbol of the dead Christ); *elevatio* (its removal from the Sepulchre on Easter Day); and *visitatio* (the enactment of the coming of the women to the tomb). These ceremonies did not necessarily exist together, but they clearly had a great deal in common. The *Life* of Bishop Udalric of Augsburg (died 973) mentions the ceremony of the 'burial' of Christ after communion on Good Friday. This was in the form of the eucharistic bread, and not, as in England, of a relic of the cross; these two variants subsequently continued for centuries in different parts of Europe.[36]

This new spirit of realism had limits. The deposition of a eucharistic host, or a relic of the cross, was a visual image of the Biblical events and not a re-enactment. S. Corbin has stressed that there was no serious dramatic element in the *depositio*: 'the whole thing turns, on the contrary, on the symbolic expression which is proper to liturgy'. This is an apt comment, and we can readily agree that it is better to speak of an Easter ceremony than an Easter play. Nevertheless, his wider generalization that 'the two ideas of symbolism and of religious drama are mutually exclusive' seems to undervalue the strength of the desire to bring the believer into more immediate

---

[35] T. Symons (ed.), *Regularis Concordia* cc. 46, 50–1 (London, 1953), 44, 49–50.
[36] *Vita S. Udalrici* (PL 135. 1020 f.).

The Visitation to the Sepulchre on Easter Morning

The date of the origin of this ceremony is hard to determine. The *Regularis Concordia* was largely based on the customs of reformed monasteries on the Continent. It seems likely that the Easter ceremony in this document was derived from Fleury or Ghent, but the early customaries of these abbeys have disappeared. In many parts of Western Europe there was a growing interest in the dramatization of the events surrounding the empty tomb. Andrew Hughes has suggested an origin in Metz or the Rhineland, which would bring it close to the centre of Carolingian liturgical reforms in the ninth century. It has also been argued that this ceremony was widespread at a an early date. It appears first in centres where there is a relatively high level of manuscript survival, and the spread of references in the later Middle Ages may reflect the dissemination of the practice of record, not the introduction of the ceremony. Its wide spread is supported by the resurrection frescoes in Saint-Pierre-les-Églises near Chauvigny (Poitou), where Mary, mother of James (*Maria Jacobi*), one of the visitors to the tomb, is shown holding the grave-clothes and announcing, '*ecce lineamenta*'.

C. Flanigan, 'The Roman Rite and the Origins of the Liturgical Drama', *University of Toronto Quarterly*, 43 (1974), 263–84, and his 'Medieval Latin Music-Drama', in E. Simon (ed.), *The Theatre of Medieval Europe* (Cambridge, 1991), 21–41; A. Hughes, 'Liturgical Drama', in Simon, *Theatre*, 42–62; J. Bärsch, 'Das dramatische im Gottesdienst', *Liturgisches Jahrbuch*, 46 (1996), 41–66; and C. Symes, 'The Appearance of Early Vernacular Plays', *Speculum*, 77 (2002), 778–831.

contact with the events at the Holy Sepulchre.[37] We should remember, too, that the widely circulated legends of the holy cross told of its burial and subsequent rediscovery by Helena: contemporaries may have thought that they were closer to the historical event than is apparent to us. In an age when other forms of participation were being denied, when the communion of the people was rare, and liturgical action was dominated by the clergy, the demand to see, which was to be so characteristic of medieval services, was emerging.

[37] S. Corbin, *La Déposition liturgique du Christ au Vendredi Saint* (Paris, 1960), 245–7.

The new pattern of worship was increasingly a liturgy of image, although not necessarily of literal depiction.

A church is a machine for worshipping in. The echoes of the Jerusalem liturgy that we have noted in Carolingian services produced their effect upon the buildings, making them memorials of the Holy Sepulchre. This was not a simple and literal representation. Liturgists aimed at a rainbow of themes and allusions, Rome as well as Jerusalem, the heavenly and earthly Jerusalem together. The distinctive architecture of the Carolingian great churches expressed this combination of traditions. They were double-enders. The apses, altars, and towers of the east end were matched by parallel provisions for worship at the west, and the more closely associated the building was with the imperial court, the more truly double-ended it appeared to be. The strong imperial connection has long been stressed by scholars, but it does not exclude the special liturgical functions associated with the distinct parts of the building, which were closely analysed by Carol Heitz. There is no very satisfactory name for the striking architectural feature: it is most usually called a westwork, sometimes a porch church or ante-church, but these terms underestimate its status. It was essentially a separate but equal facility parallel to the eastern section. Charlemagne's palace chapel at Aachen provided the model for most of these western buildings, but Saint-Riquier is the best record we have of a functional system of worship incorporating the 'church at the west end'.

Double-enders were different from our modern expectation of medieval church design. They were partly shaped by the example of the glorious past.[38] Carolingian builders were concerned to adopt the long hall in imitation of Roman buildings, but within it they wanted to incorporate a variety of functions and shrines, which in the East, and in earlier centuries in the West also, would have been separately housed: the relic of the saint, the cult of the cross, the altar of the Saviour, and sometimes the baptistery. It has been observed that 'we no longer seem to be dealing with an architecture where spaces, decorations and elements are accumulated or placed side by side, but with an architecture which aims at integration'.[39] Carolingian

---

[38] R. Krautheimer, 'The Carolingian Revival of Early Christian Architecture', *Art Bulletin*, 24 (1942), 1–38.

[39] C. Sapin, *La Bourgogne pré-Romane* (Paris, 1986), 173.

Saint-Riquier (Centula)

This great abbey, presided over by Angilbert, a close associate of Charlemagne himself, provides us with our best information about the elaboration of Carolingian worship. The surviving buildings are nothing like those of Angilbert, but a history of the abbey was written by Hariulf around 1100, and illustrated by a sketch of the monastery that appears to be reliable. This manuscript, in its turn, has been lost, but two seventeenth-century reproductions survive. So do the *Institutes* of Angilbert, which give a full account of the ceremonial. At Saint-Riquier, the eastern tower was dedicated to the saintly patron, Richarius or Riquier, and the western one to the Saviour. The monastic complex also included a small church of St Mary, which was round, in accordance with a tradition for Marian dedication. The elaborate Easter procession, presided over by the abbot in place of the bishop, involved local churches and stations within the abbey precincts, where the various parts of the buildings were treated as separate stopping-places.

The surviving material about the Centula liturgy is in F. Lot (ed.), *Hariulf, Chronique de l'abbaye de Saint-Riquier* (Paris, 1894). Carol Heitz has interpreted it, and made it a key element in the reconstruction of the worship of the Carolingian church in *Recherches sur les rapports entre architecture et liturgie à l'époque carolingienne* (Paris, 1963), and *L'Architecture religieuse carolingienne: les formes et leurs fonctions* (Paris, 1980). See the qualifications of D. Parsons, 'The Pre-Romanesque Church of Saint-Riquier: The Documentary Evidence', *Journal of the British Archaeological Association*, 129 (1976), 21–51, with comments and further references by D. Bullough, 'The Carolingian Liturgical Experience', R. N. Swanson (ed.), *Continuity and Change in Christian Worship*, SCH 35 (1999), esp. 54 n.

scholars also knew that two of Constantine's great churches, St Peter's at Rome and the basilica at the Holy Sepulchre, had their main apse and altar at the west end, and they were emboldened by the combined authority of Rome and Jerusalem to give their great churches a double orientation.

Almost all these buildings had an altar or sub-church dedicated to the Saviour. At Saint-Riquier, this was the function of the whole westwork. The cult of the Saviour was presumably derived from the cathedral at Rome, later called S. John Lateran but in Constantine's intention *basilica salvatoris*. Its wide diffusion suggests that it had a special significance in the creation of religious unity in Charlemagne's dominions: 'The cult of the Saviour determined the form of the Carolingian porch-church. This cult is essential, it was this which mobilized the masses into a common liturgical action.'[40] Most of the important churches founded in newly christianized lands during the eighth century favoured dedications to the Saviour. The Saviour-cult was linked with the major mysteries of salvation: with a Palm Sunday procession that celebrated the majesty of Christ the king, and with reverence for the cross. Most of the great churches had holy cross altars, often set in the middle of the church, sometimes significantly called *altare sancti salvatoris ad crucem*, the altar of the Saviour at the cross.[41] It is more doubtful how far these observances made any impact on the population as a whole, or even were understood by the bulk of the clergy. Liturgy has its own impetus. We cannot be sure how far lay attendance amounted to any more than simple presence at a spectacular ceremony or procession.

The celebration of Christ as king was linked with the prominence of the Paschal ceremonies, which dominate the *Institutes* of Angilbert. In great churches the chapels and relics of saints tended to be those closely associated with the historical Christ: the Blessed Virgin, John the Baptist, and St Peter. We find an extreme example of this tendency at Reichenau, which had no altar to any local saint, but filled the gap by obtaining a sample of the holy Blood. The kingship of the glorified Christ was commemorated in hymns such as that of Bishop Fulbert of Chartres around AD 1000.

> *Triumphat ille splendide*
> *et dignus amplitudine,*
> *soli polique patriam*
> *unam fecit rempublicam.*

> He triumphs gloriously on high,
> Is over all accounted great.
> The fatherland of earth and sky
> He now has made a single state.[42]

---

[40] Heitz, *Recherches*, 245.
[41] Ibid. 66–71.
[42] Raby, *Medieval Latin Verse*, no. 128, now familiar as 'Ye choirs of new Jerusalem'.

These words remind us of the political implications of the doctrine of the cult of the Saviour. Charlemagne was greeted as a new David, exercising an authority that was divinely given. From Louis the Pious onwards, this theme took more extreme forms. In Hrabanus Maurus's *Praise of the Holy Cross* about 830, he appears in the style of the victorious Christ, and later the emperor was shown as being personally crowned by Christ. By the end of the tenth century, this tradition had moved even further: Otto III was presented as elevated above the world, an embodiment of the glory of Christ.[43]

These ideas formed the basis for a distinctive Carolingian development of the spiritual interpretation of Jerusalem. Alcuin saw its vision of Jerusalem, not as a remote future promise, but as a declaration of present reality. Commenting on Revelation 11, he explained that 'the temple is open, because Christ has now been born, suffered, raised and glorified'.[44] The reality of Jerusalem was embodied in the magnificent buildings of the great churches. The idea that Jerusalem is made manifest in the baptismal community was already old. Now it was enlarged by finding the glory of Jerusalem in the victory of Christ in the world and the splendour of the great churches. An old baptismal hymn received some additional verses to make it appropriate to a church dedication ceremony:

> *Hoc in templo, summe Deus, exoratus adveni*
> *et clementi bonitate precum vota suscipe,*
> *largam benedictionem hic infunde iugiter.*

> To this temple, heavenly Father, enter as we now request,
> And with goodness and with kindness hear the prayers at our
>   behest,
> Pouring out rich benediction, making it for ever blessed.[45]

This way of thinking had consequences in the area of manuscript

---

[43] H. Mayr-Harting, *Ottonian Book Illumination* (London, 1991), i. 60–8.

[44] Alcuin, *Commentary on Apocalypse* (PL 100. 1152). The reference is to Revelation 11: 19, 'God's temple in heaven was opened, and the ark of his covenant was seen within his temple.' The biblical text closely links this with the victory-theme: 'the kingdom of the world has become the kingdom of our Lord and of his Christ, and he shall reign for ever and ever' (11: 15).

[45] Raby, *Medieval Latin Verse*, no. 63; H. Ashworth, '*Urbs beata Jerusalem*: Scriptural and Patristic Sources', *Ephemerides Liturgica*, 70 (1956), 238–41.

illumination. The Jerusalem of *Revelation* was depicted as a church, or even as a circular plan that appears to be derived from the Arculf sketches of the Holy Sepulchre.[46] It appears that artists did not think primarily of a heavenly Jerusalem that contrasted with the earthly city, but rather of the new Jerusalem, the vision of peace, which was embodied in the city where salvation had come and in the churches that represented it in the West.

Carolingian worship turned upon the 'Jerusalem events': solemn entry, passion, resurrection. These provided the fundamental message of preaching that the church could present to the newly converted German nations, whose former religion contained nothing like the Christian promise of resurrection: as the homilist expressed it, 'The resurrection of Christ is the foundation of our faith'. Rome was regarded by the reformers as the most authoritative source, but Rome pointed to Jerusalem.[47] One of its most sacred relics was the *Sancta Sanctorum*, the name in the eighth century for the chest that contained fragments from the Holy Land, each labelled with its place of origin. In any case, the cult of Christ as Saviour was rooted in the Holy Sepulchre, and the proclamation of Charlemagne as a second Constantine awoke recollections of the work of Constantine and Helena. The very fact that, at least to judge by the surviving evidence, ceremonial was focused so narrowly at Holy Week and Easter, necessarily made Carolingian worship reminiscent of that of the Jerusalem church. In this programme of liturgical renewal and church building there was no sharp separation between three constituent elements: heavenly Jerusalem, the holy places where God had wrought salvation, and the splendid new churches raised to the honour of Christ. All were expressions of the new Jerusalem. The interest of Charlemagne in the problems of the Christian community in Palestine and the negotiations with Harun ar-Raschid, which we have already considered, form a natural consequence, in the field of foreign policy, of this ideology. There were manifold links between the Holy Sepulchre and the theology and liturgy of the Western Church during the Carolingian renaissance.

[46] Heitz, *Recherches*, 133–7.
[47] H. Barré (ed.), *Homéliaires carolingiens*, Studi e Testi, 225 (Vatican, 1962), 242; H. L. Kessler and J. Zacharias, *Rome, 1300* (London, 2000), 50–1.

COMMEMORATIONS OF THE HOLY SEPULCHRE

The ceremonial of death had by no means been christianized in the years before 800, but there was a desire among influential people to be buried beside the remains of saints, *ad sanctos*. The presence of recollections of the Holy Sepulchre within cemeteries, or beside tombs, was valued.[48] It appears that the burial of an abbot Mellebaud near Poitiers, in the early eighth century, was associated with recollections of the Holy Sepulchre.

In Memory of Mellebaud

In 1878, a curious structure was discovered under some down-land near Poitiers. The local name of the site, 'le champ des martyrs', attested since the seventeenth century, presumably preserves a recollection of an early Christian cemetery in the area. Fragmentary inscriptions indicate that it was a *memoria* for an abbot Mellebaud. It is further described as a cave or *ispelunca*. It was associated with the fragments of a striking sculpture, apparently the remains of a crucifixion group, with the two thieves with bound hands; and, apart from the abbot's own tomb, there was a representation of an empty tomb within one of the walls. Stylistic criteria suggest the first half of the eighth century. The whole structure is rectangular. Its presence near Poitiers, with its celebrated fragment of the cross and a tradition of contact with Jerusalem, may be significant.

V. H. Elbern, 'Das Relief der Gekreuzigten in der Mellebaudis Memorie zu Poitiers', *Jahrbuch der Berliner Museen* 3 (1961), 148–89; J. Hubert and others, *Europe in the Dark Ages* (London, 1969), 57–62; and *Supplice*, 57–63.

In all probability there were numerous instances of the association of burials with Holy Sepulchre commemorations, but we can only recover them with the aid of a good deal of speculation. At Bologna the body of the saintly founder, Petronius, is buried within the Holy Sepulchre, but this is a structure of the twelfth century, and we cannot be certain whether it continues a more ancient situation.

---

[48] The wider question of the development of Christian cemeteries is considered in E. Zadora-Rio, 'Lieux d'inhumation et espaces consacrés', *Lieux sacrés*, 197–213.

Saint Pierre l'Estrier at Autun may have originated in a mausoleum, which was later used as a station for the processional liturgy.[49] In some cult centres, such as Grenoble in France or Disentis in Switzerland, there were circular or annular crypts which served the practical purpose of affording access to pilgrims, and conceivably the programmatic one of echoing the shape of the rotunda of the Anastasis. It has also been argued that the square crypts designed under Bishop Wilfrid at Hexham and Ripon in the 670s contained reminiscences of the Sepulchre, although the indications are slight. If we had the original decorations, we might know for sure.[50]

The funerary significance of memorials of the Holy Sepulchre continued to be important. One striking example was in the cemetery chapel at St Michael's Fulda in 822. This has usually been regarded as a very early instance of a 'copy' of the Sepulchre, but it more probably belonged to the tradition of sanctifying the burial-place with relics of Jerusalem.

With the coming of the Carolingian renaissance, we can be sure that the ground plan of the major Jerusalem buildings was widely known in educated circles in the West from the sketches of Arculf, embodied in the books of Adomnan and Bede, and that the commemoration of the Golgotha events was central to the worship of the period. But did these influences lead to the conscious imitation of Jerusalem buildings in the West? It would be a great help if we knew whether the Palatine chapel at Aachen, which was designed with a central plan and strongly influenced other major churches, incorporated pictorial references to the Holy Sepulchre, but the question has to remain unresolved.

There are signs, though, that the development of processional worship did stamp a 'Jerusalem' character upon some churches. Santo Stefano, Bologna, was first called 'Jerusalem', as far as records go, in 887, and a century later it apparently contained imitations of the holy places. Other uses of the name 'Jerusalem' were to appear in the eleventh century, and they were not the only instances of references to Palestine: the title 'Bethlehem' was given to the abbey of Saint-Pierre and Saint-Paul at Ferrières from the ninth century onwards.[51]

---

[49] C. Sapin, *La Bourgogne pré-Romane* (Paris, 1986), 166.
[50] R. Bailey, 'St Wilfrid: Ripon and Hexham', in C. Karkov and R. Farrell (eds.), *Studies in Insular Art and Archaeology*, American Early Medieval Studies, 1 (1991), 3–25.
[51] Sapin, *La Bourgogne*, 80.

A Sepulchre at Fulda?

We have excellent contemporary sources for the original dedication under Abbot Eigil in 822, including a record of the inscription composed by Hrabanus Maurus:

> This altar's mainly dedicated here
> To Christ, whose tomb will also help our tombs.
> Part of Mount Sinai, Moses' memory,
> And here the native earth of Christ the Lord.

This is a clear expression of themes we have already explored: relics from the Holy Land and a mausoleum, or at least a chapel for the cemetery of the monks. The presence later of an undoubted copy of the Sepulchre has convinced most scholars that Eigil provided one in 822. Closer examination leads to doubts. His building was a rotunda with a crypt, which is now the only surviving element. Although the new chapel, consecrated in 1092, seems to have followed the outline of the older plan, the details above ground and the relics were different, and it may be a mistake to suppose that there was already a copy of the Holy Sepulchre there. Hrabanus' inscription is primarily designed as a list of relics. Evidently the altar contained earth from the Holy Sepulchre, a type of relic that had been venerated since the fourth or fifth century and was specially appropriate to a cemetery chapel.

Texts in E. Duemmler (ed.), *MGH Poetae Latini Aevi Carolini* (Berlin, 1884), ii. *Carmina Hrabani Mauri*, 209. O. Ellger, *Die Michaelskirche zu Fulda als Zeugnis der Totensorge* (Fulda, 1988) amends the picture presented by older studies.

In 'Jerusalem and the Carolingian Liturgy' above, we have already noticed the emergence of a new tide of realism within the framework of church ceremonies, and especially the emergence of the *quem queritis* and associated rituals. This had an impact upon artists responsible for small-scale works: ivory carvings and miniatures used as a symbol of the Sepulchre, the towers or westworks in which the Easter liturgy took place. There were still no pictures of the resurrection as such, not even of the meeting of Christ and Mary Magdalen. The favourite image of the resurrection in the Greek church was the

The Palatine Chapel and the Holy Sepulchre

The probable source of its design was San Vitale at Ravenna. It has been suggested that the original mosaic in its dome was a reproduction of that in the dome of the Anastasis. There is evidence that they shared the same subject, the adoration of the Lamb in *Revelation* 5, but it is such a central feature of Christian art that its presence would not establish direct inspir-ation, let alone direct copying, from Jerusalem. Neither original survives, so we are dependent on reproductions of doubtful reliability. Alcuin wrote to Charlemagne that in Aachen 'the Temple of the most wise Solomon is constructed by God's art', but this need not be more than a reference to the grandeur of the project. Even if we accept Carol Heitz's view that the liturgy of the imperial chapel incorporated strong references to the ceremonial of Jerusalem, the presence there of pictures or architectural representations of the Holy Sepulchre remains uncertain.

On the dome mosaics, G. S. P. Freeman-Grenville, 'The Basilica of the Holy Sepulchre, Jerusalem: History and Future', *Journal of the Royal Asiatic Society* (1987), esp. 192–3.

entry of Christ into the underworld (a motif actually called the Anastasis), but this appeared quite rarely in the West at this time. Easter morning pictures, which to judge by the number of survivals must have been frequent in the treasures and perhaps on the walls of churches, showed the visit of the three Marys to the tomb. Carol Heitz has pointed out that ivories and other miniatures that showed the visit of the three women to the tomb began to depict it, not as an edicule, but as the tower of a western massif, as if the ceremony were taking place in a western porch-church. An ivory of about 870, later reused to form the book cover of a Pericope Book of the Emperor Henry II, had the traditional combination of the crucifixion and the empty Sepulchre, which is shown as a three-storeyed tower. An ivory plaque on the binding of Bibliothèque Nationale MS lat. 9453, per-haps carved about 900, has the tomb in a rotunda, with a church attached, and the 'women' look very like men, presumably the monks who were enacting the *visitatio* ceremony. Even more remarkable is

Jerusalem at Bologna

The modern visitor to St Stefano (also known as the *sette chiese*) at Bologna will find a site arranged beside an octagonal church with a large, if highly imaginative, model of the Holy Sepulchre within it. The assemblage of buildings represents the best surviving example of the episcopal group of churches that was once characteristic of major cities. Reminiscences of Golgotha and the passion of Christ are abundant throughout the surrounding cloisters and churches. The *Life of Petronius*, bishop of Bologna from about 432 to 450, claimed that he had 'symbolically created a work . . . like the Sepulchre of the Lord in the form which he had seen, and carefully measured with a rod, when he was at Jerusalem'. This work, however, was composed between 1164 and 1180, and its ignorance of the world of the fifth century is almost complete. As far as we know, the identification of Bologna with Jerusalem was first mentioned in 887 in an imperial diploma. We are subsequently told in the *Life* of St Bononius that its hero visited 'those holy places, which the blessed Petronius had created in his homeland in the image of Palestine'; and this must have been about the 970s. Unfortunately, we do not know just what was there at that time. A nearby church was then being called St John *in monte Oliveto*. It sounds as if it had come to be used as a starting-place for the Palm Sunday procession, which at Jerusalem began on the Mount of Olives. The present octagonal church of Santo Sepolcro, within the complex, contains a representation of the Sepulchre, which probably dates from the rebuilding after 1141, although we cannot exclude an earlier predecessor. The present one is an omnium-gatherum design which incorporates Calvary above the sepulchre, in which is to be found the body of St Petronius.

C. Morris, 'Bringing the Holy Sepulchre to the West: S. Stefano, Bologna, from the Fifth to the Twentieth Century', in R. N. Swonson (ed.), *The Church Retrospective*, SCH 33 (1997), 31–59, where there are extensive references to sources and modern discussions; also L. Canetti in G. Cracco (ed.), *Per una storia dei santuari cristiani d'Italia* (Bologna, 2002).

FIG 4.2 This ivory now in the Collection Carrand in the Bargello at Florence shows the Sepulchre incorporated into the west tower of a magnificent church, with the guards asleep in a pile. The date may be about 1000.

a plaque now in the Bargello at Florence, which probably originated in Northern France in the tenth century, and which shows the women, angel, and sleeping guards, all outside the west front of a church with a characteristic westwork tower, within which the empty grave-clothes can be seen rolled.[52] The same tradition was preserved in an illustration in the sacramentary produced for Bishop

---

[52] Heitz, *Recherches*, 209 ff., for references to this paragraph.

Sigebert of Minden (1022–36). There are therefore strong reasons for
thinking that the liturgical reminiscences of the Jerusalem events
shaped the way the Holy Sepulchre was imagined, and reflected a
ceremonial in which the discovery of the empty tomb took place
within the western rotunda of the church. Although the manuscripts of Adomnan and Bede, and probably the sketch plans they
contained, were well known to Carolingian communities, we should
remember that they were quite unclear in their details, and confirmed at least some of the images with a rotunda with a basilica
attached.

Physically, within the church building, the ceremony of the
Quem queritis required a Sepulchre. At first, an altar functioned as
the place for the sacrament or the cross to be deposited, perhaps
rigged up with curtains to represent a tabernacle, and located—
when possible in a western rotunda or porch-church. Subsequently
we read in the church orders that the ceremony takes place at a
monumentum or *sepulcrum*. It is reasonable to suppose that the first
building of specific copies of the Holy Sepulchre itself was designed
to satisfy this need, although it is difficult to date their emergence.[53]
Their use for the ceremony, of course, does not contradict the possibility that they were intended to provide memorials of Jerusalem
for pilgrims to visit: indeed, the two purposes would strengthen
each other.

If it is right, as was suggested earlier, to be sceptical about St
Michael's Fulda, the first well-established attempt at a direct copy of
the edicule is postponed until the middle of the tenth century, when
Bishop Conrad built one at Konstanz; and this coincides with the
date at which we have reason to suppose the existence of some sort
of reproduction of the holy places at Santo Stefano, Bologna. This
dating would correspond with the increasing realism that came
to mark the worship of the greater churches towards the end of
the ninth century. Thereafter, we begin to encounter more
evidence of the phenomenon, and it will be convenient to consider
Konstanz and other forerunners in the next chapter as part of
the sustained attempt to bring the likeness of the Holy Sepulchre to
the West.

[53] See C. Mazouer, 'Les Indications de mise en scène dans les drames liturgiques de
Pâques', *CCM* 23 (1980), 361–8.

FIG 4.3 The sacramentary of Bishop Sigebert of Minden, about 1030, may have been produced in the great monastic scriptorium of S. Gall. The tomb is shown as an open building, with a cupola shape, not unlike the western massif of the great churches. Grave-clothes are visible on the sarcophagus itself; the angel is tense and excited, the guards asleep in disorder. The women carry spice jars, but also thuribles for incense, as in the liturgy.

RELICS OF THE CROSS AND PASSION

Among all the representations of salvation in Christ, the one that most effectively brought its power to the West was the presence of a fragment of the cross. The cross had famously arrived at Poitiers in 569. Arrivals in the next two centuries were probably not common, but they were important in proportion to their rarity. One example will stand for many: the coming of the holy cross to Orléans. The date is uncertain, but is perhaps shortly before 700. The first evidence of its presence is a coin bearing the inscription SANCTA CRUS AURILIANIS, *the holy cross of Orléans*. The new cathedral built soon afterwards was dedicated to the cross. Legend soon gave it an earlier date: it was claimed that it arrived in the fourth century, and even that it was a gift of Constantine himself. The Emperor Louis the Pious twice came to the city to venerate the cross, and in 871 a list of the feasts to be kept in the diocese included 'the invention of the salvation-bringing cross, and the exaltation of the same life-giving cross', the two major feasts of the cross on 3 May and 14 September. Soon after this, we hear of popular devotions, with pilgrims spending the night before a silver crucifix in the hope of receiving healing. The relic had provided a nucleus around which legend, liturgy, and royal and popular devotion could all gather.[54]

The theme of the cross as the token of victory dominated Carolingian art and theology. John Scotus Eriugena wrote around the middle of the ninth century:

> O death, the death of life; it should be called
> Life and not death, as manifesting life,
> So I dare not say death . . .

Candidus of Fulda produced an exegesis of the Gospel narratives of the passion (the first one specifically so designed in Christian history) in his *Opusculum de Passione Domini*, interpreting it as establishing Christ's power over the universe: 'The Lord was stretched out upon the cross, to signify that his kingdom would be that of the whole world.'[55]

The cross became both the symbol of divine victory and the key to the understanding of the cosmos. Centuries before, Venantius had adumbrated the idea in some of his poems, and it was now elaborated

---

[54] Thomas Head, *Hagiography and the Cult of Saints* (Cambridge, 1990), 1, 7, 25–6, 36.
[55] R. Haussherr, *Der tote Christus am Kreuz* (Bonn, 1963), esp. ch. 9.

Hrabanus Maurus, *Praise of the Holy Cross.*

This was an immensely influential composition, at once a poem, an acrostic and a set of illustrations: it survives in more than eighty manuscripts, some of them magnificently written, like the copy produced in the abbey of Fulda about the middle of the ninth century, now housed in the Vatican Library. In its original form, it was completed about 810. For Hrabanus it was the 'first fruits' of his works, and the one to which he was most attached: he repeatedly supervised the production of new copies as gifts to influential people, including the Emperor Louis the Pious. The cross is seen as the key to human understanding, both of creation and redemption. Jean Chélini sees the book as a key work for Carolingian society: 'The cross of redemption, of which Hrabanus Maurus composed such a magnificent eulogy, dominates and integrates this society, giving a profound unity to a mosaic of races, laws and mental habits.' It is only fair to say that the work has not equally delighted all modern scholars. Michael Wallace-Hadrill thought it 'a complex and uninviting piece' with an 'intricate, even repelling, format'.

J. Chélini, *L'Aube du Moyen Age* (Paris, 1991), 507, and M. Wallace-Hadrill, *The Frankish Church* (Oxford, 1983), 316. Important recent studies include M. Perrin (ed. and tr.), *Raban Maur, De Laudibus Sanctae Crucis* (Paris, 1988), a beautifully produced volume; and H.-G. Müller in the *Beiheft, Mittellateinisches Jahrbuch*, 11 (1973).

in Alcuin's *Crux, decus es mundi* and reached its culmination in his pupil Hrabanus Maurus's great collection of poems, *Praise of the Holy Cross.*

Especially in circles closely associated with the imperial court, the cross symbolized the triumph of Christ. The custom of associating the image of the women at the tomb with that of Christ on the cross in one composition was less in evidence than it had been, or was to be again in the twelfth century: the whole mystery was contained in the cross. For Alcuin, 'cross devotion was also Easter devotion'.[56] In

[56] H. B. Meyer, '*Crux, decus es mundi*: Alkuins Kreuz- und Osterfrömmigkeit', in B. Fischer and J. Warner (eds.), *Paschatis Sollemnia: Studien zu Osterfeier und Osterfrömmigkeit (Jungmann Fs.)* (Basle, 1959), 96–107.

130 *Franks and Carolingians, 600–1000*

consequence, relics of the cross were preserved in cases of great splendour. Byzantium had already set the example by developing the staurotheca, a reliquary with a distinctive cross shape. There were certainly gold reliquaries in Carolingian churches, although few have survived. The Vatican has a splendid one in the form of a cross made for Pope Paschal I (817–24), covered with enamels depicting scenes from the life of Christ. The great relics of the passion offered protection to the servants of God against those who threatened them: Stephen II carried a fragment of the cross in procession in 756 to secure the protection of Christ against the Lombards who were threatening Rome. At Taormina in Sicily St Pancratius obtained a staurotheca from some Jerusalem merchants, which was exposed on the ramparts of the walls during a siege.[57]

A classical expression of the political significance of the cross as 'the trophy of eternal victory' was designed by Charlemagne's adviser, Einhard.

Einhard's Cross

Einhard's cross no longer survives, but it is known to us from an anonymous drawing of the seventeenth century. It was an elaborate composition in silver, some 40 centimetres tall, with the cross standing on a triumphal arch reminiscent of the Roman past. It bore the inscription, *The sinner Einhard has placed this arch to bear the trophy of eternal victory and has dedicated it to God*: Two horsemen are in attendance, presumably Constantine and Charlemagne (or Charlemagne and Louis the Pious?), thus forming an important link between the victory of the cross and the earthly triumphs of the emperors.

K. Hauck, *Das Einhardkreuz*, Abhandlungen der Akademie der Wissenschaften in Göttingen, ser. 3, 87.

The Palestinian connection of relics of the passion was emphasized in the narratives written to promote their cults. The south German abbey of Reichenau will serve us for an example. The presence there of a drop of the blood of the Lord played a crucial part in its development. A reliquary cross containing the holy blood had

[57] A. Frolow, *La Relique de la vraie croix*, Archives d'Orient Latin, 7 (1961), no. 84.

arrived in 923 or 925 from a Greek source. It was rapidly provided with a legendary origin in *Translation of the Blood of the Lord*, which was written in the middle of the tenth century and which associated its arrival in the West with Charlemagne's negotiations with Jerusalem. Abbot Alawich (934–58) built a circular chapel of the holy cross, to the east end of the abbey church, for its reverence, possibly as a conscious recollection of the Sepulchre of Christ. Otto I became interested in the area, with the marriage of his son Liudolf into the Suabian ducal house, and on 1 January 950 he gave the abbey a grant for 'the holy cross in which the blood of our Lord Jesus Christ is contained'. Reichenau was unusual in not having the body of its founder, since Pirmin was buried elsewhere; and the holy blood became its central cult.[58] A link with Palestine, as direct as possible, was emphasized by the writings of cathedrals and monasteries. At Trier, they built on their traditional links with the Empress Helena, and claimed that she had given the church one of the nails that she had found from the cross.[59]

It is in England, with its special tradition of great crosses, that we find clear indications of the pattern of devotion that they might evoke. The *Life of Willibald* reports that 'on the estates of the nobles and good men of the Saxon race, it is a custom to have a cross, which is dedicated to our Lord and held in great reverence, erected on some prominent spot for the convenience of those who wish to pray daily before it'. Such great crosses may have been a distant echo of the great floreated cross on Calvary, which had appeared in mosaics at Ravenna. The cross that Oswald erected on the battlefield at Heaven-field in 633 was an early example, but there are vestiges of many others.[60] These were triumphal crosses rather than crucifixes, although the crucifixion might form one of the sculptural themes. The Ruthwell Cross is one of the greatest survivors of this tradition,

---

[58] P. A. Manser and K. Beyerle, 'Aus dem liturgischen Leben der Reichenau', in K. Beyerle (ed.), *Die Kultur der Abtei Reichenau* (Munich, 1925), 316–437; D. Walz, 'Karl der Grosse, ein verhinderter Seefahrer: die Reichenauer Heiligbluterzählung aus dem X Jh.', F.-R. Erkens (ed.), *Karl der Grosse und das Erbe der Kulturen* (Berlin, 2001), 234–45; *Ex translatione sanguinis Domini* (MGH SS IV. 445–9); and diploma of Otto I in MGH Diplomata I, no. 116.

[59] E. G. Grimme, *Goldschmiedekunst im Mittelalter* (Cologne, 1972), 28–9 and ill. 8; *AASS*, Aug., III. 580–99; T. Head, 'Art and Artifice in Ottonian Trier', *Gesta*, 36 (1997), 65–82.

[60] P. Meyvaert, 'A New Perspective on the Ruthwell Cross: *ecclesia* and *vita monastica*', in B. Cassidy (ed.), *The Ruthwell Cross* (Princeton, 1992), 95–166.

although its date is uncertain: the claims of 685 and about 750 have both been advanced.

The great English poem, *The Dream of the Rood*, gives us a rare insight into the new pattern of devotion to the cross at an early stage of its development. It appears to offer a meditation upon a reliquary of the cross, and short extracts appear both on the Ruthwell and Brussels Cross. It celebrates a cross of victory:

> I gazed on the tree of glory,
> Royally decked as it was, gleaming brightly,
> Attired in gold: gems had covered
> Befittingly the tree of a ruler.

The sense of triumph is also permeated by an awareness of the suffering through which it was bought:

> Yet beneath that gold I could make out agony
> Once suffered at the hands of wretched men.[61]

Personal devotion to the cross was increased by the emergence of a more realistic treatment. The earlier tradition presented the cross to the faithful as a statement of the divine victory. On cross-reliquaries, the splendour of the casing proclaimed the power within; floreated crosses revealed the life that was blossoming from the wood. Pictures of the crucifix were relatively rare, and were a visible rehearsal of an old motto, supposedly from the Psalms, *regnavit a ligno Deus*, God is reigning from the tree.[62] Passion and resurrection had been understood as linked in one movement. It has been observed that Alcuin, in the manner of earlier centuries, still saw the *Triduum sacrum* from Good Friday to Easter as an undivided unity. In the later Carolingian period there were signs of a new emphasis upon the suffering involved in the cross. As yet, these themes were pursued only in a few circles, but some of them were influential. The painters of Reims between 820 and 850 began, for the first time, to show Christ with eyes closed and arms drooping. It looks as if Walafrid Strabo about

---

[61] M. Swanton (ed.), *The Dream of the Rood*, rev. edn. (Exeter, 1987); S. A. J. Bradley (tr.), *Anglo-Saxon Poetry* (London, 1982), 158–63; E. G. Stanley, 'The Ruthwell Cross Inscription', in *A Collection of Papers* (Toronto, 1987), 384–99; B. Raw, '*The Dream of the Rood* and its Connections with Early Christian Art', *Medium Aevum*, 39 (1970), 239–56, and A. E. Mahler, '*Lignum Domini* and the Opening Vision of *The Dream of the Rood*', *Speculum*, 53 (1978), 441–59.

[62] This addition to the Latin text of Vulgate Psalm 95: 10 apparently originated in Egypt, and was certainly very early, and equally certainly inauthentic. B. Capelle, '*Regnavit a ligno*', in his *Travaux liturgiques de doctrine et d'histoire* (Louvain, 1967), iii. 211–14.

850 was referring to paintings or statues of the crucifix when he wrote that 'at times we see simple and unlearned people, who can hardly be brought by words to belief in what has happened, so touched by a picture of the passion of the Lord or other miracles, that they witness by tears that the outward representations have been engraved on their hearts like letters'.[63] When Strabo wrote, the quest for the historical Jesus and the sorrow for his sorrow on the cross were still only minor influences. They do, however, lie behind a dramatic development in the next century, particularly associated with Ottonian Germany: the great cross, designed as a central feature of devotion and designed to display the suffering of Christ. The first surviving example of these mighty compositions is the Gero cross in Cologne cathedral. There is argument about whether this is in fact the one commissioned by Archbishop Gero (969–76), but it cannot be much later than his time. Its forceful representation of a dying Christ indicates the arrival of a new spirit of realism, which was to shape a sequence of great crosses in eleventh-century Germany, and to point to a new and important way of thinking about the central features of Christian belief.

---

[63] Walafrid Strabo, *De Exordiis et Incrementis Rerum Ecclesiasticarum* (MGH Leges II Capit. II appendix 484).

5

Towards the First Crusade

THE CONSEQUENCES OF CALIPH AL-HAKIM

At the end of September 1009, Caliph al-Hakim of Egypt ordered the destruction of the church of the Holy Sepulchre. It is said that he was aggrieved by the scale of the Easter pilgrimage to Jerusalem, which was caused specially by the annual miracle of the holy fire within the Sepulchre. The measures against the church were part of a more general campaign against Christian places of worship in Palestine and Egypt, which involved a great deal of other damage: Adhemar of Chabannes recorded that the church of St George at Lydda 'with many other churches of the saints' had been attacked, and the 'basilica of the Lord's Sepulchre destroyed down to the ground'.[1] It was not the first attack upon the Holy Sepulchre, but it was the most destructive one.

The demolition was thorough. The Christian writer Yahya ibn Saïd reported that everything was razed 'except those parts which were impossible to destroy or would have been too difficult to carry away'. The great church of St Constantine, as it was by now generally known, disappeared. The fabric of the Holy Sepulchre itself was damaged and the rock-cut roof demolished, to be replaced subsequently by the construction of a domed roof. The roof of the rotunda was destroyed, but the mighty pillars resisted destruction up to the height of the gallery pavement, and are now effectively the only remnant of the fourth-century buildings. It appears that some minor repairs were done to the tomb of Christ almost immediately after 1009, but a more ambitious restoration had to wait for the patronage of the Byzantine imperial authority, following an agreement in about 1037. Even so, a total replacement was far beyond

---

[1] P. Bourgain (ed.), Adhemar, *Chronicon* (CCCM 129 (1), 1999), iii. 47, 166–7.

available resources.[2] The new construction was concentrated on the rotunda and its surrounding buildings: the great basilica remained in ruins. The most original feature of the new site was the creation of a series of chapels to the east of the court of the resurrection, where the wall of the great church had been. They commemorated scenes from the passion, such as the location of the prison of Christ and of his flagellation, and presumably were so placed because of the difficulties for free movement among shrines in the streets of the city. The dedication of these chapels indicates the importance of the pilgrims' devotion to the suffering of Christ. They have been described as 'a sort of *via dolorosa* in miniature' although this looks forward to a devotion that was not developed until centuries later. Since little or no rebuilding took place on the site of the great basilica, Western pilgrims to Jerusalem during the eleventh century found much of the sacred site in ruins.

In recent years, most historians have been convinced that the primary reason for the preaching of the First Crusade at Clermont in November 1095 was the concern of Urban II for the distress of the church at Jerusalem, and the need to liberate the Holy Sepulchre from Muslim oppression. This represents a departure from an older view, represented in the classic book by Steven Runciman, that the pope was moved by the threat to Constantinople from the Turkish invasion of Asia Minor and by the appeal of the Eastern Emperor Alexius for Western assistance. It has been generally accepted, nevertheless, that the fate of Jerusalem was of importance for Western opinion as a whole, even if it was not the immediate goal of papal policy in 1095. Hans Mayer argued that originally the object of the Crusade was to help the Christian churches in the East, but very soon men had a more definite object in mind: to free the Holy Land and, above all, Jerusalem, the Sepulchre of Christ, from the yoke of heathen dominion.[3] If there was wide concern in Latin Christendom for the Holy City, one would expect the news of the destruction of the Holy Sepulchre in 1009 to be received with great distress and alarm. In reality, as John France has pointed out, the news seems to have interested only a small circle. Bernard Hamilton has also been surprised at the lack of echoes of Jerusalem in Western devotion: 'I had expected to find that the increase in pilgrimage

---

[2] On the dating of this restoration, which has usually been ascribed to Constantine IX (1042–55), see Biddle, *Tomb*, 77–9.

[3] H. E. Mayer, *The Crusades*, 2nd edn. (Oxford, 1988), 9.

to Jerusalem in the eleventh century would have influenced the mainstream of Western piety. There is no evidence that it did so.'[4] Plainly, we have a problem. There are three major pieces of evidence of a strong reaction in the West to the news of al-Hakim's act of desecration. The first is an appeal by Pope Sergius IV (1009–12) to the Italian cities to mobilize their resources against Jerusalem. It would be of great importance, if only we were sure that it was authentic.

Sergius reports that 'a messenger has come to the holy see from Eastern parts with news that the Holy Sepulchre of our Lord Jesus Christ has been destroyed by the impious hands of pagans from top to foundations'. The appeal for help rests securely on the tradition of pilgrimage: 'Many brothers, guided by love of him, seek the very place which he touched with his own feet (Psalm 132: 7), and Mount Calvary, on which he healed us with his wound, and venerate the Mount of Olives, but specially honouring with entire devotion the Sepulchre in which he lay . . .' Participants in the expedition are invited 'to follow the steps of Jesus Christ, avoiding temporal posses- sions, taking up only their cross'. This reference to Luke 9: 23 may indicate that the cross was already being used as a pilgrim badge. There are some predictions of crusading themes here, including a call to vengeance, 'to sail to Syria to avenge the redeemer and his tomb', and a plea that Christians should observe peace among them- selves. On the other hand, there is no hint of a remission of penance or indulgence; we are still a long way from the heart of Urban II's appeal in 1095.

The other two near-contemporary references in Western sources to the destruction of the Holy Sepulchre come in the chronicles of Adhemar of Chabannes and Ralph Glaber, who wrote in south cen- tral France in the 1020s and 1030s. Virtually no other eleventh- century writer mentioned the destruction of the Holy Sepulchre, and it was unknown to most of the historians of the First Crusade. The normally well-informed William of Malmesbury mentioned 'the church which contains the Holy Sepulchre, an elegant structure built by Constantine the Great, which has never suffered any injury from the enemies of the faith; they are frightened, I suppose, on account of the fire from heaven which glows serenely from the lamps

---

[4] J. France, 'The Destruction of Jerusalem and the First Crusade', *JEH* 47 (1996), 1–17; B. Hamilton, 'The Impact of Crusader Jerusalem on Western Christendom', *Catholic Historical Review*, 80 (1994), 697.

An Authentic Letter of Pope Sergius IV?

The letter has survived only in a single copy preserved at the southern French abbey of Moissac. It appears to be a direct response to the destruction of the Holy Sepulchre and it contains the first clear reference to a Western project to deliver Jerusalem by force. No other contemporary source refers to such an undertaking, and it is therefore not surprising that the document has widely been regarded as spurious. It is not a formal diploma but an appeal, indeed almost a sermon. The encyclical contains no concession of land or rights, and it is therefore difficult to see what motive there would be for its forgery. Confirmation of Sergius' concern for the Holy Land is provided by a painting on the inner wall of the façade of S. Paolo fuori le Mura at Rome, marked by a very large monogram of Sergius. It portrays Gethsemane, the carrying of the cross, the deposition, and the women at the tomb (in which the angel sits on an altar-like stone, outside a formal classical door). It is natural to understand this as an act of recollection for the destroyed holy places, although the suggestion is complicated by the appearance of his rival and successor, Benedict VIII, in the composition. Aleksander Gieysztor has suggested that the letter was composed at Moissac as propaganda for the preaching of the First Crusade in 1095. A copy might indeed have been valued as a precedent, but it is improbable that it was invented then: the circumstances were different in 1095, and the specific act of destruction had seemingly been forgotten. The weight of the evidence seems to be in favour of authenticity.

C. Erdmann, 'Die Aufrufe Gerberts und Sergius' IV für das Heilige Land', *Quellen und Forschungen aus italienischen Archiven und Bibliotheken*, 23 (1931/2), 1–21; A. Gieysztor, 'The Genesis of the Crusades: The Encyclical of Sergius IV', *Medievalia et Humanistica*, 5 (1949), 3–23, and 6 (1950), 3–34; H. M. Schaller, 'Zur Kreuzzugsenzyklika Papst Sergius IV', in H. Mordek (ed.) *Papsttum, Kirche und Recht im Mittelalter: Fs. für Horst Fuhrmann* (Tübingen, 1991), 135–53; H. L. Kessler and J. Zacharias, *Rome 1300: On the Path of the Pilgrim* (London, 2000), 172–3.

Adhemar and Ralph Glaber on the Holy Sepulchre

Both writers had a strong interest in the subject: Adhemar actually died on pilgrimage to Jerusalem. He reported the demolition of the 'basilica of the Lord's Sepulchre', while Glaber said that 'the church at Jerusalem, which contained the Sepulchre of our Lord and Saviour, was destroyed entirely (*funditus*) by the order of the prince of Babylon'—that is, the caliph at Cairo. He added that it had proved impossible to destroy the Sepulchre itself. The two accounts, while different in detail, both blame the Western Jews, who were alleged to have written to the caliph to urge him to proceed against the tomb of Christ. Evidently both writers had access to strongly anti-Semitic rumours that were circulating in different forms. Even Adhemar and Glaber did not provide a coherent account of Western responses. Glaber records generous gifts by the dukes of Normandy to the monasteries of Palestine and Mount Sinai, and a huge donation of 100 pounds of gold to the Holy Sepulchre by Duke Richard II (996–1026). It is a fair assumption that these benefactions were intended to help repair the damage done by Caliph al-Hakim, but the chronicler fails to fit them within the framework of Eastern events.

J. France (ed.), *Rodulfi Glabri Historiarum Libri Quinti* (Oxford, 1989), pp. lxv, 37, 133; R. L. Wolff, 'How the News was Brought from Byzantium to Angoulême', *Essays in Honor of Sir Steven Runciman, Byzantine and Modern Greek Studies*, 4 (1979), 139–89.

every year on Easter Eve'.[5] John France is clearly right in his conclusion that 'the destruction of Jerusalem in 1009 . . . was a forgotten event by the time of the First Crusade'. He adds that the evidence 'seems to suggest a rather distant attitude to Jerusalem in general'.[6]

To the modern observer, the contemporary ignorance of the events of 1009 must be surprising. It may, however, tell us more about their grasp of history than their attitude to Jerusalem. Pilgrims throughout the century would have seen the ruins of Constantine's basilica.

[5] Malmesbury, *Gesta Regum*, ed. R. A. B. Minors and others (Oxford, 1998), para. 367, p. 643).
[6] France 'Destruction of Jerusalem', 14.

They report the difficulties of the way, and the experience of Muslim oppression, but not the destruction wrought at the orders of al-Hakim. Their silence is evidently not produced by lack of interest; it is rather that they were not disposed to look for precise historical causes, which they could have traced had they been so disposed. We find the same phenomenon later in the century, when the Seljuk Turks invaded Anatolia and Syria. The Seljuk invasions had great implications for pilgrims, and eventually for the First Crusade, but Western writers and travellers did not record the details: even the Byzantine disaster at Manzikert in 1071 is never mentioned in Latin chronicles. They may have been uninformed historians, but it does not follow that they were lukewarm pilgrims. There is, on the contrary, evidence of a growing concern about Jerusalem in the tenth and specially the eleventh century. Most of all, we can observe an increase in pilgrimage, accompanied by an increasing enthusiasm for relics of the passion and for a new type of monumental reproduction of the Holy Sepulchre.

'AN INNUMERABLE MULTITUDE'

Glaber, always a keen observer of change, tells us how 'an innumerable multitude from the whole world, greater than any one could have hoped to see, began to travel to the Sepulchre of our Saviour at Jerusalem', and how all classes came to be involved: the populace, the middle classes (*mediocres*), kings and nobles and bishops, and 'finally, and this was something which had never happened before, numerous women, noble and poor, undertook the journey. Many wished to die before they returned to their own lands'.[7] Glaber himself ascribed the increase to the opening of a new land route to the East through Hungary, which was safer than the familiar sea route. By 1001 there was a Christian king, Stephen, who 'made the road safe for everyone, welcomed as brothers all he saw, and gave them enormous gifts. This action led many people, nobles and commoners, to go to Jerusalem.'[8] The road across the Balkans came to be regarded as the one built by Charlemagne on his legendary pilgrimage to Jerusalem. No evidence allows us to offer an estimate of numbers. The figures given by chroniclers, such as the 7,000 or even 12,000 who went on the so-called great German pilgrimage of 1064–5, are implausible. It was obviously most convenient for

---

[7] France, *Glaber* (see inset above), 199–201.   [8] Ibid. 97.

German travellers, but we also find considerable French use of the
road, perhaps because warfare in southern Italy made it difficult to
use the Apulian ports.

It is arguable whether we should think in terms of a large popular
element in these pilgrimages, as Glaber indicates. It may be that the
number of chronicle references to the activity of crowds or 'multitudes' increased from just before 1000 because there was a shift in
social awareness among writers, as a reflection of such movements
as the Peace of God and the popular appeal of heretical teaching, as
well as pilgrimage, both domestic and international. The expansion
of pilgrimage was attributed by contemporaries to apocalyptic
expectation. There is a good deal of evidence of a widespread
assumption that 1033, the millennium of Christ's passion, would be
the decisive year, and people went to Jerusalem because of it. Hervé,
archdeacon of Sainte-Croix, Orléans, had 'pondered many nights on
the frailty of life and [come] to live in fear of sudden death'.[9] The size
of the German party in 1065 was attributed by one contemporary to
'the vulgar belief' that the Last Judgement would come when Good
Friday fell on 25 March, the feast of the Annunciation.[10] There is no
simple pattern to expectation during this century. It was focused on
various dates (the incarnation year 1000, the year 1033, and the
occurrence of Easter on 25 March) and directed towards various
events: prodigies, marvels, or the coming of Antichrist.

The first half of the eleventh century was the golden age of
the land route. Pilgrims, welcomed by the Christian government in
Hungary, could enter the Byzantine empire at Belgrade and would
not need to cross another frontier until they reached central Syria,
where they would enter the dominions of the Fatimid caliphs of
Egypt. From about 1050, the slackening grip of the Byzantine
emperors in the Balkans, and still more the invasion of Anatolia and
Syria by Turkish nomads, made travel again hazardous. By 1064,
Turkish princes had torn Jerusalem from Fatimid rule. Even if we
discount overt persecution of Christians (and the extent to which this
took place is disputable) life had become far more difficult for pilgrims. Apart from Adhemar and Glaber, literary records only provide
uncertain evidence for this pattern. Later chroniclers tell us far less,
and the period has left us no guidebook or journal. It would be a

---

[9] J. Sumption, *Pilgrimage: An Image of Mediaeval Religion* (London, 1975), 133–5;
Webb, *Pilgrimage*, 43–4 (doc. 8d).
[10] *Vita Altmanni* 3 (MGH SS XII. 230).

mistake to argue from this silence that Latin Christians were not interested in going to the Holy Sepulchre. Two things emerge from the surviving records: there was a great deal of traffic, and the journey was always dangerous.

A wide scatter of evidence from the *Lives* of saints and religious, foundation charters, accounts of relics, and occasional chronicle mentions, confirms Ralph Glaber's statement about 'an innumerable multitude'. The occasional way in which references occur suggests that we may be hearing of only a small part of the traffic, and that pilgrimage had indeed become a 'custom of the time'; Glaber could comment critically on the 'vanity which inspires so many to undertake the journey merely to gain the prestige of having been to Jerusalem'.[11] Occasional details in the narratives confirm the regularity of the traffic. Journeys overlapped, and travellers bumped into others on their way back, as Bishop Lietbert of Cambrai did in Cyprus in 1056. Pilgrimage by prominent people, nobles, bishops, and abbots, which can already be evidenced in Germany in the previous century, developed rapidly. In the years after 1000, Count Fulk Nerra of Anjou travelled three times to Jerusalem. In general, the upper classes of south-western France developed a strong commitment to pilgrimage.[12] Some of the groups accompanying the bishops and nobles were large ones: the 'great pilgrimage' was a new feature of the period. Large numbers accompanied Abbot Richard of Verdun in 1027 and the German bishops in 1064. It was probably Pope Victor III (1086–7) who complained to the Byzantine empress about the exploitation of the pilgrims who were continuing to cross her territories, urging her in the name of Christ 'to put an end to the oppressive and intolerable tribute which is imposed by your officials on those who go to pray at and to visit his glorious Sepulchre'.[13] Increasingly, too, the pilgrimage attracted participants from the most distant parts of Christendom. The English knew a considerable amount about the Holy Land, and considerable Scandinavian involvement had already begun in the tenth century. Against all this evidence we have to weigh the remark of William of Malmesbury

[11] Abbot Isembard of Blois in *Acta Sancti Ordinis Benedicti* iv. 660; France, *Glaber*, 201.
[12] B. S. Bachrach, 'The Pilgrimages of Fulk Nerra, Count of the Angevins', T. F. X. Noble and J. J. Contreni (eds.), *Religion, Culture and Society in the Early Middle Ages: Studies in Honour of R. E. Sullivan* (Kalamazoo, 1987), 205–17; M. Bull, *Knightly Piety and the Lay Response to the First Crusade* (Oxford, 1993), ch. 5; Webb, *Pilgrimage*, 16.
[13] H. E. J. Cowdrey, 'Pope Victor and the Empress A.', *Byzantinische Zs.*, 84/5 (1991/2), 43–8.

that to get as far as Jerusalem in the mid-eleventh century was 'a marvellous achievement at that time, when the prowess of our Christians had not yet made those tracks passable'. This may not provide good evidence of the actual state of things: William's comment reflected a story preserved in Malmesbury tradition about a pilgrim knight, and glossed it in the light of his enormous enthusiasm for the success of the First Crusade.

It was always a dangerous enterprise. About 995, Raymond of Bousquet set sail at Luna, near modern Lucca, in the hope of reaching Jerusalem as quickly and directly as possible, and thus launched himself into a series of dramatic adventures, from which he was finally rescued by the intercession of Sainte Foy of Conques. His ship was driven to North Africa. He tried to convince his Muslim captors that he was a peasant, but his cover was blown when he turned out to be unable to dig a decent ditch, and he had to admit that he was a noble and a warrior. He was recruited into the Moorish armies, within which he obtained a prominent position, but was eventually captured fighting against Castile. He returned home after some fifteen years, to discover that his wife had long ago been told of his death.[14] The pilgrim whose visit to Malmesbury William recorded was a knight from Cologne, who was obliged to travel in the middle years of the century for parricide, bearing the armour that he had worn in committing the offence. When he was admitted to pray before the Holy Sepulchre, 'by the power of God the breastplate fell apart into fragments'. He then continued his travels and 'toured the whole of Europe'. People who departed on such an enterprise took it for granted that they might not return. In Scandinavia, a runic inscription sponsored by Ingirun, daughter of Hord, announced her intention of travelling east to Jerusalem. She was evidently providing a monument to her piety in case she did not come back.[15]

Pilgrims had to encounter all sorts of hazards. Travel by sea was dangerous, and it happened that people disappeared without trace. In 1066 or just afterwards, Count Theodoric of Trier, who had been responsible for the murder of the archbishop-elect, Conrad, set off by sea. The chronicler Sigebert later reported that his fate 'is as yet unknown', and eventually it was learned that his ship had sunk, and that he, 'cleansed by the waves of the sea from the filth of sin . . .

---

[14] P. Sheingorn (tr.), *The Book of Ste Foy* (Philadelphia, 1995), ii. 2, 115–19.
[15] *AASS*, 6 Oct., iii. 327–8; Webb, *Pilgrimage*, 36–7 (doc. 6d); J. Jesch, *Women in the Viking Age* (Woodbridge, 1991).

passed over to the Lord'. Peter Damian in 1067 reminisced about his fellow-monk Bonizo, who was saved from shipwreck during his return by clinging to a bale of cotton cloth, and about 1100 the chronicler at St Andrew's, Cambrai, recorded that their devout brother Albert, some time before 1092, had set out for Jerusalem, but 'we do not know what has happened to him'.[16] To reduce the hazards, some people settled in the East and became professional guides, like Peter of Le Puy at Ephesus, who 'knew the land and sea routes, the public roads, the ports of call, the side roads and the customs of the peoples and their languages, just as well as businessmen who travel around the various parts of the world'.[17]

The Jerusalem pilgrimage was embedded in the changing culture of the time, reflecting and shaping its pattern of devotion and its social institutions. Count Adalbert of Alsace set out for Jerusalem 'for love of the Holy Sepulchre', perhaps with Archbishop Poppo of Trier in 1028. His pilgrimage eventually produced the donation of a relic of the cross, a monastery with a holy cross dedication, with a papal blessing of the new foundation and the proclamation of a peace.[18] Hervé of Orléans, whom we have encountered already as stirred by expectations of the end, eventually joined the ranks of those who commemorated the Sepulchre in architecture and liturgy: 'I brought with me relics of the Holy Sepulchre of our Lord Jesus Christ, in veneration of which, inspired by God, I embarked on the construction of a worthy church for these relics, near the castle of my lord Landric, with his licence and permission and with the consent and agreement of my brothers Alberic and Theduin.'[19] A classic account of these pilgrimages is that of Lietbert of Cambrai.

Confirmation that the character of the personal devotion of Lietbert was shared by others comes from the quite different expedition of Ulrich, later prior of Celle, in 1062. He travelled with a servant and an almoner, with one horse for the three of them; but the Jerusalem experience seems to have been the same: 'when the holy man reached the holy places, it is impossible to tell with what emotions he beheld the monuments of the nativity, passion, resurrection

---

[16] Webb, *Pilgrimage*, 16; *Chronicon S. Andreae* iii. 15 (PL 149. 275D).
[17] Webb, *Pilgrimage*, 26.
[18] *Notitiae fundationis . . . Bosonis-villae* (MGH SS xv (2). 977–8), which was written much later. The existence of a charter of about 1030 gives substantial support to its accuracy: C. Morris, 'Memorials of the Holy Places', R. N. Swanson, *The Holy Land, Holy Places*, SCH 36 (2000), 94.
[19] Webb, *Pilgrimage*, 43–4 (doc. 8d).

The Pilgrimage of Bishop Lietbert of Cambrai (1051–76)

The account was written by Rodolf, a monk of the Holy
Sepulchre, Cambrai, who worked between 1092 and 1133. He
had excellent local sources, and much of his information rings
true. We cannot be sure whether his explanation of the
bishop's devotional ideas came from records of his sermons, or
whether Rodolf was reflecting new thinking in the years after
the First Crusade. In spite of these doubts, the account is a rich
and remarkable one. Lietbert was moved, from the beginning of
his pontificate, by meditation upon the humanity of Christ:
'The Son of God, who was of one substance with the Father,
deigned to take upon himself the whole human condition and
dwelt in us (John 1: 14).' The bishop accordingly obeyed the
words of the apostle: 'Let us therefore go forth to him outside
the camp, bearing his reproach. For here we have no lasting
city, but we seek the city which is to come' (Hebrews 13:
13–14). The words provide an interesting gloss on thought
about pilgrimage and Jerusalem, but never became part of the
central armoury of crusading thinking, perhaps because they
hardly fit a sustained attempt to keep the city of Jerusalem as a
Latin possession. Rodolf tells us of Lietbert that

with the whole force of mind he formed the desire of going to
Jerusalem; but not for the sake of seeing the stones of its towers or the
roofs of its houses, but of embracing and kissing the footprints marked
by the feet of Jesus. For he thought it blessed to see the narrow stable;
with the shepherds to adore in his mind the crying infant; to celebrate
in the church of Golgotha the mysteries of his blessed passion, crucifixion and death; to lament the death of Jesus at his Sepulchre with
the holy women; within the very bounds of the Sepulchre to water
with tears his faults and those of his people; and on the Mount of
Olives with Mary the mother of Jesus and the holy apostles to desire to
follow Jesus as he ascended above the heavens . . .

These devotions reflect the spirit of the more realistic piety of
the late Carolingian liturgy; one hears echoes of the *Quem queritis* ceremony and of the more expressive form of devotion to
the crucifix, and the Sepulchre is being treated as a memorial
of death rather than resurrection. The growth of pilgrimage to
Jerusalem would seem to be linked with the development of

new styles of worship and theology in the West, including a new conviction of the indwelling of God within the human condition.

The bishop's enterprise involved the local community, which valued his presence as 'the freedom of the fatherland, the glory of the church'. His departure was met by opposition, and required arrangements for the care of the diocese during his absence. The people flocked out with him as in 1054 he started his journey to Jerusalem, his *iter Jerosolimam versus*. In Hungary, he was the object of suspicion, 'because in those days almost nobody followed this journey'. It seems that (so the narrator thought) the land route through the Balkans was already in trouble. Lietbert had to satisfy the king of Hungary about his motives. His company was so large that it was called 'the Lord's army'. When, in Bulgaria, his people were threatened with attack by brigands, he set up the sign of the cross and addressed them as 'my fellow-soldiers': 'thus the soldier of Christ (*miles Christi*) advanced with his personal and household company, and urged the army of God not to be afraid'. Probably the choice of language was shaped by Rodolf's awareness of the crusades. The perils of the expedition continued: faced by a hostile armed force, the bishop brought to mind how the Saviour 'had undergone the passion of the life-giving cross', and desired to 'to be a partaker in the martyrdom and cup of Christ and to share in his sufferings'. They began to meet other pilgrims who had been forced to turn back because the 'king of Babylon' (the caliph of Egypt) had closed the church of the Holy Sepulchre to pilgrims, and they decided to continue by sea from Lattakiah. In Cyprus in June 1056 they were detained by the Byzantine authorities for their own safety, and encountered a group coming back with Bishop Helinand of Laon, who strongly advised them to return. During these trials, they were said to be sustained by the prayers of the church of Cambrai, and were guided by the vision of St Andrew, its patron.

The pilgrimage had a lasting impact on local piety. Gerard, Lietbert's predecessor, had established a new cemetery outside the walls of the city, and afterwards had consecrated beside it 'a church in honour of the Holy Sepulchre, and endowed it with lands and peasants, so that burial should be available there out of reverence for so great a name for the poor and pilgrims'. Gerard had intended to enlarge this foundation, but was prevented by old age and death, and Lietbert now in 1064 built a monastery on a larger scale 'in honour of our Lord Jesus Christ and his Holy Sepulchre and St Mary the mother of God and of all the saints of God'. It is reported also in a note of relics at the church of Cambrai that when Lietbert built the basilica of the Lord's Sepulchre 'he also constructed a Sepulchre for the Lord in the middle of the same basilica, round in design, that is after the pattern (*in modum*) of the Sepulchre at Jerusalem'. The marble slab was seven feet in length, like the one where the Lord's body had been placed, and was so attractively decorated within that 'any one who came with a hard heart would easily be moved to the sentiments of devotion'. The original Cambrai Sepulchre was destroyed and replaced by what to the writer was the present one, on the right side of the basilica.

The account is printed in *Vita Lietberti* xxvii–xli (MGH SS xxx (2: 853–8).

and ascension of the Lord, with what genuflections he adored them, and with what rivers of tears he flooded them'.[20] As this suggests, the element of penance had by now become prominent. Early in the century English statutes were prescribing pilgrimage as a punishment or recompense for murder, and nobles who set off for Jerusalem to secure absolution for violence included Duke Robert of Normandy in 1035.[21] This idea that the journey to the Holy Sepulchre was a suitable penance for sins of violence was to contribute to the emergence of the First Crusade. In this as well as other respects, pilgrimage to the Holy Sepulchre was rooted in the devotion of the age, and issued in new liturgical and architectural expressions.

RELICS, THE WOOD OF THE CROSS, AND PERSONAL DEVOTION

The journeys of Count Adalbert and Bishop Lietbert had brought to Alsace and to Cambrai memorials of Jerusalem and the passion of Jesus, in the shape of a building in the style of the Holy Sepulchre and 'no small part' of the cross itself. Richard of Saint-Vannes, a

---

[20] Ibid. 40–1 (doc. 8b).   [21] Ibid. 16, 26, 34–7 (docs. 6a, 6b, 6d).

Norman abbot, returned in 1027 'laden with relics gathered at Jerusalem and everywhere round about'. Some of them were contained in a bag given him by the patriarch of Jerusalem. His collection included, a little surprisingly, a stone thrown by a Saracen which fell into the Holy Sepulchre.[22] Western Europe was awash with relics, and memorials of the passion were highly prized. They knew that the best collection of all was at Constantinople. A curious letter, purporting to be an appeal from the Greek Emperor Alexius for help in defending Constantinople but definitely written by a Latin, perhaps about 1091, contained a long list of 'most precious relics of the Lord . . . which Christians ought to have rather than pagans'; they included 'a great part of the wood of the cross' and other relics of the passion, including the crown of thorns and the graveclothes found in the Sepulchre after his resurrection. At much the same time, Joseph, a monk of Canterbury, on his way back from Jerusalem, left the main party and went to Constantinople 'because he had heard that there was there an incomparable treasure of relics'.[23] The treasury at Constantinople seems to have been jealously guarded, and Joseph had to invoke the assistance of friends to gain access. While relics from Constantinople were much in demand, a Jerusalem origin was particularly valued. Two curious stories of the finding of relics will illustrate this.

A brief record entitled 'The Finding and Translation of the Blood of the Lord' reports the discovery of the holy blood at Mantua in 1048 as a result of a vision to a certain Adilbert, who had been blind from birth. He found a treasure of gold and silver, with an inscription describing the contents that asserted that they had been brought to Italy by Longinus, the blind soldier who had plunged his lance into the side of Christ on the cross. Within a stone box was a partition, which separated the holy blood and water. Pope Leo IX tried to remove the relic, 'fearing that Mantua would become a new Rome'. The inhabitants resisted, and in the end Leo consecrated the rebuilt church of St Andrew there, placing the blood under the altar in the crypt. The Emperor Henry III secured permission to remove some, and on his death it was given to Count Baldwin of Flanders, and hence to a number of other recipients. It was said to be the source of the famous holy blood at Weingarten in southern Germany.

[22] Ibid. 25.
[23] *Kreuzzugsbriefe*, ep. 1. 17 (p. 134); C. H. Haskins, 'A Canterbury Monk at Constantinople c.1090', *EHR* 25 (1910), 293–5.

Whatever we make of the real character of the discovery, there is no reason to doubt the substantial accuracy of the narrative. The wonders of the Holy Land are recreated in Mantua: just as (according to legend) Longinus had received his sight from the blood from the side of Christ, so their rediscovery gave Adilbert his sight. One can understand how the episode led to the refoundation of a great church and attracted the interest of the two leading powers of Christendom.[24]

The link with the Holy Land was also powerfully affirmed in the story of the relics of Oviedo, in northern Spain. Here, a box of relics was opened in 1075 to reveal that it contained 'an incredible treasure', including relics of the wood of the cross; the Lord's blood; the Lord's bread, that is from his Last Supper; the Lord's Sepulchre; the Holy Land where the Lord stood; the robe of St Mary and the milk of the said virgin and mother of God; the Lord's garment which was torn and his grave cloth'. The story was told that 'God, by his miraculous power and secret counsel, transported a chest, made by the disciples of the apostles out of imperishable woods and filled with numberless mighty works of God, from the city of Jerusalem to North Africa, from North Africa to Carthage, from Carthage to Toledo, from Toledo to Asturias to the church of the Holy Saviour, in the place called Oviedo.' The container itself had become a relic, made by the successors of the apostles and transported from Jerusalem by the special providence of God.[25]

Mantua and Oviedo are just two of many stories that might be told to illustrate the concern to manifest the power of apostolic Jerusalem in the churches of the contemporary West. To the modern reader they must appear bizarre, and it is worth considering for a moment the mind-set that produced them. Churchmen of the time were quite capable of being critical. Around 1019 some monks from Jerusalem appeared at Monte Cassino with a fragment of the cloth with which the Saviour had wiped the disciples' feet. Several people were sceptical about it, and the cloth was burned in a censer. When the charcoal was removed, it wonderfully recovered its original colour.[26] There was an occasion, shortly before, of the use of ordeal by fire at Trier to test a relic: this seems to be the time when the practice was introduced quite widely in Western Europe. Such instances of scepticism, however, were not given force and coherence by a grasp of the

[24] *De inventione . . . sanguinis Domini* (MGH SS xv (2). 921–2).
[25] Morris, 'Memorials', 95–7.
[26] *Chronica Monasterii Casinensis* ii. 33 (MGH SS xxxiv. 229–30).

historical period from which these objects were supposed to have survived. The relics of a great church were its *memoria*: they defined its character and the history of its foundation. Along with readings, prayers, and ceremonies, the relics clarified the Biblical history for them, for they had no alternative framework against which historical statements might be judged. They might doubt the provenance of a relic, but they were not trained to question whether it was likely that the graveclothes of Christ had been preserved, or whether the Roman army would have had a use for a blind soldier like Longinus. The past, we are told, is another country. To them, the world of the Bible was not a time which could be critically recreated, but a world of fantasy which yet was true: an enchanted forest, a Narnia to which they could gain marvellous entry by means of holy places and sacred remains.

The arrival of new relics is an important testimony to the continuing interest of the Latin West in the Holy Sepulchre, Calvary, and the other holy places of Palestine. Apart from these, there was the treasure of memorials that had been built up during the preceding centuries. John Cowdrey has drawn attention to the pilgrims' guide to the Lateran at Rome, the *Descriptio basilicae Lateranensis*, the original version of which was probably written shortly after 1073. It contained stories of Constantine and Helena and a great list of relics, many of them of Jerusalem origin. Fragments of these seem to have been given to churches dedicated by Urban II on his journey in France in 1095–6, in the course of which he was recruiting for the First Crusade: the abbey church of Marmoutier, near Tours, had a primary dedication to the holy cross, and possessed a 'particle of the most victorious cross of Christ' in one of the altars. Cowdrey observes that 'students of how the crusading mentality was formed should not overlook how, in the Lateran palace and thanks to Constantine and his mother, the popes lived in the midst of relics of the Holy Land and of Jerusalem'.[27]

This consciousness fuelled a desire to reinvigorate the ideals of the first days of Christianity. The feast of *divisio apostolorum*, kept on 15 July to celebrate the (legendary) occasion when the disciples had separated to preach the Gospel throughout the world, was increasingly observed in the tenth and eleventh centuries, and so was the

[27] H. E. J. Cowdrey, 'The Reform Papacy and the Origin of the Crusades', *Concile de Clermont*, esp. 68–71; and his 'Pope Urban II and the Idea of Crusade', *Studi Medievali* (1995), iii. 36, with a list of the Lateran relics at 740–2.

desire to reconstitute the apostolic witness in their own world. In France, the Peace of God, an attempt to restore order to a society tormented by violence, was proclaimed in front of the relics of the great churches and motivated by the memory of the Jerusalem events: 'How fair is the name of peace, and how beautiful is the reputation of unity, which Christ left to the disciples when he ascended into heaven'.[28] Monastic reform was shaped by the desire to live, as the Lateran Council of 1059 expressed it, 'the apostolic, that is the common life'.[29]

The wood of the cross was one of the most powerful links conceivable with the life of the historical Jesus. The power of the cross, though, was not confined to the churches which possessed a fragment of the real thing. In England Aelfric, resuming a point already made by Carolingian scholars, stressed that it could equally be honoured in representation:

Truly, Christian men should bow to the holy cross in the Saviour's name, even if we do not possess the cross on which he suffered. Nevertheless, its likeness is holy, and we always bow to it when we pray, to the powerful Lord who suffered for men; and the cross is a memorial of his mighty passion, holy through him even though it grew in a wood. We always honour it, to honour Christ.[30]

The cross was now shaping the devotion of monasteries. Ely in about 1075 possessed nineteen large crosses and eight smaller ones, and already in the tenth century the rule for English abbeys, the *Regularis Concordia*, provided for a regular Friday mass in honour of the cross. In England and Germany, the 'great cross' of monumental dimensions, quite often a crucifix, was becoming a standard part of church furniture.

The first assured example of these mighty compositions, displaying the dead or dying Christ, is the Gero cross in Cologne cathedral. There is argument about whether this is in fact the one commissioned by Archbishop Gero (969–76), but it cannot be much later than his time. Its forceful representation of a dying Christ indicates the arrival of a new spirit of realism, which was to shape a sequence of great crosses in eleventh-century Germany and a great deal of the devotion that lay behind the crusades. The Gero Cross was a dramatic example of the new style in 'suffering Christ' crucifixes,

---

[28] Council of Poitiers (about 1011–14), prologue (*PL* 21. 267).
[29] Lateran Council, canon 4, MGH Leges Const. I, no. 384, p. 547.
[30] B. C. Raw, *Anglo-Saxon Crucifixion Iconography* (Cambridge, 1990), 167.

but Ottonian manuscript illumination covered the whole range between triumphant crucifixes in the style of the Uta Codex from Regensburg, which showed Christ in imperial purple, to portrayals of a Christ who had reached the climax of his suffering.[31]

One of the most internationally famous of the great crosses was the Volto Santo at Lucca, the focus of a popular pilgrimage and a model for a number of imitations. It was, however, a composition that presented the solemn majesty of Christ, rather than (like the Gero Cross) the agony of his death. Once more, legend stressed its connection with the Holy Land and the biblical events. It was said to have been revealed to a Jerusalem pilgrim in 742, as being carved by Nicodemus, who had represented the sacred countenance 'not by his own art, but God's'. It was then brought back by ship to Lucca, a voyage attended by many marvels. The statue and its story fit into a period when movable, three-dimensional works, such as the 'majesties' of mother and child common in southern France, were becoming more frequent, and when a demand for exact reproductions of the countenance of the Lord, carved by angels or apostles, was growing.

The cult of the cross could still be seen as a manifestation of the victory of Christ and of the power of the emperor or king. Around the middle of the eleventh century, a portable altar made for Countess Gertrude of Brunswick associated the holy cross with four royal or imperial figures: Sigismund of Burgundy, Constantius, Helena and Empress Adelaide, wife of Otto I. If anything, the Salian emperors, who succeeded the Ottonian family from 1024 onwards, were even more inclined to associate the victory of the cross with the God-given victory of royal power than their predecessors had been. Conrad II commissioned the great Reichskreuz of 1027/9, with its inscription: 'The army of the evil one flies before the cross; so, Conrad, shall your enemies give way to you.'[32] The modern style is to read the narrative of the passion as a denial or condemnation of earthly power, but eleventh-century rulers saw a close association between their own kingship and that of Christ. Like them he was, after all, called king and lord.

Nevertheless, the focus for personal devotion seems to have been specifically on the crucifixion, seen as an expression of the suffering

[31] M. Kauffman, 'An Ottonian Sacramentary in Oxford', *Belief and Culture*, 169–86; H. Mayr-Harting, *Ottonian Book Illumination* (London, 1991), i. 126–39.
[32] P. Corbet, 'L'Autel portatif de la comtesse Gertrude de Brunswick (vers 1040)', CCM 34 (1991), 97–120.

The Santo Volto at Lucca

This magnificent carving housed in Lucca cathedral is a dignified portrayal of the crucified Christ. The statue contains a hole
for relics. We first hear of the *vultus sacrarium* in a papal grant
in 1107; before that, there are no local mentions, although we
know from England that William Rufus (1087–1100) swore by
it. So it was famous before 1100. This would exclude the possibility that it came back with the returning members of the First
Crusade, in spite of Lucca's active involvement in the movement; moreover, such monumental crosses were uncommon in
the East. This great Romanesque cross can best be dated stylistically to the twelfth century, perhaps as late as 1200, so there
must have been an earlier version at Lucca, and the ingenious
suggestion has been made (although it can be no more than a
suggestion) that the San Sepolcro Crucifix is the original Lucca
Santo Volto, removed because of its deteriorating condition.

R. Hausherr, 'Das Imerwardkreuz und der Volto-Santo-Typ', *Zs.
für Kunstwissenschaft*, 16 (1962), 129–70; A. M. Maetzke (ed.), *Il
Volto Santo di Sansepolcro* (Arezzo, 1994); J.-C. Schmitt, 'Cendrillon
crucifiée: à propos du Volto Santo de Lucques', in *Miracles, prodiges
et merveilles au moyen âge* (Paris, 1995), 241–9; M. C. Ferrari, '*Imago
visibilis Christi*: le Volto Santo de Lucques et les images authentiques
du moyen âge', *Micrologus*, 6 (1998), 29–42, and his study, 'Il Volto
Santo di Lucca', G. Morello and G. Wolf (eds.), *Volto di Cristo* (Milan,
2000), 253–75.

of a human Christ. Judith of Flanders, the wife of Tostig of Northumbria, was painted in the Weingarten Gospels in the act of
embracing the foot of the crucifix, and Queen Edith similarly
appeared in the person of Mary Magdalen at the foot of the cross.
Barbara Raw remarks that such pictures 'allowed the viewer to
experience the biblical event for himself. They were a kind of substitute for the holy places in Palestine, which provided a visible witness
to pilgrims of the truth of the bible story, or for the relics which
carried this witness to other lands.'[33] Personal prayer books were
becoming more common, and tended specially to provide 'a holy

---

[33] Raw, *Anglo-Saxon Iconography*, 31.

devotion to be read before the cross of the Lord'. There is a vivid expression of the new spirituality in the silver cross made in 1007–8 by Bernward of Hildesheim as a container for a fragment of the cross and relics of saints brought back from a pilgrimage to France: the presentation of a dying victim, designed in the spirit of the monumental Gero Cross of Cologne.[34] The change was important, although the new, more personal devotion still saw the cross as a symbol of power and victory, 'armour for the body and remedy for the soul'. The fact that so many of the late-medieval devotional works were ascribed to writers such as Peter Damian and Anselm of Canterbury has given the false impression that devotion to the wounds and suffering of Christ was fully developed by 1100. At that time, references to the wounds, the idea that the believer should feel compassion for the dying Christ, were still discreetly expressed: 'I adore you, wounded on the cross. I ask that your wounds may be a remedy for my soul.'[35]

NEW VERSIONS OF THE SEPULCHRE

Just as representations of the cross were changing, so were those of the Sepulchre. The Carolingians had expressed its presence through public worship, in great processions associated with the Easter festival. An altar or chapel dedicated to the cross or to the Saviour was the centre of this worship, and stood in place of the Holy Sepulchre. The morning visit of the women, which was the standard depiction of the resurrection in carvings and miniatures, could be shown in painting or sculpture as a visit to a tower, circular and several storeys high, recalling the form of such buildings as Charlemagne's Palatine chapel at Aachen or of some westworks. This may be a distant echo of the round shape of the Anastasis, but as far as we know there was not at this time an attempt to imitate the edicule of the tomb itself. The older tradition of rotundas was continued into the eleventh century at Saint-Bénigne Dijon and Charroux.

In neither case do we have a contemporary explanation of the purpose of this design. The use of either rotunda for the Easter liturgy, and the symbolic reference to the Jerusalem Anastasis, are hypothetical. A few other churches were built with rotundas, as at

---

[34] E. G. Grimme, *Goldschmiedekunst im Mittelalter* (Cologne, 1972), 41–2, and no. 16.
[35] J. Leclercq, 'La Dévotion médiévale envers le crucifié', *La Maison-Dieu*, 75 (1963), 119–32.

Saint-Bénigne, Dijon

The church was rebuilt by William of Volpiano between 1001 and 1018. It possessed a circular building, on three storeys, at the east end. The ground floor of this is now the only surviving part of William's construction. This is almost a unique design, although it has some partial precedents in the form of round crypts. It is probable that it was intended to stand in the rotunda tradition of churches dedicated to Mary, and the dedication day (13 May) was the same as that of the reconsecration of the Pantheon at Rome long before in honour of Mary. Carol Heitz thought that this rotunda was designed for the performance of the Easter liturgy, on the model of the Carolingian westworks. Abbot William had been responsible for the planning of a likeness of the edicule already at Fruttuaria (see below); both buildings had an 'opaion', a roof opening at the top of the dome; and the sculptures, which were not completed, referred to worship in the heavenly Jerusalem. The rotunda thus incorporated a memory of the Anastasis at Jerusalem, but the Marian intention is more probable, especially when one remembers that the original Anastasis in that year was still in ruins.

K. J. Conant, 'Cluny and Saint-Bénigne at Dijon', *Archaeologia*, 99 (1965), 179–95; M. Untermann, *Der Zentralbau im Mittelalter* (Darmstadt, 1989), 228–39; and M. Jannet and C. Sapin (eds.), *Guillaume de Volpiano et l'architecture des rotondes* (Dijon, 1996). In that volume, William's rotunda is discussed particularly in the articles by W. Schlink (35–42) and M. Bayle (59–72). An important reassessment is by C. M. Malone, 'The Rotunda of Santa Maria in Dijon as *Ostwerk*', *Speculum*, 75 (2000), 285–317.

the priory church of Lémenc in Savoy, first mentioned about 1031–2. The rotunda is at the west end of the church, designed for the accommodation of relics; but we cannot be sure whether there was a Holy Sepulchre reference.[36] There are signs of the continued awareness of the great tower or westwork as the heart of the Easter liturgy:

[36] I. Parron, 'La Rotonde de l'église priorale de Lémenc en Savoie', in Jannet and Sapin (eds.), *Guillaume de Volpiano* (see inset on Saint-Bénigne, Dijon above), 145–50.

Saint-Sauveur, Charroux

The design of this great abbey church in Aquitaine, south of
Poitiers, is distinctive. It has the standard ground-plan of the
cross, with nave, transept, and choir, but the crossing tower is
polygonal, with a circular ambulatory around it. The building
has been a ruin since the early nineteenth century, but the
mighty tower still stands, and preserves much of the detail of
its design. The characteristic dedication of the church to St
Saviour or Salvator was probably continued from its Carolingian past, and the abbey possessed relics from the Holy Land. Of
special importance was a relic of a new type, the foreskin of
Christ, claimed as a gift from the Emperor Charles the Bald at
the consecration of the church. The purpose of the centrally
planned tower building is a matter of guesswork. It could be the
centre of the Easter liturgy and site for an altar of the cross, in
line with Carolingian tradition but in a different part of the
church; a reference to the rotunda of the Anastasis is plausible
but has no contemporary support. Its date is uncertain,
because the church underwent a series of disasters and
reconstructions in the course of the eleventh century.

G. Schwering-Illert, *Die ehemalige französische Abteikirche S. Sauveur,
Charroux* (Düsseldorf, 1963); Untermann, *Zentralbau im Mittelalter*,
62–4; and M.-T. Camus, 'A propos de la rotonde de Charroux', in
Jannet and Sapin (eds.), *Guillaume de Volpiano*, 119–33.

the Tiberius Psalter, emanating from the Winchester school, represented the Sepulchre itself as a tower with a square base, and the Robert
of Jumièges Sacramentary, of about 1020, presented it as a church
with a nave and rotunda, not unlike the general layout of Charroux
and Saint-Bénigne Dijon in almost precisely the same period.

In spite of the imperfect survival of evidence, we can be sure that
there were real changes in the way architecture expressed the reality
of the Holy Sepulchre. Churches were dedicated to it. Count Fulk of
Anjou, an ardent 'Jerusalemer', founded the great abbey of Beaulieu-
les-Loches *in honore Sancti Sepulchri* on his return from his first pilgrimage. The abbey was reputed to possess a relic of the cross, torn
off by Fulk's own teeth. The probable date of its consecration is 1007.

The abbey at Noceto in Tuscany is mentioned with this dedication in 1013, and a diploma of 1022 introduces us to the way in which such a dedication was thought to bring to Italy the powers of the Holy Sepulchre. The confirmation was addressed to

the monastery acquired by us, and newly built, in the place called Noceto and dedicated in the honour of the Holy Sepulchre of our Lord Saviour—where many benefits are offered to the lowly, and miracles often take place to the praise and honour of his name, according to that prophecy which says *and his sepulchre will be glorious* (Isaiah 11: 10).[37]

Acquapendente in Lazio may not have been much later. Neuvy Saint-Sépulcre was founded in 1042, and appears as *ecclesiam Sancti Sepulcri de Novo Vico* in a bull of Gregory VII in 1079; Villeneuve d'Aveyron was a monastery dedicated to the Holy Sepulchre shortly after 1053; and at Cambrai in 1064 there was already a cemetery chapel *in honore Dominici Sepulcri*.[38] The first two of these foundations were committed to paying tribute to the canons of the Holy Sepulchre at Jerusalem. The title 'Jerusalem' was extended to still further monasteries. Shortly after 1050, we hear of a church at Tusculum in central Italy, 'which is called holy Jerusalem'; at Cambrai in 1068 the monastery appears as *Solimam nostram*; and at Saint-Hubert there was 'an oratory which is called *ad sanctam Jherusalem*' to the south of the cloister after 1076.[39] Of older dedications, holy cross continued to be common, but the Carolingian dedication to St Saviour (Salvator) seems to have fallen out of favour in new foundations.

In the great liturgical books of the later tenth century, there was much variation about the depiction of the crucifixion, but the resurrection followed a constant pattern: it was always expressed by a picture of the women approaching the tomb, with an angel sitting upon it. The consistency marks a divorce between Western tradition and that of Byzantium, in spite of the considerable elements of Greek influence upon Ottonian art. In the East, the resurrection was represented by the scene of the harrowing of hell or of Christ's descent into limbo, whereas the West remained faithful to the biblical description. The scene was almost always simplified, omitting the guards and Christ's winding sheet. Only the coffin-lid is shown. This

[37] MGH Diplomata III (repr. Berlin 1957), no. 469 (Henry II, Benevento 1022); compare nos. 276 (1013), 369 (1017), and 470 (1022).

[38] For references, see articles cited in the Bibliography.

[39] *Chronica Monasterii Casinensis* iii. 61 (MGH SS xxiv. 441); Untermann, *Zentralbau* (see inset on Saint-Bénigne, Dijon), 69.

certainly gives the impression of a coffin- or sarcophagus-burial, but the omission of other features makes it uncertain how the artists imagined the rest of the tomb. A particularly dignified version of the visit is to be found in the Pericopes Book of Henry II, made for the great church of Bamberg shortly after 1007. Within a formal frame, we see the women carrying spices, with one additionally carrying a censer, meeting the angel, seated on a sarcophagus. Few other details of the tomb itself are visible.[40]

Alongside this older rotunda tradition, a new one was emerging. The development of *Quem queritis* and other ceremonies at the tomb required a specific provision of a place that would represent it dramatically. It would most obviously be an altar, but the temptation to provide a reference to the tomb proper was very real. A number of churches were now provided with chapels that displayed some of the features of the edicule. We would be well advised not to talk about copies, because most of them were eccentric or experimental in form. If we disallow the cemetery chapel at Fulda, as was argued in the previous chapter, we have the second half of the tenth century as the time of the introduction of the first new-version Holy Sepulchres. It is not clear what there was originally at San Sepolcro at Tuscany, which eventually was to become famous as the home town of Piero della Francesca. The story was that two pilgrims, Arcano and Egidio, returning from the Holy Land, received in a dream a command to build a church, in which they placed relics from the Holy Sepulchre. Seemingly, this was some time in the middle of the tenth century. At Konstanz, Bishop Conrad, who died in 975, was said to have visited the Holy Land three times, and in the basilica of St Maurice to have founded 'a Sepulchre of the Lord in the likeness (*in similitudine*) of that at Jerusalem.'[41] The striking Sepulchre monument that is now at Konstanz is a replacement made in the late thirteenth century. The Konstanz order of service incorporated the 'sprint to the tomb' by Peter and John, of which John's Gospel tells us.[42] It must have been

---

[40] Mayr-Harting, *Ottonian Book Illumination*, i. illus. 106–7, and Möbius, *Passion*, nos. 134–5.

[41] *Vita Chounradi autore Oudalscalcho* cc. 6–7 (MGH SS IV. 432).

[42] P. Kurmann, 'Das Konstanzer Heilige Grab: sein stilistisches und zeitliches Verhältnis zu franzözischen Vorbildern', *Kunstchronik*, 25 (1972), 333–74; Erdmann and A. Zettler, 'Zur Archäologie des Konstanzer Münsterhügels', *Schriften des Vereins für Geschichte des Bodensees . . .*, 95 (1977), 31–134; and P. Jezler, 'Gab es in Konstanz ein ottonisches Osterspiel? Die Mauritius- Rotunde und ihre kultische Funktion als *Sepulchrum Domini*', A. Reinle and others (eds.), *Variorum munera florum: Mélanges F. Haefele* (Sigmaringen, 1985), 91–128.

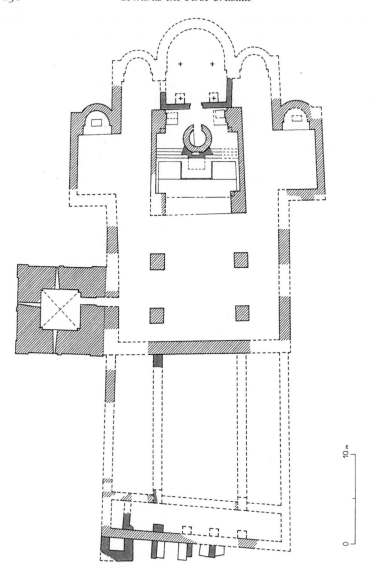

FIG 5.1 The plan of the excavations at Fruttuaria shows the position of the Holy Sepulchre in front of the main altar as part of the design of Abbot William about 1003.

FIG 5.2 The Sepulchre representation at Aquileia, from the middle years of the eleventh century, is the earliest to survive largely intact.

about this time at Bologna that Bononius was visiting 'those holy places, which the blessed Petronius had created in his homeland in the image of Palestine'.[43] At Fruttuaria in northern Italy, the church built by William of Dijon (or Volpiano) in 1003 contained a rotunda under the crossing, which the customs of the house describe as the 'Sepulchre'. Unfortunately nothing remains but the foundations, excavated recently, but the ceremonies there were specifically related to the fact that the Lord 'had bestowed on the house of Fruttuaria a part of his Sepulchre', and this relic was carried in procession during the Easter ceremonies.[44] Interestingly, the edicule at Fruttuaria was of much the same size as the slightly later one at Aquileia, where, alone among buildings of the eleventh century, something close to the original survives. The basilica was dedicated in 1031, and the first mention of the model of the Sepulchre is found in 1077. It contains

---

[43] See the inset 'Jerusalem at Bologna', Ch. 4 above.
[44] L. Pejrani-Baricco, 'L'Église abbatial de Fruttuaria à la lumière des dernières fouilles archéologiques', in Jannet and Sapin (eds.), *Guillaume de Volpiano*, 74–108. The reference to relics from the Holy Sepulchre is in L. G. Spätling and P. Dinter (eds.), *Consuetudines Fructuarienses-Sanblasianae: Corpus Consuetudinum Monasticarum*, 12(1) (Siegburg, 1985), 38, 196, 199.

Neuvy as a Reminiscence of the Holy Sepulchre

The most probable account of Neuvy's foundation ascribed it
to Odo Le Roux, lord of Déols, in 1042. He had been on pilgrimage in 1027 with a group of nobles, including Duke William of Aquitaine and Count Fulk of Anjou, and they are
reported to have brought back many fragments of the Holy
Sepulchre. What now remains is a rotunda, without a trace of
any accompanying copy of the edicule. As usual, the representation is inexact. There are eleven columns instead of the
original twelve, and the entrance is from the north. It is,
unsurprisingly, smaller than the great Anastasis rotunda at
Jerusalem. The style seems to belong to the twelfth century
rather than the eleventh, but a rebuilding then is unlikely.
Neuvy, and the province of Berry around it, became significant centres of Jerusalem devotion. Albert of Aachen tells us
that Peter the Hermit began his preaching of the First Crusade here, and the vicomte of Berry, Odo Arpin, sold the province to the Capetian king, Philip I, to finance his departure on
crusade in 1101. Neuvy is mentioned by four chronicles from
outside the immediate region, and there was still a keen
awareness in the thirteenth century of its position as a special
memorial of the Holy Sepulchre. The legate Odo of Châteauroux, on his return from the crusade of Louis IX, donated to
the church some drops of the holy blood, and some further
stones from the Sepulchre. These were built into a grotto,
with the inscription, 'These are relics of the Lord's Sepulchre
and of the place of Calvary', which survived until 1806.

J. Hubert, 'Le Saint-Sépulcre de Neuvy et les pèlerinages de Terre-
Sainte au XIe siècle', *Bulletin Monumental*, 90 (1931), 91–100;
J. Favière (ed.), *Berry Roman* (Yonne, La Pierre qui Vire, 1970), 115–19;
and C. K. Gardner, 'The Capetian Presence in Berry as a Consequence
of the First Crusade', *Autour de la 1 cr.*, 71–81.

features clearly based on the edicule: hooks for hanging lamps, and a
grave-bench inset with arch or arcosolium. On the other hand, the
twelve columns (originally) and the curved walls suggest rather the
rotunda: this curious object seems to be an all-purpose chapel

FIG 5.3 Eleven columns form the rotunda at Neuvy-Saint-Sépulcre. The dedication to the Sepulchre here was shortly before 1050, and the rotunda is clearly a reference to the Jerusalem Anastasis, which was being restored at the time. The capitals here (rather mystifyingly) look later than that.

conflating the two, in spite of the huge differences in their scale at Jerusalem. A later liturgy at Aquileia shows similarities to that of the church of Salzburg, from which Poppo, the archbishop-builder, originated.

A different example is offered by the small chapel of Le Liget, near Loches in Touraine. It is a round church, with a scheme of wall

Bishop Meinwerk at Paderborn

The present Bußdorfkirche at Paderborn is the best documented of the representations of the Holy Sepulchre created
in the eleventh century. In his charter of 25 May 1036
Bishop Meinwerk said that he had 'undertaken to construct a
church . . . in the likeness (*ad similitudinem*) of the holy church
of Jerusalem . . . in order to obtain that celestial Jerusalem'.
The charter was issued 'after the blessing of the Sepulchre
and the altar before it'. Its witnesses included Abbot Wino of
Helmarshausen, 'who brought the measures of the church and
Sepulchre from Jerusalem'. Long afterwards, between 1152 and
1165, a *Life of Meinwerk* was written at Paderborn. It was a
scholarly composition, which used both documents and local
tradition as its sources, and the author said that Wino had been
sent to Jerusalem to collect the information; but the charter,
the sole source of information available to the author of the
Life, does not say that he was specially sent for the purpose, and
his journey may well have been earlier. Apparently he had
brought back relics, as well as the measures, and the building
may have been inspired by a desire to give them a worthy
shrine. The church claimed fragments of the cross and of the
purple robe of Jesus, and a portion of the sweatband from the
tomb. There was a fire at the church in 1058, and on 21 July
1068 Bishop Imad issued a charter to celebrate its completion
or repair, dated 'at the Jerusalem church of Paderborn'. Imad
also spoke of the monastery as 'our Jerusalem', *Solimam nostram*. The use of this title is confirmed by the appearance in the
twelfth century of a 'provost of Jerusalem' there, but after that
the name disappears from Paderborn.

The Bußdorfkirche has been heavily rebuilt in later centuries, but excavation has revealed the foundations of a centrally
planned structure with four square apses. It has a vague
resemblance to the Anastasis rotunda at Jerusalem, but in
detail the differences are enormous. We do not know whether
there was originally a representation of the Holy Sepulchre
itself at the central point. Bishop Henry of Paderborn in 1126
sponsored a chapel at Helmarshausen that was quite a close
copy of the Bußdorfkirche, and where a tomb has been found

in the centre, conceivably a symbol of the Holy Sepulchre, although one which was not at all similar to the edicule. Paderborn may therefore have had a centrally planned building equipped with apses and some sort of tomb in the centre. As far as we know, it was the first time this was done, and Meinwerk might well have been proud of this likeness to Jerusalem, which to our eyes would be very different from a copy. At the (uncertain) date of Wino's journey, the church of the Holy Sepulchre may have been in course of rebuilding after the destruction of 1010, but in the light of contemporary ideas it is almost certain that his 'measurements' were designed to be incorporated as memorial relics, not to provide the basis for an architectural reconstruction.

H. J. Brandt, 'Die Jerusalemkirche des Bischofs Meinwerk von 1036: zur Bedeutung des Heilig-Grab-Kultes im Mittelalter', in H. J. Brandt and others (eds.), *Die Bußdorfkirche in Paderborn, 1036–1986* (Paderborn, 1986), 173–95; and G. Mietke, *Die Bautätigkeit Bischof Meinwerks von Paderborn und die frühchristliche und byzantinische Architektur* (Paderborn, 1991).

painting that appears to be centred on the dual representations of the deposition from the Cross and the three Marys at the Tomb.

Decorative survivals of this sort are extremely rare, and Le Liget may perhaps suggest the designs that were followed in other rotundas in the eleventh and twelfth centuries. The doublet deposition/three Marys is found prominently elsewhere, for example in the profusely painted crypt at Tavant, and this may suggest that there was a strong Holy Sepulchre reminiscence in many churches where the evidence for it no longer remains. The possibility of elaborate decorations in such chapels is strengthened by the case of Gerona, in Catalonia, where the cathedral was consecrated in 1037. It possessed a chapel of the Holy Sepulchre, with an altar of the cross. A damaged cloth survives, incorporating themes from *Genesis* and illustrations of the history of the wood of the cross; it might very appropriately have been designed for the chapel.[45] It would be nice to have had a contemporary explanation of this increasing interest in

[45] B. Baert, 'New Observations on the *Genesis* of Girona (1050–1100): The Iconography of the Legend of the True Cross', *Gesta*, 38 (1999), 115–27.

The Chapel of Le Liget

is a small, round chapel, with a diameter of about seven metres. It is clearly of eleventh-century construction. Subsequently an oblong nave was added, but this is now in ruins, whereas the original rotunda survives. The traditional dedication is to St John. No evidence remains of its foundation, but it was in the area of influence of the house of Anjou, and not far from the monastery of Beaulieu-les-Loches, established by Count Fulk Nerra in honour of the Sepulchre. The most striking element of the painting is a band depicting the life of Christ, starting from the nativity and culminating in the Tree of Jesse. The deposition and three Marys at the tomb seem to occupy pride of place on each side of the east window, and a good deal of the other decoration, such as the scrolls of the prophets, can be seen as a commentary on the passion and resurrection. Although a number of other themes are followed in the decoration, it does seem that the founder was concerned with the commemoration of the Holy Sepulchre, and that a design which, for the period, was unusually coherent was followed with this in mind.

V. Munteanu, 'A Romanesque Copy of the Anastasis: The Chapel of St Jean of Le Liget', *Gesta*, 16 (1977), 27–40.

representations of the Holy Sepulchre. The demands of worship must have played an important part. *Quem queritis* and other ceremonies at the tomb would have been more compelling with a property that looked more like a tomb than an altar. Unfortunately formal evidence for the connection is missing. We know from a service-book at Aquileia that the visitation of the tomb did take place in the eleventh century, and this would fit neatly with the provision in the new cathedral of a Sepulchre to which the women could come in their searching. We know, too, that there was a strong pilgrimage connection in these foundations. In 1053, Odilo of the Morlhon family went to Jerusalem 'to pray and see the holy places of the birth, passion, death and resurrection and ascension of Christ'. On his return, he founded a church at Villeneuve d'Aveyron with close links with the Holy Sepulchre at Jerusalem. Similarly, Konstanz was built by the three-times pilgrim Bishop Conrad. It is worthy of note that the development of indulgences assigned to particular churches began to give force to the idea that the faithful could benefit by a pilgrimage to a Western model as much as to the sepulchre at Jerusalem itself. In 1085 the foundation charter of the abbey church of Paleva in Catalonia contained the promise that whoever comes to pray there, and has given of his property or possessions to the aforesaid church, will after the confession of sins and penance for his evil deeds be granted by God such an indulgence as for the Sepulchre of our Lord Christ at Jerusalem.[46]

WAR AGAINST SARACENS

To believe that the Holy Sepulchre offers the blessings of grace, protection, and the strengthening of faith is different from a commitment to fight for its possession. The emergence of the ideal of warfare for the Holy Land has been the subject of a great deal of study, and we shall have to turn to the subject if we are to understand the most dramatic of all the impacts of the Holy Sepulchre upon Western history: the emergence of the crusades.

The ideas which had governed the court of Charlemagne are set out in a classic statement by Alcuin, written on the emperor's behalf to Pope Leo III in 796:

> It is our part, with the help of the divine mercy, outwardly to defend with arms the holy church of Christ on all sides from the incursion of the pagans and devastation of the unbelievers, and inwardly to strengthen it by the profession of the catholic faith. It is your part, most holy father, to assist our army with your hands lifted to God like Moses, that by your intercession, with God as our leader and benefactor, the Christian people may always and everywhere be victorious over the enemies of his holy name, and the name of our Lord Jesus Christ be exalted in the world.[47]

The assumption that the secular power had a duty of defence against unbelievers was dominant in the Carolingian period. It is true that there were some ambiguities: sometimes prohibitions of violence were quoted from the days of the Fathers, and penance was imposed for killing, even in lawful warfare. Such qualifications were exceptions. The assumption that the emperor and kings were called to defend Christendom was standard.

[46] Untermann, *Zentralbau*, 61.
[47] MGH Ep. Karolini Aevi II, no. 93, p. 137.

In legend at least, this imperial primacy survived. In the tenth century, it was reported that Charlemagne had received the imperial crown in the East, from the Caliph. By the eleventh century, there was a story that he had extended his empire as far as Jerusalem by means of a peaceful expedition, and as late as 1090 the imperialist writer Benzo of Alba saw the banner and keys of Jerusalem as the insignia of the Emperor Henry IV.[48] In reality, though, the imperial leadership of Christendom evaporated. The Ottonians in the tenth century were the last dynasty that was able to sustain Carolingian tradition in its earlier form. From the middle of the eleventh century, even the German monarchy had become ineffective. Henry IV (1056–1106) first had a long minority, and from 1080 was no longer recognized by the Roman Church. By 1100, no one was acknowledged as a catholic emperor, and it was one of the wonders of the First Crusade that it had no king among its participants.

The paralysis of state power may sound like a poor precondition for effective action in the eastern Mediterranean. The newly emerging class of knights was difficult or impossible for governments to control, and formed a sort of gangster society of brutality and extortion. Churchmen lamented that there was no difference between *militia* and *malitia*. In spite of appearances, there was a marked increase in the economic and military effectiveness of Western society. To trace the reasons would be a long process, but we can observe some of the indications. From about the middle of the tenth century, the barbarian raids were dying away. Lost land began to be resettled, and new lands settled within the great forests and marshes. German nobles began to create 'territories', areas under their sole dominance, within the forests. One account of the speech of Pope Urban II at Clermont depicts him as urging the expedition to create more space for settlement:

The land which you inhabit is closed in on all sides by the sea and the chains of mountains, and is crowded by your large numbers, so that it does not suffice for the supply of riches and scarcely provides food for its cultivators. That is why you quarrel among yourselves, wage war and often wound and kill each other.[49]

---

[48] H. Möhring, 'Benzo von Alba und die Entstehung des Kreuzzugsgedankens', in *Forschungen zur Reichs-, Papst- und Landesgeschichte, Peter Herde zum 65 Geburtstag . . . dargebracht* (Stuttgart, 1998), 177–86.
[49] Robert the Monk, *Historia Iherosolimitana* i. 1 (RHC Occ. iii. 728).

In 1108 the bishops and lay nobles of Saxony drafted a manifesto inviting peoples from the German lands to join in an expedition against the pagan Wends and to settle in the east: 'here you can save your souls and, if you wish, acquire the best of land to dwell in.'[50] In society generally, an increasing availability of money, much as it was lamented by radical reformers, oiled the wheels of mobility. Alexander Murray has observed that 'money, rather than being a solvent of medieval society as it might first appear, was a prerequisite for its most characteristic achievements—such as cathedrals, pilgrimages and crusades'.[51]

The movement towards new lordship was combined with increased military efficiency. Skill in horsemanship on the field of battle went back a long way, but the heavily armed knight, with metal helmet and breastplate and a formidable lance, seems to be mainly a development of the eleventh century. The Byzantine writer Anna Comnena exclaimed with astonishment that 'a Frank on horseback would go through the walls of Babylon'. The same century saw the emergence of castles, originally of wood, but later sometimes of stone. In the Mediterranean itself, the fleets of Pisa and Genoa were increasingly effective. The Pisan raids on Palermo, the capital of Muslim Sicily, in 1062, and on Mahdia in north Africa in 1087, announced a new balance of power, as did the conquest of Sicily, which the Norman settlers in southern Italy finally completed in 1091.

It would be wrong to suppose that the development of knights, castles, and fleets had made Western Europe irresistible by 1100. Contemporaries were so astonished by the triumph of the First Crusade that they thought it could only be the work of God. The changing technology had at least made the success of an expedition to the eastern Mediterranean conceivable, if scarcely probable. The knights fought their way to Jerusalem, the fleets controlled the Syrian coast and the castles held the occupied land. This background of increasing prosperity and technology coexisted, in many parts of Western Europe, with a paralysis of political authority. It was a situation that created a rethinking about the authorization of warfare. In the absence of effective royal leadership, bishops began to take the initiative in the protection of the faithful. The most striking example was the Peace of God movement in southern France. At the

---

[50] P. Knoch, 'Kreuzzug und Siedlung: Studien zum Aufruf der Magdeburger Kirche von 1108', *Jahrbuch für die Geschichte Mittel- und Ostdeutschlands*, 23 (1974), 1–33.
[51] A. Murray, *Reason and Society in the Middle Ages* (Oxford, 1978), 55.

synod of Le Puy in 975 Bishop Guy at a meeting of knights and peasants sought 'to hear from them what advice they had to give about keeping the peace', and required an oath to respect the goods of the church and the poor. A series of councils enacted peace regulations, enforced by the power of the saints, whose relics were displayed on the altars, by excommunication and other ecclesiastical penalties, and by the enthusiastic support of the laity: Raoul Glaber tells us of the cry of 'Peace', *Pax! Pax! Pax!*, with which a proclamation was greeted. The movement was at once a response to the failure of royal power and to a social change that was connected with it: the broad class of freemen, who had formed an important element in the Carolingian armies, had fragmented, and there was now a sharp contrast between the knights, who were exempt from personal bondage to lordship, and a peasantry that was increasingly subject to personal levies and arbitrary violence. It also had a theological basis in the example of the apostles. The Council of Poitiers (about 1011–14) reflected: 'How fair is the name of peace, and how beautiful is the reputation of unity, which Christ left to the disciples when he ascended into heaven.' The awareness of Christian brotherhood became explicit at the council of Narbonne in 1054: 'We warn and command, according to God's and our precept, that no Christian may kill any other Christian, because he who kills a Christian undoubtedly sheds the blood of Christ.'[52]

The church's acceptance of responsibility for peace and war was manifested by leadership in the defence of the faithful from 'pagan' attack, as they normally described it, from beyond the frontiers of Christendom. The German writer Thietmar reported that, when Saracen fleets attacked Luna in 1016, Pope Benedict VIII 'gathering all the rulers and defenders of holy mother church, asked and commanded them that they should bravely advance with him against the enemies of Christ, who were presuming to behave in this way, and with the help of God kill them'.[53] Soon after the middle of the century the initiatives of the Roman Church were strengthened as a group of reformers took control there. Its policy came to be shaped by a newly structured group of cardinals, many of them from northern Europe, and many of them monks. The sequence of monk-popes from 1073 to 1116 has hardly any parallel in the rest of papal history, and with

---

[52] Council of Poitiers, prologue (Mansi, *Concilia*, xix. 267); C. of Narbonne, c. 1 (Mansi xix. 827).
[53] MGH in usum scholarum IX. 452.

Gregory VII (1073–85) the papacy took a strongly anti-imperial direction. Popes began to see themselves as the protectors of the faithful from oppression, corruption, and the threats of unbelievers.

A simple instance of the transfer that might take place from reliance on the lay ruler to a do-it-yourself approach is provided by the actions of Pope Leo IX in face of a threat from the Normans in southern Italy, who were taking over papal territories. Leo first went to Germany to appeal for support to the Emperor Henry III in 1052, and when he was unable to secure assistance he assembled an army himself and led it against the Normans, to a disastrous defeat at the Battle of Civitate in 1053. A more extreme form of ecclesiastical initiative was the appeal by papal reformers to lay action against rulers with whom they were in conflict. To rebel against an emperor anointed by God, in defiance of an oath of obedience, was shocking to conservative opinion. Yet Gregory VII emerged as a sponsor of precisely such action. From Easter 1080 until his death in 1106, the Emperor Henry IV was regarded as excommunicate and deposed by the Gregorian popes, who acknowledged no catholic emperor. Gregory in particular appealed to sympathetic princes, obedient to the Roman Church, whom he described as 'the faithful of St Peter'. The church had moved a long way since Alcuin had defined the duty of the emperor as defending the faithful with arms, and of the pope as raising on his behalf the hands of prayer.

The formal place for new thinking about warfare was in the canon lawyers during the last twenty years of the eleventh century, notably within the *Collection of Canons* of the Gregorian Bishop Anselm II of Lucca. He devoted books XII and XIII to the right of the church to resort to coercion against its enemies, and drew most of his texts from Augustine's discussions of just war. It was much the most significant use of this material so far in medieval thought. Anselm preserved the limits that the original texts had placed on warfare: he recognized, in the rubrics he provided, that it should be waged 'with benevolence', and that the aim was 'the acquisition of peace'. Anselm's rubrics forced the texts towards the assertion of the direct power of the church: 'that the church can undertake persecution'; 'that the church does not persecute but loves in its punishments and prohibitions'.[54] It is hardly surprising that some historians have seen

---

[54] A. Stickler, 'Il potere coattivo materiale della chiesa nella riforma gregoriana secondo Anselmo di Lucca', *Studi Gregoriani*, 2 (1947), 235–85. The Latin word *persecutio* is less specific than our modern 'persecution'.

Anselm as providing the theoretical foundation for warfare in defence of the Holy Sepulchre. Yet the whole force of his thinking was directed to the right to use force against fellow Christians. It seems to have nothing to do with crusading. The canonical collections, leading to the editions of Gratian's *Decretum* in the middle years of the twelfth century, had virtually nothing at all to say about warfare with unbelievers or about the Holy Sepulchre. Conversely, crusading chroniclers and other propagandists almost never invoked texts from Augustine, or mentioned the theory of just war, when they defended the conflict with Islam as pleasing to God.

There appears to have been no problem about warfare against non-Christians, which was accepted by everybody as justifiable, not to say praiseworthy. Leo IX justified his resort to force in 1053 on the grounds that the Normans in the south, he alleged, had behaved with 'unheard-of fury and more than pagan impiety against the church of God'.[55] Leo's policy fits into a tradition of action against the Saracen threat in the Mediterranean. The defence of Bari by the fleet of Venice against Muslim attack in 1003 was said by the chronicler John the Deacon to have been undertaken 'not out of worldly fear but out of the fear of God'.[56] Pisa saw its attack on Palermo in 1063 within the framework of holy war, and used the spoils to finance its great new cathedral. Alexander II may have sponsored a French expedition against the Moors in Spain in 1064, although the precise purpose of his letter is unclear. There is enough evidence to suggest persistence in papal support for warfare against the Muslim threat in the Western Mediterranean.

Fighting for the faith raises the question of spiritual reward. Traditionally, martyrdom was reserved for those who embraced suffering for Christ to the point of death. Before the eleventh century, there were very few instances indeed of giving the title of martyr to anyone who had fallen on the field of battle, but those who fought in the armies of a Christian emperor could be seen as having a rather similar status. In 878 the Frankish bishops wrote a letter of enquiry to Pope John VIII about whether those who had been killed in recent fighting against the unbeliever could receive forgiveness (*indulgentiam*) for offences. The pope's answer was emphatic: 'we answer boldly in the mercy of Christ our God that the repose of eternal life will receive those who in the piety of the Christian religion have

[55] C. Erdmann, *The Origin of the Idea of Crusade* (Princeton, 1977), 118–25.
[56] G. Monticolo (ed.), *Cronache veneziane*, Fonti per la Storia d'Italia, 9 (1887), 166.

fallen in battle fighting against pagans and unbelievers.'[57] As expeditions came to depend less on public or feudal military duty, and more on persuasion, the assurance of reward became all the more necessary, and reserves about the term 'martyr' were stripped away. Leo IX, distressed that he had led his men to their deaths at Civitate, was reassured by visions of the slain in glory among the ranks of the martyrs:

Since they had voluntarily suffered death for the faith of Christ and the deliverance of his people in distress, he proved by many revelations that by divine grace they had everlasting joy in the heavenly kingdom. For they appeared in various ways to these same faithful of Christ, saying that they were not to be mourned by funerals and ceremonies, but were joined with the holy martyrs in glory on high.[58]

The support by the popes for warfare against Saracens leaves open the more specific question of their policy in the East. Shortly after 1010 Sergius IV, if we accept his letter as authentic, expressed a clear interest in the welfare of the Holy Sepulchre, and attempted to inspire an expedition to rescue it from the persecution of Caliph al-Hakim. Leo IX's Norman policy (badly as it miscarried) was founded on a concern for an alliance with Byzantium. A legation he sent in 1054 to negotiate with the emperor ended, immediately after the pope's death, with a bitter quarrel at Constantinople, which has often, but with exaggeration, been identified as the time when a decisive schism opened between the Latin and Greek churches. Nevertheless, it was the Western Mediterranean that commanded the attention of the popes, until the Seljuk invasions of Persia, Syria, and Anatolia profoundly changed the situation in the East. Syria and Anatolia were plunged into disorder, especially after the Byzantine emperor, Romanus IV, failed in a major attempt to expel the invaders at the disastrous battle of Manzikert in 1071. Three years later, the *Register* of Gregory VII contains a series of letters planning an expedition to redress the situation. Gregory wrote of the bearer of one of his letters that 'we have learned from him, as we have learned from many others, that a pagan people has prevailed strongly against the Christian empire, that they have already cruelly laid waste and occupied

---

[57] E. Caspar (ed.), *Registrum Iohannis VIII Papae* (MGH Ep. Karolini Aevi v, no. 150, pp. 126–7). See also the statement of Leo IV that later became a text of canon law: MGH Ep. Karolini Aevi iii, no.28, p. 601.

[58] Wibert (?), *Vita Leonis Papae*, ii. 11, J. M. Watterich (ed.), *Pontificum Romanorum Vitae* (Leipzig, 1862), 166.

everything almost to the walls of Constantinople'. He concludes that as Christ laid down his life for us, 'we ought to lay down our lives for the brethren'.[59] The emphasis on the suffering of the Eastern brethren is the recurrent theme in these letters, and suggests that the dominant concern was the Turkish threat to Constantinople, but in an optimistic report to Henry IV he extended his view: 'if they have me as leader and pontiff on the expedition, they will rise up in arms against the enemies of God and reach the Lord's Sepulchre under his leadership'.[60]

This is the sole reference to the Holy Sepulchre within the brief collection of Gregory's surviving correspondence about a Mediterranean expedition. Gregory's Eastern policy ended as a catastrophic failure at the time of his death in 1085. He had neither assisted in the defence of Constantinople nor, if it was ever in his mind, protected the church at Jerusalem from oppression. Gregory's correspondence contains no indication that he concerned himself directly about the difficulties that Jerusalem pilgrims were experiencing. Urban II was a close confidant of Gregory in his later years, and when he became pope in 1089, his circular letters announced that he would stand in the footsteps of his great predecessor. He could not himself have been involved in the 1074 project, as he only joined the papal curia in 1080, but the letters in the *Register* would certainly have been available to him. In the event, his interventions in the eastern Mediterranean were to draw upon much wider ambitions than Gregory had entertained, and were to assume a very different character.

THE FIRST CRUSADE

The triumph of the First Crusade was the capture of Jerusalem on 15 July 1099, but it has been doubted whether this was originally part of Pope Urban's intentions. The pope was undoubtedly concerned with assisting the Eastern brethren, harassed as they were by Turkish invasions, and Carl Erdmann, in his great book *The Origins of the Crusading Idea* (1935) posed the crucial question: 'was the aim to assist the Byzantine Empire, or only to free the Holy Sepulchre?' Hans Mayer thought that Jerusalem was an addition to Urban's original plan: 'Originally the object of the Crusade was to help the Christian churches in the East . . . But very soon men had

---

[59] Caspar (ed.), *Registrum Gregorii VII*, I. 49 (75).
[60] Ibid. *Registrum*, II. 31 (165–8).

a more definite object in mind: to free the Holy Land and, above all, Jerusalem, the Sepulchre of Christ, from the yoke of heathen dominion.'[61]

The uncertainties cannot exactly be put down to the lack of sources, because the events of the First Crusade are much more fully described in near-contemporary literature than anything else in the period. Unfortunately the chroniclers did not know much about the events leading up to its proclamation. Some historians have confused matters further by treating as reliable the five versions of Urban's sermon or speech which the chroniclers attributed to him at the Council of Clermont. As one would expect from the conventions of the period, they are later constructs, even if they reflect the assumptions of writers who lived through the events.

The Decree at Clermont in November 1095

The full text of the canons of the Council, always supposing that one was ever compiled, does not survive. In his letter to Bologna Urban II made it clear that he was reporting the Council's decision, and the text is close to summaries provided by eyewitnesses of the proceedings. There are, in addition, five lengthy accounts of his speech or sermon there, by Robert the Monk (who was certainly present himself), Baudri of Bourgueil, Guibert of Nogent, Fulcher of Chartres, and William of Malmesbury, but there is no reason to think that any of them is close to a verbatim report. They were composed at periods between about 1106 and 1120, and convention did not require the literal reporting of the spoken word.

For early reports of the relevant decree of the Council, R. Somerville, *The Councils of Urban II, i. Decreta Claromontensia* (Amsterdam, 1972), 74, 108, 124 n.

The decision to authorize an expedition of princes to the East was not a sudden response to a single appeal. Urban, inspired by recent advances in Sicily and Spain, was conscious of the possibilities of Christian restoration in the Mediterranean world. He set out his

[61] Mayer, *The Crusades*, 9.

hopes on 1 July 1091 for Archbishop Berengar of Tarragona, in which he declared that God

'transfers kingdoms and changes seasons' (Daniel 2: 21). Once he saw fit to exalt the glory of the city of Tarragona. He saw fit, in the same city, to visit the sins of his people . . . But behold, after 390 years have passed since the people of the Hagarenes made desolate that city, he has deigned to inspire the hearts of his princes to undertake the restoration of the city, according to the command of the apostolic see.[62]

Urban several times used such language. Liberation, restoration, exaltation were his words for God's action on the frontiers of Christendom.

Such thinking does not in itself explain the presence of the Holy Sepulchre among Urban's military objectives. Its recovery by Christians had been envisaged by the prophetic writings of Pseudo-Methodius and his successors, but plans for action had been few and doubtful. The collapse of the Byzantine position, which had already produced the abortive project of 1074, led to further interest in the East. The new Byzantine Emperor, Alexius I, was keen to obtain Latin help, and wrote a series of letters to secure it. Alexius' best-known appeal is that of his ambassadors to the Council of Piacenza in Lent 1095, where they 'humbly implored the lord pope and all the faithful of Christ, that they should give him some help against the pagans for the defence of holy church, which the pagans had now almost wiped out in those parts, and had overrun them up to the walls of Constantinople'.[63] There is so little detailed information about the various appeals from Alexius that they offer a rich field for speculation. The safety of Constantinople must have been a primary concern in his mind: whether any of his appeals mentioned Jerusalem, we do not know. The idea, which has attracted a number of writers, that in 1095 Alexius was seeking 'mercenaries' who would be a spearhead for a counter-attack into Asia Minor belongs to the realm of the historical novel, for the passage quoted above is the totality of our knowledge.

It was only in 1094 that the stranglehold of imperialist forces in central Italy had been broken, and Urban (whatever previous hopes

---

[62] J. von Pfugk-Hartung (ed.), *Acta Pontificum Romanorum Inedita* (Stuttgart 1884), no. 176, ii. 142–3. The important and unusual quotation is discussed by I. H. Ringel, '*Ipse transfert regna et mutat tempora*: Beobachtungen zur Herkunft von Daniel 2:21 bei Urban II', *Deus qui mutat tempora: Menschen und Institutionen im Wandel des Mittelalters: Fs. für Alfons Becker* (Sigmaringen, 1987), 137–56.

[63] Bernold of Constance, *Chronicon* under 1095, MGH SS v. 461.

he may have entertained for the eastern Mediterranean) was finally able to make plans for Lombardy and France. Common sense suggests that the presence of Greek ambassadors at Piacenza was a response to a papal invitation: in that case the pope would appear in the role of originator of the discussions. Piacenza was chosen because it was a secure place for the pope's supporters and free from the danger of attack by his imperialist enemies, and had a tradition well designed for the project under discussion. It was an important link in the pattern of pilgrim travel, whose known connection with pilgrimage to the Holy Sepulchre went back to the sixth century. A monastery dedicated to the Holy Sepulchre existed there in the middle of the tenth century, and was rebuilt about 1055: 'in the said church we have constituted a Sepulchre in honour of the Saviour, that those who see it may be mindful of the God who suffered and was buried for us and, considering it in their minds, may renounce their previous ills and do penance.'[64] If there is any force in these speculations (and speculations they are) Urban presumably summoned the council, and invited Byzantine representations, with Jerusalem in mind. According to Bernold, who was present, the pope persuaded his hearers to take oaths to go to assist the emperor 'against the pagans', but that does not conclusively establish that Jerusalem had definitely entered into the pope's plans.

Piacenza was followed almost immediately by plans to summon a council at Clermont, in southern France, whose broad agenda would include an expedition to the East. The pope had direct information about Jerusalem from returning pilgrims. A strange document, circulating in the West, had apparently originated in the circles of Count Robert of Flanders, who had been in Jerusalem in the years before 1090, but the most influential report may have been that of Peter the Hermit. According to the chronicler Albert of Aachen, Peter visited Jerusalem, was horrified by the condition of the Christians there, and in the church of the Holy Sepulchre had a dream in which Christ charged him to carry back from the patriarch an appeal for help 'to cleanse the holy places of Jerusalem and to restore the offices of the saints'. The pope, moved by the appeal, set out for France, where the princes 'agreed to God's request for an expedition at their own expense to the Sepulchre itself'.[65] This whole story of Peter's

---

[64] P. M. Campi, *Dell'Historia ecclesiastica di Piacenza* (Piacenza, 1651), i. 513–14, no. 89; J. Heers, 'Bourgs et faubourgs en Occident', *Jérusalem, Rome*, 205–15.
[65] Albert of Aachen, *Historia Hierosolymitana* i. 2–5, RHC Occ. iv. 264 f.

pilgrimage was for a long time dismissed as legend, but recent research has rehabilitated Albert as a serious source. He saw Peter as 'the first author' of the Crusade, and (even if we suppose this to be an overstatement) it is likely that the Hermit was at least the carrier of influential news. It is interesting, too, that the Aleppo chronicler al-ʿAzimi, in the rather fragmentary notes that survive from his writings, reports that in 1093–4 Frankish and Byzantine pilgrims who had landed at the ports of Syria were prevented from continuing to Jerusalem, and the reports of those who survived led the Franks to prepare for war.[66]

We have no precise statement of Urban's objectives written before the Council of Clermont. That is hardly surprising, since one does not find records of events made before they have occurred. A variety of materials, which can be assembled from the years 1095–8, provide strong confirmation that the recovery of Jerusalem was at the fore-front of the minds of the crusaders. Urban's own summary of the decision at Clermont was sent to Bologna on 19 September 1096:

> To all who set out thither [i.e. to Jerusalem], not for desire of earthly reward but solely for the salvation of their soul and the liberation of the church, we have granted, through the mercy of Almighty God and the prayers of the Catholic church . . . total penance for sins of which they have made a true and perfect confession, since they have endangered their property and their persons for love of God and their neighbour.[67]

This is close to reports we have from the notes of other participants in the Council. Confirmatory evidence comes from accounts in local chronicles of Urban's preaching in 1096. At Saumur in January, we are told, he 'publicly and privately invited the people to the Jerusalem journey against the pagans who had advanced to Constantinople, and to rebuild the holy places which had been destroyed'.[68] This sounds similar to the account that Urban himself gave of his inten-tions at Clermont in a letter to Flanders, which is probably to be dated to the preceding December:

> you have already heard some time ago from the reports of many that the rage of barbarians has devastated with wretched persecution the churches of God in Eastern parts, and has moreover delivered the holy city of Christ,

---

[66] C. Hillenbrand, *The Crusades: Islamic Perspectives* (Edinburgh, 1999), 50.

[67] Letter of Urban II to Bologna, 19 September 1096, *Kreuzzugsbriefe*, ep. III. 4 (p. 137).

[68] G. T. Beech, 'Urban II, the Abbey of St-Florent of Saumur, and the First Crusade', *Autour de la 1c*, 60–1.

enlightened by his passion and resurrection, to intolerable servitude (shame to say) with its churches. Grieving with anxiety at this calamity, we have visited the provinces of Gaul and urged its princes and subjects to the liberation of the Eastern churches.[69]

It is not surprising to find the same pattern of ideas expressed in the charters of departing crusaders, as for example in a charter to the abbey of Saint-Victoire Marseille: 'Therefore I, Godfrey, and my brother Guigo, seeking Jerusalem both for the sake of pilgrimage and to extinguish, with God's protection, the wicked and furious rage of the pagans . . .'[70] When we begin to have available letters from the military leaders of the Crusade, it becomes clear that the objective in their mind was to advance through Antioch to Jerusalem. In June 1097, Count Stephen of Blois, after the capture of Nicaea, wrote confidently that 'we shall advance from Nicaea to Jerusalem in five weeks, unless Antioch resists us'. That is a clear statement of intent, even if it proved to be sadly overoptimistic.[71] On 11 September 1098, after they had overcome the long and bitter resistance at Antioch, the leaders as a group summarized to the pope what they regarded as their mission statement:

We urge you, our spiritual father, who initiated this way and by your sermons made us all leave our lands and earthly possessions, and commanded us to follow Christ, bearing crosses, and admonished us to exalt the Christian name, to come to us and complete what you planned . . . Thus fulfil with us the way of Jesus Christ, which we began and you preached, and open to us the gates of both Jerusalems and make the Lord's Sepulchre free, and the Christian name exalted above every name.

With this view of their calling, they described themselves as the 'Jerusalemers of Jesus Christ', *nos Hierosolymitani Iesu Christi*.[72]

That is not to say that the crusading princes did precisely what Pope Urban originally intended. Common sense (although not documentary evidence) suggests that he had not envisaged the acute tensions that developed between the leaders and the Byzantine Emperor Alexius, and we do not know what view the pope was taking over the princes' reluctance to hand back Antioch to Byzantium; nor do we know whether he had envisaged the replacement of Greek

[69] *Kreuzzugsbriefe*, ep. II. 3 (p. 136).
[70] M. Guérard (ed.), *Cartulaire de . . . St-Victor de Marseille* (Paris, 1857), i. 167, no. 143.
[71] *Kreuzzugzbriefe*, ep. IV. 14 (p. 140).
[72] Ibid., ep. XVI. 13–14 and 2 (pp. 164–5, 161).

by Latin patriarchs at Antioch and Jerusalem. Yet amid the doubts a firm backbone of certainty remains. Urban had proclaimed a pilgrimage or journey (*via, iter*) to Jerusalem which was designed to relieve the suffering churches of the East, to deliver Jerusalem from pagan oppression, and to win pardon or 'indulgence' for those who responded to his call. No one could call the evidence complete, but it does seem unambiguous.

Jerusalem, for contemporaries, meant the Holy Sepulchre. There was no other shrine to rival it. Albert of Aachen remarked that the Turks had used the Temple for their own rites, and only 'the temple of the Lord's Sepulchre' and the church of St Mary of the Latins had been left to the Christians, and those because they could extract revenue from the pilgrims there. In the rest of the oratories of the city, Catholic worship had been wiped out.[73] This was not an accurate account of the history of the holy places, for there had never been a Christian cult on the Temple Mount, but it was what the crusaders believed. The Holy Sepulchre was the shrine of outstanding importance, and virtually the only one that still existed as a centre of Christian worship.

The evidence of recruiting confirms its special status. The chronicler of Saint-Pierre at Le Puy reported that Urban

lamented to the faithful how the Sepulchre of the Lord had for a long time been kept under the oppression of the Saracens, who afflicted the pilgrims who went there with great injuries and troubled the Christians in those parts, taking from them lands, possessions and the other goods which they possessed ... (He addressed them) with sorrow about the Lord's Sepulchre and the miseries of the poor captives who lived in the lands of Outremer. All who heard this, placing the banner of the holy cross on their right shoulders ... said that they were ready to live and die for Christ.[74]

The centrality of the Sepulchre was echoed in the charters of recruits. In May 1096 Guigo of Romulas announced that 'I desire to go in the service of our Lord Jesus Christ to the Lord's Sepulchre'. In 1098, Aymeric Bruno expressed his wish 'to go to fight with the Christian people against the Saracens, and to visit the Sepulchre of

---

[73] Albert of Aachen, vi. 25 (RHC Occ. iv. 480–1). The same account was given by Baudri in his version of Urban's speech at Clermont, i. 1 (RHC Occ. iv. 13). In addition, there was an ancient Christian church on Mount Sion, but the Franks at first regarded this as outside the city wall (*Gesta Francorum*, ed. R. Hill (repr. Oxford, 1979), 100).

[74] Cited C. Lauranson-Rosaz, 'Le Velay et la croisade', *Concile de Clermont*, 33–64.

the Lord, which is in Jerusalem'.[75] Count Raymond of Saint-Gilles was said to have gone 'on pilgrimage to wage war on foreign peoples and defeat the barbaric nations, lest the Holy City of Jerusalem be held captive and the Holy Sepulchre of the Lord Jesus be contaminated any longer'.[76] Even in Spain, where they had their own campaign of liberation to occupy them, the Holy Sepulchre was high among their concerns. In June 1100 an intending traveller obtained a loan from the monks of Sahagun 'to visit the Sepulchre of the Lord in Jerusalem'.[77]

The author of the anonymous *Gesta Francorum* was writing shortly after the capture of Jerusalem in 1099. As a Norman from southern Italy, he had not observed the original preaching at first hand, but he was well placed to reflect the attitudes of the triumphant expedition. They remembered the essential message as being that 'if any one, with all his heart and mind, really wanted to follow God and faithfully to bear his cross after him, he should make no delay in taking the way of the Holy Sepulchre immediately'.[78] The idea of warfare for the deliverance of the Holy Sepulchre was a new feature in the thought of Christendom.

[75] *Cartulaire de Lérins* ccxxv, p. 229; A. Sohn, *Der Abbatiat Ademars von S-Martial de Limoges* (Münster, 1989), 347.
[76] J. Riley-Smith, 'The Idea of Crusading in the Charters of the Early Crusaders, 1095–1102', *Concile de Clermont*, 156.
[77] S. Barton, 'Patrons, Pilgrims and the Cult of Saints in the Medieval Kingdom of Leòn', *Pilgrimage Explored*, 57–77.
[78] *Gesta Francorum*, i. 1, ed. Hill, 1, citing Matthew 16: 24.

6

Latin Jerusalem, 1099–1187

The capture of Jerusalem by the First Crusade in July 1099 created much closer links than ever before between the West and the Holy Sepulchre. Within twenty-five years, Western dominance had been established over the eastern coast of the Mediterranean, and there were four principalities, of which the kingdom of Jerusalem enjoyed the greatest prestige and importance, controlled by an aristocracy predominantly Frankish or French in culture. Westerners were not at first sure what to call their conquests. They referred to the whole vast enterprise as designed to assist 'the Asian' or 'the Eastern (Oriental) churches', but this was too imprecise. They searched for other vocabulary. In December 1099 Pope Paschal II spoke of the need to reinforce 'those who had remained in the lands, formerly of the Philistines or Canaanites', thus calling Biblical language to his assistance.[1] Once their territories had become relatively stabilized, they came to describe them by the new term, Overseas (*Outremer, Oltramare*), or by the traditional Latin term Syria. In particular, the Christian inhabitants were normally referred to, by the Westerners, as 'Syrians'.

From the very beginning we can discern two distinct Western reactions to the fate of Outremer. Settlers in the East, and enthusiasts for the cause, frequently complained of neglect. They complained that there were renegades who had committed themselves to the journey and then failed to depart, or had abandoned their colleagues during the crisis at the siege of Antioch in 1097–8; some of these missing colleagues continued to remain in the West. Other frontiers, too, had to be protected in the interests of Christendom, and kings and barons

---

[1] *Kreuzzugsbriefe*, xix. 2, p. 175.

always had their own territories to consider. Against these cries of neglect must be placed the huge commitment to the welfare of Jerusalem and the other Latin possessions in the East which persisted for two centuries, and—in a transformed situation—for much longer than that. Renegades were required to fulfil their vow; a very large (if very unsuccessful) 'follow-up' expedition was mounted in 1101; and Bohemond's appeal for a further campaign, however obviously shaped by self-interest, won wide support in France in 1106–8. Although in previous centuries there had been a long-standing concern for Jerusalem, there was nothing in the past remotely like the huge involvement that the West was henceforth to assume in the affairs of the eastern Mediterranean. This was a new thing in the history of Europe.

THE LIBERATION OF THE HOLY SEPULCHRE

The fall of Jerusalem seemed to observers to be a great and unprecedented act of God. Contemporaries could not fail to be astonished at the success of a march of 2,000 miles, led by no king or emperor but only by those who had willingly placed themselves at the disposal of God. The march was accompanied by wonders, assisted by saints, and attended by visions. Participants came to be seen as *milites Christi*, soldiers of Christ—a title that had earlier been given to monks. It has been suggested that Urban gave the participants this description. It certainly appeared early in crusading vocabulary, for it is prominent in the *Gesta Francorum* (completed perhaps in 1101 or 1102) and was adopted by chronicles that derive from it.

The central concern of this warfare was the liberation of the Holy Sepulchre. Raymond of Aguilers vividly described the arrival of the conquerors at the Temple of Solomon and the Holy Sepulchre:

It suffices to say that in the Temple and porch of Solomon they rode in blood to their knees and up to the reins of their horses. By a most just judgement, the same place received their blood, whose blasphemies it had borne to God for so long a time ... With the fall of the city, it was a delight to see the devotion of the pilgrims before the Lord's Sepulchre, how they clapped their hands, rejoicing and singing a new song to the Lord.[2]

---

[2] Raymond, *Liber*, 150–1. The description of the bloodshed echoes Revelation 14: 20: 'blood flowed from the wine press, as high as a horse's bridle', and Isaiah 63: 'I trampled down peoples in my anger. I crushed them in my wrath, and I poured out their lifeblood on the earth.'

To the modern reader, these words are notable for their savagery. They rested on the older view, which we have encountered already, that warfare between Christian and 'pagan' was natural and normal. The duty to maintain peace applied almost wholly to relations with other Christians. At the same time, we note a rise in the level of triumphal violence among contemporary historians of the First Crusade, the result of appropriating the language about warfare in the Old Testament in the light of a new confidence that God has given to the new Israel, as to the old, the possession of the holy city and land. The new rhetoric led writers to exaggerate the cruelty of the crusaders and the number of casualties they had inflicted.[3] We must return to this characteristic triumphalism, observing for the time being the central place occupied within it by the recovery of the Holy Sepulchre. An early manuscript of the *Gesta Francorum* expressed this by including, after the end of the narrative, an itinerary of the holy places, material for a mass 'in veneration of the Holy Sepulchre', and a diagram of the height of the body of Christ 'taken from the Lord's Sepulchre at Jerusalem'. This small compilation, which John Wilkinson calls 'the First Guide', offers the pilgrim a handbook to the many sacred sites of the city.[4] The early scribe saw it as the culmination of the long endeavour: *explicit itinerarium Hierosolimitanorum*, 'the end of the Jerusalemers' journey'.

The central significance of the Sepulchre was evident to people outside the Christian ranks. The Jewish chronicler of Mainz who described the persecution of his people in the cities of the Rhineland, recorded that the Franks 'planned to ascend, to rise up like an eagle, to wage war and to clear the way to Jerusalem, the Holy City, and to arrive at the Sepulchre of the crucified, a trampled carcass that can neither profit nor save, because it is vanity'.[5] French accounts of the varied expeditions led by Prince Bohemond of Antioch (who seems rarely to have put a foot wrong in his expressions of piety) stressed the importance of the Sepulchre. He is said to have urged his original recruits in 1096, 'O knights, who now are mine, be knights of

[3] D. Hay, 'Gender Bias and Religious Intolerance in Accounts of the "Massacres" of the First Crusade', M. Gervers and J. M. Powell (eds.), *Tolerance and Intolerance: Social Conflict in the Age of the Crusades* (Syracuse, 2001), 3–10.

[4] R. Hill (ed.), *Gesta Francorum* (repr. Oxford, 1979), 97 n. and 98–103; Wilkinson/Hakluyt, 4–6.

[5] S. Eidelberg (tr.), *The Jews and the Crusaders* (Wisconsin, 1977), 99. See also R. Chazan, 'Jerusalem as Christian Symbol during the First Crusade: Jewish Awareness and Response', Levine, 382–92.

God, and begin with me the way of the Holy Sepulchre.'[6] When Bohemond returned to the West in 1106 to assemble another expedition, his purposes were once again presented—whether honestly or not—as 'to preach the road to the Holy Sepulchre'.[7] The centrality of the Sepulchre as a theme persisted throughout Europe in the next generation. In 1137 a grant from a Spanish lord to the canons of the Holy Sepulchre, presumably echoing their teaching, declared that

> Our fathers have told us, as they have learned from the Gospels, that the holy church of the Resurrection of the Lord should be held in greater esteem than all others because our Lord Jesus Christ consecrated it, not through the witness of the prophets nor through the blood of the martyrs, but he dedicated it to himself through his own presence and by the shedding of his own blood and by the glory of his resurrection.[8]

In spite of the amount of eleventh-century pilgrimage, there had been no true itineraries or first-hand descriptions of the Holy Land. With the new possibilities of going to the Sepulchre, new itineraries began almost at once. The so-called First Guide made a good deal of use of the earliest record of all, that by the Bordeaux pilgrim. Since his journey had been almost 800 years previously, it must have been of limited use to contemporary readers. Saewulf in 1101–3 referred to the title of the church of the Holy Sepulchre as the *martyrium*, which he took to mean that it was evidence for the Christian revelation 'because it is more celebrated than any other church, and this is meet and right, since all the prophecies and foretellings in the whole world about our Saviour Jesus Christ were all truly fulfilled there'.[9] Theoderic about 1170 was apparently misunderstanding the traditional name when he assumed that *martyrium* meant martyrdom, 'because it is illuminated by the presence there of our God and Lord Jesus Christ and of his good mother, and the fact that all the patriarchs, prophets and apostles have lived and taught and preached and suffered martyrdom there'.[10] Other traditions were carefully preserved, and indeed improved. Saewulf already had recorded a new legend that linked directly with the historical Jesus the belief that the church contained the centre of the earth: 'Not far from the place of

---

[6] Robert the Monk, ii. 4 (RHC Occ. iii. 741).
[7] N. Housley, 'Jerusalem and the Development of the Crusade Idea, 1099–1128', *Horns of Hattin*, 30–1.
[8] G. Bresc-Bautier (ed.), *Le Cartulaire du chapitre du Saint-Sépulchre de Jérusalem* (Paris, 1980), 220, no. 101.
[9] Saewulf, 9 (Wilkinson/Hakluyt, 101).
[10] Wilkinson/Hakluyt, 276.

Calvary is the place called "Compas", where our Lord Jesus Christ
with his own hand marked and measured the centre of the world.'
He illustrated the idea with the standard quotation of Psalm 74: 12.[11]

The descent of the Holy Fire at the Easter ceremonies was the most
dramatic expression of the central importance of the Holy Sepulchre.
The significance of this ceremony was underlined in the curious
episode at Easter 1101, when the miraculous fire failed to descend
upon the Sepulchre and 'a sorrow, lamentation and fear greater
than any since the earliest days of the Christian religion seized all,
so much so that some almost fell into despair'. The general view
was that this failure was a response to the sins of the victorious
Christians, but the hard-nosed Daimbert of Pisa argued that it was a
mark of the new era, in which such marvels were no longer needed:
'God makes miracles for unbelievers, not for the faithful.'[12]

'A NEW DAY'

Nothing in the Scriptures, nothing in Christian tradition or literature, had prepared the church for what happened on 15 July 1099. In
a providential way, the City of God had been given back to God's
people. Instantaneously, the writers who had shared the agony and
final triumph of the pilgrims looked for an explanation in the sacred
writings and tradition. The author of the *Gesta Francorum* thought
that the great expedition had been directly predicted in the preaching
of Christ: 'When the time had drawn near which the Lord Jesus daily
points out to his faithful, especially when he says in the Gospel, "if
any one wants to follow me, let him deny himself and take up his
cross and follow me", there was a strong movement through all parts
of Gaul.'[13] A striking variant of this idea appears in the *Song of
Antioch*. There are problems about the text and authorship of this
poem, but it contains a remarkable prediction of the First Crusade by
the crucified Christ:

> 'Friends!', says our Lord, 'You know for certainty
> 'That a new race will come from overseas.
> 'No pagans will live here or in the East;
> 'The Franks will then deliver all the land,

[11] Saewulf, 12 (Wilkinson/Hakluyt, 103).
[12] B. McGinn, '*Iter Sancti Sepulchri*: The Piety of the First Crusaders', in B. K. Lack-
ner and K. R. Philp (eds.), *Essays on Medieval Civilization* (London, 1978), 33–71.
[13] *Gesta Francorum*, 1, quoting Matthew 16: 24.

'And those who go on this great pilgrimage (*errement*),
'Their soul will enter our salvation.'[14]

Without doubt, the most splendid of these first announcements of a new age was the lyrical passage of Raymond of Aguilers (see inset below).

Urban II did not live to hear of the fall of Jerusalem, and we do not know what theological interpretation he would have offered of the victory. He had been thinking in terms of a change in the course of history designed by God, who was offering liberation to the oppressed churches of the East and Spain, but those who were at present at the events of 15 July went beyond this, finding in the Scriptures and history the deep plan of God to restore Jerusalem to his people. Raymond's account must have been completed by 1105, at the latest. Already at the end of 1099 Archbishop Manasses of Reims, like Raymond, had seen the victory as a divine act, writing of the report he had received, 'which we believe to have come not by human power, but from the divine majesty, that is that Jerusalem is standing on high with the joy and delight which it has in our days so gloriously received from its God': a reference, if rather an imprecise one, to the liberation language of Isaiah.[15]

Even those of conservative disposition could rejoice in the victory. Albert or Adalbert of Aachen was a senior member of the imperial collegiate church there and the author of the largest of all the histories of the Crusade, the *Historia Hierosolymitana*. It represented the German or Lotharingian tradition of thought, which was to have a major impact on crusading historiography. Albert offered a largely traditional interpretation of what had happened, using categories that would have been familiar in Carolingian and post-Carolingian thinking. The expedition was interpreted as a pilgrimage. Its source lay in the pilgrim traffic, specifically in the distress of the pilgrim Peter the Hermit at the desolation which he had found in the church of Jerusalem and the appeal that he brought back to the West on its behalf. The word 'pilgrim' occurs seventy-six times in Albert's first six books, which were devoted to the events of the Crusade itself. *Milites Christi* was a new confection, which Albert did not care to use: his standard word for the crusading host was simply *Christiani*. Papal privilege, indulgences, and repentance for sin had no place, or only a marginal place, in his thought about the Crusade. While he certainly did not deny the proud title of 'martyr' to those who fell in war

[14] S. Duparc-Quioc (ed.), *La Chanson d'Antioche* (Paris, 1976), xi. 27.
[15] *Kreuzzugsbriefe*, xx. 175–6.

Raymond of Aguilers on 15 July

His words deserve full quotation:

With the fall of the city, it was a delight to see the devotion of the pilgrims before the Lord's Sepulchre: how they rejoiced, exulting and singing a new song to the Lord, for their mind offered to the victorious and triumphant God sacrifices of praise which they could not express in words. A new day, new gladness, new and everlasting happiness, the completion of labour and devotion, demanded new words and new songs from everyone. I say that this day, to be famous in all ages to come, turned all our sorrows and labours to joy and exultation. This day, I say, saw the abolition of all paganism, the confirmation of Christianity, the renewal of our faith ... On this day the apostles were expelled from Jerusalem and dispersed throughout the world. On this day the sons of the apostles reclaimed for God and the fathers the city and homeland (*patriam*). This day, 15 July, is celebrated to the praise and glory of the name of God, who gave to the prayers of his church the city and homeland which he promised to the forefathers and restored to their children in faith and blessing. On this day we sang the office of the resurrection, because on this day he who rose from the dead by his power, revived us by his grace.

In these words there are many echoes of Biblical passages, especially from the Psalms, which provided the references to the 'new song' (Psalms 33: 3, 96: 1, and 144: 9) and the 'new day' (Psalm 118: 24: 'this is the day the Lord has made'). Raymond, however, is not engaged in a search for proof-texts to define the theology of the unexpected liberation. He seeks for a devotional expression of it from the liturgy and history of the church. The singing of the office of the resurrection on the day is significant, for this was the day when the empty Sepulchre was recovered for Christendom. Raymond invokes the history of the apostles: the feast *divisio apostolorum* was celebrated on 15 July to mark the departure of the apostles from Jerusalem to preach the Gospel throughout the world, and the return of the Christians to Jerusalem could be seen as part of the divine plan. It is tempting to think that the reference to the celebration of 15 July already indicates that it had at once become a special feast of the church of Jerusalem.

For the text, see Raymond, *Liber*, 151.

against the unbeliever, his interpretation of martyrdom was cautious. A speech by Bishop Adhemar at the siege of Nicaea represented this approach: 'O people dedicated to God, you have left everything for the love of God, riches, fields, vineyards and castles. Here and now there is perpetual life for every one who is crowned with martyrdom in this battle.' There is a strong echo here of the Gospel message that 'every one who has left houses or brothers or sisters or father or mother or children or lands for my name's sake, will receive a hundredfold, and inherit eternal life' (Matthew 19: 29). Albert did not embrace the more excited ideas of martyrdom that are found in some crusading literature: he sometimes used *martyrium* simply for suffering, and he several time emphasized the traditional style of burial given to one of the crusading leaders, accompanied by 'a handsome distribution of alms for the salvation of their soul'.[16] The idea of the crusaders as pilgrims was certainly not confined to the pages of Albert, although other authors found the combination of pilgrim and warrior paradoxical. Robert of Reims reported a dispute between a group of Egyptian ambassadors and the leaders of the Crusade. The ambassadors expressed their shock at an unwelcome innovation: 'they are astonished that you thus seek the Sepulchre of your Lord in arms, wiping out their people from territory which they have long possessed, indeed—what is obscene for pilgrims—killing them with the edge of the sword'. The reply was that 'no sensible person should be surprised if we come with arms to the Sepulchre of our God, and wipe out your people from those lands; because any of our own who used to come here with wallet and staff were insulted with shocking ridicule, and bearing the shame of mockery were even put to death'.[17] Robert was evidently reflecting Western concern about the militarization of pilgrimage. For him the heart of the matter was that peaceful pilgrimage had become impossible, and that its safety had to be guaranteed by military action.

The first decade after the conquest of Jerusalem saw the composition of three major works on the First Crusade by Abbot Guibert of Nogent, Abbot Baudri of Bourgueil (also archbishop of Dol), and Robert, monk of Reims. The three have strong family resemblances. They were all written by Benedictine monks from the north of France, and all drew on the *Gesta Francorum*, amplifying it from

---

[16] C. Morris, 'The Aims and Spirituality of the First Crusade as Seen Through the Eyes of Albert of Aachen', *Reading Medieval Studies*, 16 (1990), 99–117.

[17] Robert the Monk, v. 1–2 (RHC Occ. iii. 791–2).

interviews with returned crusaders. They were written with the intention of dignifying the lame style of their source with more elevated writing. These historians of the First Crusade addressed themselves to answering the question, What was God's purpose in bringing about this new dispensation? The most systematic, and to modern minds the most far-fetched, explanation was offered by Guibert. Drawing on a version of the 'last emperor' prophecies, he explained that the world could only come to an end when the Christians had been persecuted by Antichrist in Jerusalem. Accordingly, the victory of 1099 came to have a central role in the divine purpose for history. Closer to the main line of thinking, Baudri of Bourgueil reported a sermon preached outside the walls during the siege of the city which glorified its historical role: 'In this city, which stands before us, Christ redeemed you; in it, God instituted Christianity; and from it the mystery of Christian faith came out to us. We have come from our own lands, to pray here and kiss the Sepulchre of our God. This, which you see, is the cause of all our labour.' Its greatest glory, however, was to bring to the minds of men the Jerusalem above: 'Yet this Jerusalem is heavenly: this is the form of that city to which we aspire . . . Indeed, if you will consider it rightly and duly, this Jerusalem which you see, to which you have come, where you are standing, prefigures and signifies that city in the heavens.'[18] This does not mean that Baudri was confusing the two Jerusalems. The function of the earthly Jerusalem was to bring men to the heavenly one: in the context of the Crusade, that meant that they must bravely offer their lives for its capture. The thinkers of the time were concerned to define the relationship of the two Jerusalems, but the victory of 1099 did not lead them to confuse them.

The most interesting comments on the new situation were perhaps those made by the German writer Ekkehard of Aura in his *Hierosolomita*. He pointed out how there were now to be found on all lips prophecies that had long been almost forgotten, such as Isaiah 66: 10–11: 'Rejoice with Jerusalem, and be glad for her, all you who love her; rejoice with her in joy, all you who mourn over her; that you may suck and be satisfied with her consoling breasts.' He then explained the new significance such words had assumed:

These and a thousand other prophecies, although they refer by analogy to that Jerusalem, our mother, which is above; yet they urge the weaker members, who have drunk from the breasts of that consolation which has been

---

[18] Baudri, iv. 13 (RHC Occ. iv. 100–1).

proclaimed or will be proclaimed, for the contemplation of or participation in such a great joy, to submit themselves to danger literally (*historialiter*) by actually going. For example, we know a man who thought in a vision that he was singing that canticle *I was glad* with the alleluia . . . By this he was so inspired to that pilgrimage that his spirit had no rest until by many tribulations he could adore in bodily presence, having arrived where the feet of the Lord had stood.[19]

The thought here is close to that of Baudri's sermon to the crusading army: the conquest of the earthly city, and pilgrimage to it, offered a road that laymen could take, while monks were pursuing the way of contemplation to the Jerusalem above. Even while symbolic use was made of the name of Jerusalem, a commonsense awareness of the distinction between the two cities continued to prevail. When Bishop Altmann of Trent died in 1149 after he came back from the Second Crusade, it was noted that 'after his return from the Lord's Sepulchre, desiring to behold the heavenly Jerusalem . . . he left the world and went to the Lord'.[20]

Some of the main histories of the Crusade, including Albert of Aachen, Fulcher of Chartres, and William of Tyre, continued their narrative well beyond 1099. In this sense, they expressed the idea of God's continuing care for the brethren in the East and of the lasting responsibility of Westerners for them. Yet, even in these works, we sense that a chapter had finished in 1099, and that there has been a change in the character of history. The sense of providential guidance that was so marked a feature of the progress of the crusaders is not sustained in subsequent decades. A description of a divine act has been replaced by a the history of a kingdom: Latin Jerusalem.

REBUILDING ZION[21]

The city which the crusaders conquered was in a poor condition, the result of long neglect, the depredations of Caliph al-Hakim, and the damage done in the conquest of June 1099. The view of the crusaders of the conditions they inherited is reflected in Baudri's report of Urban II's address at Clermont:

[19] Ekkehard, *Hierosolymita* xxxiv (RHC Occ. v. 38–9). The 'canticle' is one of the so-called 'pilgrim' psalms, 122: 1: 'I was glad when they said to me, "Let us go to the house of the Lord." '

[20] E. Curzel, *I canonici e il capitolo della cattedrale di Trento* (Bologna, 2001), 61 n.

[21] I have borrowed the title for this section from Bernard Hamilton in 'Rebuilding Zion', SCH 14 (1977), 105–16.

Of holy Jerusalem, brethren, we dare not speak, for we are exceedingly afraid and ashamed to speak of it. This very city, in which, as you all know, Christ himself suffered for us, because our sins demanded it, has been reduced to the pollution of paganism and, I say it to our disgrace, withdrawn from the service of God . . . Who now serves the church of the Blessed Mary in the valley of Josaphat or Jehoshaphat, in which church she herself was buried in body? But why do we pass over the Temple of Solomon, nay of the Lord, in which the barbarous nations placed their idols contrary to human and divine law? Of the Sepulchre of the Lord we have refrained from speaking, since some of you have seen with your own eyes to what abominations it has been given over. The Turks violently took from it the offerings which you brought there for alms in such vast amounts, and in addition they scoffed much and often at your religion . . . How precious would be the longed-for, incomparable place of the Lord's burial, even if God failed there to perform the yearly miracle.[22]

We cannot say with confidence how much of this content would have been familiar to Urban himself. Nearly everything in the speech that Baudri assigned to him became prominent in the thought of the First Crusaders: the interest in the Temple, the presence of idols there, the desolation of the Holy Sepulchre, the levies on pilgrims, and the importance of the Easter fire. It sounds as if the speech is also addressing the failure of the fire to materialize in the year after the victory of the Crusaders. How much of this was baggage that they carried in their heads from the West, how much developed in the course of the expedition, it is impossible to say.

The new arrivals, then, found a scene of desolation. Most of the places sacred to Christian memory were now marked, if at all, by the ruins of Byzantine chapels. Saewulf, one of the first pilgrims to arrive after the Latin conquest, recorded his impressions of the ruins of former churches outside the walls of the city:

There is a very beautiful church built there. But this church has been totally destroyed by the pagans . . . This too had a very noble and lovely church, but it is in ruins because of the pagans . . . [At Bethlehem] nothing habitable is left there by the Saracens, but it is all ruined, exactly as it is in all the other places outside the walls of Jerusalem, except the monastery of the Blessed Virgin Mary.[23]

Services were quickly established or re-established after 1099 in a series of sites of major importance, in addition to the shrine churches

---

[22] Baudri, i. 4 (RHC Occ. iv. 13); tr. A. C. Krey, *The First Crusade* (Gloucester, Mass., 1958), 33–4.

[23] Saewulf, 21–2 (Wilkinson/Hakluyt, 108).

at Jerusalem. Bernard Hamilton has argued that 'the public performance of the Latin liturgy in the churches of Syria was the justifica-
tion of the crusading movement'.[24] It has often been suggested that
the desolate state of the holy places led to a rapid campaign of
rebuilding, but there were considerations pulling in the opposite direction: the desire to provide a magnificent site for the liturgy may
have been balanced by a desire to preserve what was left from the
sacred buildings of the past. The most obvious place for the new
Latin rulers to begin their building work would have been the fabric
of the Holy Sepulchre, but the character and date of their work there
is uncertain.

Whatever hesitations the Franks felt about interfering with the
sacred fabric, there were reasons that drove them towards the extensive redesign of the site as a whole. Even the Muslim conquerors who
recovered Jerusalem in 1187 acknowledged how the Franks had
transformed the city:

Islam received back a place which it had left almost uninhabited, but which
the care of the unbelievers had transformed into a Paradise garden . . . Those
accursed ones defended with the lance and sword this city, . . . where they
had founded churches and the palaces of the Templars and the Hospitallers
. . . One sees on every side houses as pleasant as their gardens and bright
with white marble and columns decorated with leaves, which make them
look like living trees.[25]

The Augustinian regular canons who were introduced in 1114
required accommodation and a church adapted to their liturgy. This
in itself was a major project, but still more important were the sanctity of the place and the triumphalist spirit of the time, which
required a construction to equal or surpass anything in the Mediterranean world. At the heart of the new building, an innate conserva-
tism continued to be displayed: the great dome and the surrounding
area were preserved as they were. So (perhaps) was the edicule which
it protected. The great dome was echoed by a new and smaller one,
belonging to the crusader church. Robert Ousterhout has
emphasized that the twelfth-century rebuilding preserved many features because they were seen as sacred, even when they appeared
clumsy in the context of the new designs: 'the architecture . . . had
come to be regarded as sacred, and . . . the building itself had become

---

[24] B. Hamilton, *The Latin Church in the Crusader States* (London, 1980), 361–2.
[25] Saladin's companion, al-Fadel, cited Hamilton, 'Rebuilding Zion', in SCH 14
(1977), 116.

The Crusaders and the Edicule

The edicule, or fabric surrounding the Holy Sepulchre itself, had been extensively demolished by al-Hakim at the beginning of the eleventh century. We have some quite good sources for its appearance in the twelfth century after its restoration. Visiting pilgrims such as the Russian Abbot Daniel (1106/8) and the German Theoderic (1169/74) provided descriptions of the whole church, and especially of the edicule, and there are exact representations of its fifteenth-century state in the West. We therefore have a record of the new design: but who built it and when?

Its reconstruction may well have been undertaken as part of the general repairs carried out by Byzantine emperors in the first half of the eleventh century. No contemporary tells us this, but common sense connects many of the new details with the situation at the time. The edicule was covered with marble, very possibly because its surface had been ravaged in the time of al-Hakim. This meant, however, that pilgrims could no longer touch the sacred rock itself. Hence, the marble slab on the face was pierced by three 'port-holes' to enable pilgrims to reach the rock of the tomb. These port-holes became a sort of trademark for Western representations. A cupola was built over the edicule. This would provide a valuable shelter for the tomb, perhaps at a time before the repair of the dome above it. There are therefore quite strong reasons for supposing that the basic structure of the Holy Sepulchre was inherited by the Franks from the Byzantines. The only thing that Abbot Daniel specifically ascribed to the Franks was the provision of a large figure of Christ on the edicule. If he is right, it must have been placed there quickly after the fall of Jerusalem; and in any case, it was not to be a permanent feature. There are other options for the timing of the new edicule. Virgilio Corbo argued for its extensive rebuilding in 1119. Presumably (on this interpretation) it was at this point that the statue of Christ disappeared and the leading medieval features, which we have mentioned above, were built. Certainly the Latin inscription around the cornice must be the work of the Franks, and it seems that the mosaic work in the outer chamber, including the scene of the burial of

Christ and of the three Marys at the Tomb, had a Latin inscription. A dating to 1119 is speculative, and Martin Biddle is
dubious about it. By the mid-twelfth century the edicule had
taken a form that it largely retained until the end of the Middle
Ages, but the main features may be associated with the earlier
Byzantine reconstruction.

Biddle, *Tomb*, 89–91.

a venerated relic'.[26] A striking feature was the inclusion of the sacred
sites under one roof, which would now cover the Sepulchre, Calvary,
the chapel of St Helena where the holy cross had been found, the
navel of the world or *omphalos*, the prison of Christ, and the stone of
anointing: for William of Tyre, this union of sites was the most
remarkable feature of the work of the Latins. The church was richly
decorated with wall-paintings and mosaics. These have largely disappeared, and their loss prevents us from discovering how large an
influence its style had upon the development of church decoration in
the West.

One of the major considerations in the great rebuilding was
undoubtedly pilgrim demand. The overall design of the Augustinian
church echoed that of the pilgrimage churches that were being built
in the West during the twelfth century. A south portal was designed
to give access to the rotunda and (by an outside staircase) to the
Calvary chapel: to Westerners, familiar with south entrances to transepts, it would be an obvious arrangement, but it was a striking
innovation in the context of Jerusalem. The lintel over the doorway
should probably be seen as a sculptural address to pilgrims. Given the
disappearance of so much of the internal decoration throughout the
church, the lintel forms one of our best pieces of evidence of the
programmatic intentions of the canons in the new building: but
unfortunately its message is problematic.

The completion of the new building has usually been dated from
an inscription at the entrance to the Golgotha chapel, which gives
the date as 1149, but it is probable that this refers only to the chapel
itself. The finishing of the whole vast project can be more naturally
dated to the period around 1167. This date would tally with the

---

[26] R. Ousterhout, 'Architecture as Relic . . .: The Stones of the Holy Sepulchre',
Journal of the Society of Architectural Historians, 62 (2003), 13.

The South Transept Lintel

There were really two lintels. One, over the eastern doorway, was a vine scroll. The other was historiated, presenting a series of biblical events to the viewers. Both went long ago to the Rockefeller Archaeological Museum in Jerusalem, where they seem to have taken up permanent residence The historiated lintel is badly damaged in its central areas, which were already difficult to decipher by 1345. Reading from left to right, its themes begin with the resurrection of Lazarus at Bethany and (secondly) the meeting of Christ with Mary and Martha on the way there. If we disregard the sections that are difficult to decipher, we come at the other end to the entry of Christ into Jerusalem and finally the Last Supper. This order seems wrong: the meeting on the road to Bethany should precede the raising of Lazarus there, and not follow it. The selection is odd, too: the meeting can scarcely be viewed as a central element in the Holy Week drama. The most probable explanation of a difficult collection of scenes is that the lintel was intended to illustrate to pilgrims the Palm Sunday procession, beginning at Bethany, passing the place of meeting and of the summons to collect the ass and colt (a possible interpretation of the damaged section), and arriving into the city through the Golden Gate. Even on this interpretation, the use of the Last Supper as the final scene is surprising, since it was traditionally located at another of the Augustinian houses, the one at the Cenacle on Mount Sion.

A. Borg, 'Observations on the Historiated Lintel of the Holy Sepulchre, Jerusalem, *JWCI* 32 (1969), 25–40; H. Buschhausen, 'Die Fassade der Grabeskirche zu Jerusalem', J. Folda (ed.), *Crusader Art in the Twelfth Century* (Oxford, 1982), 71–96; N. Rosen-Ayalon, 'The Façade of the Holy Sepulchre', *Rivista degli Studi Orientali*, 59 (1985), 289–96; N. Kenaan-Kedar, 'The Figurative Western Lintel of the Church of the Holy Sepulchre in Jerusalem', in Goss (ed.), *Meeting of Two Worlds*, 123–32; and M. Lindner, 'Topography and Iconography in Twelfth-Century Jerusalem', *Horns of Hattin*, 81–98.

FIG 6.1 View of the crusader church of the Holy Sepulchre from the south-east. The great dome of the Anastasis can be seen left centre; on top is the section that was originally the opening or opaion; to its right, the smaller dome of the twelfth-century church of the canons of the Holy Sepulchre, and beyond that the crusader apse. The bell-tower and doorway are in front of front of the Anastasis.

representation of the new building, with the divine hand blessing it from heaven, on the coinage minted under King Amalric I (1163–74).[27] Around the Holy Sepulchre a whole series of sites were identified and provided with stories and places of worship.

The new attitude to Jerusalem was manifested by the treatment of the Temple area. The Byzantine emperors had left this in ruins, thus advertising the destruction of the Temple as part of the divine purposes. The building of the Dome of the Rock there, along with the al-Aqsa mosque, had turned it into a Muslim response to the Christian city. The area was now captured for Christianity. A chapter of secular canons was created there about 1105. The actions of

[27] Biddle, *Tomb*, 81–98; Folda, *Art of the Crusaders*, ch. 7.

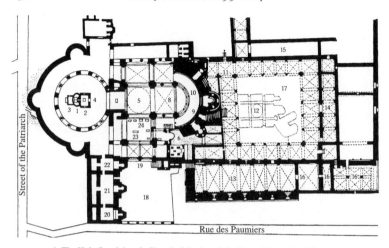

1. The Holy Sepulchre; 2. Chapel of the Angel; 3. Altar; 4. Rotunda; 5. Dome;
6. Golgotha; 7. Chapel of the Raising of the Cross; 8. Choir of the Augustinian
Canons; 9. Stairs to the Crypt of St Helena; 10 Stairs to the Augustinian cloister;
11. Entrance to the cloisters; 12. Dome of the Crypt of St Helena; 13. Refectory;
14. Chapter Room; 15. Dormitory; 16. Kitchen, office, stores; 17. Cloister
quadrangle; 18. Southern atrium; 19. Main entrance to the Basilica; 20. Chapel of St
James; 21. Chapel of St John, former Baptistery; 22. Chapel of the Forty Martyrs;
23. Stone of Unction; 24. Royal tombs

FIG 6.2 Plan of crusader church. The tomb and Anastasis rotunda are preserved on the left (west): to the east, a choir is now provided for the canons,
with the Calvary chapel brought inside. The design, because of the special
needs of the building, is unique.

FIG 6.3 A denier of Amalric, issued in the 1160s. The image shows the
(newly completed?) church of the Holy Sepulchre, and can be interpreted,
starting from the top, as the hole or *oculus*, the ribs of the dome, the main
fabric of the church, and/or the Sepulchre itself. Coin in author's possession.

Christ that were supposed to have taken place in the Temple were enriched by new identifications: it was regarded, for example, as the place where Jesus had been circumcised. The destruction of the Temple in AD 70 was, however, well known and made the identification of the site of events awkward. Legend accordingly held that it had been 'restored' by a later builder, rather than replaced as was in fact the case. The fully fledged account is to be found by about 1130.[28] The sacred rock was covered with marble, and the building was used as the choir of a house of Augustinian canons. Much of it was left intact, but the Temple was turned into a Christian church, with Latin inscriptions replacing those of the Koran and an inscription from the hymn *Urbs beata Jerusalem.* The great gold cross placed above the dome specially horrified Muslims. The al-Aqsa mosque (identified as the Temple or Palace of Solomon) became the Templar headquarters. The treatment of the Temple area was part of a project to restore (or more accurately to create) a wholly Christian city with the Old Testament sites absorbed into the new revelation, but the Temple was not the most important of the shrines. When Theoderic described his visit to the city, he 'thought it best to begin at the Holy of Holies, that is at the Sepulchre of the Lord'.[29]

The accounts which were given of the history of the Temple site warns us that the attempt to identify the locations of historical events produced some strange distortions. Some supposed events referred to parables, such as that of Dives and Lazarus, and others were fictional episodes such as the meeting with St Veronica on the road to the crucifixion. Sometimes, though, important elements of history were preserved in the narrative. The extension of the walls that brought the Sepulchre inside was still known, even if some writers ascribed it inaccurately to Hadrian. The anonymous text of about 1220, the *Citez de Jherusalem,* noted that 'Jerusalem is no longer in the place where it stood when Jesus Christ was crucified and was raised again from death to life. When Jesus Christ was on earth the city of Jerusalem was on Mount Sion, but it is no longer there . . .

---

[28] *Work on Geography* (Wilkinson/Hakluyt, 199). The Russian pilgrim Abbot Daniel (1106–8), knew that 'the church which is there now was built by a Saracen *chieftain* called Amor ['Umar]' (132).

[29] A. J. Wharton, 'The Baptistery of the Holy Sepulchre in Jerusalem and the Politics of Sacred Landscape', *DOP* 46 (1992), 324; Y. Friedman, 'The City of the King of Kings: Jerusalem in the Crusader Period', *Centrality,* 190–216; Theoderic in Wilkinson/Hakluyt, 278.

The church of the Holy Sepulchre as it is now, and Mount Calvary, were, when Jesus Christ was crucified, outside the wall.'[30]

The building campaign spread throughout and around Latin Jerusalem. In the south of the city the Byzantine church at Mount Sion was repaired, and extensive buildings added to it—it was supposed to be the house of St John, the scene of the last supper, the coming of the Spirit, and the dormition of the Blessed Virgin. There were many improvements in the facilities of the city such as a better water supply, accommodation, and market arrangements. There are relatively few twelfth-century houses surviving, perhaps because the conquerors seized existing dwellings by placing their arms on the doors, and did not need to do a great deal of domestic building. Away from Jerusalem, there was reconstruction at important shrines, as well as the discovery of other sites for Biblical events. The church at Bethlehem was given an ambitious decorative scheme by a Syrian painter and mosaic worker, Ephrem the monk, to celebrate the marriage of Amalric with the niece of the Byzantine Emperor Manuel I in 1167. On occasions, new buildings commemorated pilgrim history itself: the burial-place of Samuel, in the Judaean hills, came to be known as Mountjoy because those travelling the road from Jaffa caught their first glimpse of the holy city from there, and it became the site of a Premonstratensian abbey. This programme was financed by the munificence of local crusaders, donations by pilgrims, and in some cases magnificent endowments by Western kings and princes. Until recently, the assumption was that the art and culture of the crusading states were almost totally Western in character. The cultural mix at Bethlehem was always undeniable, but it was regarded as an exception. The work of scholars such as Bianca Kühnel has now, however, suggested that the process of rebuilding Sion was not a pure intrusion of Western styles. Designs were responsive to local tradition. The church of the Holy Sepulchre itself had an ambulatory with radiating chapels, reflecting (or inspiring?) the churches of the Compostela roads in France. Yet nowhere else in Palestine was this matched. All other churches retained the locally traditional design of a square east end issuing in three chapels standing side by side, as at St Anne (Jerusalem). Even the design of the Holy Sepulchre site was special in having its focus at the western end of the building. Church decoration responded to Syrian and Byzantine influences, as well as to the particular character of the pilgrimage site.

---

[30] Anon, *City of Jerusalem*, PPTS 6. 2–3.

The pattern of worship followed by the canons of the Holy Sepulchre has been clarified in an outstanding study by Cristina Dondi. From the beginning, they followed a Latin rite, primarily extracted from books brought with them by French clergy. The orders of service consequently preserved technical features distinctive of some diocesan usages in northern France and favourite French saints. Subsequently, the influence of Augustinian uses can naturally be traced in their liturgy. We know that there was a *magister scholasticus* at the Holy Sepulchre by 1103, and this suggests a concern to produce service books and to train clergy in their use. A later breviary (Vatican 659) recorded that it was compiled from a series of books and then revised by the common and unanimous consent of the canons, although it is not clear when this took place. These observances designed for the canons, which to our eyes curiously understate the special character of the Holy Sepulchre, were accompanied by public ceremonies recorded in a thirteenth-century manuscript preserved at Barletta in Apulia.[31] These included inheritances from the Greek past and elements reflecting the new order in Jerusalem. On Palm Sunday the patriarch went in procession before daybreak to Bethany 'where the Lord resurrected Lazarus'. He was accompanied by the heads and congregations of the houses of Mount Sion, the Mount of Olives, and St Mary of Josaphat. They returned to Jerusalem with the patriarch personally carrying the cross, and all singing suitable hymns such as Theodulph's 'All glory, laud, and honour'. They entered by the Golden Gate, and the ceremonies ended with a procession to the Temple of the Lord and a station there. The ceremonies had a Jerusalem ingredient, which would have made them particularly impressive. The Holy Saturday liturgy was arranged round the need to wait for the coming of the new fire. On Easter Day, the *Quem queritis* could be staged outside the Holy Sepulchre itself. Some of the Jerusalem features were simply retentions of ceremonies that existed in 1099. This was notably true of the ceremony of the new fire on Easter eve. It is more difficult to account for the elaborate public processions, which could not have continued throughout the centuries of Muslim dominance. One wonders if there was a deliberate revival of some of the rituals described by Egeria, whose work was certainly known to Peter the Deacon at Monte Cassino during the first half of the twelfth century.

[31] C. Kohler (ed.), 'Un rituel et un bréviaire du St-Sépulcre de Jérusalem', *Revue de l'Orient Latin*, 8 (1900–1), 383–500. See the inset 'The Barletta Compilation', Ch. 10 below.

There were other major festivals peculiar to Jerusalem. The most distinctive was the celebration of the fall of the city, on 15 July each year, *in liberatione sancte civitatis Ierusalem*. There is no reason to doubt that this celebration went back to the fall of the city, and it has been remarked that in it 'one observes . . . an impressive adoption of the traditional attributes of Old Testament Jerusalem in a new Christian city, with none of the reservations and qualifications that were evolved during centuries of mainly spiritual interpretation of Jerusalem'.[32] The procession left the city and 'turned to the place where the city was taken', the point on the walls where Duke Godfrey had forced an entry, and which was now marked with a cross. There, a sermon was preached to the people. The Barletta manuscript rarely mentions pilgrims specifically, but the ritual, with its dramatic evocations of Biblical and historical events in the places where they were thought to have happened, would have been highly meaningful to them. It has been said of the 15 July festival that 'the entire service seems to have been designed primarily with the Jerusalem pilgrimage in mind'.[33] There were also days of special commemoration for those who died on the First Crusade and for Duke Godfrey, the first Latin ruler.

PILGRIMS

The First Crusade did not restore the old pilgrim route through Constantinople. Anatolia was still divided among contending Christian and Muslim powers. The main expansion in the pilgrim traffic took place by sea, beginning with arrivals at Jaffa recorded by the pilgrim Saewulf in 1101/3. Pilgrimage was, at first, a perilous enterprise. The dangers of the Mediterranean crossing were exacerbated by the inadequacy of Jaffa as a harbour and by the insecurity of Christian control in the Syrian waters, where at first many of the main harbours remained under Muslim government. Saewulf tells us how, just after he had landed, twenty-three of the thirty ships in the harbour were wrecked in a storm, and his ship only just escaped capture on the way back. After 1104 Acre provided pilgrims with an excellent harbour, and gradually the whole coast was brought under control: the last two ports, Tyre and Ascalon, fell in 1124 and 1153

---

[32] A. Linder, 'The Liturgy of the Liberation of Jerusalem', *Mediaeval Studies*, 52 (1990), 130.
[33] Ibid. 129.

respectively. Ascalon had posed a particularly severe problem to pilgrims, because it was a major Egyptian military base, and the road from Jaffa to Jerusalem was less than a day's ride away. Saewulf complained that 'the Saracens, who are continually plotting an ambush against Christians, were hiding in the caves of the hills and among rocky caverns', and gave a horrendous account of the bodies that were to be seen lying unburied beside the road.[34]

The danger and expense of the journey did not prevent the growth of a large pilgrim traffic. Within a few years, the Russian visitor Daniel was recording deaths at the Holy Saturday ceremonies because of the overcrowding in the congregation, and two generations later John of Würzburg was amazed at the mixture of visitors he found at Jerusalem: 'Greeks, Bulgars, Latins, Germans, Hungarians, Scots, people of Navarre, Britons, Angles, Franks, Ruthenians, Bohemians, Georgians, Armenians, Jacobites, Syrians, Nestorians, Indians, Egyptians, Copts, Capheturici, Maronites and very many others.'[35] It is noteworthy that this account comes from the period after the Second Crusade, when it is sometimes supposed failure had made pilgrimage less popular. In 1169 Pope Alexander III observed that the Holy Sepulchre is famous 'because it is much visited'. In 1181 he said that he derived his knowledge of events in Syria from the 'common report of travellers'.[36] Theoderic mentioned that on one day, Wednesday of Easter week, a season when the number would be at its largest, he saw over seventy pilgrim ships in harbour at Acre. They must represent thousands of Latin visitors.[37]

True, there was a reservation in the minds of some writers. Monks, who were committed to the search for the heavenly Jerusalem, should not leave their community to travel to Palestine. Pope Urban himself had been opposed to their participation. 'Going to Jerusalem', observed Abbot Geoffrey of Vendôme, 'is commanded to laymen and forbidden to monks by the apostolic see. I know this', he added with conviction, 'because I personally heard the speech of the lord Pope Urban when he ordered the laity to go on pilgrimage to Jerusalem, and forbade that pilgrimage to monks.'[38] At almost all periods

---

[34] Saewulf, 7–8 (Wilkinson/Hakluyt, 100).
[35] Wilkinson/Hakluyt, 167, 273.
[36] ep. 626 (*PL* 200 600A); ep. 1504 (*PL* 1294C).
[37] Wilkinson/Hakluyt, 310.
[38] G. Giordanengo (ed.), *Geoffroy de Vendôme: Œuvres* (Turnhoult, 1996), ep. 196, probably 1122–4.

there were monks who made the earthly journey, but the practice was often criticized.[39] Reservations were expressed about laymen, too. Bishop Hildebert of Le Mans protested when Count Geoffrey of Anjou set out for Compostela in 1127: 'whoever undertakes government is bound to obedience, against which he offends if he abandons it.' In the same way, Abbot Suger and other advisers urged Louis VII not to participate in the Second Crusade. It was only too possible, moreover, to go on pilgrimage for the wrong reasons. Honorius' *Elucidarium* warned its readers against those who finance their journeys by extortion, or who 'gad about holy places out of idle curiosity or a desire for human praise'.[40]

The expansion in pilgrimage led to its increasing codification. The insignia of a pilgrim was his staff and wallet (the *pera* or *scarsella*), and these had been the accepted signs for some centuries. There was at first no formal blessing of them; the first known German formulary for the ceremony is from the early eleventh century. The crusades led to a rapidly expanding demand for it. Shortly after the First Crusade Ekkehard commented on the innovation of giving a sword as well as staff and wallet to pilgrims: 'among these peoples, massing at the churches in greater hordes than can be believed, a priestly blessing bestowed, according to a new rite, swords with staffs and wallets'. It is not clear whether Ekkehard was describing the whole rite as innovation, or whether the innovation was the inclusion of the sword.[41] The bestowal of the cross was slow to appear in liturgical books. A further element in the formalization of pilgrimage was the appearance of badges, which apparently originated in the practice of bringing back palm-leaves from Jericho or scallops from northern Spain as the sign of a completed pilgrimage. In the course of the twelfth century, ecclesiastical authorities began to require these as proof of a completed pilgrimage, and metal badges came to be worn by participants. A striking statue designed for the priory of Belval in Lorraine about 1160 appears to show Count Hugh of Vaudémont being greeted by his wife on his return from the Second Crusade. He is wearing a cross on his chest and a wallet, with a pilgrim staff, and his hair and clothing are noticeably bedraggled. Philip II of France took the staff and wallet in 1190 when he set out on the Third Crusade, and he must surely have been wearing the cross; but on his

[39] A. H. Bredero, 'Jérusalem dans l'occident médiéval', *Mélanges offerts à R. Crozet* (Poitiers, 1966), i. 259–71.

[40] Webb, *Pilgrimage*, 246 (docs. 1, 2).

[41] Ekkehard, *Chronicon universale*, year 1099 (MGH SS VI. 214).

FIG 6.4 The walls beside the steps to the chapel of St Helena (where the cross was traditionally found) are incised by many crosses, mostly by pilgrims in the twelfth century.

premature return from the expedition he was welcomed with his followers by Pope Celestine III 'and although they had not fulfilled their vow, he gave palms to them and hung crosses on their necks, declaring that they were pilgrims'.[42] It is worth noticing that the terminology of pilgrimage remained standard among those who were undoubtedly expecting to fight. In charters issued in Burgundy on departure for the East, it was only at the time of the First Crusade that the donors spoke of their intention 'to fight against pagans and Saracens for God': the predominant language after that was simply of pilgrimage.[43]

The interest in travel to the East was reflected in the demand for guidebooks, the output of which increased hugely in the twelfth century. Some visitors give us a more serious description of the architecture than survives from any earlier century, perhaps because in

[42] N. Kenaan-Kedar and B. Z. Kedar, 'The Significance of a Twelfth-Century Sculptural Group: *Le Retour du Croisé*', *Dei gesta per Francos*, 29–44; E.-R. Labande, 'Pellegrini o crociati?', *Aevum*, 54 (1980), 217–30.

[43] C. Robin, 'Le motivazioni dei crociati', *Crociate*, 133–40.

the West they were living in an architectural boom and were more
familiar with the subject. Saewulf (1101/3), an Englishman by his
name, and the Russian Abbot Daniel (1106/8) both provided valuable
information, and so, after them, did John of Würzburg and Theoderic
(both about 1170). Such accounts are specially informative for the
modern historian, but the interests of most pilgrims lay elsewhere.
They wanted to know about how the sites related to the Gospel
events: 'it was the outer cave into which the women entered when
they said, "Who will roll the stone away for us?" ' They were also
keen on measurements, presumably because they wanted to rehearse
them back at home, and incorporate them in memorial buildings:
'The church of the Holy Sepulchre is round, and has the pre-
eminence. It is 74 feet in diameter between the columns, apart from
the apses, which project 30 feet away all round.'[44] They wanted
routes, as well. Odo of Deuil's major history of the Second Crusade
was written in part to provide advice for later travellers: 'Never will
there fail to be pilgrims to the Holy Sepulchre, and they will, I hope,
be more cautious because of our experiences.'[45] Other writers had
in mind the needs of those who were unable to travel to the East.
Theoderic said that he had written

in order to satisfy . . . the wishes of those who cannot personally follow us
there, and cannot reach the places with their eyes or hear them with their
ears. Every reader will realize how much trouble this work has been to me, in
order that in reading it, or having read it, he may learn to have Christ always
in mind.[46]

His purpose was to lead them to salvation: 'Having him in mind he
must be eager to love; loving him who suffered for him, he must
suffer with him.'

   Pilgrim accounts did not follow a standard pattern. John of
Würzburg began with the Temple, and seems to be structuring his
description around the sequence of events in the Gospel, in so far
as these could be put in topographical order. A few years later,
Theoderic began immediately with the most important objective
of all, the church of the Holy Sepulchre. There are even curious
discrepancies within an individual narrative. Saewulf announced
clearly that 'I was on my way to Jerusalem in order to pray at the

---

[44] A brief anonymous account, PPTS 6. 21–2.
[45] V. G. Berry (ed.), *Odo of Deuil, De profectione Ludovici VII in orientem* (New York, 1948), 28–30.
[46] Wilkinson/Hakluyt, 274.

Lord's tomb', but in the event he said little about it, and spent more time on the Byzantine alterations to the church. Presumably these surprised him because they were not in the older account by Bede, which he knew. The classic guides were a series of interrelated editions originated, it would seem, by Fretellus, apparently a canon of Nazareth. They were designed for Western patrons around 1130; manuscripts survive in considerable numbers.[47] What was valued by the twelfth-century observer is made clear in the narrative of Nicholas, who was to become abbot of Thvera in Iceland, and who travelled about 1140:

Then it is up to Jorsalaborg; it is the most splendid of all the cities of the world . . . There is there the church in which there is the Lord's Sepulchre and the place where the Lord's cross stood, where one can clearly see Christ's blood on the stone as if it were newly bled . . . Men receive light down from heaven there on Easter eve. It is called the church of the Holy Sepulchre and it is open above over the Sepulchre. The centre of the earth is there, where the sun shines directly down from the sky on the feast of St John. Then there is the Hospital of St John the Baptist, which is the most magnificent in the whole world.[48]

THE DEVELOPMENT OF CRUSADING IDEAS

The sense of God's deliverance of his holy places dominated twelfth-century thinking, shaping ideas of Jerusalem, the nature of its architecture, and the experience of pilgrimage. In the course of the century, two new phenomena challenged contemporary ideas. The Second Crusade in 1147–9 was a vast international project. It was also a catastrophic failure, thus demanding a further assessment of God's intentions for his people and his land. In addition, from Jerusalem there emerged a series of international orders knitting the Holy Land into the fabric of Western society: the canons of the Holy Sepulchre, the Hospitallers, and the Templars. Into these innovations (the Second Crusade and its failure, and the new orders) a variety of Western writers, above all Abbot Bernard of Clairvaux, universal spokesman for the highly successful order of the Cistercians, interposed their views and convictions.

In the course of the century, noble houses and cities in the West

---

[47] The text is summarized as *The Work on Geography* in Wilkinson/Hakluyt, 12–15.
[48] J. Hill, 'From Rome to Jerusalem: An Icelandic Itinerary of the Mid-Twelfth Century', *Harvard Theological Review*, 76 (1983), 175–203.

committed themselves to continuing the work of conquest in the East. Even in Spain, the warfare against the Moors came to be envisaged as a war for Jerusalem:

Just as the soldiers (*milites*) of Christ, the faithful sons of holy church, opened the way to Jerusalem with much labour and much bloodshed, so we too should be soldiers of Christ, and—defeating his enemies the foul Saracens— should open a way which is short and much less burdensome through the regions of Spain to the Sepulchre of the Lord, assisted by his grace.[49]

The obvious occasion for the Second Crusade was an appeal from the Latins in the East because of the loss of Edessa to the Moslem leader, Zengi, in 1144. The international commitment began with Louis VII of France, but his intentions remain unclear: separately from the defence of Syria, he had in any case resolved on a peniten- tial pilgrimage. Pope Eugenius III's letter of 1145/6, *Quantum pred- ecessores*, was the first crusading bull, and was to be used as a model by subsequent popes. Eugenius seems to have been conscious that his initiative was a momentous one, and he referred no less than three times to the precedents created by Urban II. He recalled how his predecessors had 'worked for the liberation of the Eastern church', and how the Latins had 'freed from the filth of the pagans that city in which it was our Saviour's will to suffer for us and where he left us his glorious Sepulchre as a memorial of his passion'. Unhappily, 'because our sins and those of its people demanded it', Edessa had fallen to the Muslims, and we must 'recognize how great the danger is that threatens the church of God and all Christendom because of it'.[50] Given that the sins of Westerners, as well as the Eastern Christians, were to blame for what has happened, it was natural that Eugenius renewed the remission or indulgence granted at the time of the First Crusade.

Eugenius was a Cistercian, and an even more outstanding member of the Order, his former master Bernard of Clairvaux, masterminded the preaching of the Crusade. We have Bernard's ideas especially in two 'encyclicals' he issued, for the benefit of those to whom he could not personally preach.[51] In Bernard's exposition, Eugenius' proclamation of forgiveness became the occasion for an appeal for

---

[49] N. Jaspert, 'Pro nobis qui pro vobis oramus, orate', *Santiago, Roma, Jerusalén*, 189–91.

[50] *Quantum predecessores* (1146), Riley-Smith, *The Crusades*, 57–9.

[51] J. Leclercq, 'L'Encyclique de saint Bernard en faveur de la croisade', *Revue Bénédic- tine*, 81 (1971), 282–308.

conversion. Bernard also dealt with the objection, which was only too evident to the contemporary mind, that God could perfectly well save his own land without human help, and he wove his answer into a statement of God's design for human salvation that fits into his own theology of love and persuasion:

It is at his disposal to do everything he wishes, but I tell you that the Lord your God is testing you. He looks upon the sons of men, if perchance there is anyone who understands, and asks, and grieves on his behalf. God has compassion on his people, and provides to those who have greatly fallen a saving remedy.

This thinking led Bernard into a recruiting policy that did not give primary place to the military needs of the expedition: to him, the crusade was rather 'a day of abundant salvation'. The message is perhaps related to another divergence from *Quantum predecessores*: the prominence of Jerusalem in Bernard's letters. Bernard warned his hearers that Jerusalem was in danger (a threat that had not specifically appeared in the appeal of Eugenius). This threat was given a strongly feudal connotation: 'The God of heaven has begun to lose his land. His land, I say, where he was seen and spent more than thirty years as a man with men; in which the first flowers of the resurrection appeared.' Although Bernard did insert a reservation that it would not be right to fight the Saracens if they did not threaten the Christian possessions in the East, he was virtually blessing warfare against the unbeliever. Unlimited warfare also appeared in other statements about the Crusade in Palestine. One group in the army defined the purpose as 'to visit the Holy Sepulchre and . . . to wipe out our sins with the blood or the conversion of the pagans'.[52] The Cologne chronicle summarized the aims of the crusade in slightly less sanguinary terms: 'All the kingdoms of the West were moved and fired with a desire to go to Jerusalem and to visit the Sepulchre of the Lord and to fight against the Gentiles and to extend the bounds of the Christian empire in the East.'

A French poem written as a piece of recruiting propaganda indicates that many of these themes (such the desecration of the holy places and the promise of salvation by war) were being enthusiastically presented to the fighting nobility:

Pris est Rohais, ben le savez,	You heard about Edessa's fall.
Dunt crestiens sunt esmaiez.	The Christians are sore oppressed.

---

[52] Riley-Smith, *The Crusades*, 95–8; Berry (ed.), *Odo of Deuil*, 71.

Les mustiers ars e desertez:	No churches are in use at all;
Deus n'i est mais sacrifiez.	God's sacrifice is nowhere blessed.
Chivalers, cher vus purpensez,	Knights, think of this, delay no more,
Vus ki d'armes estes preisez;	All you who are accounted brave;
A celui voz cors presentez	But give your bodies to his war,
Ki pur vus fut en cruiz drecez.	Who on the cross his life once gave.
Ki ore irat od Loovis	If you with Louis will arise,
Ja mar d'enfern avrat pouur,	You need not fear the hell of fire;
Char s'alme en iert en pareïs	Your soul will go to paradise,
Od les angles nostre Segnor.	Rejoicing with the angels' choir.[53]

The international project ended in international disaster. No territory had been gained or recovered in the Holy Land, and all there remained to show for the whole effort were some advances in the Iberian peninsula. Christendom was left to make sense of God's apparent abandonment of a great enterprise. It certainly provoked anxiety and concern among writers, and seems to have had a practical impact on public opinion: in England, donations to the Cistercians and Templars were much reduced after the Crusade, while the Hospitallers were favoured instead, presumably because of their charitable work for pilgrims and others in need.[54] Similarly, a marked reduction in the number of 'departure charters' confirms the degree of disillusion with Jerusalem in the years between 1150 and 1180.[55] True, it was not the first time Christendom had known failure, for there had been bad moments in the First Crusade; but this was catastrophe on a larger scale, and it occasioned the first major debate in the West about its causes—a subject that circumstances guaranteed would be a regular theme for anxious discussion in later years.

Some writers found historical or political reasons for what had happened, blaming it on the greed of the Eastern Franks (as Gerhoh of Reichersberg did) or the treachery of the Greeks (Odo of Deuil). Odo, a confidant of Louis VII, seemed unaware of the challenge it presented to faith. In the circumstances, his remark that Louis's expedition was an 'example set forth by God for future kings' can only be regarded as fatuous.[56] The issue under discussion was a narrower one than we might have anticipated. No one at all expressed

[53] H. Gelzer, 'Zum altfranzösischen Kreuzugslied *Chevalier, mult estes guariz*', *Zs. für Romanische Philologie*, 48 (1928), 438–48.

[54] M. Gervers, 'Donations to the Hospitallers in England in the Wake of the Second Crusade', in his *The Second Crusade and the Cistercians* (New York, 1992), 155–61.

[55] C. Robin, 'Le motivazioni dei crociati', *Crociate*, 133–40.

[56] Berry (ed.), *Odo of Deuil*, 4–5.

doubts about the rightness of using force in defence against pagan attack, nor was there any scepticism about the West's duty to preserve the Holy Sepulchre from Saracen defilement. The glorious triumphs of the First Crusade remained unquestioned. As a result, not much emerged in the debate about the theological explanations of failure, with one important exception: Bernard and his sympathizers argued that it had really been a success, because it opened a way to heaven for all those who fell in the course of the expedition.[57] Otherwise, the agonizing questions were more immediate ones: whether it had been right to summon the Second Crusade at all and whether a new project for another campaign in the East, championed by the French church, should be supported.

Eugenius III had no doubts. Writing to Abbot Suger of Saint-Denis in 1150, he called the disaster 'the most severe injury of the Christian name which the church of God has suffered in our time'.[58] His successor Hadrian IV was even sharper:

On that occasion, when Conrad . . . and you . . . undertook the journey to Jerusalem with little caution, you did not receive the expected result and hoped-for reward . . . How great a disaster and loss resulted from that to the church of God and almost all the Christian people! And the holy Roman church, because she had given you advice and support in this matter, was not a little weakened by it; and every one cried out against her in great indignation, saying that she had been the author of so great a peril.[59]

'MIXING KNIGHTHOOD WITH RELIGION'

Another new feature to emerge in the course of the century, alongside the experience of failure, was the growth of great international religious orders associated with the Holy Sepulchre. From early days, the great arrivals of pilgrims were important for the defence of the kingdom of Jerusalem. In his history of the kingdom, Fulcher of Chartres repeatedly mentioned the help provided by the pilgrims in beating off attacks, even as late as 1113, when the Turks waited for two months for an opportunity, 'but in vain, because in that season the pilgrims from overseas were arriving as was customary, and our army grew from day to day'. We hear that Hugh of Lacerta went to Jerusalem 'in order to fight for Christ and never to return from there

---

[57] Bernard, *De Consideratione* (Riley-Smith, *The Crusades*, 61–3).
[58] Eugenius III, ep. 382 (PL 180. 1414c).
[59] PL 188. 1615–17.

to his own possessions', and that 'the man of God was sometimes a knight and sometimes a pilgrim'. These pilgrims, skilled in war, who came to stay beside the Holy Sepulchre, gave rise to a new religious phenomenon.[60]

The whole situation at the Holy Sepulchre was essentially new, and demanded a new military and religious structure. Although Greek and Syrian clergy retained some access to the churches, it was to be a Latin establishment. The Greek patriarch, Simeon, had left the city in advance of the arrival of the First Crusade, and in his absence he was replaced, immediately upon the fall of the city, by a Latin. There were reservations about the creation of a lay government in so holy a place. One group among the clergy demanded that a patriarch or 'spiritual vicar' should be elected before a king was chosen. They were not successful in this proposal, but no one was immediately given the royal title, Duke Godfrey apparently being elected as prince. Although neither Daimbert nor his successors were able to enforce the more absolute claims of spiritual headship or rights of secular jurisdiction, the patriarch was left in a privileged position, with a considerable area in the north-west of the city recognized as 'the land of the Holy Sepulchre', *terra sancti sepulchri*.

A sense of apostolic renewal was in the air, excited partly by the fact that the city fell on 15 July, the feast of *Divisio apostolorum*. The chapter of canons of the Church of the Holy Sepulchre stood at the centre of this renewal. In 1114 Patriarch Arnulf decided to turn the canons into a regular community, living according to the Rule of St Augustine. He announced in grandiose terms that 'I notify to all living throughout the Christian world the privilege which in the year 1114 . . . we have instituted and confirmed for the renewal of the Church of the Holy Sepulchre.'[61] Arnulf was plainly conscious of doing something for Christendom, not merely for the local church, and the canons created 'confraternities' or agreements for prayer with a considerable number of Western communities. The canons of Barcelona noted in the thirteenth century a traditional alliance of this sort: '3 March: on this day a general commemoration of all canons and brethren of the Holy Sepulchre, Jerusalem; they also make the same commemoration on this day for all canons of this house'. Some of the enormous wealth of the canons of the Holy

[60] G. Constable, 'The Place of the Crusader in Medieval Society', *Viator*, 29 (1998), 380.

[61] Folda, *Art of the Crusaders*, 57.

Duke Godfrey and the Holy Sepulchre

Traditionally, it has been supposed that Duke Godfrey of Lorraine was elected to secular authority under the title 'Advocate of the Holy Sepulchre'. At first sight, this startling piece of information seems clearly established, since in a joint letter from the crusading leaders in September 1099, Godfrey is listed as *ecclesiae Sancti Sepulchri nunc advocatus*. The title is explained elsewhere by the chronicler Raymond of Aguilers as the consequence of the refusal by Count Raymond of Saint-Gilles to accept the kingdom, since 'he trembled at the name of king in that city'. As a result, they 'elected the duke, and offered him to the Lord's Sepulchre', a curious phrase that is naturally understood as a ceremonial admission, rather than the granting of an unprecedented title. Other writers do not support the existence of the title of advocate. The *Gesta Francorum* simply reported that 'they elected Duke Godfrey prince of the city (*principem civitatis*) to defeat pagans and protect Christians'; Fulcher called him 'prince of the realm'; and Albert of Aachen said he was 'promoted to keep the principality of the city'. The occurrence of the title 'advocate' in the letter of 1099 is not a convincing proof of its official standing. Godfrey was not present and Daimbert of Pisa, who masterminded the letter, was probably anxious to limit the authority of Godfrey. Moreover, the text may have been actually composed by Raymond of Aguilers. Daimbert subsequently claimed that Godfrey had 'become the man of the Holy Sepulchre' and that he had secured from him a conditional grant of the city to the patriarch. When after Godfrey's early death his brother Baldwin succeeded him, he was crowned by Daimbert in the basilica of the Nativity at Bethlehem on Christmas Day 1100 and did homage to the patriarch. Presumably this was a compromise that enabled Baldwin to secure the royal title while leaving ambiguous his lordship over Jerusalem or the Holy Sepulchre.

J. Riley-Smith, 'The Title of Godfrey of Bouillon', *BIHR* 52 (1979), 83–6; J. Prawer, 'The Patriarch's Lordship in Jerusalem', *Crusader Institutions* (Oxford, 1980), 296–314; J. France, 'The Election and Title of Godfrey de Bouillon', *Canadian Journal of History*, 18 (1983), 321–9; R. B. C. Huygens (ed.), *Guillaume de Tyre: Chronique*, CCCM 63–63A

(Turnhoult, 1986), 10. 4, pp. 456–7; A. V. Murray, 'The Title of Godfrey of Bouillon as Ruler of Jerusalem', *Collegium Medievale*, 3 (1990), 163–78; and L. Ferrier, 'La Couronne refusée de Godefroy de Bouillon', *Concile de Clermont*, 245–65.

Sepulchre was inherited from their Greek predecessors. When Baldwin I confirmed to them thirty villages near Jerusalem, which his predecessor Godfrey had granted, he was almost certainly continuing their ownership of properties that had belonged to the Holy Sepulchre before 1099.[62] Apart from their endowments in the Holy Land, the reformed canons proved to have international appeal, as Arnulf's proclamation had intended, and they were given extensive estates throughout the West. The most extraordinary single gift was the decision by Alfonso I of Aragon in 1131 to 'grant and give all my kingdoms completely to the Sepulchre of Christ, the Hospital of the Poor and the Temple of the Lord so that they have it and possess it in three equal shares'. This remarkable proposal was not implemented, but it is a striking sign of the reputation of three new institutions that had recently emerged from Jerusalem and the Holy Sepulchre: the canons, the Hospitallers, and the Templars.

Formally speaking, the canons did not differ greatly from other Augustinian houses, but their international wealth and prestige put them in a special class and their public ceremonial was shaped by their responsibility for the Holy Sepulchre. The Augustinian canons were influential in the Holy Land; as well as the Holy Sepulchre, their communities served the Temple (*Templum Domini*), Mount Sion, Bethlehem, Nazareth, Tripoli, and Hebron. By 1200, we are told that the canons of the Holy Sepulchre had established themselves 'in all kingdoms where the name of the crucified is acknowledged'. In Syria, they were large proprietors of landed endowments. In the West, in addition to their land, there were important houses of canons associated with them or dependent on them. Their international prestige was illustrated by the acceptance of prominent crusaders at Jerusalem as brothers, *fratres*, of the house. King Baldwin II died in the habit of a canon. In the late twelfth century, we hear of German nobles who went to the Holy Land and 'perpetually dedicated themselves to the service of the Holy Sepulchre', although

[62] R. Röhricht (ed.), *Regesta Regni Hierosolimitani* (Berlin, 1893), no. 74, p. 12.

in what capacity is not clear. Confraternities of the Holy Sepulchre emerged in the West. As early as the 1120s there was a 'fraternity of the Holy Sepulchre' at Cambridge which was involved in the building of the round church which still exists there, and about 1140 William of Warenne, in the process of founding the priory of the Holy Sepulchre at Thetford, mentioned the existence of pilgrim brethren, *fratres palmiferi*, there.[63] The canons' financial situation was probably less impressive than all this suggests. In Outremer, they were able to accumulate enough capital to purchase additional estates, but on nothing like the scale of the Templars and Hospitallers. The houses of canons in the West probably did not contribute much income, and the scattered gifts of estates by devout pilgrims must have been difficult to exploit economically. Their significance at the heart of the crusading kingdom is illustrated by the story that circulated in the thirteenth century, that a great code of statutes, the *Letres dou Sepulcre*, had been deposited in the church, and lost when Saladin captured the city. The story may merely illustrate the standing of the church in later thinking, although it is certainly possible that it acted as the place for the deposit of laws or *assises* enacted in the royal court. It was the place of the coronation, and the burial-place of kings, for most of the twelfth century. The prestige of the canons would have helped to make the title of 'church of the Holy Sepulchre' even more standard in Latin usage, although the Greek and Arabic title was not forgotten among the Latins: the Patriarch Heraclius in the 1180s had on his seal the title 'Heraclius patriarch of the church of the Holy Resurrection'.[64]

From the leaders at Jerusalem, including the nobles, patriarch, canons of the Holy Sepulchre, and pilgrims, emerged two more institutions, more radically original than the regular chapter. About 1070 a group of merchants from Amalfi had founded a Hospital for the care of poor pilgrims arriving in Jerusalem. By the time of the First Crusade it had acquired a dedication to John the Baptist and considerable independence under the rule of its administrator Gerard, described in his epitaph as 'the humblest man in the East and the father of the poor'. From its early days, it had a special dedication to the service of the poor, and the rule later required the brethren to dress humbly, 'for our lords the poor, whose servants we acknowledge

---

[63] K. Elm, 'Kanoniker und Ritter vom Heiligen Grab', J. Fleckenstein and M. Hellmann, *Die geistlichen Ritterorden Europas*, VuF 26 (1980), 141–69.
[64] B. Dichter, *The Orders and Churches of Crusader Acre* (Acre, 1979), 65.

ourselves to be, go naked and meanly dressed. It would be shameful if the servant was proud and his lord humble.' Soon after the conquest of Jerusalem, the Hospital received handsome donations, including a gift by Baldwin I of one-tenth of all his revenues—a striking illustration of the importance he assigned to pilgrims. During these early years, the link between the Hospital and the Holy Sepulchre was close. Grants were made, for example, 'to God and the Holy Sepulchre and the Hospital of Jerusalem'.[65] By 1113, the Hospital had become the owner of a list of hostels in the West, especially in pilgrimage ports such as Bari, Otranto, Taranto, Messina, and Pisa. The early Hospitallers may have been a lay group, bound by a simple oath to serve the poor. In 1113 Paschal II's bull *Pie postulatio voluntatis* guaranteed the Hospital the possession of its properties in the West and the freedom to elect its own master. H. Prutz, the pioneer of modern studies of the religious orders, saw this bull as creating the Hospital as an integrated international order. It was his conviction that the papacy sponsored the order to be auxiliaries (*Hilfstruppen*) of the pope. This is too political: the aim was rather to support the Holy Land and the pilgrims to the Holy Sepulchre. It was from the 1130s that the Order acquired exemption from the authority of the diocesan bishops, and soon after that we hear of the brethren as 'living under rule', *regulariter degentes*.

In the course of the twelfth century, the Hospitallers acquired enormous endowments. They had estates in virtually every Western country, and their landholdings in Syria were enormous. The pilgrim Theoderic expressed his amazement at it:

Apart from the properties they have in foreign lands . . . the number of which can scarcely be counted, both the Templars and they have acquired almost all the cities and villages which once belonged to Judaea and were destroyed by Vespasian and Titus, with all their fields and vineyards, with an army spread throughout the whole region and castles strongly fortified against the pagans.[66]

The status of the Hospital was reflected in legends that circulated about its foundation. It was supposed to have been founded in Old Testament days, with Judas Maccabeus as its patron, and among its

---

[65] R. Hiestand, 'Die Anfänge der Johanniter', Fleckenstein and Hellmann, *Die geistlichen Ritterorden*, VuF, 26 (1980), 46–8.
[66] Wilkinson/Hakluyt, 287–8. There are lists and maps of the Hospitallers' properties in the East in J. Riley-Smith, *The Knights of St John in Jerusalem and Cyprus* (London, 1967), 477–507.

earliest governors, it was claimed, were Zacharias, the father of John the Baptist, and St Stephen the first martyr. Pope Celestine III, in a confirmation of privileges issued on 16 July 1191, accepted the truth of these stories. It has been suggested that the creation of this legendary past was an answer to the claims for an Old Testament foundation for the Templars, which were, however, differently based.[67] The Hospital itself never became a major centre of pilgrimage in the way that the Temple did.

Nevertheless, its maintenance was the first charge on the large revenues of the order. John of Würzburg gave a glowing description of what was happening there:

A great crowd of sick people is collected, some of them women and some men. They are cared for, and every day fed at vast expense. The total of persons at the time when I was present I learned from the servitors talking about it, and it was two thousand sick persons. Between night and day there were sometimes more than fifty corpses carried out, but again and again there were new people admitted. What more can I say? This house feeds so many human beings outside and within, and it gives so huge an amount of alms to poor people, either those who come to the door, or those who remain outside, that certainly the total of expenses can in no way be counted, even by the stewards and dispensers of this house.[68]

The Hospital at Jerusalem was the first Western institution to have medically qualified staff permanently retained on its strength, and it has been suggested that it was inspired by Islamic example, and thus passed the idea of full-time medical care to Western Europe. It is attractive to think of the National Health Service as the ultimate result of pilgrimage to the Sepulchre, but the suggestion is speculative, for Western cities were also developing hospitals at the same time on a much smaller scale; the Jerusalem establishment was the largest of them all, and the inspiration for others.

It is likely that the order of the Temple also emerged in co-operation with the canons of the Holy Sepulchre, and it certainly arose out of the ambiguous situation of the pilgrim knights. The two major accounts of its origins are both late. Bernard the Treasurer wrote about 1232, but he had access to an earlier source. According to him, knights present in Jerusalem after the end of the First

---

[67] S. Schein, 'The *Miracula* of the Hospital of St John and the Carmelite Elianic Tradition—Two Medieval Myths of Foundation?', M. Goodrich and others (eds.), *Cross-Cultural Convergences in the Crusader Period: Essays . . . to Aryeh Graboïs* (New York, 1995), 287–96.

[68] Wilkinson/Hakluyt, 266–7.

Crusade offered themselves to the service of the canons of the Holy Sepulchre, living in obedience to the prior of the Holy Sepulchre with a status of lay brethren or half brothers, *semifratres*. William of Tyre, about 1180, told how a group of nine knights, led by Hugh of Payns, took an oath to the patriarch to defend pilgrims and protect their routes. The details are quite different, but both versions agree that the Templars emerged from the heart of the new church establishment at Jerusalem. Their link with the Sepulchre is evidenced by the earliest version of the Rule, which required them to worship 'according to . . . the customs of the regular masters of the Holy City of Jerusalem'.[69] It was apparently at the Council of Nablus in January 1120 that formal approval was given to the group by the princes and bishops.[70] They provided a nucleus for noble pilgrims who joined them temporarily on visits, but their expansion was at first relatively slow. Their earliest title, 'fellow-soldiers of Christ', *commilitones Christi*, gives some hint of their original philosophy. No claims for ancient foundation were advanced, as in the case of the Hospitallers, because the Temple itself carried with it a strong link with the events of the Old Testament and the life-time of the Christ. Hugh of Payns came to Western Europe to seek approval for their way of life, and to recruit. Their customs, with some amendments, were confirmed at the Council of Troyes in January 1129, and endowments began to flow in with remarkable speed. In 1139, the bull *Omne datum optimum* granted almost complete freedom from episcopal authority, and by this time the knights had become known as the Templars from their principal headquarters. The remarkable feature of this new order was its combination of religion and warfare: 'religious order has flourished and is revitalized in the order of knighthood'.[71] Within a short time, the Templars had been matched by the emergence within the Hospitallers of knight brothers devoted to the defence of the Holy Land.

These orders were original creations. Contemporaries were by no means happy with the concept of mobile monks. For conventional thinkers, 'stability', life in one place, was of the essence of the monastic life. The idea of killer monks was a great deal more startling, but

---

[69] J. M. Upton-Ward (tr.), *The Rule of the Templars* (Woodbridge, 1992), para. 9.

[70] S. Cerrini, 'Il faut une nouvelle règle pour concilier prière et combat', *Les Templiers et la vérité: Historia*, 53 (1996), 16–25, and R. Hiestand, 'Kardinalbischof Matthäus von Albano, das Konzil von Troyes und die Entstehung des Templarordens', *Zs. für Kirchengeschichte*, 99 (1988), 295–325.

[71] Upton-Ward, *Rule*, para. 2.

was warmly welcomed by some thinkers. The Carthusian Guigo, far from regarding the combination of monasticism and warfare as shocking, actually saw enrolment into a religious order as the thing that made righteous warfare possible: 'Let us take possession of ourselves first, beloved, that carefree we may then fight enemies without; let us purge our minds from vice, and then our lands from the barbarians.'[72] The Templar Rule regarded members of the order as having a special vocation or election, as 'those whom God has chosen from the mass of perdition and whom he has ordered through his gracious mercy to defend the holy church'.[73] This idea was worked out fully in the widely read treatise of Bernard of Clairvaux, *In Praise of the New Militia*, perhaps written before 1129. Bernard was clear about the originality of the Order:

It seems that a new knighthood (*militia*) has recently appeared on the earth . . . This is, I say, a new kind of knighthood and one unknown in the ages gone by . . . I am not sure what I should call them, monks or knights (*milites*), unless I should perhaps name them as both, since it is clear that they lack neither the meekness of the monk nor the courage of the knight.[74]

Such a view could easily slide into an unconditional defence of total war, as in the privilege of Innocent II for the Templars issued in 1139: 'How many and great are those who, taking up warlike arms, have bravely fought for the inheritance of God and the defence of the laws of their fathers; and who, consecrating their hands to the Lord in the blood of unbelievers after the stress of war have received the prize of eternal life.'[75]

These views were not shared by everybody. Writers as prominent as John of Salisbury and William of Tyre criticized the Templars, although their complaints were more about excessive privilege than warfare. More startling is an attack in a sermon of Isaac de l'Étoile, who, although he was a follower of Bernard of Clairvaux, attacked the 'new militia' as a 'new monstrosity', 'to compel unbelievers to the faith with lances and weapons, and lawfully to despoil and religiously to kill those who do not bear the name of Christ'.[76] Nor was there

---

[72] Letter of Guigo to Hugh, 'master of the holy militia', about 1129, *Lettres des premiers Chartreux*, i (SC 88 (1962), 154).

[73] Upton-Ward, *Rule*, para. 19.

[74] P.-Y. Emery (ed.), *Bernard de Clairvaux, Éloge de la nouvelle chevalerie* (SC 367 (1990), i. 1, p. 50; iv. 8, p. 72).

[75] R. Hiestand, *Papsturkunden für Templer und Johanniter* (Göttingen, 1972), 207.

[76] A. Hoste and others (eds.), *Isaac de l'Étoile, Sermons* (SC 339 (1987)), Sermon 48, pp. 158–60.

anything ambiguous about the assault on the Templars by Walter
Map, a satirist at the Angevin court, in the years after 1180:

Nowhere save at Jerusalem are they in poverty. There they take the sword to
protect Christendom, although Peter was forbidden to take it to defend
Christ. There Peter was taught to pursue peace in patience; I do not know
who taught these men to overcome violence by force. They take the sword,
who perish by the sword. But, they say, all laws and all codes permit the use
of force to repel force. Yet he renounced that law who, when Peter struck a
blow, would not call out the legions of angels. It would seem as if these men
had not chosen the better part, when we see that under their protection our
boundaries in those regions are always being narrowed, and those of our
enemies enlarged.

Taken literally, this passage constitutes an attack on the whole concept of the armed defence of the Holy Sepulchre. The conventions of
rhetoric allowed writers to develop a theme without qualifications,
and Walter was probably less of a pacifist than he sounds; but it is
impossible to escape the existence of strong reservations.

The Military Orders were a striking example of the way in which
the defence of the Holy Sepulchre required new structures and new
thinking in Western Europe; a process that we must consider further
in the next chapter.

7

Christendom Refashioned

Scholars have doubted whether the crusades contributed much to the new Christendom: 'probably the apricot was the only benefit brought back from the crusades by the Christians'. Even this negative judgement pales in the light of the onslaught upon the crusades delivered in the closing pages of Steven Runciman's monumental history, where he argues that 'seen in the perspective of history the whole crusading movement was a vast fiasco'.[1] These perceptions were formed from the distant landscape of the twentieth century; indeed, Runciman's judgement seems to be delivered in the light of eternity. The changes produced upon ideals and culture within Western Europe were not a major part of his subject, and when he considered them, he found that here, too, the positive impact of the crusades was slight. Outremer, he said, did not 'contribute to the progress of Western art, except in the realm of military architecture and, perhaps, in the introduction of the pointed arch'. There were many influences, from other times and other regions, shaping Western Europe. Among intellectuals, contacts with Islamic writers in Spain were much more significant than similar encounters in Syria. More generally, images of warfare between good and evil were shaped by classical antiquity and contemporary Spain. The *Psychomachia*, the battle between virtue and vice handed down from the fourth century in manuscripts of Prudentius, fed the artistic visions of conflict, and so did the immensely popular stories of Roland's conflict with the Moors in the time of Charlemagne. All the same, scholars have emphasized the impact of crusades on Western art, arguing that 'there is a "crusader art" back home. It is frankly

---

[1] J. Le Goff, *Medieval Civilization, 400–1500*, tr. J. Barrow (Oxford, 1988), 67; S. Runciman, *A History of the Crusades* (Harmondsworth, 1954), iii. 469.

eclectic, cluttered with any number of borrowed themes and forms.'[2]
To appreciate what is involved, we have to bear in mind two general
considerations about the medieval approach to art.

Images were immensely important to them, in part because they
were a means of addressing a largely illiterate population. Gregory
the Great had said so about 600, and his *topos* was frequently quoted
by later writers. There are plenty of pictures and sculptures that we
can interpret primarily as 'crusade propaganda', although it is often
difficult to be sure of the precise date and circumstances. One striking
example is the set of windows in the abbey of Saint-Denis near Paris,
to commemorate the First Crusade.

Another public statement was placed on the west front of Saint-
Maria della Strada, in the province of Molise in central Italy, which
was consecrated in 1148. Here, diverse borrowings were combined
into a statement of the perils of pilgrimage: Jonah is in trouble at sea,
Alexander in the air, and by land a knight is attacked by wild beasts.

The First Crusade Window at Saint-Denis

The window no longer survives, but we have a series of
engravings published by Bernard de Montfaucon in 1729. Of
the panels that he illustrated, two were scenes from the legendary pilgrimage of Charlemagne, and ten were from the First
Crusade. These were concerned, not with the spiritual objectives of the Crusade, but its military history: the capture of
Nicaea, Antioch, and Jerusalem, and the crowning victory at
the Battle of Ascalon. There may have been two windows, but
one seems more likely. Abbot Suger's new choir would be in
process of glazing in 1144; the Second Crusade set out in 1147;
and Suger was trying to sponsor another expedition to the East
in 1150. The window could therefore have been a thanksgiving
for the First Crusade, or it may have had the function of propaganda for a new crusade.

L. Grodecki, *Les Vitraux de S. Denis* (Paris, 1976), 115; E. A. R. Brown
and M. W. Cothren, 'The Twelfth-Century Crusading Window of the
Abbey of St. Denis', *JWCI* 49 (1986), 1–40.

---

[2] L. Seidel, 'Images of the Crusades in Western Art: Models and Metaphors', in Goss
(ed.), *Meeting of Two Worlds*, 377–91.

The church was close to pilgrim routes to Bari, and thence to the journey to Outremer, although the carvings do not make specific the shrines that the patrons had in mind. Their principal purpose was to advertise the protection which Our Lady offered to all travellers on the roads.[3]

The rich and varied symbolism devised by Carolingian illustrators was elaborated and presented to a wider public during the twelfth century. Images were not standard. The view of Émile Mâle that painters and sculptors worked to an agenda dictated by theologians and preachers is only partly true; on the contrary, the thirteenth-century liturgist Durandus remarked that 'the various stories both from the Old and New Testament are represented by painters just as they like'.[4] The connection between the symbol and the message could at times be arbitrary. Peter Bartholomew, the charismatic prophet who spoke for the poor on the Crusade, had a series of visions, of which the last was the sight of the five wounds of Christ, which he interpreted to mean the five groups in the crusading army. More usually, there was a more natural link, which would readily be understood by the beholder. The cross and crucifix became the symbol of crusading: indeed, the word *crux* eventually came to mean 'crusade'. The Holy Sepulchre could stand both for the saving event of the resurrection and for the Jerusalem pilgrimage. The entry of Jesus to Jerusalem on Palm Sunday could be code for the triumph of the First Crusade. Other symbols could be borrowed from traditional imagery or recent legend to illustrate crusading themes. The story that when the Christ-child entered a city in Egypt the idols fell from their temples contained the promise of Christian victory in the holy war, and became important in the thirteenth century, when Egypt became the focus of expeditions. For our present purposes, we are most concerned with the use of the cross and the Holy Sepulchre as a linkage between Jerusalem and the West; but, before turning to that, we must look at the change in the more general self-awareness of the European community.

Historians of the early church have often spoken of the making of Christendom. The term is an appropriate description for the way in which Europe and parts of Asia came to be studded with shrines as

[3] R. Lejeune and J. Stiennon, *The Legend of Roland in the Middle Ages* (London, 1971); E. Jamison, 'Notes on S. Maria della Strada at Matrice, its History and Sculpture', *Papers of the British School at Rome*, 14 (1938), 33–97.

[4] J. Baschet, 'Inventivité et sérialité des images médiévales', *Annales HSS*, 51 (1996), 110.

the focus of sanctity and bishops and monasteries became centres of authority. In the period of the crusades, there was a movement towards creating Christendom in a new and more literal sense. 'Christian' was certainly not a new word, for it had an apostolic origin going back to Acts 11: 26, but it was rarely used in the centuries before the crusades. It certainly was not, as it is today, a standard term for a member of the church. When Gregory VII (1073–85) was addressing members of the church, his normal terms were *fideles*, faithful, *credentes*, believers, or *subditi*, subjects. The word *christianitas* occurs only twenty-seven times in the massive texts generated by the papal reform movement and the dispute with the empire during the second half of the eleventh century. In contrast, in the chronicles of the First Crusade terms cognate with 'Christian' were adopted as a basic description of the participants in the Crusade. In Albert of Aachen's narrative the Crusaders appeared as *christiani* over 210 times. He did not often favour the more abstract and theological concept *christianitas*, but other writers did, in both of the modern senses of 'Christianity' and 'Christendom'. These were not the only distinguishing concepts that suddenly emerged into common use for the emerging West. We encounter 'Westerners', *occidentales*; Franks, *Franci*; Gauls, *Galli*, in Albert of Aachen. Western Europeans were more aware of themselves as culturally different, charged by God with the protection of their Eastern brethren and the defence of the Holy Sepulchre.[5]

The veneration for the Holy Sepulchre, and the crusades movement, were illustrations of general tendencies that can be observed throughout the West. Institutions were becoming international. The popes, whose feet had once been planted firmly in the Roman earth, were after 1046 rarely of Roman origin themselves, and by the end of the twelfth century they presided over an administration that received appeals from every part of Europe. The former independent status of monasteries was replaced by international orders such as the Cistercians and the Franciscans. The papal concern for the churches of the East, and the structures developed by the canons of the Holy Sepulchre, the Hospitallers, and the Templars, were characteristic of the new period. Religious movements fed, and themselves fed upon, socio-economic progress. The abundant chronicles of the

---

[5] J. van Laarhoven, 'Chrétienté et croisade', *Cristianesimo nella Storia*, 6 (1985), 27–43; P. Rousset, *Les Origines et les caractères de la première croisade* (Geneva, 1945), 102–4; C. Morris, 'The Aims and Spirituality of the First Crusade as Seen through the Eyes of Albert of Aachen', *Reading Medieval Studies*, 16 (1990), 106.

First Crusade, which exceeded in volume almost the whole of the rest of contemporary historical writing, opened a new chapter in Western self-conscious. One must never underestimate the influence of local centres in medieval society, but there was now a much stronger sense of a common culture binding them together.

MEMORIALS IN THE WEST: RELICS

An important element in this new self-awareness was the multiplication of commemorations of the cross and Sepulchre in the West. Almost every sort of reminiscence can be found. Returning crusaders and pilgrims built churches dedicated to the Holy Sepulchre, polygonal or round in shape in memory of the great rotunda at Jerusalem, or created representations of the Sepulchre. Orders and brotherhoods devoted to the Holy Land did the same. Votive churches or inscriptions offered prayers or thanks for visits to the East, and provided propaganda for new expeditions. Older centres of Jerusalem devotion produced justificatory histories or legends. While exact attempts at reproduction of Jerusalem architecture remained rare, the number of reminiscences was vast.

The greater closeness between the Holy Land and the churches and aristocracy of the West encouraged the transfer of relics. The desire was there from the beginning. The contents of the imperial relic collection at Constantinople were eagerly listed. At the crisis in the fortunes of the First Crusade in 1098 the discovery of the Holy Lance reinvigorated their spirits and became the symbol for the completion of the expedition. That was followed by the new finding, immediately after the end of the First Crusade, of the wood of the cross. The main part of this wood was believed to have been taken to Constantinople by Heraclius in face of the advance of Islam, and the details of the new discovery are obscure. In all probability what was found was a substantial fragment in one of the Palestinian shrines. In any event, it was used as the emblem of the kingdom of Jerusalem, carried with the army to invoke divine protection, until it was captured by Saladin in 1187 on the field of Hattin.

The significance of such relics in the culture of the time can be illustrated by four examples. Ansellus (or Anseau), a canon of Notre Dame, Paris, had set off at the time of the First Crusade, and had become cantor in the community of Augustinian canons at the Holy Sepulchre. He sent back to his old church, by the hands of one Anselin, whom he had met at Jerusalem, a fragment of the holy cross within a silver reliquary—a later inventory hopefully listed it as 'a great part of the Lord's cross'. Its reception in its new home on 1 August 1120 was privileged with a plenary indulgence by the papal legate, Cardinal Conon of Praeneste, as the feast of the translation. Soon afterwards, Ansellus wrote again, giving an account of the history of the cross, and sending a relic from the Holy Sepulchre in a further reliquary. He explained these magnificent donations by his affectionate memories of his old church:

In my mind I am still fervent in your love, and live in my mind with you in your church. I have always talked with those who over the years have come from you to us, who knew you and were known to you, and inquired eagerly about the condition of your church, and what you were doing, and how you are, especially of those whom I saw and knew . . . Often in dreams I seem to be taking part in your ceremonies and processions, and at your daily matins and offices, and to be saying the psalms with you.

This was an age when the art of distant friendship was seriously practised, and Notre Dame was for Ansellus his first home, where he had been educated and trained. The canons were also interested in expanding their international connections : it was part of their 'mission statement'. The gift had a significant impact on northern French society. The great fair of Lendit was granted a royal privilege (*indictum*) in 1124. It was a major occasion, combining the relics of Saint-Denis and Notre Dame, and influential in developing the prosperity of Paris and its region. There may have been an impact on crusading ideology: it has been suggested that the epic poem, *The Pilgrimage of Charlemagne*, which told the story of his supposed journey to bring to the West the Paris relics, was composed within the context of the Lendit fair, around the time of the Second Crusade.[6] The arrival of relics from the Holy Sepulchre and Golgotha helped to shape economy, pilgrimage, and ideology in this region which was the base of Capetian royal authority in France.

The nobles of southern Germany had a tradition of support for the Gregorian papacy, and some personal links with Urban II. They were active supporters of the First Crusade and subsequent expeditions to the Holy Land: Abbot Gerhard of Allerheiligen, under pressure from imperialist partisans, left for Jerusalem in 1101, and became a canon of the Holy Sepulchre there. A Suabian pilgrim, Berthold, resolved to

[6] G. Bautier, 'L'Envoi de la relique de la vraie croix à Notre Dame de Paris en 1120', *Bibliothèque de l'École des Chartes*, 129 (1971), 387–97; Folda, *Art of the Crusaders*, 83. Bautier's view of the date is convincing.

establish a community at Denkendorf which would be dedicated
to the Holy Sepulchre, and directed by the canons. As part of the
process, a reliquary was sent by Patriarch Gormond containing
fragments from the cross and the Holy Sepulchre. The date of the
reliquary appears to be a little before 1130. It is interesting as providing another of several instances where relics of the cross and
Sepulchre are closely associated, and it is the earliest one to survive
from those made by craftsmen at Jerusalem itself.[7]

The new building at San Clemente, Rome, was consecrated in 1118
or 1119, and one of its most striking features was its enormous apse
mosaic. This included several themes characteristic of early Roman
tradition. It borrowed from the past the images of the rivers of paradise, lambs, Bethlehem, and Jerusalem, and a flowering (vine-scroll)
cross. The apse of 1118–19 could well have been an imitation of the
one in the old church of San Clemente which was in ruins. In at least
one way, however, the decoration of the new apse incorporated what
was, for Italy at least, an innovation. The figure upon the crucifix was
a representation of the dying Christ, the first known example south
of the Alps. The crucifix was attended by Mary and John. There was
no narrative sequence of the events of the passion here: it stands as a
powerful theological presentation of the suffering Christ as the centre
of salvation. In a process of restoration in the 1930s, it was discovered that there was a hole in the breast of Christ, which can be
most readily explained as damage done in the eighteenth century in
the process of recovering relics that had been inserted there. The
architectural embodiment of relics was not common at this time, and
only one previous example is known in Italy: Monte Cassino, consecrated in 1071, had 'within the Saviour's halo, the wood of the
Lord and stones from the Holy Sepulchre'. There were personal
connections between the two churches. The provenance of the
San Clemente relics is unknown: at a guess, they could have been
donated from Monte Cassino.[8]

The reliquary cross now at Scheyern in Germany has been largely
transformed over the centuries, but the account of its transfer to the

---

[7] K. Elm, 'St Pelagius in Dendendorf, in K. Elm (ed.), *Landesgeschichte und
Geistesgeschichte: Fs. für Otto Herding* (Stuttgart, 1977), 80–130; Folda, *Art of the
Crusaders*, 97–100. The reliquary is now in the Württembergisches Landesmuseum
at Stuttgart.

[8] W. Telesko: 'Ein Kreuzreliquiar in der Apsis?', *Römische Historische Mitteilungen*, 36
(1994), 53–79; and A. Dietl, 'Die Reliquienkondierung im Apsismosaik von S. Clemente
im Rom', R. L. Colella and others (eds.), *Pratum Romanum: Richard Krautheimer zum
100 Geburtstag* (Wiesbaden, 1997), 97–111.

West in 1155/7 throws further light on the cultural exchanges of the time. It was designed to be the centre of a processional tour of fund-raising. Fulcher, patriarch of Jerusalem, and Amalric, the prior of the church of the Holy Sepulchre, sent with it greetings to all in the West and a promise that they would be remembered at the glorious Sepulchre of Christ. The letter thus expressed the sense of mission to the whole Western world, and it stressed how many of those who desire or promise to visit the holy places of the passion and resurrection are prevented by sickness or poverty or other concerns. The senders say that they have gathered relics from all the holy places, Bethlehem, the Temple, Gethsemane, Calvary, and the Sepulchre, and enclosed them with a piece of the wood of the cross within a reliquary cross. They are sending it by the hand of their canon, Conrad, and whoever makes an offering at this cross will receive the same reward as he would have done if he had made it at the Holy Sepulchre. The project miscarried: Conrad was attacked and robbed of the proceeds, and the sacred object ended, by what process is not clear, at the monastery of Scheyern. It was, however, a striking expression of the sense of universal commitment at the Holy Sepulchre for the well-being of their Western brethren, and the financial opportunities that this connection offered. Although this reliquary had an unusual history, it was a representative of a family of cross-reliquaries produced at Jerusalem in the middle years of the twelfth century to enclose gifts of high prestige to the authorities of the Latin world.[9]

Frequently reliquary treasures and other objects contained a deliberate attempt to point to the connections between the cross and the Holy Sepulchre. The second Master of the Hospitallers, Raymond of Le Puy, already had in the 1130s a seal which on the obverse showed him kneeling in veneration of the cross, and on the reverse had an image of the Holy Sepulchre. At Agrigento in Sicily, a portable altar preserved a double cross design characteristic of Jerusalem reliquaries, and, at its foot, a lamp hanging over the Sepulchre, which was here distinguished by its three typical 'port-holes'. Some fragments discovered in England in 1833 may well have originated as figures in a combined crucifix and Holy Sepulchre, although they were erroneously given the name of the Temple pyx, and only the knights

---

[9] Folda, *Art of the Crusaders*, 291–3; A. Legner, *Reliquien in Kunst und Kult zwischen Antike und Aufklärung* (Darmstadt, 1995), 59–60; A. Reichhold, *Das heilige Kreuz von Scheyern* (Scheyern, 1981), 15 ff.

FIG 7.1 This reliquary now in the Louvre is a good representative of a class that combines the cross with a representation of the Holy Sepulchre at the base of the shaft. The two large figures are Constantine and Helena. Crucifixes in the modern period have often preferred to show symbols of the eucharist, not the empty tomb, at the base of the cross.

survive, now in the Burrell Collection at Glasgow.[10] Urban myths, too, associated some of the great cities with the Holy Sepulchre. In the late Middle Ages, the florid development of legends at Florence makes the exact dating impossible to establish, but at its heart were stones from the Sepulchre, the size of a hazelnut, which may have been brought there in the course of the twelfth century.

There was a revival, too, of the vases or ampullae which centuries

---

[10] G. Zarnecki and others (eds.), *English Romanesque Art, 1066–1200* (London, 1984), no. 234; Folda, *Art of the Crusaders*, 292–3.

Florence and the *Scoppio del Carro*

There is no evidence that a contingent from Florence took part in the First Crusade. At that time, it was not a city of primary importance in the Italian scene. There were certainly Florentines in the Holy Land later in the twelfth century: the Florentine Haymar was a prominent churchman there in the later part of the century, and eventually became titular patriarch of Jerusalem. He would be an obvious source for the gift of stones from the Sepulchre, but that is a pure assumption. In the later Middle Ages, the stones from the Sepulchre became the basis for a series of legends and ceremonies, according to which the Florentine Pazzino Pazzi was first over the walls of Jerusalem in 1095, and was rewarded with the gift of relics. In the fourteenth century Villani reported an ancient custom of carrying the new fire to all the houses of the city, as had been done at Jerusalem—although this ceremony was followed in a number of Western cities, and was not distinctive of Florence. By Villani's time, the Pazzi family were acting as sponsors of this ceremony, but they had only become prominent relatively recently, and the story of their heroism on the First Crusade is pure fiction. The festivities were later amplified to include the descent of a mechanical dove from the west front of the cathedral, which set fire to a cart of fireworks. Ceremonial use of these carts is characteristic of Renaissance Italy, and the legend does not seem to be recorded in its completed form until as late as 1736.

Neri, 74–80; F. Cardini, 'Crusade and "Presence of Jerusalem" in Medieval Florence', *Outremer*, 332–46; S. Raveggi, 'Storia di una leggenda: Pazzo dei Pazzi e le pietre del Santo Sepolcro', in F. Cardini (ed.), *Toscana e Terrasanta nel Medioevo* (Florence, 1982), 299–31.

before had been used to bring back dust from the Holy Sepulchre or oil from the lamps there. It is unlikely that there was a continued manufacture of these during the long period of Islamic supremacy at Jerusalem, but they reappeared in the twelfth century. Surviving examples were once again made of a lead/tin material, and unlike their distant predecessors were equipped with small handles or ears which served to attach a belt for easy carrying. One of the images impressed on such ampullae was an image of the Sepulchre, marked by its three 'port-holes', and upon it the body of Jesus, wrapped in winding-cloths and surmounted with a halo. Behind this image were the three towers of the church of the Holy Sepulchre: the opaion of the Anastasis rotunda, the belfry and the dome with a cross—a representation, that is, of the buildings as they stood after the crusaders' rebuilding. On the other side might be a portrayal of the visit of the women to the tomb. Another theme was the figure of the risen Christ, the Anastasis motif characteristic of Greek art. In their tiny and damaged form some of these impressions have a striking resemblance to illuminations in the Psalter made for Queen Melisende in the middle of the century. Although, as we have seen, there are good reasons for doubting whether the ampullae from the Patristic period were copies of mosaics, the likelihood that these provided the source for the twelfth-century vessels is strong. Ampullae quite often had summary inscriptions in Greek. Not many of these vessels survive from the crusader period, but it is likely that their original number was large, and may have acted as examples for the design of those for the Canterbury pilgrimage to the shrine of Thomas of Canterbury.[11]

The provision made by contemporaries for the display of relics not infrequently leaves us uncertain about their precise intention. There is, for example, a puzzling monument in the church of Saint-Jean, Aubeterre in Charente, western France, which was excavated out of rock in the twelfth century. This has a semi-circular choir, with a two-stage monument, nearly twenty feet high: a lower stage, which contains a table for offerings, and an upper storey that seems to be designed as a place for the exposition of relics.[12] If it was supposed to be reminiscent of the form of the Sepulchre, it was wide of the mark, yet there are sufficient general similarities for us to think that this was perhaps the intention. In this particular case, there is no contemporary record to establish a clear connection with pilgrimage or crusade. But there are many cases where the design, or literary accounts, make clear the intention to bring the commemoration of the Holy Sepulchre to the West.

---

[11] L. Kötzsche 'Zwei Pilgerampullen aus der Kreuzfahrerzeit', *Zs. für Kunstgeschichte*, 51 (1988), 13–32.

[12] M. Aubert, *Romanesque Cathedrals and Abbeys of France* (London, 1966), pl. 131.

COMMEMORATIONS OF THE HOLY SEPULCHRE

In the twelfth century, monasteries were thought of as pictures of Jerusalem. This was not only so in a vaguely metaphorical sense. Some writers saw an abbey plan as an echo of the topography of the city: as Master Honorius explained, 'the cloister building beside the house is taken from the portico of Solomon built beside the Temple'.[13] Detailed recollection, however, could be much more specific than this. There are several round churches that can plausibly be ascribed to a patron returning from the First Crusade, and can be understood as representations of the rotunda above the Holy Sepulchre at Jerusalem.

Bishop Landulf of Asti, returning from the Holy Land in 1103–4, seems to have commemorated his journey by the creation of the church of San Sepolcro there: a cupola stands on a circular arcade of eight arches, which provide a covered ambulatory. This church was long regarded as a baptistery, and still appears as such in some current guidebooks, but almost certainly that is wrong. It was later given to the Hospitallers, but by the time of the transfer it must

St Sepulchre, Northampton

This parish church was built by Earl Simon of Senlis on his return from the First Crusade. While there is no documentary proof of his responsibility, the circumstantial evidence is strong. He was lord of the town, and the style of the building fits the first decade of the twelfth century. The nave was circular in form, with a central ring of eight pillars that provided for an ambulatory on the ground floor and a gallery above: the form of the church thus approximately echoed that of the rotunda at Jerusalem, although it was not planned as a precise copy. There would have been space for a model of the Sepulchre itself in the centre of the circular nave, but there is no evidence that one existed. The gallery was rebuilt in the later Middle Ages, but fragments of Norman windows confirm that there was one from the beginning. Unfortunately the roof of the rotunda was replaced in 1868, so we do not know if any attempt was made to represent the dome at Jerusalem.

---

[13] Honorius, *Gemma animae* i. 148 (*PL* 172. 590B).

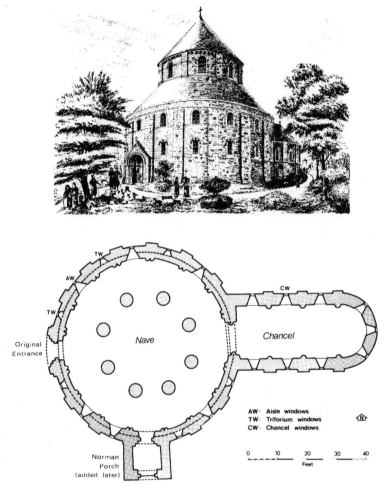

FIG 7.2 The church of the Holy Sepulchre, Northampton has been greatly altered, but its original appearance (above) can be reconstructed with some confidence.

already have been in its present form. It has been suggested that the building was planned to commemorate the visit of Urban II in 1096 during his preaching of the Crusade, but foundation by the bishop on his return seems a more likely conjecture.[14] The massive church at

[14] S. Casartelli-Novelli, 'L'Église du S-Sépulchre ou le baptistère S.-Pierre-Consavia', *Congrès archéologique*, 129 (1977), 358–63.

Lanleff in Brittany is clearly an imitation of the rotunda of the Holy Sepulchre. There is no documentary history of its foundation, so its attribution to a lord returning from the First Crusade is a guess, but a plausible one.[15] In contrast, the small round churches in Lombardy, whose style would fit a date around 1100, cannot be given a firm connection with crusaders and pilgrims, and they may represent a local building tradition unconnected with Jerusalem.

At least once, we know of a foundation by (so to speak) a frustrated pilgrim. Bishop Henry of Paderborn (1084–1127), where the eleventh-century church was already a commemoration of Jerusalem, recorded that 'I conceived a desire to vow to go to Jerusalem and to see and frequent the holy places of the birth and passion and ascension of Christ . . . When I discussed this with spiritual and wise men, they unanimously answered that it would be better to use the expenses which I had prepared for this expedition, to build an oratory in honour of some saint, whom I could honour as patron and champion.' He therefore founded the church of St John at Helmarshausen, which not only echoed the design of the Bussdorfkirche at Paderborn, but contained in its crypt a representation of the tomb of Christ.

Quite often, the design of such a memorial was the result of the initiative of a fraternity or a religious community. At Cambridge, Abbot Reinald of Ramsey granted a site to three men of the *fraternitas Sancti Sepulcri* to build a church 'in honour of God and of the Holy

---

The *Rotonde* of Lombardy

The only one of this group whose dedication suggests a Palestinian reference is Santa Croce at Bergamo. Tradition assigns the splendid small church of San Lorenzo, Padua, to the Countess Matilda; the striking *rotonda* in Brescia cathedral is early twelfth century in style, but uncertain in intent; the beautifully situated San Tomè, Almenno, is of obscure origin. These and other churches, to make matters more difficult, have been extensively reconstructed.

L. Bertinelli and A. Truzzi, *La rotunda di S. Lorenzo in Mantova* (Mantua, about 1993); S. Chierici, *Italia Romanica: la Lombardia* (Milan, 1984) 284, 291, 295.

---

[15] L. M. Tillet, *Bretagne Romane* (La Pierre qui Vire, 1982), 241–6.

Helmarshausen

The donation of 1126, from which the words of Bishop Henry are quoted in the text, is probably a forgery in its present form, but contains much of the original. There are reasons for thinking that the building had made good progress by 1107. Seemingly, then, Bishop Henry's desire to go to Jerusalem was not a recent thing. The chapel was circular, 13.20 m. in diameter, with rooms in all four directions to make a cross, and thus basically similar to the Bussdorfkirche, although externally Helmarshausen is round rather than octagonal. It is now in ruins, but in the 1930s a crypt was discovered with an arcosolium in the north wall, presumably a version of the Holy Sepulchre. Bishop Henry had already, in 1115, built a chapel on the cliffs at Externsteine, with at its foot a representation of the Tomb, again in the form of an arcosolium.

G. Mietke, *Die Bautätigkeit Bischof Meinwerks von Paderborn und die frühchristliche und byzantinische Architektur* (Paderborn, 1991).

Sepulchre'—the 'Round Church' which still exists. The style suggests a date no earlier than 1130. It had eight thick short round piers and a gallery with twin openings, but it is impossible to say whether there was a representation of the Sepulchre in the middle of the rotunda. We do not know precisely what the 'fraternity of the Holy Sepulchre' was. It may have consisted of returned pilgrims and crusaders: in any case, it clearly was an association of people devoted to the Sepulchre. At Imola in Lombardy, another lay community had by 1143 established a 'hospice of the Holy Sepulchre', which in 1169 was transferred to the Hospitallers and appears as the *domus et hospitale Sancti Johannis de Imola ordinis domus Sancti Sepulchri seu Sancti Johannis Jerusalemi*.[16] At Brindisi, the impressive round church of San Giovanni al Sepolcro can most probably be ascribed to the canons of the Holy Sepulchre, who held the building from about 1125 onwards.[17] Alongside these major constructions, there must have

---

[16] N. Pevsner, *The Buildings of England: Cambridgeshire*, 2nd edn. (Harmondsworth, 1970), 230–1; J. Heers, 'Bourgs et faubourgs en Occident', *Jérusalem, Rome*, 210.

[17] B. Sciarra, *La chiesa di S. Giovanni al Sepolcro in Brindisi* (Brindisi, 1962).

been innumerable minor memorials that are no longer recorded. An inscription at Saint-Jean-de Montierneuf at Poitiers tells of a monk who in 1102 built an altar and tomb 'on his return from Jerusalem; he brought with him relics of the Lord's Sepulchre and many others'.[18]

A number of churches in Spain seem to have similar connections with fraternities or Orders.

Spanish Round Churches

These very possibly did incorporate a reminiscence of the Holy Sepulchre, although date and purpose are sometimes obscure. A testament of February 1058 mentions the foundation of 'the church built in honour of the Lord's Holy Sepulchre near Tallada' (Catalonia), and by the next century this church was subject to the canons of the Holy Sepulchre. The Santo Sepolcro church of Torres del Rio (Navarre) is mentioned by a bull of Innocent III in 1215, and its style suggests that a date in the 1160s is likely. It has a distinctive cupola, which has been thought to be a reminiscence of Islamic architecture, or alternatively as belonging to a tradition of cemetery lanterns. At Segovia, what is now the church of Vera Cruz has an inscription dated to 1208, but it does not establish clearly that this was the true date of the completion of the church. It was a two-floored building, round inside and twelve-cornered outside, and the dedication inscription described it as the church of the Holy Sepulchre. In spite of its shape, it was not a Templar foundation—at least, it was ascribed to them only in a forged document of 1224—and in the later Middle Ages it certainly belonged to the canons of the Holy Sepulchre. Whatever its original date, it seems to belong to an interest in copies of the Holy Sepulchre more characteristic of the twelfth century than of the thirteenth.

D. Stephanie, 'Die Kirche la Vera Cruz', *Mitteilungen der Carl Justi Vereinigung*, 5 (1993), 92–121; N. Jaspert, Vergegenwärtigungen Jerusalems in Architektur und Reliquienkult', *JerKonflikte*, 219–70.

---

[18] R. Favreau and J. Michaud (eds.), *Corpus des inscriptions de la France médiévale: 1. Ville de Poitiers* (Paris, 1974), no. 75.

The most famous cases of communities whose churches commemorated the Holy Sepulchre are the Hospitallers and, even more, the Templars. To some extent this has become a myth. For a considerable time, architectural studies of the Templars rested on the assumption that all round churches belonged to the Order, and conversely that all Templar churches (unless there was absolute evidence to the contrary) had originally been round. The fact is that most churches and chapels belonging to these two orders were of ordinary local design. There were, however, exceptions. In England, the Hospitaller priory of Clerkenwell has a rotunda, as did their Essex preceptory at Little Maplestead. Both twelfth-century Templar buildings in London, the Old and New Temple, were round, and there were rotundas at the Templar houses of Temple Bruer and Aslackby in Lincolnshire, Garway in Herefordshire and Dover in Kent. It is not certain whether these were designed as commemorations of the Temple (or Dome of the Rock) at Jerusalem or of the Holy Sepulchre, but the latter is more likely, since it would be better known in the West.

Some memorials reflected the close links between a city, a religious community, and the Holy Land. The fascinating church of San Sepolcro is a small octagonal building on the south bank of the River Arno at Pisa, with eight central pillars that serve to support a small drum. It was apparently built at the same date, 1153, and by the same architect, as the great baptistery beside the cathedral, which is arguably the one baptistery whose design unambiguously recalls the Church of the Holy Sepulchre.

The sites we have visited so far were based on general recollections of the church of the Holy Sepulchre. They did not contain a version of the Sepulchre itself; or this has disappeared; or (in the case of Helmershausen) it was extremely unlike the original. Eichstätt, in southern Germany, is another matter.

These were all new buildings. Established centres of devotion to the Holy Sepulchre were expanded. At Santo Stefano, Bologna, an imaginative memorial of the Sepulchre was provided in the octagonal church now dedicated to Santo Sepolcro. Dates are difficult at Bologna, but there was probably an extensive rebuilding in the years after 1141, and the main fabric of the Sepulchre looks stylistically as if it had been built then. (It also contains fourteenth-century work, but this is clearly a later addition.) When a *Life* of the founding saint, Petronius, was composed between 1164 and 1180, the author claimed that Petronius had visited Jerusalem, and then built his

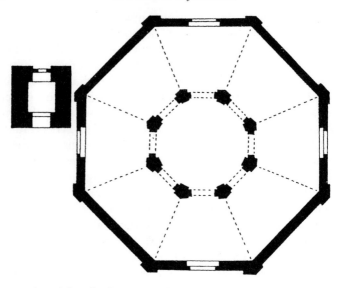

FIG 7.3 Plan of church of Santo Sepolcro at Pisa, by Diotisalvi about 1153.

church at Bologna in the likeness of the Holy Places. This story went back at least to the tenth century, but the author appears to be incorporating the legend of Petronius' foundation into a fantasy-history of the fifth century. The imitation of Jerusalem was evidently a central memory, legendary or historical, of the local church.[19]

We find a similar evolution of Holy Sepulchre tradition at Konstanz, although on a somewhat different time-scale from Bologna. Oudals-calch wrote his *Life of Conrad* in 1120s, and provided an account of the bishop's ambitious building activities, which brought to Konstanz the splendours of Rome and 'a Sepulchre of the Lord in the likeness of that at Jerusalem'. The material for this life is better than that of the *Life of Petronius* at Bologna. The Sepulchre remained intact throughout the twelfth century, but later its chapel was reconstructed, and the Sepulchre itself was replaced about 1300.

The Holy Sepulchre could also be invoked in the West by painting and statues. It is likely that such depictions were far more common than survivals suggest. Sometimes they were probably directed to the specific purpose of propaganda for a crusade. We hear of this,

---

[19] See the inset 'Jerusalem at Bologna', in ch. 4.

Diotisalvi and the Holy Sepulchre

In the middle years of the twelfth century, Pisa had close links with Palestine, and many Pisans had undoubtedly visited the Holy Land as merchants or pilgrims. By 1113 the Jerusalem Hospital already had a hostel in the city, and in 1138 it was specified that they possessed a church there. There is an inscription on the (unfinished) bell-tower at San Sepolcro ascribing the building to Diotisalvi in 1153, although we can only guess whether or not this refers to the entire church. It is impossible to doubt that San Sepolcro is a memorial of the rotunda of the Holy Sepulchre. Diotisalvi was, at the same time, involved in the building of the baptistery, and it is probable that the civic government of Pisa was acting as his patron. Not only was the baptistery a major civic project, but San Sepolcro was the meeting-place of the judges appointed by the consuls. We do not know whether Diotisalvi had himself visited the Pisan community in Palestine.

U. Böck, 'Das Baptisterium zu Pisa und die Jerusalemer Anastasis', *Bonner Jahrbücher des Rheinischen Landesmuseum in Bonn*, 164 (1964), 146–56; A. Caleca and A. Amendola, *La dotta mano: il Battistero di Pisa* (Bergamo, 1991).

surprisingly, from Muslim sources. It was reported that Conrad of Montferrat, recruiting in Europe, carried with him a placard:

He had a picture of Jerusalem painted showing the *qumama* . . . Above the tomb the marquis had a horse painted, and mounted on it a Muslim horseman who was trampling the tomb, over which his horse was urinating. This picture was sent abroad to the markets and meeting-places; priests carried it about, clothed in their habits, their heads covered, groaning, 'O the shame'.[20]

This is plausible, and one would hardly expect such transient placards to survive. As far as our evidence goes, the crusades were advertised more often by pictures of the battle of good and evil, such as the increasingly popular St George and the dragon or the fight of virtue against vice.

[20] Baha' al-Din, in F. Gabrieli, *Arab Historians of the Crusades*, tr. E. J. Costello (Berkeley, 1969), 208–9. *qumama* is the (abusive) Muslim name for what Arab Christians called the 'church of the Resurrection'.

Eichstätt

An act of 1194 by Bishop Otto referred to Walbrun, who 'built a
hospital . . . in a suburb of the city of Eichstätt, where he . . .
placed a piece of the life-giving wood of the cross'. He reported
that a church had recently been consecrated 'in honour of the
holy cross and Holy Sepulchre'. It is a reasonable guess that
Walbrun was on the Second Crusade, and that he founded the
hospital on his return, about 1149; but the church itself can be
dated only to some time in the following half-century. A number of descriptions survive from the later Middle Ages. Two
annual processions there, on the feast of the Invention of the
Cross (3 May) and on Good Friday, continued until it was
closed, as being in need of repair, in 1611. The edicule must
have been built at the same time as the church. The Jerusalem
pilgrim Hans Tucher in 1479 described the church at Jerusalem as 'very like that of Eichstätt'—a curious reverse comparison. The edicule was transferred to the Capuchin church in
the town and rebuilt there in 1623. The appearance suggests
that the twelfth-century fabric survives reasonably intact,
and it is probably the closest copy of the contemporary Holy
Sepulchre we possess before the fifteenth century. It is, however,
not a precise imitation: the arches outside the circular end, for
example, are lower than those at Jerusalem and take a different
form.

Dalman, *Das Grab Christi*, 56–65; H. Flachenecker, *Eine geistliche Stadt:
Eichstätt vom 13 bis zum 16 Jahrhundert* (Regensburg, 1988), with his
article, 'Das Schottenkloster Heiligkreuz in Eichstätt', *Studien und Mitteilungen zur Geschichte des Benediktinerordens und seiner Zweige*, 105
(1994), 65–95; and Biddle, *Tomb*, 29–31.

There were, however, plenty of illustrations designed to keep
Golgotha and the Holy Sepulchre in the minds of the faithful. An
interesting early example is to be found on the sculptures of the west
front of the abbey of Saint-Gilles-du-Gard. Work was proceeding on
this in the middle part of the twelfth century, and over the right
doorway is a lintel that shows the three Marys buying spices from the
chemist (the first known sculptural copy of this theme), and then
at the Sepulchre, which is shown as a sarcophagus, but with the

FIG 7.4 The commemoration of the Holy Sepulchre at Santo Stefano, Bologna, in its present form. It combines a memorial of the tomb with one of the Calvary, which surmounts it. A staircase offers access to the Calvary, and on the far side is an ambo or pulpit. The whole is contained within a rotunda. The basic design is twelfth century in form, perhaps the result of a rebuilding after 1141, with later sculptural additions.

Jerusalem 'port-holes', and with grave-clothes hanging out of it. The façade contains a number of reminiscences of the Jerusalem story.[21]

A fairly recent rediscovery alerts us to the probability that many memorials of the Sepulchre have disappeared. Under the crossing arches at Winchester Cathedral there was known to be a chapel of the Holy Sepulchre, but it was only in the 1960s that it was discovered that, beneath the thirteenth-century decoration, there was a complete scheme of twelfth-century designs, which had been hidden for 700 years. The east wall of this chapel gives a powerful impression of one possible way of commemorating the Holy Sepulchre. The lower tier contains a combined painting of the deposition of the body of Christ in the tomb (which is represented as a coffin or sarcophagus) with the visit of the three Marys, and the angel's revelation to them of the resurrection. The association of deposition and visitation in one picture is unusual, and presumably reflects the purpose of the altar as the place where the two Easter ceremonies took place.

There is a striking survival of an elaborate Sepulchre chapel at Gernrode nunnery. At the entrance stands Mary Magdalen, below a frieze with Peter and John on the way to the Tomb. The figures include the long-established three Marys and the angel, along with the rather newer theme of the meeting of Christ and Mary Magdalen. There is, however, no real attempt to reproduce the edicule, to which the only real similarity is the double chamber included within the structure: the emphasis is rather on telling the story by representing the figures. This composition can be dated only from its style, which appears to be close to 1120.[22]

Representations of the Holy Sepulchre and the resurrection were not, of course, confined to specifically dedicated chapels. The holy women appeared on the first stone pulpit in Pisa cathedral, carved by Guglielmo just after 1159, which proved to be a major influence on later Tuscan sculpture.[23] There is, for example, a splendid carving on a capital that originated at Saint-André-de-Rosans in the Hautes

---

[21] C. Ferguson O'Meara, *The Iconography of the Façade of S. Gilles-du-Gard* (New York, 1977).

[22] Möbius, *Passion*, pls. 112–16; G. Schiller, *Iconography of Christian Art*, ii. *The Passion of Jesus Christ* (London, 1972), 181–4; and L. Kötzsche, 'Das Heilige Grab in Jerusalem und seine Nachfolge', *Akten XII*, 284–7, where it is dated about 1080. For depictions of Mary's meeting with the risen Christ and her purchase of spices in the early twelfth century, see W. Tydeman, *The Theatre in the Middle Ages* (Cambridge, 1978), 39–40.

[23] D. F. Glass, *Portals, Pilgrimage and Crusade in Western Tuscany* (Princeton, 1997), 8–10.

Winchester Cathedral

The style of the architecture and original painting suggests that the chapel of the Holy Sepulchre was inserted into the crossing some time around 1180. The top layer of the east wall showed the deposition of Christ from the cross. The lower tier illustrated the entombment, the visit of the Marys to the Sepulchre, and to the side the harrowing of hell by Christ (a theme very commonly associated with the resurrection in the East, but less frequent in the West). The rest of the chapel may have been decorated with episodes from the passion story, but these survive only in the form of the sketches or *sinopie* designed to underlie the fresco—a survival that is technically interesting because so rare at this date, but which is impossible to decipher with confidence. There is no reason to think that the construction of the chapel marked any particular public event. It is more probable that it reflected a desire to have a splendid place for the Easter ceremonies in one of England's greatest churches.

D. Park, 'The Wall Paintings of the Holy Sepulchre Chapel', in *Medieval Art and Architecture at Winchester Cathedral: British Archaeological Association*, 6 (1980/3), 38–62.

Alpes and is now in the museum of Gap.[24] The Auvergne, in central France, seems to have been a particularly rich area for representations of the Holy Sepulchre. There are records of several chapels with this dedication, which do not now survive. The major churches of the region preserve a fine series of capitals, including some showing the tomb with the visiting Marys and the attendant angel and the guard of soldiers, depicted as knights. The tomb is in most cases presented as a two-storey edifice, with lamps and an upper turret, as in the capital at Saint-Nectaire, where it is accompanied by other capitals illustrating the events of the passion story. Unfortunately, these works cannot be dated, apart from a chapel at Joligny (now destroyed), which was founded in 1037. We are therefore not sure whether they express a background of piety that encouraged local recruiting to the First Crusade, or whether they were created by

---

[24] There is a list of southern French examples in Y. Esquieu, 'Théâtre liturgique et iconographie', *Cahiers de Fanjeaux*, 28 (1993), 215–31 and fig. 61.

returned crusaders. The style of the capitals suggests an early twelfth-century date, but there is no way of being sure.[25] Tuscany had a number of Holy Sepulchre dedications in its parishes, which can be dated only by the chance survival of the first reference to each. There had already been an oratory *in onore Sancti Sepucri* [*sic*] *et sancte Marie* near San Gimignano in 1034, and now we find S. Gersolé (properly S. Pietro in Gerusalemme) by 1156; the *plebes Sancti Yerusalem* at San Donnino near Certaldo by 1192; and, in the thirteenth century, the *ecclesia Sancti Viti de Yerusalem*, also near Certaldo. In these cases, we are not able to say whether the churches had been named for a monument, decoration, or relic, or all of these together.[26] The same applies to the twelfth-century church of Forshem, Västergötland, Sweden, which was built *in honore Domini nostri Jesu Christi et dominici Sepulcri*.[27]

It was possible also for architecture to introduce the Jerusalem events by enacting the solemn entry by Christ. This was an evocative moment, because it was rooted in the ceremony for welcoming the visit of a king or bishop. The entry of a king into a city or monastery was attended with hymns and lauds that transformed the space into an image of the heavenly Jerusalem, the king into a figure of the triumphant Christ. It was a favourite theme in the portals of cathedrals in Tuscany, sometimes accompanied by the representation of the raising of Lazarus (the opening of the events of Holy Week in John's Gospel), sometimes showing the apostles with censers, to make clear that the event was interchangeable with the Psalm Sunday procession. Tuscan carving, in fact, was moving in a different direction from the west fronts of the new French cathedrals, which often represented the Last Judgement: for Tuscany, they favoured rather the recollection of the Jerusalem events.[28]

It is almost true to say that before 1100 the resurrection of Christ was never depicted in Western art: the three Marys at the tomb always stood in its place. In just a few instances, when a specific text about the idea of resurrection was being illustrated, there actually was a depiction of Christ emerging from the tomb, but the focus on

---

[25] A. Hayman, 'The Representation of the Holy Sepulchre in Auvergnat Romanesque Sculpture', *Autour de la 1c*, 633–42.

[26] F. Cardini and G. Vannini (eds.), *San Vivaldo in Valdelsa* (Valdelsa, 1980), 18–19; S. Gensini, 'La "Gerusalemme" di S. Vivaldo', in L. Vaccaro and F. Ricardi (eds.), *Sacri Monti* (Milan, 1992), 76–7.

[27] Dalman, *Grab Christi*, 13–21.

[28] G. Koziol, *Begging Pardon and Favour* (Ithaca, NY, 1992), 84; Glass, *Portals, Pilgrimage and Crusade*, 19–62.

F I G 7.5 A two-storey Holy Sepulchre guarded by knights, on a capital at Saint-Nectaire, Auvergne. The apertures show the lamps (valued, no doubt, as a source of holy oil for pilgrims). It has to be seen as a distant reminiscence of Jerusalem, and the occurrence of this motif on capitals in a church in the Auvergne confirms the interest of the aristocracy of the region in the Holy Land around the time of the First Crusade.

the moment of resurrection essentially began in the twelfth century. 'The great iconographic novelty . . . is the new version of the resurrection theme which visualises Christ rising bodily out of his tomb.'[29] In England, the only surviving representation from that time is on the porch of Malmesbury Abbey. The theme of the three Marys was certainly not abandoned, but by the thirteenth century the figure of the triumphant Christ, striding out of his sarcophagus, carrying a banner of victory, with the guards asleep or fainting at the side, was becoming a major topic for painters. The Klosterneuburg altar of about 1180 contains parallel images of Samson carrying the gates of Gath and Christ rising triumphantly from the tomb: conceivably,

---

[29] O. Pächt, *The Rise of Pictorial Narrative in Twelfth-Century England* (Oxford, 1962), 56.

the Samson 'antitype' helped to reconcile artists to the unfamiliar version of the resurrection.[30]

Meanwhile, representations of the tomb itself were changing. It had first appeared, in the early centuries, as a version of Constantine's edicule at Jerusalem, and in the Carolingian period it had often taken the form of the church building where the resurrection ceremonies were enacted. An illustration of Christ emerging from his sarcophagus can be found on an enamel shoulder-piece now in the Louvre, dating from about 1180, and in a crudely drawn but dramatic representation of the theme in a thirteenth-century calendar at Dresden in the Landesbibliothek.[31] This was a truly dramatic change in the way the Holy Sepulchre was represented, and it is difficult to be sure why it happened. It may be that there are fundamental reasons for the shift. Throughout the twelfth century, depictions of the crucifix focused attention increasingly upon the suffering Jesus, and the cross as a symbol of triumph became less common. If there was to be an unambiguous proclamation of victory, it would be natural to turn to the moment of resurrection itself. This would be a plausible explanation for an important iconographic change, but it is not one that can be demonstrated.

The proliferation of images of the Holy Land and of the historical events that had taken place there had the effect of bestowing a special sanctity upon parts of Western Europe as well. Monastic tradition had seen cities as places of disorder and greed, and some of the twelfth-century orders, including the Cistercians, responded to urban growth by founding their houses in what they called 'the wilderness'. Yet there was another image of cities: as far back as the ninth century, Hrabanus Maurus had written that 'citizens are called to come together and live as one, and to live the common life with more dignity and safety'.[32] The sense of dignity, or even holiness, of the cities was expressed in a wide variety of ways. The earliest surviving city seal in Europe was at Trier, dating from about 1150, and contains the inscription 'may the Lord bless the people and city of Trier'. On the Neutor, built in the first half of the thirteenth century, was an image of Christ blessing the city, which was represented as a model held by its patron, St Eucherius. In 1166 Frederick Barbarossa's

---

[30] For the Samson possibility, I am indebted to a lecture by Dr Sally Dormer, of the Victoria & Albert Museum.
[31] S. Collon-Gevaert and others (eds.), *A Treasury of Romanesque Art* (London, 1972), pl. 52; Möbius, *Passion*, pl. 145.
[32] Hrabanus Maurus, *De universo* (PL 111. 451).

diploma on the canonization of Charlemagne greeted Aachen as a
'sacred and free city'. Some cities commemorated their glory in 'city
praises', *laudes urbium*, a style of composition that went back to the
classical past. One of the themes that appeared in these—although it
certainly did not dominate them—was the participation of the city in
the glory of Jerusalem: Bamberg in about 1010 was said to 'share in
the glory of Jerusalem'.[33] On the whole, the references seem to be
more to the earthly Jerusalem than the heavenly one. It was conceived that the city, protected by its saints, visited by pilgrims, committed ideally to the struggle for the Holy Land, could be a holy place,
after the model of Jerusalem itself. Cities acquired commemorative
names that linked them with the East and with the events of the
crusades. Piacenza, in addition to its monastery of the Holy Sepulchre, had a convent of Nazareth, a Cistercian house of Galilee, and
a hospice of St Mary of Bethlehem. Reims had a Rue de Barbâtre,
perhaps commemorating the Spanish expedition in 1064, and a suburb of Venise, founded just after the Fourth Crusade, in which Venice
had played such a central part. Huy in the Low Countries, apart from
the foundation of Neufmoutiers, which was dedicated to the Holy
Sepulchre, soon after 1200 acquired a Constantinople gate and a
tower of Damietta. Even in the fifteenth century the walls of Padua
reminded a writer of those of Jerusalem.[34] Rome, as one might
expect, was special. There, the Lateran basilica incorporated the
sanctity of the Temple of the Old Testament, whose sacred vessels it
claimed to possess.[35] The sanctity of the holy places had begun to
place its stamp upon cities that contained memories of the sacred
East.

THE INTERNAL PILGRIMAGE

The new Christendom rested in part upon a new spirituality, and to
this the experience of visits to the Holy Sepulchre made an important
contribution. Accounts of journeys to Palestine were meant to provide practical information, and are somewhat reticent about what

[33] *Haec Jebusaice partem capit inclita doxae*, MGH Poetae 5, 397–8.
[34] A. Haverkamp, ' "Heilige Städte" im hohen Mittelalter', F. Graus (ed.), *Mentalitäten im Mittelalter*, VuF 35 (1987), 119–56; S. Collon-Gevaert and others, *A Treasury* 55; P. Raedts, 'The Medieval City as a Holy Place', *Omnes Circumadstantes*, 144–54; J. Heers, 'Bourgs et faubourgs en Occident: les pèlerinages et dévotions au Saint-Sépulcre', *Jérusalem, Rome*, 205–15.
[35] S. de Blaauw, 'The Solitary Celebration of the Supreme Pontiff: The Lateran Basilica as the New Temple', *Omnes Circumadstantes*, 120–43.

the visit meant in personal terms. The underlying motivation is clear
enough: 'I stayed in Jerusalem on pilgrimage for the love of our Lord
Jesus Christ.'[36] The sanctity of the place depended upon its role in the
history of salvation; new building, ambitious as it was, was secondary. The inscription painted in gold letters in 1149 above the entrance
to the Golgotha chapel emphasized this:

> *Est locus iste sacer, sacratus sanguine Christi,*
> *Per nostrum sacrare sacro nichil addimus isti.*
>
> This place is sacred, consecrated once
> By Christ's own blood; and we add nothing more.[37]

In most pilgrimage there was a penitential element, but this was
particularly prominent in the Holy Land. A popular saint's life in the
twelfth century was the story of Mary the Egyptian: Honorius 'of
Autun' preached a sermon on her, there is a verse life ascribed to
Hildebert of Tours, and her history is illustrated in the capitals of
Saint-Etienne, Toulouse. Mary was a prostitute who wished to visit
the church of the Holy Sepulchre, but found herself physically
unable to enter the building. Realizing her unworthiness, she went to
the point on the Jordan where Christ had been baptized, and crossed
the river, to live the life of a hermit on the other side. The themes of
pilgrimage, penitence, the baptism in the Jordan, and the hermit life,
which are entwined here, were prominent in the experience of visitors to the Holy Land. The ceremony of bathing in the Jordan was a
normal part of the pilgrim tour, and it carried with it the connotation
of a new baptism. Theoderic wrote of seeing 60,000 pilgrims
('according to our own estimation of the number') by the river,
standing in the dusk with candles in their hands, in an echo of the
baptismal liturgy.[38] Mary Magdalen, the model penitent, appears frequently in pilgrim accounts; so does Rahab the harlot of Jericho, who
was treated (with some forcing of the original meaning of Joshua 6:
17) as a model of penitence. The Mount of 'Quarantaine', where
Jesus was supposed to have spent his forty days of fasting in the
wilderness, became a centre of pilgrimage where a priory of the Holy
Sepulchre was built. Along with other remote places, it attracted the
settlement of hermits. The old monastic settlements from centuries
before had largely disappeared, although some of them lived on as

---

[36] John of Würzburg, Wilkinson/Hakluyt, 244.
[37] Biddle, *Tomb*, 93.
[38] *PL* 171. 1322–40; Wilkinson/Hakluyt, 304.

monasteries of the Orthodox church. Beside them, now sprang up a new generation of Latin religious houses and hermitages.

In particular, the ceremonies at Jerusalem brought pilgrims into direct association with the life, death, and resurrection of Christ. They visited Bethany for the raising of Lazarus, entered the city in the Palm Sunday procession, and crowded Calvary on Good Friday for the veneration of the Cross, and the Holy Sepulchre the following evening to wait for the new fire of the resurrection. This reverence for the historical Jesus was a fundamental feature of the pilgrim experience. It was often summed up in the desire to be 'where his feet have stood', *ubi steterunt pedes eius*, Jerome's much-quoted version of a text of the psalms. The idea was already familiar to Ekkehard of Aura shortly after the First Crusade, when he declared that Christ had 'consecrated that place . . . more than the earthly paradise itself by his incarnation, miracles, passion, resurrection and ascension'.[39]

As we saw long before, in considering the travels of Paula in the days of Jerome, seeing and physical contact were fundamental to the pilgrim experience. 'Port-holes' were provided in the side of the marble covering of the Sepulchre to make the saving rock accessible to pilgrims. The German visitor Theoderic recorded about 1170 how pilgrims attempted to make a direct physical link with the passion of Christ and his second coming. They would press their heads into the hole at Calvary where the cross had been fixed, and leave crosses brought from their homes in a great mound on the rock there: the guards had the job of burning them every Saturday. Similarly they left stones in the valley of Hinnom in order to take their seats there at the day of judgement.[40] The walls of the staircase down to the chapel of St Helena are still covered with crosses that pilgrims engraved to mark their arrival, a custom that assuredly began in the decades after the First Crusade. Processions and public ceremonies similarly helped the participants to see the saving events as present, rather than as episodes of the distant past: 'the great number of processions which took place indicates that Western crusaders . . . did not simply encounter splendid churches and monasteries at the holy places, but also a truly magnificent and well-ordered Latin worship.'[41]

---

[39] Ekkehard, *Hierosolimita* (MGH SS VI. 267).
[40] Wilkinson/Hakluyt, 285–6, 305.
[41] A. Schönfelder, 'Die Prozessionen der Lateiner in Jerusalem zur Zeit der Kreuzzüge', *Historisches Jahrbuch*, 32 (1911), 597.

In some unusual instances we do have a description of the trans-
forming character of the pilgrim experience. The devotion to the
historical Jesus, in particular, could have a dramatic impact on a
visitor's lifestyle. Ranieri of Pisa came to the Holy Land initially for
business purposes, but he was a devout man, and while there he
experienced a profound conversion. In the course of the ceremonies
in which he participated, he began to live the life of Christ. The Holy
Spirit descended upon him in the form of a dove; he fasted forty days
and nights in the wilderness; and lived as a hermit on Mount Tabor,
where he experienced the transfiguration as Christ's disciples did.
Ranieri was surrounded by prophecies that suggested that in him the
ministry of Christ was being renewed. At Sidon on Christmas Day
1139, he heard the bishop announce: 'Hear, most dear brothers: you
know in truth that now God is among us, who put on the flesh of one
of you for the salvation of all Christians.'[42] This remark, which
sounds like a straightforward reference to the incarnation, was taken
by Ranieri to be a mention of himself. The whole sequence of events
strikingly illustrates the close links between the pilgrim experience
and a growing pattern of spirituality in Western Europe: the sacred
sites seem to have shaped him into a sort of forerunner of Francis, for
whom also the pursuit of a ministry in the Holy Land would be
important in the next century. Ranieri eventually returned to Pisa
and devoted himself to poverty and preaching until his death in
1160, although the establishment there seems to have captured him
for its own purposes, turning him into a patriotic saint whose miracles supplied the needs of Pisans, and who became, next to the
Blessed Virgin, the patron saint of the city.

There are significant similarities between the experience of Ranieri
and those of Raimondo Palmario in the next generation. They both
reflect a conviction that a ministry of compassion is better than life at
the Holy Sepulchre. Such reservations about pilgrimage were not
new: they go back to Jerome himself, and to the legislation of the
Carolingians. One feature is different: the stress on works of mercy, a
characteristic feature of twelfth-century humanism. This is somewhat obscured in our records of Ranieri by the determination of his
hagiographer to turn him into a Pisan patriot. With Raimondo, it is
very clear. He was a native of Piacenza, for a long time a major centre
in the pilgrimage movement, and had travelled widely to holy

---

[42] R. Grégoire (ed.), *San Ranieri di Pisa in un ritratto agiografico inedito del secolo XIII*
(Pisa, 1990), 123–4; C. Morris, 'San Ranieri of Pisa', *JEH* 45 (1994), 588–99.

shrines. He was living rough at Rome when Christ appeared to him in the guise of a pilgrim, 'as first to the two disciples whom he accompanied to Emmaus' (Luke 24: 13–35):

'Raimond my servant . . . up to this moment I have satisfied your pious desires for pilgrimage . . . You have now seen all the holy places you most wanted to see, nor is there any vow remaining except that you should return to my most Holy Sepulchre. But I do not approve of this plan. I want you to occupy yourself with things more useful, that is works of mercy . . . I do not want you henceforward to wander round the world, but to return to your own land of Piacenza, where so many poor, so many abandoned widows, so many who are ill and worn down by various calamities demand my mercy.'[43]

From the beginning, there was an awareness of the Holy Sepulchre as something that could be treasured as an internal spiritual experience. In the sermon outside the walls of Jerusalem reported by Baudri of Bourgueil, the hearers are urged to 'keep . . . the incomparable treasure in the sepulchre of your heart'. At this early period, the stress was a practical one. It was the basis for recollecting the need for courageous action: 'boldly seize [the city] from those wicked crucifiers.'[44] A more spiritual meaning was in the mind of Peter the Venerable, half a century later. In his treatise *In Praise of the Holy Sepulchre* he came close to demythologizing the Sepulchre altogether, urging his hearers themselves to 'be Christ's Sepulchre': 'truly, he will never be separated, because, when all else is despised and rejected, Jesus will be my rest, Jesus my life, Jesus my food, Jesus my joy, Jesus my home, Jesus my glory, Jesus my all.' Peter, as abbot of Cluny, was a contemplative and teacher of contemplatives. All the same, his idea of the interior sepulchre continued to embody the intention to make war which was present in Baudri's sermon: 'Knowing all this, you have come to the Sepulchre of our Lord and God and of your creator and redeemer . . . and with your devout swords have cleansed from the filth of the impious the place and habitation of heavenly purity.'

Peter's work was the most sustained discussion of the theology and spiritual significance of the Sepulchre published in the twelfth century. In it he re-examined the nature of reverence for holy places: 'It is not for its own merit that we praise the Lord's Sepulchre, but because it was chosen to receive the Lord's body; it was made holy by the Lord's body itself. For we call "holy", not only angels and men

---

[43] Webb, *Pilgrimage*, 247–8 (doc. 3).
[44] Baudri, iv. 13 (RHC Occ. IV. 101).

who please God, but we also call holy the places which have been sanctified by God.' Among all holy places, the Sepulchre was supreme: 'The Lord's Sepulchre is given precedence not only over the Temple, not only over the Ark of the Covenant, not only over the Lord's birthplace, but it is also preferred without any exception to all holy places.'[45] Abbot Bernard of Clairvaux ended his treatise for the Templars, *In Praise of the New Militia*, with a meditation on the holy places. Like Peter the Venerable, Bernard gave the pre-eminence to the Sepulchre: 'Among the holy and desirable places the Sepulchre in a way holds the primacy. Somehow devotion is felt more keenly where he rested in death than where he lived in converse with men . . . The life of Christ is for me a rule of living; his death is a redemption from death.'[46] Peter and Bernard firmly linked the crusades with the personal devotion to the crucified Jesus that was becoming important in the spirituality of their time.

This personal devotion was closely associated with the presentation of the suffering Christ upon the cross. About the middle of the century, the popular preacher Ralph Ardens explained the growing strength of this theme: 'For this reason the image of the crucifix is now painted in church so that, seeing that our redeemer bore for our salvation poverty, weakness, reproaches, spitting, blows and death, we burn increasingly to love him in our heart.' By the 1180s, the canonist Huguccio was pointing out how the painting of the crucifix brought before the faithful what in later centuries would be called the arms of the passion: 'The painting and carving of the cross recalls (*rememorat*) the passion. The sun and moon in eclipse recall the suffering on the cross. The thieves are painted there, the nails, pincers, wounds, lance, blood and water, the title and the crown and purple garment, which are all insignia of the passion.'[47] The devotion of the twelfth century bound together a series of interlocking circles: personal sorrow for the suffering of Christ, the dying-Christ crucifix, meditation upon the events of his passion, relics of the cross and other memorials from the Holy Land, and the experience of pilgrimage.

Biblical commentators such as Peter Comestor, working after

[45] G. Constable (ed.), *Petri Venerabilis Sermones Tres, Revue Bénédictine*, 64 (1954), 243, 247, 234–5.

[46] P.-Y. Emery (ed.), *Bernard de Clairvaux, Éloge de la Nouvelle Chevalerie* (SC 367, (Paris, 1990), xi. 18, p. 98.

[47] A. M. Landgraf, *Dogmengeschichte der Frühscholastik* (Regensburg, 1952–5), 24–30.

1160, were more interested than before in exploring the literal meaning of the Gospels. To do this, he assembled a mass of evidence. Apart
from a detailed examination of the biblical texts, he went back to
Paschasius Radbertus, who had used the descriptions of the tomb to
clarify the Easter narratives. Comestor knew more than Paschasius
about the topography of the Holy Land: he was familiar with some of
the pilgrim narratives, notably with one of the editions of Fretellus'
standard guide. His treatment was critical: for example, he rejected
the speculative idea that the Temple had been rebuilt after its destruction by Titus. The most striking feature of his work, however,
was the way in which he read back the ceremonies of the church into
the exposition of the Gospel events: 'his account of the entry into
Jerusalem, the Last Supper, the crucifixion and the resurrection read
like a commentary on the liturgy for Holy Week and Easter, both in
the *Scholastic History* and in the lectures.' Comestor's work was well
known among subsequent scholarly writers on the Holy Land, such
as Willibrand of Oldenburg and Burchard of Mount Sion. There
is force in Bernard Hamilton's view that the changes in 'religious
sensibility occurred at least in part because throughout most of
the twelfth century Jerusalem had been a Western Catholic city, and
it had been possible for the pilgrims . . . to appreciate the Gospel
narratives on a literal level'.[48]

The way in which so many of these themes came together can be
illustrated in the Waltham Chronicle, which was composed after
1177 to record the legendary discovery, more than a century before,
of the holy cross that was placed in Waltham Abbey. An image of the
crucified Christ was found buried, carved with such wonderful skill
'that you might think it the work of the supreme craftsman himself'.
The lord of the estate, Tovi, addressed his personal devotion to the
image: 'O Lord who, to save the world, sacrificed your body and blood
on the altar of the cross, a holy victim pleasing to God, who allowed
the crown of thorns to be placed on your head for the salvation of
the faithful . . . O source of my delight, O peace and joy of my heart.'
Effectively the image was Christ's true body. When studs were
inserted into it to secure gold plating, blood oozed from the stone
of which it was made. Some of this was caught in a cloth, thus

---

[48] B. Smalley, 'Some Gospel Commentaries of the Early Twelfth Century', and 'Peter
Comestor on the Gospels', *Recherches de Théologie Ancienne et Médiévale*, 45 (1978),
147–80, and 46 (1979), 84–129; and B. Hamilton, 'The Impact of Crusader Jerusalem
on Western Christendom', *Catholic Historical Review*, 80 (1994), 713.

generating a local cult of the holy blood. Anachronistically, these events led Tovi to fasten his sword round the image, 'henceforth to fight for him'.[49] The cult encouraged a group of pilgrims to set out. As they explained to the king: 'We your servants, desiring to visit the holy places ... chose by divine mercy to travel to Jerusalem ... to adore with heartfelt and sincere devotion, to the best of our ability, the traces of his holy nativity, passion, resurrection, ascension and the mission of the Holy Spirit to the apostles.' Such overlapping themes of devotion inescapably led contemporaries to attach great importance to the protection of the Holy Sepulchre itself from what was perceived as defilement by the unbeliever.

THE THREAT TO THE HOLY SEPULCHRE

For those who were planning military action to defend or recover the Holy Land, the Sepulchre accordingly remained the centre of their interest, and the most promising subject for public appeal. As the position of the Latin kingdom became more precarious in the face of Saladin's growing power, a high-level embassy, consisting of the Patriarch Heraclius and Roger des Moulins, the Master of the Hospitallers, came in January 1185 to offer Philip II of France and Henry II of England in turn, the keys of the city of Jerusalem and of the Holy Sepulchre and the banner of the holy cross. Apart from the serious level of Muslim pressure, the internal position of the kingdom was insecure, with a leper king, Baldwin IV, an infant heir and bitter controversy among the magnates. The objects the representatives brought could be seen as relics: the chronicler Ralph of Diceto regarded them as reminders (*memorialia*) of the birth, passion, and resurrection of Christ. Other writers, in more political terms, thought they implied an offer of 'the crown of the kingdom and the allegiance of its people'. The intention of this offer is still not clear, but it is plain that the symbols expressed, to the minds of contemporaries, the Latin dominion at Jerusalem that the faithful were called to defend.[50] A thirteenth-century manuscript of the crusading history of William of Tyre summed up the movement in a diagram that contained miniatures of the preaching of Urban II at Clermont, the crucifixion,

---

[49] L. Watkiss and M. Chibnall (eds.), *The Waltham Chronicle* (Oxford, 1994), 9–13, 19–21, 39.
[50] J. Phillips, *Defenders of the Holy Land* (Oxford, 1996), 257–9, and C. Tyerman, *England and the Crusades, 1095–1588* (London, 1988), 50–1.

a pilgrim at the Holy Sepulchre, and Muslims worshipping a naked idol on a column.[51]

Westerners therefore saw themselves as both protectors of, and protected by, the Holy Sepulchre. An ancient German pilgrim song, which continued in use throughout the Middle Ages, prayed;

In gotes namen fara wir	In God's name we make our way,
seyner genaden gara wir.	And we journey in his grace.
Nu helff uns die gotes kraft	Power of God help us today
und das heylig grab,	And the Holy Grave
da got selber ynne lag	In which God in person lay.
Kyrieleis.	Kyrie eleison.[52]

For Bernard and Peter the Venerable alike, for all their concern with the spiritual meanings of Jerusalem, it was of great importance that the Holy Sepulchre should be kept safe and in Christian custody:

What is holy should not be given to dogs, lest the places where his feet stood, who brought salvation into the midst of the earth, should again be trampled by the feet of the wicked . . . lest the very cross of salvation, now besieged by the wicked, it is said . . . should be seized; lest the very Sepulchre of the Lord, which up to now was the glory of the whole world, should perchance be destroyed completely as they threaten.[53]

Such sentiments explain the horror that possessed Western European society when the Sepulchre and the Cross were lost in 1187, at Saladin's capture of the city.

---

[51] S. Lloyd, The Crusading Movement', *Oxford Illustrated History of the Crusades* (Oxford, 1988), 44.

[52] U. Müller, *Kreuzzugsdichtung* (Tübingen, 1969), no. 8.

[53] G. Constable (ed.), *The Letters of Peter the Venerable* (Cambridge, Mass., 1967), ep. 166, i. 399–400, with references to Matthew 7: 6; Psalms 132: 7 and 74: 12; and Isaiah 11: 10.

8

Failure and Endeavour, 1187–1291

The later twelfth century was the period when the struggle between two visions of Jerusalem, the Muslim and the Christian, came to be fully defined. Within Islam, as within Christianity, there had been periods of indifference to the fate of the city, but the career of Saladin, his recovery of Jerusalem, and his defence of it against the Third Crusade was supremely the time when it was identified, on both sides, as the Holy City. For Christians, this had become a favoured description: for Muslims, *al-Quds*, the holy, was used (and still is used) as its proper name.

The ground of the sanctity of the city was different in Christianity and Islam, although there was a common inheritance of Old Testament associations. The Muslims understood the central significance of the Holy Sepulchre for Christians. When al-Harawi visited Jerusalem in 1173, he observed that

> as for the places of Christian pilgrimage, the most important of them is the dung-church . . . For the Christians, the tomb is situated there which they call the tomb of the Resurrection (*qiyyaama*), because they locate in that place the Resurrection of the Messiah. In reality the site was *qumama*, the place of dung, because the sweepings of the area were thrown there. It was a place outside the city where the hands of malefactors were cut off and thieves were crucified; that is what the Gospel says.

Qadi al-Fadil, at the time of Saladin, reported to the caliph at Baghdad that the crusaders' aim had been 'to liberate the tomb and restore the *qumama*', and at the same time Imad-al-Din presented the Franks' absolute commitment: 'We will die beneath the tomb of our Lord.'[1]

---

[1] Hillenbrand, *Perspectives*, 317–18.

The underlying Muslim veneration for al-Quds had not been very evident during the first half of the twelfth century. There were no *Fada'il al-Quds* (Praises of Jerusalem) composed in those decades, and language of the holy war (*jihad*) was little used in official circles until Zengi's recovery of Edessa in 1144. From then onwards the conviction that the service of Allah demanded the recovery of Jerusalem became powerful. Nureddin built a magnificent *minbar* (pulpit) in 1168–9, with the intention that it should be brought to the al-Aqsa mosque when it was recovered, and the decisive campaign of Saladin was launched by a public reading of one of the eleventh-century 'Praises' in April 1187. The conquest of the holy city was greeted by an outpouring of joy throughout the Muslim world: it was celebrated in sixty letters that still survive, and a dozen poems. In far-off Baghdad, Ibn al-Jawzi wrote a long 'Praises' work: 'he who visits Jerusalem, moved by devotion to the place, will enter paradise'. The special grounds for this reverence were stated in a letter that, according to Ibn Shaddad, Saladin wrote to Richard I in 1192: 'Jerusalem is to us as it is to you. It is even more important to us, since it is the site of our Prophet's night journey and the place where the people will gather on the day of judgement.' When Saladin entered Jerusalem, a solemn *khutba* or sermon was delivered by Ibn al-Zaki of Damascus, in which he stated the glories of the city more fully:

It was the dwelling-place of your father Abraham; the place from which your blessed Prophet Muhammad mounted to heaven; the *qibla* towards which you turned to pray at the commencement of Islam, the abode of the prophets, the place visited by the saints . . . It is the country where mankind will be assembled for judgement, the ground where the resurrection will take place.[2]

For the Muslims, the presence of the Christians in the sacred place was a defilement. Each side wrote of the impurities perpetrated by the other. The long-repeated pun on *qiyyaama* and *qumama* was not just a nasty joke, but expressed a reality: the presence of the empty tomb was, for Islam, the corruption of al-Quds. Matters were made worse when buildings with a long history of Islamic devotion were turned over to the Christian cult. The great cross erected above the Dome of the Rock provoked particular horror, and the adaptation to Templar use of the al-Aqsa mosque led Imad-al-Din to the outrageous charge

[2] Ibid. 189–92.

that they had employed the *mihrab*, which indicated the direction of Mecca, as a lavatory. (Other accounts indicate that in reality it had been left intact, but concealed by a wall.)[3] The descriptions of Saladin's victory stressed the care with which the Temple mount and al-Aqsa mosque were ceremonially purified.

That victory was effectively won on 4 July 1187, when the army of the kingdom of Jerusalem was destroyed at the Battle of Hattin. The wood of the cross, which had protected the Franks since its rediscovery in 1099, was captured. Within a few days Acre, the most important of the coastal cities, had been surrendered. Jerusalem was poorly garrisoned and was now without a standing army to protect it, but it was gallantly defended until it, too, fell on 2 October. Saladin entered the city, according to the Muslim calendar, on 27 Rajab, the anniversary of the night journey. The collapse should not have come as a great surprise to the West. Letters and delegations from the Latin East had long been warning of its approach; the crown and nobility of the kingdom were in bitter dispute among themselves; and the uniting of the Muslim world by Saladin had created an enemy of overwhelming strength. Pope Gregory VIII, looking back to 1144 with the benefit of hindsight, remarked sadly that 'these things could first have been feared when Edessa and other land passed into the power of the pagans'.[4]

Nevertheless, the defeat was greeted in the West with shock and horror. Gregory VIII, who at first was not sure what had happened to the city itself, spoke of 'the severe and terrible judgement' that had fallen upon the land of Jerusalem, and of 'those savage barbarians thirsting after Christian blood and using all their force to profane the holy places and banish the worship of God from the land'. Peter of Blois turned angrily upon God: 'Where are your former mercies? How have you been forgetful of your compassion? . . . For now you have become not sanctifier and redeemer, but slayer and destroyer.' The lamentations spread through the chronicles of the West and were repeated in poems and songs. To Prévostin, the head of the schools at Paris, it seemed that God was no longer on the side of the Christians:

The Holy Sepulchre knew glorious days, but because of our sins has lost its sacred halo . . . Demons dance round the Sepulchre; they lead their choirs, and sing: 'where is the God of the Christians?' The Saracens have not lost

---

[3] Ibid. 300.   [4] *Audita tremendi* (Riley-Smith, *The Crusades*, 65).

their God, but the God of the Jews has fallen asleep, and the God of the Christians is dead.[5]

Although the orthodox explanation for what had happened was to blame the sins of Christians, there was thus an undercurrent that suggested that God did not intend the recovery of the Holy Sepulchre. When Richard I died in 1199, before he could carry out his project of a renewed crusade in the East, the song-writer Gaucelm Faidit saw it as marking the disappearance of the hope of freeing the Sepulchre:

Et mais ert tart lo Sepulcres conqés	The Sepulchre will not be freed for now.
Qe Dex non vol; et se il lo volgués,	God does not want it—if he had desired,
Qe vos seignor, vesquisaz senz faillir,	My lord, you would be flourishing and whole.
Se's conveguez de Surie foïr.	Then they would have to flee from Syria.[6]

Whereas in 1099, the Christians drew on the triumphant prophecies of Isaiah, they now appropriated the psalms of lamentation for their sermons and liturgies. They ceaselessly had on their lips, 'If I forget you, O Jerusalem, let my right hand wither! Let my tongue cleave to the roof of my mouth, if I do not remember you, if I do not set Jerusalem above my highest joy!' (Psalm 137: 5–6); and 'O God, the heathen have come into thy inheritance; they have defiled thy holy temple; they have laid Jerusalem in ruins . . . Why should the nations say, "Where is their God?" ' (Psalm 79: 1, 10). An English participant on the Third Crusade (1189–92) reflected the same spirit, quoting from Lamentations 1: 12: 'There is no sorrow like this sorrow, when they possess the Holy Sepulchre but persecute the one who was buried there; and they hold the cross but despise the crucified.'[7]

When Jerusalem was recovered by Frederick II in 1228, it was a precarious and ambiguous success, and at the overrunning of the city again in 1244, the same sense of despair prevailed. A Spanish poet told of the horror with which the news was received by the pope, seemingly at the First Council of Lyons (1245):

---

[5] Ibid. 64–5; Peter of Blois, *De Hierosolymitana peregrinatione acceleranda* (PL 207. 1058); G. Lacombe, *La Vie et les œuvres de Prévostin*, (Paris, 1927), 199–200.

[6] F. Collins, *A Medieval Songbook* (Charlottesville, 1982), 58.

[7] *Itinerarium Peregrinorum*, i. 9, p. 39.

Léesse la carte en el conçilio santo:	The council read the
	message they received;
papa e cardenales fazian grand	The pope and cardinals
llanto,	were deeply grieved.
rompen sus vestidos	Their garments all were rent,
dan grandes gemidos	They gave a loud lament
por Jherusalem.	For Jerusalem.[8]

Latin writers assumed that the conquerors were determined to desecrate the holy places. Gregory VIII had set the note in his attack upon the 'savage barbarians', and Conrad of Montferrat had a placard painted of the humiliations inflicted on the Holy Sepulchre. In the same way, the poet of *Ay, Jherusalem*, describing the events of 1244, told how the conquerors massacred and tortured the Christian inhabitants and desecrated the Holy Sepulchre. Such comments were often written close to the events, but they were shaped by the needs of propaganda, or merely by what Western Christians expected Saladin to do. The Muslims did not in fact behave in this way.

The savage warfare during the thirteenth century between Mongols, Latins, and Mamluks, which culminated in the elimination of the Latins from the Holy Land, did a great deal of damage to the substructure on which the former prosperity of Palestine had rested: the pilgrims of the later Middle Ages were startled to observe the desolation that prevailed in the land of milk and honey they had expected to find. More immediately, Christian shrines suffered a great deal from the events of 1187. Saladin had recovered the city in a spirit of *jihad*, and the restoration and extension of the faith was central to his intentions. A sequence of pilgrimage certificates, originally deposited in the great mosque at Damascus, recorded the visits of the faithful to Mecca, Medina, and Jerusalem. Many of these certificates survive only in fragments, but those that can be dated cover the period of the recovery of Jerusalem from 1193 to 1229.[9] The Dome of the Rock and the al-Aqsa mosque almost immediately were ritually purified and restored to Muslim worship. Christian decorations, such as the cross on top of the Temple, were torn down. The abbey of Mount Sion was damaged, and the church of Our Lady of Josaphat was virtually demolished. Two major Christian centres were soon appropriated for Islamic purposes: the church of St Anne was

---

[8] D. M. Rogers, 'Christians and Moors in *Ay Jherusalem*', *Journeys towards God*, 127–34.
[9] J. Sourdel-Thomine, 'Une image musulmane de Jérusalem au début du XIIIe siècle', *Jérusalem*, Rome, 217–33.

transformed into a madrasa, the *Salahiyah*, and the house of the Latin patriarch was taken over as a *sufi* centre. The willingness of Saladin's heirs to compromise with the Christians over his greatest triumph and to surrender Jerusalem strikes a curious note, even given the promise of political security that it offered. The reason was partly, as al-Maqrizi argued, that the 1229 treaty preserved for Islam its own sacred places: 'The Haram and the Dome of the Rock and the Aqsa mosque which lay therein should remain to the Muslims, with no Franks allowed to enter except as visitors . . . All the practice of Islam, with the call to prayer and the prayers themselves, should continue to be observed within the sacred area.'[10] Since the properties and rents that sustained the Latin church had been transferred to the use of the new owners, the old establishment found it difficult to restore the old order after 1229. At the Holy Sepulchre the canons lost their properties in the town, and were obliged to move to Acre. It was reported by a Muslim writer that Saladin and his advisers considered the possibility of demolishing the church, but had decided against it. This was partly out of respect for 'Umar, the caliph who had first conquered Jerusalem and left the Holy Sepulchre intact, and partly because it was realized that it was the site that was holy, not the structures, whose loss would exasperate the Franks but not destroy the place's importance for them.

The events of the late twelfth century created a new balance of power at the Holy Sepulchre. For almost a century, decisions about worship had been made by the Latin establishment. After Saladin's reconquest, the Greek Emperor Isaac Angelus (1185–95) at first hoped to shape the Christian presence at the Sepulchre, but his own political problems and the Latin conquest of Constantinople in 1204 fatally weakened Byzantine influence. In the power vacuum, local clergy (that is, Greek Orthodox clergy of Syrian use) were allowed to conduct services at the Sepulchre. Some limited Latin influence remained: from 1192, at the request of Archbishop Hubert Walter, Latin priests were given access to the altars. The kingdom of Georgia emerged as a significant player on the scene, and Georgian clergy obtained access to altars in some of the major remaining shrines. As to the admission of pilgrims, we have limited information. Perhaps from 1187 onwards, only pilgrims who were willing to pay a considerable fee were allowed access to the Holy Sepulchre; this was certainly the case when Willibrand visited in 1212. The effect of this

---

[10] Hillenbrand, *Perspectives*, 380.

custom was to limit access to tourist parties, and to exclude local Christians except when the church was opened for the Easter ceremonies. The church became essentially a private chapel for small and privileged groups of clergy, with only pilgrim access on special occasions. Except between 1228 and 1244, this was the regime enforced continuously from Saladin onwards.[11]

THE THIRTEENTH-CENTURY REASSESSMENT

The crusades continued to be massively present to the minds of clergy and nobles in Western Europe. Indeed, the fate of the Holy Land was a more persistent theme than it had been in the twelfth century. Every monastic library contained reading about the crusades. Sometimes they would have a copy of one of the classic crusade narratives, such as that of Robert of Reims on the First Crusade, sometimes a compilation of crusade histories. The imagination of the aristocracy was fed by crusading epics contained in the *First Cycle of the Crusades*. The European courts were interested in reading the French version of William of Tyre and its various continuations. We have more sermon material for the thirteenth century: there was more preaching, and it was better organized. The handful of sermons that survives from the period up to 1200 comes from chronicles, and they no doubt are constructing free versions. The evidence brings us closer to the preachers of the thirteenth century. Christoph Maier counts twenty-one complete surviving sermons. In addition, there is a collection of materials for use in sermons circulated in England in about 1216, rather inappropriately known as the *Ordinacio*, and the massive tract by Humbert of Romans, *On the Preaching of the Holy Cross*, prepared in 1266–8.

In the decades after 1187, the Latins responded with a series of expeditions without parallel in their strength and persistence. The aid currently provided by Western Europe to the Third World is feeble in comparison with the huge effort devoted by our predecessors to the aim of recovering the Holy Sepulchre. From 1189 to 1192, in the Third Crusade, the Emperor Frederick Barbarossa, and Kings Philip Augustus of France and Richard I of England led armies that recovered a substantial part of the former Latin posses-

---

[11] A. Jotischky, 'The Fate of the Orthodox Church in Jerusalem at the End of the Twelfth Century', *Patterns of the Past*, 179–94; M. L. Bulst-Thiele, 'Die Mosaiken der Auferstehungskirche in Jerusalem', *Frühmittelalterliche Studien*, 13 (1979), 442–71.

sions along the coast, notably the great port of Acre, and occupied
the island of Cyprus, but which failed to reach Jerusalem. In 1197 a
major campaign planned by the Emperor Henry VI was wrecked by
his sudden death from fever on the point of departure. In 1202–5
the largely Franco-Italian Fourth Crusade occupied Constantinople
and partitioned the former Byzantine Empire, but never proceeded
to the Holy Land. The Fourth Lateran Council generated an international attack on Egypt in 1217–21 commanded by the papal legate Pelagius, which captured the major port of Damietta but
achieved no further success, and did not significantly alter the situation in Syria. In 1228–9 the Emperor Frederick II negotiated with
the sultan a truce that returned Jerusalem to Christian lordship.
Latin control was left insecure under this agreement, signed when
Frederick himself was under papal excommunication, and the
terms of the settlement were condemned by the Latin patriarch.
After the loss of the city in 1244, Louis IX of France led another
major expedition to Egypt which, despite a spectacular success in
the instantaneous capture of Damietta in 1249, ended in total disaster. Records do not enable us to state the precise size of these
armies, but they were substantial: the army of Louis IX has been
estimated as 15,000 men, and these were serious professional warriors, maintained by royal resources, who should (although the
event proved differently) have been a disciplined and formidable
force.

Thinking about the new situation was consolidated in three papal
bulls: *Audita tremendi* of Gregory VIII (October 1187), and *Quia maior*
and *Ad liberandam*, issued by Innocent III in 1213 and 1215 in connection with the Fourth Lateran Council. The promise of forgiveness
to participants was virtually unchanged: 'to those who with contrite
hearts and humbled spirits undertake the labour of this journey and
die in penitence for their sins and with right faith we promise full
indulgence of their faults and eternal life.' The exhortation not to
'make your way there for money or for worldly glory, but according
to the will of God who taught by his own action that one ought to lay
down one's life for one's brothers' went back to the first decades of
the twelfth century. The insistence that 'the Lord could save (the
Holy Land) by his will alone, but it is not for us to ask him why he
has acted thus' is pure Bernard of Clairvaux. In these important
senses, the response to the crisis was to reassert traditional values.[12]

---

[12] Riley-Smith, *The Crusades*, 66.

Tradition continued to prevail in some of the expressions of devotion, such as the 'Palestine song', *Palästinalied*, of Walther von der Vogelweide:

Allerêrest lebe ich mir werde,	Now my life has found a purpose,
sît mîn sündic ouge siht	For my sinful eyes behold
daz reine lant und ouch die erde	That pure land and holy country
der man sô vil êren giht.	Of which wondrous things are told.
mirst geschehen des ich ie bat	My desire is granted now:
ich bin komen an die stat	I have seen the place which God
dâ got mennischlichen trat.	In a human body trod.[13]

These lines may have been written in the context of Frederick II's recovery of the Holy City, but we do not know that Walther took part in that expedition. He may never have been to Palestine, and have been giving poetic expression to long-held ideals.

Christians devoted themselves to serious attempts to understand what God was doing in the Holy Land. Politicians, preachers, and propagandists had to make sense of projects that did not appear to have been blessed by God. It was already conventional to explain failure by sin: sometimes crusaders, sometimes the *poulains* or Franks settled in Outremer, had betrayed the holy cause by their wickedness. Without exempting the settlers from all responsibility, papal thinking now took a large step forward. The defeat, it was said in *Audita tremendi*, was the result of 'not only the sins of the inhabitants but also our own and those of the whole Christian people'. Gregory seems particularly to have had in mind the conflicts within Christendom that were to continue to delay the departure of the kings on the Third Crusade: 'we hear from all parts of the world about quarrels between kings and princes, cities against cities, and about scandals.' Preachers also continued to use an excuse already formulated by Bernard of Clairvaux at the time of the Second Crusade. God is perfectly well able to defend his own land, but he wishes to test the faithful, and thereby to offer them an opportunity of repentance through his service: 'The Lord is indeed injured in the loss of his patrimony, but wishes to test his friends, and discover if his vassals are faithful. For whoever holds a fief of his liege lord, if he fails him

---

[13] P. Stapf (ed.), *Walther von der Vogelweide: Sprüche, Lieder* (Wiesbaden, [n.d.]), no. 171.

when he is attacked and his inheritance is taken from him, deserves to lose his own fief.'[14]

New ideas sprang from the disaster of 1187, and were developed by Innocent III into a philosophy of church government. It was widely accepted that a responsibility rested on the whole Western church to commit itself to repentance and to the deliverance of the Holy Land. Westerners were helped to understand what was going on by their familiarity with the custom of the humiliation of images. In response to need, distress, or attacks upon a church, the cross and statues of the saints would be placed on the floor, surrounded by thorns. When in 1197, for example, the church of Dublin was confronted by excessive exactions by Count John, the future king of England, the archbishop ordered a ritual humiliation. In the course of it, one of the images joined in the lamentations. Upon one of the crucifixes, the face reddened, drops fell from its eyes, and blood and water were shed from its side.[15] This way of thinking was echoed in crusading propaganda. Henry of Albano wrote of the 'the holy ground upon which the Lord once has set his foot and which now is abandoned to defilement by the pagans', and of the desecration of the cross. 'How would the redeemer have tolerated the rape of the cross by the pagans unless he was ready to let himself be crucified again by them? Thus the mystery of our redemption repeats itself.'[16]

Throughout the pontificate of Innocent III (1198–1216) reform and the liberation of Jerusalem were the two connected endeavours to which he devoted his attention: 'Among all the good things which our heart can desire, there are two in this world which we value above all: that is to promote the recovery of the Holy Land and the reform of the universal church.'[17] Francis of Assisi was actively concerned for the fate of Jerusalem, and went with the Fifth Crusade to preach to the sultan at Cairo. When Louis IX was setting out for his own crusade, he saw it as necessary that first he should reform the operation of the royal government in France, and set in motion a 'restitution' of things wrongly taken from the people by royal officers. All these expeditions ended in marginal success or total failure. The central explanation that this was the result of sin continued, but wore increasingly thin. Spiritual crisis is visible in the attempt of the papal legate Cardinal Odo of Châteauroux, who was expert in the

---

[14] James of Vitry, sermon 47 (Riley-Smith, *The Crusades*, 134).
[15] L. Little, *Benedictine Maledictions* (London, 1993), 123–4.
[16] W. Zander, *Israel and the Holy Places of Christendom* (London, 1971), 16.
[17] Innocent III, *Register*, xvi. 30 (PL 216. 824A).

New Thinking at the Papal Curia

The placing of the Third Crusade alongside the cross and Sepulchre as a central event of salvation history points to a radical agenda behind the thinking of the papal curia in 1187–9. Peter of Blois, who was in residence there when the news of the Battle of Hattin arrived, addressed himself to the need to embrace poverty as part of the penance that a new crusade would demand. He claimed that others were following the same path: 'the cardinals, with the assent of the lord pope, have firmly promised among themselves that, having renounced all wealth and luxuries, they will preach the cross of Christ not only by word, but by deed and example'. Peter, in his crusade preaching, embraced the ideals of poverty that were circulating among the more radical religious reformers: 'Nothing weighs down and suffocates the fruit of penance so much as the afflu- ence of possessions and the eminence of human rank.' He even, at one point, said that the church should abandon the wealthy as a source of support and turn to the poor. In the age of the Humiliati, the Waldensians, and the emerging friars, poverty had a radical edge to it, and became an essential elem- ent in the general reform of Western society which would be pleasing to God and secure his blessing for the recovery of the Holy Sepulchre.

This was the central thrust of new thinking promoted by the curia. There were other analyses. Immediately after 1187, the Englishman Ralph Niger wrote his treatise, *Warfare and the Threefold Pilgrimage to Jerusalem, De re militari et triplici via per- egrinationis Ierosolimitanae*. Ralph was not disposed to excuse the wickedness of the Franks in the East: he has a section uncompromisingly entitled 'on the just punishment of Pales- tine'. But he had severe doubts about the wisdom of warfare in the East, while corruption plagued the West, and while heresies such as dualism were left to flourish there: 'what advantage is there if the earthly Jerusalem is built up and meanwhile our mother Zion is laid waste; if Palestine is liberated from the Saracens, and meanwhile the malice of unbelief grows fat at home; if while unbelief is overcome abroad, the purity of the faith is destroyed and corrupted?' Ralph insisted so strongly that only defensive measures should be taken against the Saracens, who were to be converted by words, not force, that his response stands clearly outside the tradition of crusading thinking. Even amongst reformed and radical groups, the insistence on Christendom's duty, to recover the Holy Land by force remained dominant. The friar Stephen of Bourbon argued that, as we are spiritual descendants of Adam, 'the land is ours by right of succession as far as we are the true children of God', and that 'the land belongs to us by the right of purchase and acquisition; for Christ bought it for us by his blood, has expelled the Jewish people from it by the might of the Romans and has handed it to Christendom'. The overwhelming opinion was that the disaster of 1187 required a new endeavour, accompanied by repentance and reform, to recover the Holy Sepulchre.

G. B. Flahiff, '*Deus non vult*: A Critic of the Third Crusade', *Medieval Studies*, 9 (1947), 162–88; L. Schmugge (ed.), *Radulfus Niger:* De re militari et triplici via peregrinationis Ierosolimitanae (Berlin, 1977); W. Zander, *Israel and the Holy Places of Christendom* (London, 1971), 17–19; R. W. Southern, 'Peter of Blois and the Third Crusade', H. Mayr-Harting and R. I. Moore (eds.), *Studies in Medieval History presented to R. H. C. Davis* (London, 1985), 207–18; M. Markowski, 'Peter of Blois and the Conception of the Third Crusade', *Horns of Hattin*, 261–9.

affairs of the Holy Land, to explain the catastrophic defeat of the army of St Louis at Mansurah on 8 February 1250. It was obvious that if the Holy Land had to wait for someone more saintly than Louis, it would have to wait a long time, and Odo found, so far from ascribing the defeat to the sins of the French army, he was obliged to defend its actions as pleasing to the will of God: 'These nobles were waging a just war, intending to recover the land which the wicked Saracens had taken from Christians. But the Saracens were waging an unjust war. So how comes that God allowed injustice to overcome justice, and impiety piety?' Among the explanations which Odo offered the most prominent was still that of sin, and since the crusaders could hardly be seen as sinful, he had to underline still more strongly that God had acted 'to point out to the whole Christian people how gravely they had offended him . . . Thus the son of God willed to be killed by a most foul death, to show how grave our sins were.'[18]

The conviction that the recovery of Jerusalem depended on the conversion of Christendom involved the whole of the Western church in preparation for further crusades. When Innocent III was planning the Fifth Crusade, he incorporated a large element of spiritual preparation and financial commitment by all Christians. There were already some opportunities in Western liturgy for commemorating the Holy Land in special or 'votive' masses, but these were now widely extended. The process began at once: a *clamor pro Terra Sancta* seems to have been started at London in 1188. The term suggests that its champions were aware of the parallel between ritual humiliation of the crucifix and images and the humiliation of the cross and Sepulchre in 1187. Provisions for this new type of service were extended throughout Europe by papal authority. Massive papal direction of this sort was only conceivable with techniques of government which were only newly available, and of which Innocent himself was an outstanding master. He provided for universal prayer and a liturgy directed to remembering Jerusalem:

We ought to fight in such a conflict not so much with physical arms as with spiritual ones. And so we decree and command that once a month there must be a general procession of men . . . and women separately, praying with minds and bodies humbly disposed and with devout and fervent prayer, that merciful God will relieve us of this shameful disgrace by liberating from the hands of the pagans that land in which he accomplished the universal mystery of our redemption . . . And every day during the celebration of mass . . . everyone, men and women alike, must humbly prostrate themselves on the ground and the psalm 'O God, the heathen are come into thine inheritance' (Psalm 79: 1) should be sung loudly by the clergy.

A prayer for the restoration of the Holy Land to Christian worship was then to be said over the altar. Associated with the endeavour to stamp a crusading piety upon the awareness of the West was the prescription that a chest be provided in each church for alms for the Holy Land, and requests (or demands) for financial contributions from the clergy. This universality of response was underlined by an important extension of recruitment. A preaching ministry for the crusade was carefully regulated. Moreover, whereas previous popes

---

[18] P. Cole, D. L. D'Avray, and J. Riley-Smith, 'Application of Theology to Current Affairs: Memorial Sermons on the Dead of Mansurah and on Innocent IV', *Historical Review*, 63 (1990), 227–47.

had been selective in admitting only suitable warriors, Innocent appealed for everyone to join, 'except persons bound by religious profession'.

All of this had very practical consequences. There was a general recruitment, accompanied by the assumption that unsuitable recruits would be dispensed by papal authority and contribute appropriately to the costs of the expedition. Systematic taxation, in effect, came to Western Europe through the pressure of the attempt to recover Jerusalem. The kings of France and (much more success-fully) England levied a heavy charge, the 'Saladin tithe', to finance the Third Crusade. There was little previous history of the papal taxation of the clergy, but Innocent made heavy demands for money, originally voluntary but increasingly exacted by papal officers. In the thirteenth century levies for crusading, many of them controlled or exploited by the kings, became a major element of political conflict. There was, moreover, a link between the need for finance and the appeal for wider recruiting. Payments made by those who had taken the cross, but were not usefully able to join the expedition, were an important source of finance, and amounted to the sale of forgiveness of sins in order to support the expedition. It was an amalgamation of repentance and finance that was one of the originalities of thir-teenth-century crusading.[19] This whole range of administrative developments encouraged contemporaries to see the crusades as a much more coherent movement than had been the case in the twelfth century. They never were clearly distinguished from pilgrim-age, but they acquired their own terminology (*crux, crucesignati, croisade*), and a body of law based on the papal privileges and defined by some of the major canonists. Pilgrimage and crusading were also recognized as legal entities, which had to be taken into account by the law courts. Starting shortly before 1200, English and Norman law courts accepted pilgrimage as an 'essoin', or legitimate reason for non-appearance; and soon distinctions were made between journeys to the Holy Sepulchre and shorter journeys, and between personal pilgrimage and involvement in a full-scale military operation.[20]

The expeditions we have mentioned so far were designed to retake the Holy Sepulchre from the heathen, but one cannot escape the impression that people were ready to fight for the Holy Land

---

[19] *Quia Maior* (Riley-Smith, *The Crusades*, 122–4); Tyerman, *England*, 75–83; C. Morris, *The Papal Monarchy* (Oxford, 1987), 558–9; S. Lloyd, *English Society and the Crusade* (Oxford, 1988).

[20] For examples, see Webb, *Pilgrimage*, 84, 99–100, 163–4.

everywhere but in Palestine. Crusade 'diversions' (that is, papally authorized expeditions with objectives other than Jerusalem) were not new. They became much more prominent for several reasons. One was the changed political position in Syria. The collapse of Latin Syria in 1187 had transferred into Muslim hands the great southern fortresses such as Kerak, which had formerly protected Jerusalem from conquest from the armies based in Egypt, and which moreover had impeded communications between Cairo and Damascus. Without these fortifications, it was necessary for crusaders to defeat the powerful armies of the Ayyubid empire, or to seek other bases in the eastern Mediterranean. It was true that some hope was offered by the split between two branches of the Ayyubids, but the project was formidable.

Richard I had been aware during the Third Crusade that Jerusalem could not be held as long as Saladin's military power remained intact, and he had taken a first step towards securing new resources by his conquest of Cyprus. The leaders of the Fourth Crusade in 1202/3 were right to argue that 'in Syria you can do nothing . . . The land of Outremer will be recovered, if recovered it is, by the land of Babylon [Egypt] or by Greece'.[21] The original plan named Egypt as the objective, but events directed the fleet and army to Constantinople, and led to the destruction of the Byzantine empire. Egypt was once again the target of Cardinal Pelagius' Damietta crusade. Frederick II's crusade applied the same logic in a different way in 1228–9, by securing a peaceful transfer of Jerusalem, but without the fortresses that would have offered a guarantee of continued occupation. In 1249 Louis IX, in reaction, at first refused all negotiation with the enemy, until the disaster in Egypt forced him to come to terms.

The military situation in the eastern Mediterranean therefore obliged armies that were intended to reach the Holy Sepulchre to attempt an indirect approach. Diversion itself demanded further diversion. The rickety Latin empire, which had been created at Constantinople in 1204, increasingly needed support from the West against the threats of Byzantine revival or conquest from the Balkans. The belief that a necessary precondition for success in the East was reform and peace in the West led to attempts to coerce

---

[21] M. R. B. Shaw (tr.), *Joinville and Villehardouin* (Harmondsworth, 1963), 51. 'Babylon', one of the component districts of Cairo, was a standard French usage for Egypt.

the recalcitrant, who appeared as enemies of catholic unity, above all the Albigensian heretics in southern France and the German imperial house of Hohenstaufen, whose Italian objectives clashed bitterly with those of the papacy. These papally directed wars in the West went back to the pontificate of Innocent III, who left them as a deadly inheritance to his successors. The new structure of crusade organization made such undertakings more practical. Popes now had the power to give spiritual and financial support to an undertaking, almost irrespective of its objective. Popes might also be pulled in the direction of diversions by secular interests, such as the ambitions of the northern French nobles in the south and the fierce rivalries of the Italian cities: fired by such motives, the elimination of the great enemy of papal interests in Italy, that 'viper brood' the Hohenstaufen family, became a rooted part of the policy of the curia.

The defence and recovery of the Holy Land never disappeared from the awareness of thirteenth-century leaders, but the provision of practical help became increasingly difficult, as the last fortresses and ports were lost, until the fall of Acre in 1291. This final catastrophe drove out of Outremer those interests and orders that were most committed to its welfare. The canons of the Holy Sepulchre moved to a new centre in Italy, although they remained an important international order with liturgies that celebrated the Holy Land. The Templars and Hospitallers moved westward to Cyprus and eventually Rhodes. The Teutonic Order moved its centre to Venice, and eventually to Marienburg in Prussia.

The lamentation after the disaster of 1187 embraced alike the capture of the cross at Hattin and the subsequent loss of the Holy Sepulchre and the city of Jerusalem. Devotion to the Sepulchre was strong in Richard I's army:

It was the custom in the army that each night before they went to bed someone who had been assigned to this duty would shout out loudly in the middle of the army the popular cry, 'Holy Sepulchre, help us'. At this cry everyone would shout together, repeating the same words, and holding their hands towards Heaven begging with copious tears for God's mercy and aid.

Similarly, in the wretched conditions of the march towards Jerusalem,

only one comfort was left: they hoped they were very soon going to visit the Lord's Sepulchre, for they had an indescribable yearning to see the city of Jerusalem and complete their pilgrimage . . . An absolutely enormous horde flocked together from all over the place so that they could visit the Lord's

Sepulchre with the army. This hope alone overcame all their other discomforts.[22]

From this time onwards the Holy Sepulchre seems to have been given less prominence in the literature of crusading. It continued to be said that the objective of many of the major expeditions was the recovery of Jerusalem and the Holy Land. When Oliver of Paderborn was preaching in 1214, one of his hearers, receiving a vision, announced, ' "Now the Holy Land has been recovered", as though the event provided a certain prophecy.'[23] The Sepulchre slipped out of the conventional crusade vocabulary. 'Taking the cross' became the standard term: it provided a clear sign that a man had joined up, and it offered an opportunity for appeals based on the suffering of Christ, in line with the increasing devotion to the passion. The *Ordinacio* or collection of sermon notes designed for England about 1216 is full of references to the cross and to the blood of Christ, but the preachers had much less in their brief about the Holy Sepulchre. James of Vitry associated the cross which the crusaders wore with the cross on which Christ suffered. It was characteristic of him to found his sermons on prophecies from the Old Testament, and it was only in this context that he spoke of the Sepulchre to his hearers:

> It is clear that Christ has the sign of the living God, so that he may sign his soldiers; he also wanted to be signed first with the cross, so that he could precede all others with the banner of the cross. God the Father signed him, to whose flesh the cross was fixed with iron nails, which is fixed with a soft thread to your coats. Whence Isaiah: 'The root of Jesse, standing as a sign for the people: the nations will beseech him and his sepulchre will be glorious.' The root of Jesse, that is Christ, stood as a sign for the people, namely on the cross, with which God's people are signed. . . . The Sepulchre in which he lay is glorious, because it is held in honour by all the followers of Christ, in as much as many, after they have taken the sign of the saving cross out of love of Christ and devotion, labour by land and sea so that they may see and honour him bodily.

Gilbert of Tournai went further, and subsumed devotion to the Sepulchre within devotion to the cross: 'The Sepulchre of Christ is made glorious, when people take the cross out of love and devotion, that they might see it and honour him.'[24] The shift of attention from

---

[22] *Itinerarium peregrinorum* i. 9, p. 39; iv. 12, p. 240; iv. 35, p. 279.

[23] Riley-Smith, *The Crusades*, 136.

[24] R. Röhricht, Ordinatio de Predicatione S. Crucis in Anglia, *Quinti Belli Sacri Scriptores Minores* (Paris, 1879); James of Vitry, Sermo 1. 7 (C. T. Maier, *Crusade Propaganda and Ideology* (Cambridge, 2000), 86–9, referring to Isaiah 11: 10); Gilbert of Tournai, Sermo i. 8 (Maier, 180–1).

the Sepulchre to the cross was real. Some authors expressed a definite reserve about visiting the Holy Sepulchre while it remained in the power of the heathen. Joinville reported how the advisers of Louis IX discouraged him from visiting Jerusalem under safe-conduct, for fear that 'if he, who was the greatest of all Christian monarchs, went on pilgrimage to Jerusalem, without delivering the city from God's enemies, then all the other kings and pilgrims coming after him would rest content with doing no more than he had done, and would show no concern for delivering the holy city'. They supported the argument by referring to the example of Richard I who, having realized that he would be unable to take the city, declined to go there under the terms of the truce, or even to look at the city from the surrounding hills.[25] The knowledgeable Franciscan friar, Salimbene de Adam, described how Louis assumed the insignia of a pilgrim, but defined his intentions more precisely:

The lord king assumed this pilgrimage and signing with the cross in honour of our Lord Jesus Christ, and to bring help to the Holy Land, and to fight against the enemies and opponents of the faith and of the cross of Christ, and to the honour of the universal church and of the whole Christian faith and for the salvation of his soul and of all who should journey with him.[26]

The recovery of the Holy Sepulchre has an ambiguous place in Joinville, and Salimbene does not mention it at all.

Acre now became in effect the new capital. The canons of the shrine churches in and around Jerusalem established themselves there. In 1211 Willibrand of Oldenburg remarked on the presence of patriarch, king, bishops, and religious orders, 'to such an extent that it has become the main city of the Franks in Syria'; Bernard Hamilton has remarked that it 'came to resemble Jerusalem in exile'.[27] The hasty withdrawal from the Holy City in 1187 was not matched by any eagerness to return after the truce of 1229. Some saw the reoccupation as precarious and ill-judged: it rested on a ten-year agreement that had involved concessions to the Muslims and been condemned by the patriarch, who complained that 'not a single foot of land has been restored to the patriarch, or to the house of the Holy Sepulchre, outside the city'. The restoration of the major houses of canons would have required them to secure revenues and to resume their old buildings, and this was not feasible in the Jerusalem of the 1230s. It

[25] Shaw, *Joinville and Villehardouin*, 304.
[26] Salimbene, *Cronica* (MGH SS XXXII. 223).
[27] B. Hamilton, 'The Way to Rome and Jerusalem', *Santiago, Roma, Jerusalén*, 142.

appears that the enforced residence at Acre reduced the significance of the canons of the Holy Sepulchre. Although they had many affiliated houses in the West, they had lost most of their property in Outremer, and inevitably lost the prestige that had arisen from their important task of presiding over the Jerusalem pilgrim ceremonies. It was the Franciscans and Dominicans who took the opportunity to create new houses in Jerusalem after 1229, on a much more modest scale than the old shrine communities. These orders reflected a new movement of devotional interest in the West, corresponding with the concern for poverty that we noticed in crusade propaganda: 'People in the Frankish East, and for that matter in the Catholic West as well, had radically changed their attitudes towards the role of religious communities in the Holy Land'.[28] Most of the religious houses that had been forced to migrate to the relative security of Acre stayed there, and offered substitutes for the visits which could be made only with difficulty to the old sites, while the Hospitallers provided pilgrims with a great new hospital, and the hostel of St Mary of the Germans and other pilgrim facilities were developed. A record of the 'pilgrimages and pardons of Acre' was apparently composed about 1260, and survives in a single manuscript. It recorded processions and indulgences at some forty churches in the city, which could, it seems, be combined into a single tour. Presumably these pilgrimages catered for visitors who could not reach the holy sites because of warfare and Muslim occupation, but they fell far short of the great plenary indulgences that were to be a prominent feature of the late-medieval pilgrimage to the Holy Sepulchre.[29]

Nevertheless, Acre was not a replacement for the Holy City. When James of Vitry arrived in 1216 he was bewildered by the huge number of church authorities domiciled there, and complained that 'I have discovered that Acre is like a monster, or a beast with nine heads, each one at odds with the other.' He was also very clear that Acre was not part of the Holy Land: 'I have not yet visited the land of promise, the desirable and Holy Land, although the city of Acre is not far from the place where Jesus lived and was conceived and was brought up . . . that is, Nazareth.'[30] It could be said in 1251 (that is, after the second loss of the city) that ever since 1187 'the holy places of the kingdom of Jerusalem, and especially Nazareth, have been

---

[28] B. Hamilton, 'Ideals of Holiness: Crusades, Contemplatives and Mendicants', *International History Review*, 17 (1995), 693–712.

[29] D. Jacoby, 'Pilgrimage in Crusader Acre: the *Pardouns dAcre*', *De Sion*, 105–17.

[30] R. B. C. Huygens (ed.), *Lettres de Jacques de Vitry* (Leiden, 1960), 89–90.

neglected and left without clergy, and have suffered great and irreparable damage ... through the neglect and indeed the total absence of canons, for so far scarcely any one, or no one suitable, could be found who was prepared to devote his life there to the service of God'.[31]

For a long time after 1187 the number of pilgrims fell greatly from the high level of the twelfth century, although it is clear that pilgrimage continued, and the interest is reflected in the writing of new pilgrim itineraries, although in smaller numbers than in the past. The dominant spirit is the recording of traditional information about the sacred places. James of Vitry, bishop of Acre from 1216 to 1228, was interested in many aspects of Eastern life, and a committed advocate of crusading; but when he wrote of Jerusalem he had in mind primarily the Biblical prophecies and the nature of the sacred sites. He did not draw attention to such major changes in the life of the city as the dismantling of the walls in 1219.

At the same time, we can notice in thirteenth-century writers some interest in both the changing facts of Palestinian life and the collection of information to satisfy the curious. The authors of the *Citez de Jherusalem* up-dated news about the conditions at the shrines and recalled what the city was like 'at the time when Saladin and the Saracens took it from the Christians'. They warned pilgrims of the new restrictions. They were admitted only by the small St Lazarus postern, near the ruined church of St Stephen on the north side, 'so that they could go covertly to the Sepulchre. For the Saracens did not wish that the Christians should see the business of the city: wherefore they admitted them by the gate which is in the street of the Holy Sepulchre, but would not admit them by the master gate.' In some of the manuscripts, a passage added that the visitors were heavily charged for access to the church of the Holy Sepulchre, so much so that, alarmed by the heavy tribute, the Latin authorities imposed a sentence of excommunication on those who paid it.[32]

These new interests seep into the itineraries from various directions. Willibrand, having taken his vow of pilgrimage in 1211, was charged by Otto IV with an embassy to Cilician Armenia, and his account of his journey there from Acre forms the longer part of his account, and is a new form of travel document. His description of the Holy Land was concentrated on the Biblical foundations of the sacred

[31] E. Berger (ed.), *Les Régistres d'Innocent IV* (Paris, 1884–1921), 5, no. 538.
[32] Anon., *The City of Jerusalem*, 16, second section of PPTS 6.

sites, but his journey to Armenia contains a good deal of material about the landscape and people; it is this part of his work that has led Graboïs to call him 'the first pilgrim to give a realistic portrait of the Middle East'. The concern to report facts about the situation in Asia generally is evident in the travels of the friars to the Mongol court, which we must notice later. Ricoldo of Monte Croce, late in the century, was still observing the same division as we can see in the work of Willibrand. He went to the Holy Land in 1288, and his account of the sacred sites is traditional in character. But his main purpose was to take the Gospel to Asia, and his report of his journey to Baghdad included a mass of information about the Eastern Christians and other peoples.[33] Even the thirteenth-century writing on the Holy Land did show a number of new features: there is a spirit of interest in serious historical evidence, thanks to the influence of scholarly writers such as Peter Comestor, and even (in James of Vitry and Ricoldo) a desire to record classical legends that could be domiciled in Syria.[34] Towards the end of the century, these new tendencies were brought together in the work of Burchard of Mount Sion.

The combination of a traditional account of the shrines with a new realism and curiosity and also an evolving spirit of piety helped to define the future character of pilgrim writing. Although it is not really possible to think in terms of the late medieval pilgrimage system until after the settlement of the friars in Jerusalem in the 1330s, the writing of Burchard can be seen as the bridge between the two periods.

The continued strength of the pilgrim interest can be seen in a variety of places in thirteenth-century life. It was, for example, sufficiently strong to encourage fraudulent imitators, who 'say that they have been at Jerusalem, and carry palms and wear their robe, but may never have seen the eastern Mediterranean, nor completed even a half of their journey'.[35] Pilgrimage was also a major influence in providing a language for the developing theology of the church.

In spite of the changed conditions at the Holy Sepulchre, crusaders in the thirteenth century still saw themselves as pilgrims.

---

[33] R. Kappler, 'L'Autre et le prochain dans la *Pérégrination* de Ricold de Monte Croce', in I. Zinguer (ed.), *Miroirs de l'altérité* (Geneva, 1991), 163–72.

[34] Graboïs, *Pèlerin occidental*, 43–4, 110–12, 125–8; 'Terre Sainte et Orient latin vus par Willebrand d'Oldenbourg', *Dei gesta per Francos*, 261–8; and 'Burchard of Mount Sion', *Outremer*, 285–96.

[35] M. E. O'Carroll, *A Thirteenth-Century Preacher's Handbook: Studies in Ms Laud Misc. 511* (Toronto, 1977), 150 n. 76, in a sermon of 1283.

Burchard of Mount Sion

Burchard was a German Dominican who lived in the Holy Land for about ten years from 1275 to 1285. He emphasized that he recorded only what he had seen with his own eyes, and his description of Jerusalem and the Holy Sepulchre was greatly superior to anything else written in the thirteenth century. He also took a more realistic view of the actual character of society in Outremer, of which he was highly critical. In the past, criticisms of the Franks of the East, although there were plenty of them, had usually not been incorporated into the pilgrim itineraries, which concentrated on the holy places. He was also acid about the failure of Latin settlers to defend it. Graboïs sees Burchard as writing 'the first manual of "Palestinography" '. Burchard was no mere transient visitor, but a resident, who found it necessary to warn the West of the impending disaster in Syria. Along with this realism, he caught the spirit of new devotions that were growing in the West, and which turned on meditations on the life of Christ. He expressed confidence that the memory of these events was specially accessible to believers in the holy places themselves. The traveller, he says,

should return afterwards to Jerusalem, to see and hear Jesus preaching in the Temple, teaching the disciples on the Mount of Olives, singing at Mount Sion, washing the feet of his disciples, giving his body and blood, praying at Gethsemane, sweating blood, and kissing his betrayer; how he was taken captive, mocked and spat upon judged, carrying his cross, falling under the weight of his cross in the part of the city as we can see it today, following after Simon of Cyrene, celebrating for us at Calvary the mysteries of his passion. Of each and every one of these places there is thus still a full and manifest memory, just as happened on that day when they were done in person.

S. Mähl, 'Jerusalem in mittelalterliche Sicht', *Die Welt als Geschichte*, 22 (1962), 11–26; J. Folda, 'Jerusalem and the Holy Sepulchre through the Eyes of Crusader Pilgrims', Levine, 158–64; A. Graboïs, 'Christian Pilgrims in the Thirteenth Century and the Latin Kingdom of Jerusalem', *Outremer*, 285–96.

The Church Militant and the Church on Pilgrimage

The idea that the believer is called upon to fight (*militare*) against evil, and to travel (*peregrinare*) to the kingdom, are biblical ideas, but the twelfth and thirteenth centuries saw significant changes in the way the nature of the church was viewed. They arose primarily within Cistercian circles, where Augustine's great work *The City of God* (*De Civitate Dei*) was favourite reading. Two major Cistercian writers offered rewritings of Augustine's theology of the church: Otto of Freising and, more significant still, Henry of Albano, whose book *The Pilgrim City of God* was written at much the same time as the disaster at Jerusalem, having perhaps been started at the papal curia about 1185, and completed in 1188. His design in revising Augustine was quite conscious:

Saint Augustine wrote without distinction of the two cities, the one on pilgrimage on earth and the one reigning in heaven, although they are actually only one . . . About that part of the city of God which is now in triumph, of the saints and spiritual beings who judge all things, I abstain from writing. I . . . propose to write about the city of God militant on earth.

Henry's primary choice of word, as in the title, is 'on pilgrimage', *peregrinans*, but the two words, pilgrim and militant, are synonyms for him. The pilgrimage and crusade has formed a model for his conception of the nature of the church.

Y. M. J. Congar, 'Église et cité de Dieu chez quelques auteurs cisterciens à l'époque des croisades', *Mélanges offerts à Étienne Gilson* (Paris, 1959), 173–202.

Villehardouin, in his history of the Fourth Crusade, repeatedly referred to the members of the expedition by that word, although few pilgrims missed their mark more completely than his company did. Preachers thought of pilgrimage as a spiritual ideal, which was expressed in actual travel. The crusading preacher James of Vitry reflected upon Abraham as 'the first pilgrim', and in one of his sermons (directed, seemingly, to an audience of monks or clergy) he dwelt on the character of human life as pilgrimage. This was not a rejection of the validity of the literal pilgrimage to Jerusalem, but a way of seeing within it a deeper reality. Indeed, it became a common-place to understand pilgrimage as the model of human life:

Travellers and pilgrims, especially when they are very far from their own country, beseech God diligently every day that he will faithfully lead them . . . But we all, who are gathered here, are travellers, because day by day we journey on our pilgrimage towards death, because we dwell in this exile, far from our land of paradise or heaven.[36]

Shortly after the middle of the century Humbert of Romans elaborated this theme. There is, he said, a general pilgrimage, in which every human being can be said to be involved. There are special pilgrimages, directed to the shrines of saints. Finally, there is a pilgrimage of 'prerogative excellence', that is of the crusaders (*crucesignati*), who travel far for the common good of Christendom. Humbert is thinking here of armed expeditions, and he made no distinction between a peaceful pilgrimage and a crusade. Strikingly, in a context where a reference to the Sepulchre would once have been obligatory, he mentions only Calvary, and even that is not meant to be a geographical goal.[37]

Liturgies for prayer for the Holy Land used Psalm 79 as an indispensable element. It came to be more than a devotional expression: rather, it was a precise prediction of what had happened in 1187 and 1244. Humbert of Romans, in his *Opus Tripartitum*, just after 1272, saw it as an exact statement of fact: '*They have poured out their blood* (Psalm 79: 3). What blood, may I ask? Not Jewish, but Christian blood, redeemed by the blood of Christ'. The dominance of the psalm in prayer for the crusading effort lasted until late in the thirteenth century.[38]

Some of the features we have noticed in the thirteenth century were the subject of angry controversy. This was particularly true of the diversion of crusades to objectives other than the Holy Land. Contemporaries varied in their attitude to this great diversion movement. By some, it was bitterly resented. All over Europe, writers condemned the financial exactions organized by the papacy to sustain the military effort, and the fact that nothing was achieved in the Holy Land added fuel to the flames of criticism. Troubadours such as

---

[36] Ibid. 157 n. 76, in a sermon of 1277.

[37] D. J. Birch, 'Jacques de Vitry and the Ideology of Pilgrimage', *Pilgrimage Explored*, 79–93; Humbert of Romans (Maier, *Crusade Propaganda*, 210–13).

[38] A. Linder, '*Deus venerunt gentes*: Psalm 78 (79) in the Liturgical Commemoration of the Destruction of Latin Jerusalem', *Medieval Studies in Honour of Avrom Saltman* (Jerusalem, 1995), 145–71.

Guilhem Figueira were horrified as armies marched to Avignon, Toulouse, and Carcassonne, and ruined their own lovely land of Provence. They suspected with reason that the crusades there were sustained in large part by the political ambitions of the French crown and aristocracy:

> Rome, to Saracens you turn the other cheek.
> All your victims are Latin or else Greek.
> In the pit of hell, Rome, is your true location,
>> sitting in damnation.
>> God knows I want none
>> of your pilgrims' dispensation
>> if their stated destination
>> is at Avignon!
>
> Rome, you understand why my words are biting,
> since with tricks against Christians you are fighting.
> Tell me in what text do you find it written,
>> Christians should be smitten?
>> God, you are true bread
>> for us every day,
>> bring down what I pray
>> on the Romans' head.[39]

There was another view. Papal letters insisted that these so-called 'crusades against Christians' were essential for the recovery of the Sepulchre, which would be hopelessly jeopardized if the West lost the resources of the Latin rulers of Constantinople. Nor, it was claimed, could the Sepulchre be secured while the Roman Church was being threatened at home by unscrupulous enemies. This view commanded wide support. Sincere people perceived a spiritual coherence in the defence of the church from enemies within and without. The people of Venice were invited in 1256 to take the cross in northern Italy 'that deeds should be performed like those you did at Ferrara, and that your ancestors did at Tyre, and throughout Syria, and as they did at Constantinople, always in the service of holy church'.[40] The Saracen community at Lucera, which formed an important part of the Hohenstaufen army, helped propagandists to present the Italian wars as if they mystically re-enacted the fate of the Holy Land. When Orvieto was being besieged by the Hohenstaufen

[39] Guilhem Figueira, *D'un sirventes far*, R. T. Hill and T. G. Bergin (eds.), *Anthology of the Provençal Troubadours* (New Haven, Conn., 1941), no. 122, pp. 178–9.
[40] Doge Ranieri Zeno of Venice, cited N. Housley, *The Italian Crusades* (Oxford 1992), 162.

Manfred in 1264, cloths that were believed to be marked with the blood of Christ, miraculously revealed in the mass at Bolsena, were placed in the cathedral. At Orvieto, as in the Holy Land, the relics of the passion were threatened by the Saracens. Even before that, St Clare had defended San Damiano outside Assisi against the Saracen colony in Lucera, who served in the Hohenstaufen army, with a pyx containing the consecrated eucharist.[41] It has been argued that such diversions of crusading endeavour created a disillusion which turned public opinion altogether away from the crusade. Whatever the truth of that, by the mid-thirteenth century Outremer was already in a hopeless military position. The resources of the papal curia were extensive, but in the end it could command only so much finance, so much political credit, so much religious obedience. If these were directed towards Constantinople, Italy, and Provence, there would be little left for the recovery of Jerusalem. Whether or not the diversions were intended eventually in the interests of the Holy Sepulchre, in practice it was likely to wither on a distant branch.

While crusading activity was becoming increasingly diversified, another approach to the unbeliever was developing, for which the Holy Sepulchre was almost an irrelevance: peaceful preaching. The concept was not totally new. Before the middle of the twelfth century, the hermit Stephen of Obazine urged his companions that they should go to convert the Saracens by preaching, or 'themselves be killed for Christ by the unbelievers', and Ralph Niger had criticized crusading by force because it yielded no converts.[42] Yet the conversion of the unbeliever had originally played virtually no part in the aims of crusaders. Their language about 'the expansion of Christendom' expressed an intention to extend the observance of Christian worship, which they thought was threatened by the government of Muslims. The first half of the thirteenth century saw the beginning of major attempts to proclaim the Gospel outside Europe and to formulate a theory of mission. The idea of preaching, combined with the ready acceptance of martyrdom, became influential with the growth of the Franciscan and Dominican friars. The fact that this missionary activity was in the long run unfruitful should not lead us to neglect it, because the ideas that shaped it shifted attention away from the Sepulchre and eventually influenced the expansion of the church through the great Atlantic explorations. Gregory IX's

---

[41] F. Cardini, 'Gilberto di Tournai', *Studi Francescani*, 72 (1975), 40–1.
[42] *Vita S. Stefani Obazensis* c. 10, ed. M. Aubrun (Clermont-Ferrand, 1970), 60.

decretal of 1235, *Cum hora undecima*, formulated, in a way that had not been done before, the missionary function of the church, and, in an enlarged form issued by his successor Innocent IV, it was repeatedly copied in later centuries. The most obvious reason for the emergence of a missionary initiative was a technical one. The church now had religious orders at its disposal who could be sent where they were needed. This new element had emerged with the Hospitallers and Templars in the medical and military fields; now, they were supplemented by the huge and flexible human resources of the friars. Both Francis and Dominic saw their mission as extending beyond the boundaries of Christendom: 'I say to you in truth that the Lord chose and sent the friars for the profit of the souls of everybody in the whole world, and they are to be received not only in the lands of the faithful but also of the infidel.'[43] Most contemporaries did not regard crusades and missions as contradictory: some people, like Gregory IX and Innocent IV, were keen advocates of both. Nevertheless it was possible, if rare, to see the two in opposition. The radical Franciscan Roger Bacon stated around the middle of the century the objections to the use of warfare:

If the Christians are victorious, no one stays behind and defends the occupied lands. Nor are non-believers converted in this way, but killed and sent to hell. Those who survive the wars, together with their children, are more and more embittered against the Christian faith because of this violence. They are indefinitely alienated from Christ and rather inflamed to do all the harm possible to Christians.[44]

The turning towards missions was associated with a change in Western ideas about Asia. The assumption that Christianity and Islam occupied most of the surface of the planet was disturbed by the discovery that in Asia behind the Islamic barrier there was a network of Nestorian churches and great populations to whom the faith could be brought. The first news of Prester John arrived in 1145, brought by the bishop of Gabala in northern Syria. The report was almost certainly based on the defeat of the Seljuk Sultan Sanjar in 1141, which rumour falsely ascribed to a great Christian emperor. Prester John's kingdom was located by legend in Asia, until, centuries later, report placed it Ethiopia, where there genuinely was a Christian kingdom. In the next century, the emergence of the Mongol empire

---

[43] Francis of Assisi to Cardinal Hugolino, *Scripta Leonis Rufini et Angeli sociorum*, ed. R. B. Brooke (Oxford, 1970), 233.
[44] S. Menache, *Vox Dei* (Oxford 1990), 121.

revolutionized the European understanding of Asia. In 1219 a Mongol army overran Persia and ravaged its cities. In 1240 European Russia and a good deal of the east of the continent was overrun by a great Mongol host, but in the spring of 1242 their armies withdrew eastward. Europe was left to speculate on the likelihood that they would return. It was Innocent IV who undertook the collection of information about the East. One of the major purposes of the assembly of the Council of Lyons in 1245 was 'to find a remedy against the Tartars and other despisers of the Christian faith'.[45] Innocent promised aid in the event of a renewal of the Mongol offensive, and sent friars to establish contact with their rulers. The most remarkable of these missions was that of the Franciscan John of Carpine, who produced the first great narrative of Asiatic travel. Leaving Lyons in April 1245, he arrived in Mongolia in July 1246 in time to be present at an assembly to elect a new khan. The reply of the great khan to the papal initiative was hostile, for he demanded recognition of his universal supremacy. Other envoys received similar responses, but there were a few meetings with Nestorian Christian officials, members of a church widely spread in Asia, some of whom were influential in the government of the empire. The ground had been prepared for great missionary and commercial journeys that were to follow, and a new world-view was emerging. The tradition that Jerusalem was the centre of the world was so established that it was not readily forgotten, but it was evident that there were prospects and perils that tended to move the military situation in the Holy Land out of the heart of world history.

The weakening of the political establishment in Outremer led the papal curia to take a much more directive role there. One might have expected this to produce a keener attention to the affairs of the Latin church, but it did not. For one thing, popes were not well informed about the true situation of the communities in Syria. They were asked to confirm long lists of possessions, which often were not really producing revenue: the canons of the shrine churches were often in more serious financial straits than was realized at Rome. There was also a more fundamental problem. The activity of papal government was impressive in its scope, but it was designed to respond to initiative from outside. Popes could respond to petitioners, but they had little machinery for legislation, or even for continuity in planning. This

---

[45] Letter to archbishop of Sens 3 January 1245: H. Wolter and H. Holstein, *Lyon I et Lyon II* (Paris, 1966), 250–1.

system of administration, which is sometimes called 'rescript' government, was geared to the issue of letters or rescripts in response to
petitions from outside the curia, and these often simply echoed the
wording of the request. It was the task of officials to ensure that the
answer was in accordance with the law, but there was no investigation of the facts nor assessment of the wider impact of the decision. A
picture of this kind helps us to understand the popes' remarkable
failures (as it may seem to historians) to reform the Western church,
to sustain an effective defence of the Holy Sepulchre, or to regulate
the affairs of the Latin church in Syria. The heart of the problem lay
not in the corruption or indifference of the curia, but in the failure to
design a structure for the application of consistent policies. It was, for
instance, only in 1256 that Alexander IV discovered that there were
no longer enough canons to sustain a proper liturgical service at the
church of the Holy Sepulchre at Acre. The election of James of Pan-
taleon as Pope Urban IV in 1261 confirmed the importance attached
at Rome to the affairs of the Holy Land. James had been titular
patriarch of Jerusalem for several years, and was visiting Rome at the
time of the election in connection with the business of Latin Syria.
His devotion to the Holy Sepulchre formed a prominent part of
his spirituality and was reflected in the preamble of a number of his
bulls, and in his decision to remain patriarch of Jerusalem during his
pontificate (1261–4). In so short a time he issued no less than forty-
nine grants and confirmations to the canons, and he employed the
prior, Hugh of Nysam, as a personal adviser. He showed a strong
interest in Eastern affairs, especially in negotiations with the new
Greek emperor at Constantinople, but the shortness of his pontificate, as well as the inadequacies of the papal machinery, meant that
no effective new policy was put in place.[46] Clergy appointed to the
Latin states tended increasingly to be Italian, often had little previous
association with Outremer, and were seeking promotion and an
income, sometimes by seriously corrupt means.[47]

A slender and poorly organized Latin establishment in the East
meant that there was less support for pilgrims. As it became more
difficult for them to visit and worship at the holy places, Western

---

[46] B. Hamilton, *The Latin Church in the Crusader States* (London, 1980), 299–307;
G. Bresc-Bautier, 'Bulles d'Urbain IV en faveur de l'Ordre du Saint Sépulcre (1261–4),
École Française de Rome, Miscellanea, 85 (1973), 283–310.

[47] For an example, see P.-V. Claverie, 'Un cas de trafic de reliques dans le royaume
de Jérusalem au XIIIe siècle: l'affaire «Giovanni Romano»', *Revue historique de droit
français et étranger*, 75 (1997), 627–37.

Europe developed new institutions to incorporate in its own life and devotions the salvation that came from the East.

THE PASSION AND SEPULCHRE IN THE HOLY NATION

The disaster of 1187, followed by the misdirection of the Fourth Crusade in 1204, made a dramatic change to the flow of relics from the eastern Mediterranean. In the twelfth century, Jerusalem had been the obvious source, but in the thirteenth century the great relics came from Constantinople. The sacking of the city and its churches produced a wonderful set of relics and treasures, to which the crusading knight Robert of Clari dedicated pages of description. The new Latin Emperor Baldwin I observed that 'the whole Latin world did not possess so much'. Under the terms of the treaty between Venice and the Franks, the Venetians acquired a handsome share, which helped to make their treasury of San Marco the best museum of medieval Byzantine art. There is a description in the Cologne Chronicle of the way in which the relic of the cross in the imperial chapel was 'divided by the bishops present and shared out with other precious relics among the knights; later, when they returned home, they were given to churches and cloisters'. The knight Henry of Ulm seized a superb staurotheca, a cross-shaped reliquary, made at Constantinople in 964–5, and brought it back to the nunnery at Stuben, on the Mosel, where his sister was abbess. It is now in the treasury at the cathedral of Limburg an der Lahn. Another relic was to have a striking role in the history of Western symbolism. The wood of the cross presented to the abbey of Boissière in Anjou was contained in a staurotheca with the typical form containing two parallel arms (the upper one presumably representing the title). This double-armed cross became the symbol of the princes of Anjou, and then eventually the 'cross of Lorraine', adopted by Charles de Gaulle as the symbol of French freedom in 1940.[48] The Western conquest of Constantinople released, not only an immediate flood of relics, but a series of subsequent deposits, because the Latin emperors were obliged to abandon the jealousy with which their Greek predecessors had administered their treasury. The new order made possible the creation of the Sainte-Chapelle.

---

[48] A. Legner, *Reliquien in Kunst und Kult zwischen Antike und Aufklärung* (Darmstadt, 1995), 67–9; E. G. Grimme, *Goldschmiedekunst im Mittelalter* (Schauberg, 1972), 30–5; J. Rauch, 'Die Limburger Staurothek', *Das Münster*, 8 (1955), 201–40; and Gaborit-Chopin, 'La Croix d'Anjou', *Cahiers archéologiques*, 33 (1985), 156–78.

The Sainte-Chapelle at Paris

The crown of thorns may appear to be an unlikely survival, but to thirteenth-century rulers it had a supreme importance. Louis IX of France purchased it, through the intermediary of the Venetians, from the Latin Emperor Baldwin II, and it was solemnly received at Paris on 18 August 1239. It was accompanied by other major relics of the passion, including a large portion of the wood of the cross and a reliquary box with stone from the Holy Sepulchre. Louis determined to build them a suitable shrine, and adjoining the royal palace he began in 1239 one of the most perfect Gothic buildings of all, consecrated on 26 April 1248, when the king was actively preparing for his Crusade. The confirmatory charter of foundation was issued at the moment when Louis was taking ship. The immediate inauguration of the building was therefore in the context of the Crusade, but there is no strong reason to connect the whole building and its iconography directly with crusading. It was a design on two storeys, a plan for which there were few parallels in France. It has been suggested that the two storeys echoed the two storeys of Calvary (although one can scarcely imagine a building looking less like the church of the Holy Sepulchre than this one does). In practical terms the design may simply have been required by the need for the upper chapel to communicate directly with the apartments of state in the adjoining palace. This chapel was provided with a magnificent set of windows, which incorporated, among other themes, the history of the wood of the cross. At its east end was the great shrine for the sacred relics. The surviving treasury lists mention twenty-one Byzantine reliquaries which arrived in Paris shortly after 1239. The whole collection was dispersed, and in most cases destroyed, in 1793. There survives only the silver-gilt Greek inscriptions, now in the Louvre, from the box containing the material from the Holy Sepulchre; they consisted of the text of an Easter hymn, with a presentation of the holy women and the angel before the Tomb. The crown of thorns is in the treasury of Notre Dame, provided now with a nineteenth-century setting. An excellent picture of the crosses displayed to view was painted in the fifteenth century. The treatment of the relics influenced the rebuilding of the Santa Sanctorum by Nicholas III (1277–80) at the Lateran, and the shrine in particular was partly echoed at S. Paolo fuori le Mura at Rome. A most elegant representation of the *Visitatio* ceremony, set within a chapel, in engraved silver, is found at Pamplona in Navarre. It was designed about 1290 to accommodate relics of the shroud, and appears to be Parisian work, with a strong influence from the Sainte-Chapelle.

S. J. Morand, *Histoire de la Sainte-Chapelle royale du Palais* (Paris, 1790); A. Vidier, *Le Trésor de la Sainte-Chapelle: inventaires et documents . . . (Mémores de la Société del'histoire de Paris et de l'Ile de France,* 34–7 (1907–10); M. Aubert, *Les Vitraux de Notre-Dame et de la Sainte-Chapelle de Paris* (Paris, 1959); K. Gould, 'The Sequences *de sanctis reliquiis* as Sainte-Chapelle Inventories', *Medieval Studies,* 43 (1981), 315–41; Gauthier, nos. 91 and 94–5; C. Billot, 'Le Message spirituel et politique de la Sainte-Chapelle de Paris', *Revue Mabillon,* NS 2 (1991), 119–41; M. Müller, 'Paris, das neue Jerusalem? Die Ste Chapelle als Imitation der Golgotha-Kapelle', *Zs. für Kunstgeschichte,* 59 (1996), 325–36; and D. H. Weiss, *Art and Crusade in the Age of St Louis* (Cambridge, 1998), with an important review by C. Bruzelius, *Speculum,* 76 (2001), 813–15.

Louis saw the crown of thorns as an emblem of sacred royal authority, and its possession as an affirmation of the dignity of the kingdom of France. The archbishop of Sens, Walter Cornut, remarked of its arrival: 'Just as . . . Christ chose the land of promise for the mysteries of our redemption, so he seems to have chosen our Gaul for the devout veneration of the triumph of his passion.' This does not suggest that France will entirely replace the Holy Land in God's purposes; that would be a surprising view to hear from a confidant of the crusader Louis. It is rather that God has chosen to transfer to France the special commemoration of his passion:

> This family is loved by God:
> His cross and crown of thorns,
> The passion's nails and iron and lance
> Are held in faithful guard.[49]

[49] Walter Cornut, 'Historia susceptionis coronae spineae Christi', F. Duchesne (ed.), *Historiae Francorum Scriptores* (Paris, 1649), v. 407–11; C. Beaune, *Birth of an Ideology: Myths and Symbols of Nation in Late-Medieval France* (Berkeley, 1991), 177.

The Sainte-Chapelle embodied two major themes of contemporary devotion: the commemoration of the relics of the passion and the reverence for sacred kingship, embodied in the feast of the holy crown each 11 August: *tua corona spinea tuos coronat aurea*: 'Your crown of thorns crowns your people with gold.' Marie-Madeleine Gauthier's view is an extreme one, but has a good deal to be said for it:

The transfer of the crown of thorns from Constantinople to Paris may be regarded as the most significant act to have taken place in the whole of the thirteenth century. For if we view kingly rule in the perspective of a political anthropology, it was the crown of thorns of a tortured God that now guaranteed the validity of the crown of gold and precious stones worn by the kings of the West.[50]

The new status of France was reflected in the foundation of sanctuaries that celebrated the nation. The royal spirituality of the thirteenth century had a new focus: it linked the Christian nation with the relics of the Holy Land, and predominantly it was the passion rather than the Holy Sepulchre that provided the medium for the transfer of sacred power. This was now a claim on behalf of the nation, of the entire community, and not simply on behalf of the shrine and the religious who serve it, and applied more widely than the kingdom itself. The *Anonymous Chronicle of the Kings of France* linked relics and sovereignty: 'God showed his love for (Louis IX) and the kingdom of France when he allowed such precious holy things to be brought to the crown and realm of France . . . The king of France and the kingdom . . . will be, if God pleases, the chief of Christian princes.' A new chapter was opening in the coming of Jerusalem to the West.

Alongside the Sainte-Chapelle, there is another major, but controversial, source of information on Louis's thinking about the Holy Land: the *Life* or *History* by John of Joinville.

One crucial point in Joinville's picture comes with Louis's return from the crusade, after a long stay in the Holy Land. At Hyères, the king summoned the Franciscan Hugh of Digne to preach before him. Brother Hugh was a follower of Joachim of Fiore, with his teaching of a new age to come. Joinville was not aware of the full inwardness of this, but he was sufficiently impressed to record Hugh's message that no kingdom had ever fallen 'except where justice had been

---

[50] Gauthier, 162–3.

Joinville on Saint Louis

The composition and purpose of Joinville's book present us with problems. It was written when the author was an old man, long after Louis's death in 1270, and after he had been officially acknowledged as a saint. Joinville wrote at the request of the queen, Joan of Champagne, seemingly between 1305 and 1309. All of that would suggest that he is presenting us with the official Louis of royal and papal ideology; but there is a complication. The two men were close companions on Louis's Crusade to Damietta and Acre, and the personal exchanges recorded in the book, even if improved by more than fifty years of shifting memory, are unlikely to be pure invention. What is more, the crusade reminiscences are different in character from the general observations on Louis's piety and kingship. It has been suggested that they give us 'the real St Louis', and even that they may have been recorded separately, perhaps shortly after the king's death. While the specially personal character of the crusade narrative is clear, it is incorporated into Joinville's main purpose of displaying Louis as a saint and model king. He was not entirely satisfied with Louis's canonization: he thought that, in addition, Louis ought to be reverenced as a martyr, and he deploys his arguments to this effect both in the introduction and in the narrative of events during 1248–54. It looks like a personal memoir shaped by ideological conviction, composed as a whole fifty years after its hero's death in 1309.

J. Monfrin (ed.), *Jean de Joinville, Vie de Saint Louis* (Paris, 1995); J. Evans (tr.), *The History of Saint Louis by Jean Sire de Joinville* (Oxford, 1938); M. R. B. Shaw (tr.), *Joinville and Villehardouin: Chronicles of the Crusades* (Harmondsworth, 1963); J. Le Goff, *Saint Louis* (Paris, 1996); J. Dufournet and L. Harf (eds.), *Le Prince et son historien: la* Vie de Saint Louis *de Joinville* (Paris, 1997); and C. Lucken, 'L'Évangile du roi: Joinville, témoin et auteur de la *Vie de Saint Louis*', *Annales HSS*, 56 (2001), 445–67, followed by response by Le Goff, 469–77.

ignored', and to record a determined, but unsuccessful, attempt to persuade him to stay at the royal court. Christopher Lucken's verdict on this episode is that it proved 'indispensable for the kingdom of France to become, instead of the city of Jerusalem which God had not given to the crusaders . . . the image on earth of the celestial city which the king had gone to seek in the Holy Land'.[51] Joinville did not really go so far as to say that for Louis, France had become the Holy Land: but he took a significant stride in that direction. The prominence of the French monarchy in crusades against unbelievers and heretics (in which five kings in succession took part) led, even during the thirteenth century, to the conviction that France was a kingdom specially beloved by God. James of Vitry claimed that 'there are many Christian nations, but the first among them is France, and the French are pure Catholics'. The popes did not dissent, calling Louis in 1239 and 1245 'a most Christian prince, head of a very devoted people'. The title 'Most Christian King' was not unique to the French monarchy, but in the course of the thirteenth century it came to be used very frequently, even in contexts that were not specifically designed as royal propaganda. France was a sacred nation, as well as enjoying the blessing of a Christian monarch: Nogaret, the adviser of Philip IV, claimed that God 'had chosen it as his peculiar kingdom', and in his bull *Rex gloriae* in 1311 Pope Clement V agreed: 'the realm of France has been chosen by God as his peculiar people for the execution of his heavenly commands.'[52]

During the time of Louis IX the public image of the saint-king, and in all probability his own intentions, continued to be shaped by older crusading traditions. He made a second, although misdirected, attempt at the recovery of the Holy Land in the Tunis Crusade of 1270, on which he died. A statue of about 1290 depicts him and his wife, Margaret of Provence, as a happily married couple. Louis is armed, holding in his right hand a copy of the Holy Sepulchre, and in his left a shield with the insignia of the Capetian royal family.[53] It seems also that Louis inspired a new venture in artistic propaganda in Syria. After a modest manuscript production in the East during the first half of the century, the first splendidly illustrated manuscript from Acre contained passages from the Bible in French translation,

---

[51] Lucken, 'L'Évangile dur voi', 463–6 (see inset, 'Joinville on Saint Louis', above).

[52] Beaune, *Birth of an Ideology*, 174–5; J. R. Strayer, 'France: the Holy Land, the Chosen People', *Medieval Statecraft and the Perspectives of History* (Cambridge, Mass. 1971), 311–14.

[53] See R. Delort, *Life in the Middle Ages* (London, 1974), 115.

and was clearly planned under Louis's patronage. It began a tradition of ambitious illumination in the scriptorium at Acre: even in the dying decades of the kingdom, its manuscripts were celebrating the triumphs of the First Crusade and the past importance of the Holy Sepulchre.[54]

In the twelfth century, the reproduction, or commemoration, of the Holy Sepulchre had been one of the powerful ways of bringing salvation from the East. It has been said that 'the movement for the construction of these churches came to a halt with the conquest of Jerusalem by Saladin', and—even while allowing for problems of dating of individual constructions—that seems to be a sound judgement.[55] Instances of 'Holy Sepulchres' are hard to find in the thirteenth century. A spectacular chapel in Magdeburg cathedral has been claimed as a Holy Sepulchre memorial, but its dedication and purpose are unclear.

One existing chapel that certainly was rebuilt in the later thirteenth century was that at Konstanz. It was reconstructed with

---

The Gothic Chapel in Magdeburg Cathedral

This distinctive, polygonal chapel was originally in the nave, but was moved in 1826. It is sixteen-cornered with Gothic windows, and its style suggests a date of about 1250. It has been suggested that it could be a replacement for a former building, but the relatively recent date of the church as a whole does not make that an attractive speculation. No medieval source mentions it as dedicated to the Holy Sepulchre. Indeed, a ceremonial from the early fifteenth century described it as *capella S. Maria Rotunda*. A late-medieval source does mention it as the goal of the Good Friday procession, and this suggests, whatever its first purpose, it may have functioned liturgically as a Sepulchre.

Dalman, *Grab Christi*, 34–5; Möbius, *Passion*, pl. III.

---

[54] M. A. Stones, 'Secular manuscript illumination in France', in C. Kleinhenz (ed.), *Medieval Manuscripts and Textual Criticism* (Chapel Hill, 1976), 82–102; H. Buchtal, *Miniature Painting in the Latin Kingdom of Jerusalem* (Oxford, 1957); C. Bruzelius, review of D. H. Weiss, *Speculum*, 76 (2001), 813–15.

[55] G. G. Stromsa, 'Mystical Jerusalems', Levine, *Jerusalem*, 356–8.

FIG 8.1 The existing Sepulchre at Konstanz was built shortly before 1300, on
the same site as Bishop Conrad's. This eighteenth-century lithograph shows
the monument which still exists, although the statue on the summit, which
was added later, has been removed.

rich statuary recalling the Gospel events, and particularly those connected with the Sepulchre itself: the twelve apostles, the Nativity, and
inside it the three Marys, the angel, soldiers in thirteenth-century
armour, and the women visiting the apothecary to buy ointments.
The last was a favourite scene in Easter plays, and the whole decoration suggests familiarity with them. The preferred date among local
historians is 1260, but there is only the style to go by, and the dating
could really be any time in the later part of the century. At Bologna,
the Sepulchre, in all probability built after 1141, was decorated by
reliefs of the women and the angel, which look late thirteenth-
century. This is a tiny list compared with the previous generations.
The pattern was to change once again, as we shall see, in the course
of the later Middle Ages.

While the passion was now more central in Western devotion,
there was still a real desire to bring to the faithful the events of Easter
Day. They were, however, pictured according to the type of burial
familiar in medieval society. The use of a sarcophagus or coffin in
scenes showing the resurrection or the visit to the tomb became very
general in the thirteenth century, and it emphasized the distancing of
the geographical, and even of the historical, Jerusalem. The Holy
Sepulchre was increasingly seen in the light of the sacrament of the
altar, and could be represented in manuscripts by a sarcophagus with
a ciborium behind it to express the presence of the Holy Body and
Blood.[56] The play *The Holy Resurrection* was perhaps first composed in
England shortly before 1200, but it became widely popular in both
England and France in the following century, and may fairly be seen
as representative of the piety of that time. As its name implies, it was
centred on the Sepulchre and in particular on Joseph of Arimathea. It
contained instructions for setting the scene: within the 'playing place'
the action needed a series of 'stages', or sets as we would call them:

> First, for the crucifix find room: the next house is the Holy Tomb:
> Outside, a guard, four soldiers brave, and Marys visiting the grave.

The action describes the preparation of a stone sepulchre, but clearly
one of a 'sarcophagus' type: 'the slab of rock must go on top'. The
memory of the real Jerusalem was no longer effectively present in
their minds.[57]

---

[56] R. Hauscher, 'Templum Salamonis und Ecclesia Christi', *Zs. für Kunstgeschichte*,
31 (1968), 101–21.
[57] R. Axton and J. Stevens (trs.), *Medieval French Plays* (Oxford, 1971), *La Seinte
Resureccion*, opening section.

More radical thinkers envisaged a new order, in which God had abandoned the Holy Land for the West. Louis IX had been influenced by the preaching of Hugh of Digne: but the tradition of Joachim stood for much more than social justice. The *Life* of Joachim of Fiore tells how, on a visit to the Holy Land, he received a revelation from God about the nature of the Biblical revelation. Joachim then visited the religious houses around Jerusalem, and condemned them for their errors. 'Guided by divine grace, he understood that God had now cast out that land from his sight.' Appearing before Pope Lucius III, Joachim prophesied the fall of the Jerusalem. It is a nice question whether his biographer credited him before 1187 with a foresight that he did not possess, but he certainly began to think in terms of a 'transmigration' of Jerusalem. He prophesied that the Temple of God would be rebuilt 'from living stones by the sons of the new transmigration, who do not forget Jerusalem'. We are told that he founded his abbey of Fiore in Calabria to provide for 'new fruit of the Holy Spirit in Nazareth', and he described the monks, who were to initiate the third age in the life of the church, as 'new Israelites'.[58]

Joachim's position that Jerusalem had now come to the West, that the Holy Land had been replaced by the family of holy monks, was an extreme one, but it does stand at one end of a new spectrum of thought. This has been described as the *crux cismarina*: the cross (or crusade, since the word can mean both) on this side of the sea. The life of the Holy Land, the sufferings of Christ, and the armed struggle for Jerusalem, were being absorbed into the spirituality of Western Europe. What was more, although the arrival of relics from the East was still valued, they were no longer the sole, or even the predominant, means of linking East and West. The new attitudes had deep roots. Bernard of Clairvaux had taught that the victory of the Christian consisted in the overcoming of evil in himself, and Innocent III had presented the suffering Christ as the model for crusaders. By no means were these views intended as alternatives to the armed defence and recovery of the Holy Land, but they opened the way to the conviction that the life of Christ within the believer mattered more than the capture of Jerusalem. Early in the thirteenth century, a spectrum of thought had emerged that combined commitment to the Holy Land with enthusiasm for a communal life of poverty, and that increasingly looked to spiritual means of overcoming the foe.

[58] S. Wessley, 'The Role of the Holy Land for the early Followers of Joachim of Fiore', SCH 36 (2000), 183 n., 189 n.

James of Vitry, later bishop of Acre, had close links with Mary of Oignies and the early Beguines movement. These Beguine mystics represented a change in the current of medieval piety. Their devotion was centred on vivid personal experiences, in contrast with the monastic writers of the past who were shaped by liturgy and learned exegesis. When they meditated on the cross, the Lord showed them his wounds, placed his arm round them, kissed them mouth to mouth, and marked them with his own wounds. The sense that God had brought into being a new work was strong among Joachites, Beguines, and Franciscans: 'At the new year we hope for the new season, that will bring new flowers and new joys manifold.'[59]

The new spirit did not dismiss the Holy Land: only a few extreme followers of Joachim took this view. Yet there was confidence among such thinkers that they were already living in spiritual union with Christ in his passion, and their assumptions about warfare for the cross were less simplistic than in the past. James of Vitry said that Mary of Oignies wore the cross, not on her clothing, but on her heart. Lutgard of Tongres undertook a fast of seven years for the conversion of the Albigensian heretics of Languedoc. This was indeed a sort of crusade, but one waged within the West and under-taken, as far as she was concerned, by spiritual means. The Beguine devotion to the eucharist was a further instance of their sense of the presence of Christ, in the West: the new feast of Corpus Christi was promulgated to the church as a whole in 1264 by Urban IV, a pope with Beguine connections, who had himself been patriarch of Jerusalem. Margaret of Cortona, in the last years of the century, was a special example of the new perceptions. She was one of the first people to follow what would later be the *via dolorosa* or stations of the cross: 'for although on every day she made in order a cycle of the passion, yet she specially renewed this in her heart on every Friday, on which she said that on such a day no Christian should be joyful.' Margaret saw Cortona as an embodiment of Jerusalem, and resided like a 'new Mary Magdalen' beside the church of San Francesco there. She greeted the noble Guglielmino Casale, a frequent visitor, with the words, 'behold the holy knight', and urged him to give thanks because Cortona would not fall into the hands of strangers: 'It will be a new Jerusalem: *ella sarà Gerusalem novella*'. Like the arrival at Loreto in Italy of the holy house of the Blessed Virgin from Nazareth, the Beguine devotion 'tended to bring into being in the lands of the faithful those places, or indeed those images, which the unbeliever was making inaccessible to the devotion of Christians'. While not being expressly opposed to warfare for the holy places, Margaret said that when she prayed 'for the Tartars, Saracens and other unbelievers, I feel sweetness and warmth in my heart'. We are seeing the emergence of the *crux cismarina*, the coming of the holy places to reside in the West, and this in circles widely distinct from those of the royal propagandists who were shaping a new image of sacred kingship.[60]

Even when, in the fourteenth century, the holy places once again became more accessible to pilgrims, they were serviced by Franciscans, who had been fashioned in this same type of devotion. The function of the holy places was to enrich the piety of the West: and at Cortona, as in France, they sanctified a city or a nation. Many of the pilgrim narratives in the late Middle Ages breathe the air of thirteenth-century *crux cismarina* spirituality. But to this we must turn in the next chapter.

---

[60] G. Mancini (ed.), *Cronache cortonesi di Boncitolo e di altri cronisti* (Cortona, 1896), 19; A. B. Papi, ' "Margarita filia Ierusalem": Santa Margherita da Cortona e il superamento mistico della crociata', in F. Cardini, *Toscana e Terrasanta nel Medioevo* (Florence, 1982), 117–37; and J. Cannon and A. Vauchez, *Margherita of Cortona and the Lorenzetti: Sienese Art and the Cult of the Holy Woman in Medieval Tuscany* (Pennsylvania, 1999).

9

The 'Great Pilgrimage' in the Later Middle Ages, 1291–1530

The final loss of Latin Syria took place on 28 May 1291, when the last resistance collapsed in the great port of Acre. The Mamluk rulers of Egypt and southern Syria had been eroding the Latin strongholds for more than thirty years. Since 1258, there had been a formidable Mongol presence established in Persia, a serious threat to the Mamluk dominions, and Mongol–Christian alliance several times resulted in common action between the Mongols, Antioch, and Armenia. The fall of Acre was rapidly followed by the abandonment of the few remaining Latin strongpoints.

The defeat did not mean the end of Christianity in Syria. There was no special reason for the Mamluks to be hostile to the indigenous Christians, who were able to continue worshipping in their local churches. Even in the sixteenth century there was a substantial community of Arab Christians in Jerusalem, and they formed a majority in the small town of Bethlehem. The continued status of the holy places in Jerusalem, which had been under Mamluk control since 1244, is not easy to determine. Many, certainly, were in ruins. The church of the Holy Sepulchre normally remained locked, but it was opened to local Christians and Eastern pilgrims from Good Friday to Easter Day, above all to celebrate the miraculous descent of the holy fire on Easter Eve. The relative Mamluk tolerance towards Eastern Christians is illustrated by the concessions that gave Georgian clergy a modest place in maintaining the liturgy within the church of the Holy Sepulchre.

For the Latins, the loss of Acre was a disaster. They were primarily a military presence, depending on the fortresses and army of the military orders and on armed assistance from the West. After the loss of Acre, they had no base for recovery on the Asian mainland, and they lost the substitute devotional places that the religious orders had maintained there. Such groups as the canons of the Holy Sepulchre were, from that time onwards, wholly based in Western Europe, where their presence and their ceremonies helped to keep alive the memory of Jerusalem. The resident native Christians of the Holy Land could with good reason suppose that the Latin intervention in Palestine had been a brief and unhappy episode in the millennial history of the native Christian churches. 'The crusader occupation and its passing were epiphenomena, mere changes of pace that did not, after all, disturb the slow rhythms of Orthodox liturgical life.'[1] Such a perception reveals the enormous differences in the way Greek (or Arab) East and the Latin West perceived the structure of Christian history.

There was a startling footnote to the Latin defeat. In the spring of 1300 the news arrived in the West that the Mongols had conquered the Holy Land, and were ready to return the Holy Sepulchre to the Christians. Pope Boniface VIII eagerly circulated the report, and many Western chroniclers recorded it. It was said that the victors had celebrated with a mass at the Holy Sepulchre: 'and on the following Easter Day, it is said, the Christians celebrated divine service in Jerusalem with exultation and joy', although this may simply have been the regular Easter ceremony. The reports did have some factual basis. The armies of the Mongol Ilkhan of Persia, Ghazan, had swept the Mamluks out of Syria, occupied Damascus, and raided as far as the frontiers of Egypt. Ghazan invited King Henry II of Cyprus and the masters of the military orders to campaign with him. The illusion was quickly shattered when the Mongols were forced to withdraw from Syria. In any case, Ghazan himself became a convert to Islam. While Syria under the Mongols might have offered a more favourable prospect for Christian access to the holy places, the opportunity, such as it was, quickly vanished. No Christian army was to enter Syria and Palestine until General Allenby captured Jerusalem in 1917, and until then the holy places remained under a Muslim government, subject to the regulations they made for control of the church of the Holy Sepulchre and for pilgrim access.

The perilous position of the Latins had been apparent to Westerners since the death of Louis IX on the Tunis Crusade in 1270. The election in 1271 as pope of Gregory X, who was actually on crusade

---

[1] A. Jotischky, 'The Fate of the Orthodox Church in Jerusalem at the End of the Twelfth Century', *Patterns of the Past*, 194.

at Acre at the time, set the defence and recovery of the Holy Land high on the church's agenda. Gregory initiated a great debate on the subject, originally intended as preparation for the Second Council of Lyons in 1274. The loss of Acre in 1291 released a stream of treatises designed to plan a serious attempt to retake the Holy Land. Franco Cardini described them as the *crociata d'inchiostro*—'paper crusade'. Many of these works were serious studies written by people with a good grasp of the subject. Fidenzio of Padua, who dedicated his *Book of the Recovery of the Holy Land* to Pope Nicholas IV in 1291, mentioned that at Lyons Gregory X 'commissioned me . . . to put in writing how the Holy Land could be acquired from the hands of the unbelievers and could then be held by the faithful of Christ'.[2] He had travelled widely in the East and had a solid knowledge of recent crusading history. Such reports shaped the terms in which projected crusades were discussed, but it was another matter to set on foot a successful expedition.

It has been a long-standing tradition among historians that the crusades ended in 1291. Although Steven Runciman's classic, *A History of the Crusades*, identified the failure of the expedition of Pius II in 1464 as marking the point when 'the crusading spirit was dead', he firmly labelled the years after 1291 as 'Epilogue', and covered them in only some forty pages out of a three-volume work. Hans Mayer's book, *The Crusades*, ends firmly in 1291. A study of Florentine wills by P. Pirillo provides a useful illustration of the range of reasons on which such an analysis was based. He notes that in the final quarter of the thirteenth century, a total of about 400 wills survives in Florence. Of these, 13 per cent, a significant proportion, contain bequests *pro passaggio*, 'for the crusade'. After 1300 such bequests became much less frequent. Pirillo thought that the immediate explanation was the indulgence issued for the Holy Year of 1300 at Rome, while the long-term explanation was the difficulty, if not the impossibility, of recovering the Holy Sepulchre by military means: 'in the course of the fourteenth century the idea of the liberation of the Holy Land progressively weakened in the awareness of those who were drawing up their last wills.'[3] It was tempting for the church and secular powers to retain Jerusalem as a pious aspiration, which cost little to mention and which would give both

[2] P. G. Golubovich (ed.), *Liber Recuperationis Terrae Sanctae: Biblioteca Bio-bibliografica della Terra Santa e dell'Oriente francescano*, 2 vols. (Florence, 1906–27), pref.
[3] P. Pirillo, 'La Terrasanta nei testamenti Fiorentini del duecento', F. Cardini (ed.), *Toscana e Terrasanta nel Medioevo* (Florence, 1982), 57–73.

moral authority and access to crusading taxes; but it must now seem to us that the prospect of a successful invasion of the Asiatic mainland was remote. No expedition even arrived there, let alone succeeded in recovering Jerusalem. In spite of this, recent studies by such scholars as Norman Housley and Christopher Tyerman have shown that the aspiration to recover Jerusalem was being seriously entertained in a variety of forms. The desire for Jerusalem could still function as the source of political initiatives and religious aspirations.

People hoped for the recovery of the holy places. Anselm Adorno (1471) met a friar at Jerusalem who was 100 years old, never used a stick, and 'always affirms that before his death he would see the Temple and city in Christian hands'.[4] Some political leaders certainly took seriously the prospects of reconquest. One of the projects which came closest to realization was the Mediterranean crusade of Philip VI of France, which he was planning between 1332 and 1336, and which was abandoned only in face of a growing quarrel with England. King Peter I of Cyprus, inspired by his chancellor, Philip of Mézières, and encouraged by his own title as king of Jerusalem, travelled to the West to appeal for a 'general passage' or crusade in 1362. In command of a large fleet and army, he succeeded in seizing the port of Alexandria in 1365, and demanded the surrender of the kingdom of Jerusalem as part of the conditions for a peace treaty. This proved in the event to be the last expedition to take place with the specific and central objective of the recovery of Jerusalem.[5]

By this time the position in the eastern Mediterranean was being transformed by the expansion of the Ottoman Turks, who by the middle of the century had overrun much of Anatolia and were poised to enter the Balkans. Western kings who were concerned for the welfare of Christendom had to focus on the Turkish menace, as the Ottomans occupied Serbia and finally took Constantinople itself in 1453. In 1516 they destroyed the Mamluk Sultanate, which had controlled Egypt and Syria. The Hospitaller outpost of Rhodes fell in 1522–3. After the conquest of Hungary, Vienna was besieged in 1529, and the new Hospitaller base at Malta was fiercely assaulted in the siege of 1565. The Turkish failure in these two sieges marked the high-water mark of Ottoman expansion, but the war with Venice for the complete control of the eastern Mediterranean continued for a long time afterwards.

---

[4] *Anselm Adorno*, 262–4.   [5] Housley, *Later Crusades*, 39–42.

Even in this new political order the aspiration to recover Jerusalem lingered. Philip of Mézières, the chancellor of Cyprus at the time of the Alexandria Crusade, remained a champion, and under his influence, Charles VI of France proposed to Richard II of England 'that you and I, for the propitiation of the sins of our ancestors, should undertake a crusade to succour our fellow Christians and to liberate the Holy Land'. The idea was still present in the crusading projects contemplated during the middle years of the fifteenth century by the court of Burgundy. The Burgundian agent Bertrandon de la Brocquière after 1432 travelled back from Palestine through the Ottoman dominions to study Turkish power at close quarters. He recorded his concern that the sultan's dominion in Jerusalem was 'to the shame and grief of Christendom', and in dedicating his book to Duke Philip of Burgundy, he explained that he wrote 'in order that if any king or Christian prince should wish to make the conquest of Jerusalem, and lead thither an army overland, or if any gentleman should be desirous of travelling thither, they may be acquainted with all the towns, cities [and] regions'.[6] The chance of a recovery continued to nag at the thinking of the devout. Paul Walther (1483) provided a 'heartfelt prayer for the recovery of the Holy Land by Christians', and the Swiss pilgrim Ludwig Tschudi (1519) commented that 200 armed men would be enough to capture Jerusalem, although this remark strikes one as extremely optimistic.[7]

Meanwhile new explorations and acquisitions beyond the Atlantic Ocean were being made possible by improved maritime technology, and were motivated in large part by hope of direct access to the supply of slaves and gold from West Africa, which had hitherto been available only through the merchants of Morocco. By 1500 these ambitions had expanded to linking up with the Indian spice trade and exploiting the resources of the Atlantic islands as profitable sugar plantations. The most active promoters of exploration were still moved by ideals of military crusade and the recovery of Jerusalem. Prince Henry of Portugal, later named Henry the Navigator, saw himself above all as a warrior of Christ. His public career began with

---

[6] De la Brocquière in T. Wright (ed.), *Early Travels in Palestine* (London, 1848), 283, 287; on his thinking, see D. M. Vaughan, *Europe and the Turk, 1350–1700* (Liverpool, 1954), 50–3.

[7] M. Sollweck (ed.), *Fratris Pauli Waltheri Guglingensis Itinerarium* (Tübingen, 1892), 310; B. Esch, 'Vier Schweizer Parallelberichte von einer Jerusalemfahrt im Jahre 1519', N. Bernard and Q. Reichen (eds.), *Gesellschaft und Gesellschaften: Fs. für U. im Hof* (Berne, 1982), 184.

the spectacular seizure of Ceuta in North Africa in 1415. The expeditions that he later sent to the African coast were inspired in part by the desire to conquer and convert pagans and to find a route to the supposed empire of Prester John, in the hope of a joint Christian expedition to the Holy Land. That at least was Prince Henry's mission statement: some modern historians have accepted that these were sincerely held objectives, while others suppose that they were a disguise for a desire for slaves and gold.

Even the discovery of the New World did not point, as one might expect, to the abandonment of the recovery of Jerusalem as an ideal. On the contrary, it offered the prospect of rich resources that might make possible the long-held dream, and implied a providential intervention that promised the culmination of history. The ideas of Joachim of Fiore, complicated by other currents of eschatology, had entered Spain through the preaching of the friars. Christopher Columbus was a highly practical man who combined talented seamanship with a grasp of navigation and a knowledge of late medieval cosmology. He was also influenced by eschatological speculations that looked for the recovery of Jerusalem. He claimed that initially he had advised Ferdinand and Isabella, his sponsors, 'to spend all the profit of this my enterprise on the conquest of Jerusalem', and he grew increasingly confident of his special role, not merely in discovering new territories, but equally in opening the way to the Sepulchre: 'in this voyage to the Indies', he wrote, 'our Lord wished to perform a very evident miracle in order to console me and the others in the matter of this other voyage to the Holy Sepulchre.' The providential recreation of a Christian Holy Land was close at hand: 'The prophets tell us that Jerusalem and Mount Sion are to be rebuilt by the hand of a Christian.' Columbus's concern with Jerusalem remained real, and he promised Ferdinand and Isabella in 1502 that 'you are assured of certain victory in the enterprise of Jerusalem if you have faith'.[8] King Ferdinand of Aragon several times announced his intention to recover Jerusalem: 'the conquest of Jerusalem belongs to us', he wrote in 1510, 'and we have the title of that kingdom.'

Conquest, exploration, and acquisition were not the only way. A few people recognized that the recovery of Jerusalem was a lost

---

[8] Housley, *Later Crusades*, 311–12; V. I. J. Flint, 'Christopher Columbus and the Friars', *Intellectual Life in the Middle Ages: Essays Presented to Margaret Gibson* (London, 1992), 310; P. M. Watts, 'Prophecy and Discovery', *American Historical Review*, 90 (1985), 85.

cause. Felix Fabri, writing after his second journey to Jerusalem in 1483, remarked that 'the Holy Land has been so utterly lost to us that now no one so much as thinks about recovering it, and there is no longer any way to recover it, unless it should please God to work some miracle to that end'. Even so, he was distressed at the control of the holy places by the unbeliever: 'It is a great confusion that Christ's faithful worshippers should be let into Christ's church by Christ's blasphemers . . . I confess that while I was passing between them into the church I was filled with confusion and covered with blushes, nor could I look them straight in the face by reason of the shame which I felt.'[9] Fabri accordingly provided his reader with a history of the crusades. Yet while some aspiration for a military success remained, there emerged another approach: peaceful pilgrimage. A number of events and influences came together to create a well-organized and remarkably persistent new pattern of pilgrimage: the settlement of a community of Observant friars on Mount Sion, who formed a close link between the developing piety of the West and Jerusalem; a planned tour of visits, which did not change much in two centuries; an insatiable demand for indulgences; and the organization for pilgrims of Venetian maritime traffic to the East. The new pilgrimage was different from that of the twelfth century because the great shrines, with their communities and liturgies and public celebrations, were no longer in existence. Modest processions were now directed by the accompanying friars from one holy place to another, in search of devotion and indulgences.

The prospects for Latin pilgrimage to Jerusalem appeared poor in the early fourteenth century. If the Mamluks did not have a determined policy of excluding Latin pilgrims, they regarded them with suspicion. There were Western reservations about the pilgrimage, too. The prospect that pilgrims would put money into the hands of the Muslim powers worried the papacy, and there were long-standing papal requirements of a dispensation to make the Jerusalem pilgrimage, and the minimum expenditure needed to make the visit possible. At least nominally, to go without permission carried with it the penalty of excommunication.[10] Although two important accounts of the Holy Land were written in the closing years of the thirteenth century by Burchard of Mount Sion and Ricoldo of Monte Croce, neither of

[9] *Felix Fabri*, PPTS 7–8. 341.
[10] For papal prohibitions, and the dispensations they required, in particular for England, see Webb, *Pilgrimage*.

them was a pilgrim in the normal sense. After 1310, we do hear of visitors, such as the Irish friar Symon Semeonis in 1322 and the German William of Boldensele in 1334. Both of these were able to have Latin mass said in the church of the Holy Sepulchre by members of their party, but they mention the presence only of Georgian clergy, with no regular Latin service; and Symon Semeonis in particular had to face suspicion and difficulty on the part of the authorities, from which he was only rescued by sympathetic local Christians. Public observances continued to be restricted: Niccolò of Poggibonsi in 1345 indicated that the Palm Sunday procession, the whole essence of which was the solemn entry into the city, had to be confined within its walls—although he may have been describing the Latin version, because we know that shortly before the Armenians were being allowed to conduct the full procession. By that time, a new structure of pilgrimage was emerging.

While chivalry had long seen war with the unbeliever as one of the principal Christian virtues, the idea of securing the Holy Sepulchre by negotiation and truce had already been important in the thirteenth century. It went back most obviously to the treaty negotiated by Frederick II in 1229, and even earlier had a place in the policy of Richard I. In the fourteenth century it was in the interest of the Mamluks to find Western allies, and Westerners found advantages in negotiations with Egypt. Most Mediterranean powers in practice had to do diplomatic business with Egypt, and some sent regular embassies there. Commerce, too, required agreements between Christian and Muslim. For centuries, Venice paradoxically combined a commitment to crusading with a concern for peaceful trade with Egypt, and subsequently with the emerging power of the Ottoman Turks. Pius II at the Congress of Mantua in 1459 complained to the Venetians that 'too much intercourse with the Turks has made you the friend of the Muslims'. As an overall judgement of Venice that was unfair, but it expressed an undoubted ambiguity in the city's policy. Alongside these secular interests there were new spiritual ideals, and the new interest in missionary work which had emerged among the friars.

King James II of Aragon was on good terms with the Mamluk sultans in Egypt, and sent a series of embassies there between 1293 and 1327. The basis of his policy was to establish a house of friars at Jerusalem, but without asking for any territorial concessions: in that sense, the new establishment was to be much more modest than the Frederick II's treaty a century before. An attempt to establish a house of Dominican friars met with insoluble problems in 1323, and in 1327 James II was still writing to the sultan to ask him for action: 'We also have a great devotion for the Holy Sepulchre of Christ. We have heard by the mouth of . . . friars minor recently returned from Jerusalem that the church of the Holy Sepulchre is not served as decently or sufficiently as is proper.' King James died, however, before any action was taken on this request. The settlement was finally negotiated by a group of Franciscans led by brother Roger Guérin from Aquitaine in 1333. The proposals were strongly supported by the royal house of Naples, which could build on good relations with Egypt going back to the times of Frederick II and Charles of Anjou. Unfortunately, copies of the treaty do not survive: most of the archives of the Franciscans at Jerusalem were lost when the brothers were imprisoned by the Ottoman authorities in 1537. Nevertheless, the outline is clear. The Franciscans were to be allowed to occupy a house on Mount Sion, on the site (the 'cenacle') which was believed to be that of the upper room where the Last Supper had taken place and the Spirit had descended upon the apostles. They were given liberty to serve several major holy places: the Holy Sepulchre, Calvary, the church of the Nativity at Bethlehem, and the tomb of the Virgin. While they failed to secure a monopoly in face of the established Georgian privileges, particularly at the Holy Sepulchre itself, they became the recognized representatives of Latin Christianity. The sultan was induced to make the concessions by a large monetary payment from Naples and by the advantage of obliging a Western ally and thus of reducing the likelihood of another crusade. Final papal approval of the new order was issued only some years later, in two bulls of Clement VI on 21 November 1342, and Ludolf of Suchem found the friars well established when he visited Jerusalem in 1350. Even in the twentieth century Catholic writers regarded the treaties and bulls as 'the fundamental basis of the rights which catholicism can claim over the holy places of Palestine in general'.[11] The Franciscan house on Mount Sion was eventually organized into a 'custody of the Holy Land' within the administration of the order, although their tenure there was insecure, being challenged several times in the fifteenth century, and terminated altogether in the sixteenth.

[11] For the documentation of this section, see S. de Sandoli, 'La Libération pacifique des lieux saints au XIVe siècle', *Studia Orientalia Christiana Collecta*, 21 (Cairo, 1988), 73–159.

To the Venetians, good relations with their trading partners in the Middle East were fundamental. Already in 1304, the emir of Acre had written on behalf of Sultan en-Nāsir Muhammad: 'This is my lord's command, that I should preserve, guard and honour the men of Venice above all others in the world. If any of your people wish to go as pilgrims to the Holy Sepulchre, we will provide them with an escort to go there and back without any danger at all.' Venice was crucial in the system of pilgrim sailings. Passengers negotiated with the Venetian shipmaster their transport and keep. The package included a Muslim escort to Jerusalem, and guided visits to the sites conducted by the resident Franciscans. Hostels such as the *fundaco dei Tedeschi* catered for residence while passengers waited for the galleys to sail: frequently two of them, competing for custom, and leaving just after the feast of the Ascension. Pilgrims were incorporated into civic ritual, and were given an honoured place in the great Corpus Christi procession. The dominance of Venice lasted into the sixteenth century, when Francesco Suriano, a friar very experienced in conditions in the Holy Land, recommended this passage as much the fastest, 'due to the great amount of merchandise carried from Venice to these ports'. Still later, in 1533, Greffin Affagart from Maine in northern France, although conscious that the continuation of the pilgrimage was now in question, wrote that 'if someone simply wants to go on the journey to Jerusalem, I advise him to take the pilgrim ship . . . from Venice'.[12] Not everybody was enthusiastic about this service. Anselm Adorno (1470) advised his readers against 'the pilgrim galleys which are prepared every year at the Ascension at Venice'. They were too narrow, he said, and what is more, the mixture of nationalities tended to spread infection on board. Anselm noted, with a certain grim satisfaction, the casualties among his companions who, 'fearing to follow a route other than the standard one', had travelled through Venice, whereas he himself had successfully taken ship at Genoa.[13] Other travellers arranged a completely different route, negotiating their own arrangements for passage on cargo vessels in preference to the package offered by Venice. They would commonly go through Alexandria, and visit Cairo and Mount Sinai before reaching the Holy Land proper.[14]

The friars had a modest establishment at Mount Sion. Leading the

---

[12] *Francesco Suriano*, 32; *Affagart*, 26.
[13] *Anselm Adorno*, 54.
[14] C. Schefer (ed.), *Le Voyage d'Outremer de Jean Thenaud* (Paris, 1884), introduction.

pilgrim parties was one of their major functions, and Mariano da Siena (1431) recorded some of the prayers they used. Canon Pietro Casola from Milan encountered a community of twenty friars in 1494, but commented that they were not allowed to keep their buildings in repair. Himself a scholar of liturgy, he did not think much of their ministry:

I do not mention that any antiphons or prayers were said there, because those fathers did not say any. They only explained in Latin and the vernacular what those places were and nothing else. Many itineraries, however . . . mention that formerly antiphons and prayers appropriate to the places visited used to be said. I only say that in fact this was not done. I can well believe that as the friars were in such a hurry to show us those places, they omitted some of the usual ceremonies.[15]

A few years earlier, Felix Fabri was making use of a ' "processional for pilgrims in the Holy Land" . . . wherein are marked all the versicles, collects, responses, hymns and psalms which ought to be said or sung at all the holy places and throughout the course of a pilgrimage beyond sea'.[16] Fabri himself, in fact, complained about the hurried circumstances of his first journey in 1480—after which, he observed, he hardly knew whether he had been at Jerusalem or not—and had much more time available on his second journey of 1483. He assumed that visits to the holy city should be followed by a further journey to the River Jordan, which 'is the end of the pilgrimage of Jerusalem'. The energetic traveller could also add to this inclusive programme optional excursions, as they would now be called, including the monastery of St Catherine on Mount Sinai, which involved a long desert journey. These enterprises were generally unpopular with the captains of the ships, whose interest was in securing a rapid return to the West for their whole party, and who even tried to persuade their customers to leave out the Jordan expedition, which friar Felix admitted could be dangerous.

The new order was described by the German canon Ludolf of Suchem on the occasion of his visit in 1336. He reported that the keys of the edicule of the Holy Sepulchre were in the hands of the Georgians, who opened it to pilgrims for a Venetian denier each. The cenacle on Mount Sion (which, he commented, was once a house of regular canons) was by then occupied by the Franciscans, who were

---

[15] *Mariano da Siena*, 105; and *Pietro Casola*, 246–7, 254. The introduction to this volume includes a particularly good history of the Venetian pilgrim service.
[16] *Felix Fabri*, PPTS 7–8, 290.

supported partly by alms and partly by gifts from the royal house of Naples. There were times during the long Mamluk ascendancy when the underlying hostility between Christian and Muslim powers disrupted the precarious balance. The most dramatic was the capture and sack of Alexandria in 1365, which led to the imprisonment of the Mount Sion Franciscans at Damascus and the closure of the church of the Holy Sepulchre for a number of years. This may have been the background to the misfortunes of Isolda Parewastel of Bridgwater in Somerset, who had visited the Holy Places for three years, 'and has there been stripped and placed head downwards on a rack and beaten'.[17] In 1523, the custody was obliged to move from its normal base in the church of Mount Sion, and in 1510, after the Hospitallers from Rhodes had attacked an Egyptian fleet, the sultan threatened the closure of the Holy Sepulchre, but did not carry out his threat. In spite of these crises and of the growing disruption of navigation produced by the rise of Ottoman sea-power in the later fifteenth century, the pilgrimage operated on a reasonably stable basis from the agreement of 1333 until the Mamluks lost control of Jerusalem to Ottoman conquest in 1516.

THE GREAT PILGRIMAGE, 1330–1530

Two galleys a year from Venice seems to have been the norm, and of course two galleys do not make a mass pilgrimage. Mariano da Siena (1431) says that on his ship there were 125 pilgrims and 300 personnel in all including sailors, and that another vessel travelled as well. Hans Roth (1440) actually provides us with a list of the pilgrims' names, and there were ninety-one of them on his ship. Francesco Suriano (1481 and later) said that there were about 300 on board each galley, but was probably including the crew. To those who chose the standard package, we must add parties travelling with great nobles who hired their own ship, and a wholly unknown number who went by other routes There is no way of making an impressive total out of these casual indications: Cordula Nolte's estimate of 300–500 Latin pilgrims to Jerusalem is probably close to the mark, and one must remember that there were some years when naval warfare made it impossible for even this number to travel.[18]

---

[17] Webb, *Pilgrimage*, 186.
[18] *Pietro Casola*, 11; *Mariano da Siena*, 75–6; *Hans Roth*, 312; *Francesco Suriano*, 36; C. Nolte, 'Erlebnis und Erinnerung fürstliche Pilgerfahrten nach Jerusalem im 15 Jahrhundert', *Fremdheit und Reisen*, 65–92.

FIG 9.1 A French manuscript of the fifteenth century shows the arrival of pilgrims at the church of the Holy Sepulchre. It echoes the narratives of Jerusalem travel. The participants are carrying staff and wallet, and are paying the Saracen doorman for entry. On the other hand, the church is very different from the reality. Angels are in process of removing the tomb-slab from a sarcophagus, and the Sepulchre is located under a Western-style apse.

In some ways, 'great pilgrimage' is therefore a misnomer, for it was certainly not as numerous as in the high crusading days of the twelfth century. Twelfth-century pilgrims included the large parties that we more usually reckon as crusades. It remains true that the Jerusalem pilgrimage between 1330 and 1530 had a profound importance in shaping the culture of the West. Travellers, if not numerous, were influential. Many of them were nobles, senior clergy, or learned friars, well placed to shape the thinking of the societies in which they lived. Voyagers began to produce literary accounts of their experiences on a scale totally without previous parallel. The visiting of shrines was conducted on a programme, providing a regulated experience which helped to form all who came on the Jerusalem pilgrimage, even to those who continued their travels elsewhere. All of this helped to shape a pilgrim culture that pervaded the spirituality, liturgy, and art of Western Europe, and the character of Christian devotion, and continued with remarkable persistence for a long

period. Franco Cardini has described these centuries as 'a homo-
geneous moment, within which a systematic study of the scope of
Western pilgrimages can be undertaken with good results'.[19]

The Palestine pilgrimage in the late Middle Ages was dominated
by the aristocracy. The participants included people from the highest
ranks of society, such as the visionary Birgitta, a member of the
Swedish royal family resident in Italy in 1372, and Henry of Boling-
broke, the future Henry IV of England, who followed a campaign in
Prussia with a visit to Jerusalem in 1392 for a brief stay. In contrast,
Duke William III of Saxony travelled in 1461 with a company of
ninety-one, and Duke Frederick the Wise went in 1493 with a party
of about a hundred, including two painters to record what he saw
and a fool for his entertainment. He was joined by other princes,
and a massive party of 189 people set sail from Venice. The six-
month journey seems to have included only six days at Jerusalem,
allowing the minimum time required for the completion of the visits
there.

Occasionally we can form an intimate picture of the circumstances or the membership of a company of pilgrims. The young
south German noble Jörg von Ehingen was called, one day in 1494,
to his father's room, 'which still stands above the gate, and had long
and agreeable speech . . . concerning the state of knighthood, and
in what manner I should comport myself'. His father wanted him
to accompany a 'splendid expedition' under the knights of St John
(the Hospitallers) to Rhodes, for he himself 'had been possessed
throughout his life with a great desire to see the Holy City and
Land', but had never found the occasion to go. He therefore urged
Jörg to continue there from Cyprus, promising to fit him out
appropriately. No one from the court wanted to go with him, and he
travelled with a knightly company from France and Spain.[20] Some
burgher families established a long-standing tradition of pilgrimage
to Palestine. The Ketzels of Nuremberg went to the Holy Land nine
times over the period of a century, and normally marked their
return by creating a monastery or other pious foundation. Georg
Ketzel in 1459, six years after his return, founded a chapel of the
Holy Sepulchre in one of the hospitals—a custom to which we must
return later.[21]

---

[19] F. Cardini, 'Pellegrini medievali in Terra Santa', *Rivista della Storia d'Italia*, 93
(1981), 5–10.
[20] M. Letts (tr.), *Jörg von Ehingen* (London, 1929), 23.
[21] T. Aign, *Die Ketzel* (Neustadt, 1961).

Friar Felix Fabri provides us with a list of the twelve people in his company at Venice on his second pilgrimage in 1483. The group, he says, 'held together inseparably and lived at the common expense of the four lords' who were the heads of the party. Their retinue included their barber (who was also a good musician), their steward, a man-at-arms, an interpreter (a trader who had been a galley-slave), and Felix himself as their chaplain, along with 'a good simple fellow, patient under hardships'.[22] The sources record little about cut-price travel for poorer pilgrims. Acts of charity to the poor can often be illustrated by the foundation of hospitals, alms-houses, and other social institutions, but there are few mentions of the rich seeking merit by defraying the expenses of the journeying poor. It was customary for people in the West to pay for substitutes to perform pilgrimages when they were prevented by ill health or business, or even to carry them out after their death; but that is by no means the same thing. There is almost no sign of a mass pilgrimage of the poor, although people of modest means did go to Jerusalem. The long-suffering companions of Margery Kempe in 1413 do not sound like a party of the privileged, and Margery herself was at first at a loss how she could afford the journey. Niccolò of Poggibonsi (1346) refused, as a friar, to carry money and tried to work his way, but was in trouble because he could not pay his dues in Palestine; and we hear of a Benedictine monk who had to beg his passage money from sponsors.[23] But none of these people can really be seen as poor. Margery herself came from the burgess class in the substantial port of King's Lynn. Religious were professionally poor, but they normally came from the upper classes, and could reduce their expenditure by acting as chaplains or guides. The fact was that ship passages and the dues demanded for access to the holy places were expensive. Writers and preachers repeatedly cite a proverb that pilgrims had to take with them three bags, filled with faith, patience, and money. Statements of costs are quite numerous in our records. While they are difficult to reconcile with one another, it is clear that a Jerusalem journey would have cost a pilgrim of modest social rank the equivalent of several years' normal income. They were also uncomfortable and dangerous. Some people then, as now, dismissed a pilgrimage as a sort of holiday, but Felix Fabri indignantly denied that this was true of the Holy Land: 'all men may see clearly how untrue is the common saying that the passage by sea from Venice to the Holy Land is a mere

---

[22] *Felix Fabri*, PPTS 7–8. 81–2.   [23] *Niccolò of Poggibonsi*, introduction and 8.

pleasant excursion with little or no danger . . . It requires courage and audacity to attempt this pilgrimage.'

The journey of a noble household was deeply shaped by its aristocratic character. When Fabri's party reached the church of the Holy Sepulchre, the Father Guardian of the Franciscans instructed them in appropriate behaviour: 'we must not break anything off at the holy places, nor must any man draw his coat of arms there, lest by their means the holy places should be defiled'—a prohibition widely disregarded.[24] There is a marked contrast between the innumerable anonymous pilgrim crosses at the entrance to the chapel of St Helena, and the desire of the late medieval nobility to record their coats of arms and names. A curious sketch-book commemorating the life of Richard Earl of Warwick, which focused largely on his pilgrimage to Jerusalem, devoted a page to show 'howe he offered in Jherusalem at our lordes sepulcre and his Armes were set up on the north side of the Temple'.[25] The desire to leave an armorial record was found less objectionably in 'the books in which the arms of many lords were recorded' at a pilgrim hospice in the Alps, where Hans Roth was delighted in 1440 to see 'my father's blessed arms'. He was so excited that, for the only time in his account, he burst into the first person singular.[26] The institutional heart of these aristocratic pilgrimages was the prospect of being dubbed as a knight of the Holy Sepulchre, and thus being admitted into an unstructured but prestigious order. The distinction which has sometimes been made between travel for chivalric adventure and true pilgrimage is invalidated by the importance of obtaining knighthood at the Sepulchre.

THE LITERATURE OF PILGRIMAGE

One of the most striking features of the late-medieval pilgrimage was the volume of literature that it generated. The precise count must depend on which categories are included. Ursula Ganz-Blättler finds 262 narratives of Jerusalem pilgrimage written between 1301 and 1520. During the fourteenth century there was a steady but slow stream, growing until the period from 1460 to 1520, which saw the

---

[24] *Felix Fabri*, PPTS 7–8. 344–6.

[25] Viscount Dillon and W. H. St John Hope (eds.), *Pageant of the Birth, Life and Death of Richard Beauchamp Earl of Warwick, 1389–1439* (London, 1914), illus. xvii. The drawing was probably executed well after Richard's death. 'Temple' here undoubtedly meant church of the Holy Sepulchre.

[26] *Hans Roth*, 307–9.

FIG 9.2 Another imaginative fifteenth-century depiction of worship at the Holy Sepulchre, probably drawn in the late 1480s. It shows how Earl Richard of Warwick 'offered in Jherusalem at our lordes sepulcre and his Armes were set up on the North side of the Temple' (which here means the church). The representation is wholly conventional, with a simple hall with lanterns and a sarcophagus-style tomb.

production of more than half the total. Almost every Western language is represented in this outpouring of literature, and almost all the works were composed by writers who had actually been to Jerusalem.[27] Sometimes there was a startling accumulation of accounts of particular pilgrimages. R. J. Mitchell was able to combine six in describing the 'spring voyage' of 1458, and Helen Prescott had three lengthy sources available for the Sinai journey of 1483. There is so much material here that it qualifies to be seen as a literary tradition in its own right.

Such literature has sometimes been disregarded because it contains a good deal of common material, specially in the accounts of the visits to holy places in and around Jerusalem. It has been suggested that a standard guidebook or Baedeker, available at Venice, was used and extensively cited by later writers, and Josephie Brefeld has endeavoured to reconstruct its text. The similarities among the accounts are indeed marked, and it is clear that writers frequently used earlier works as a source of information. But the master Baedeker itself seems to be a phantom: there is no single, generally available, guide for the Jerusalem journey on the model of the *Wonders of Rome*, the *Mirabilia Romae*, which served visitors there.

The central core is normally provided by the 'pilgrimages' on which they went, under Franciscan guidance, all round the Holy City; the plural is almost always used for the visits to the multiplicity of sites. The variations in these tours are slight, and one can quote texts composed anywhere in the period 1330–1530 to illustrate a persistent tradition. The Spaniard Pero Tafur (1435–9) mentions, as do so many others, the escort of friars who came to Jaffa to conduct the pilgrims: 'When the pilgrim ship arrives at Jaffa the fact is known almost at once to the prior of Mount Sion, who sends two or three friars to the governor of Jerusalem, who return with the sultan's safe-conduct.'[28] Many travellers had to wait in a cave near Jaffa, whose filthy condition impressed itself on their memory. Muslim officers noted the names of the pilgrims before their departure. The visits around Jerusalem were tightly organized by the friars of Mount Sion. Narratives such as those of Sir Richard Guylforde (1506) were dominated by lists such as 'pilgrimages of Mount Sion', 'pylgrymages within the Temple of the Holy Sepulchre', and 'pylgrymages within Jerusalem'. A decade later, Sir Richard Torkington echoed much the same list: at the Mount Sion, within the place of Mount Sion, to the

[27] Ganz-Blättler, 39–43.   [28] *Pero Tafur*, 54.

'Vale of Josophat', at the 'Mount of Olivete' and within the Temple of the Holy Sepulchre. The *Via Dolorosa* along which Christ carried his cross was nothing like as distinctive as it was eventually to become, but it was beginning to emerge. The 'stone of anointing', which became a special place for mourning the death of Christ, was first described by Poggibonsi. By the time of Guylforde it could be said that 'we vysyted all ye longe wey by the whiche our Savyour Christe was led from the hous of Pylate unto the place of his crucifyinge'.

The church of the Holy Sepulchre was the main objective of all these visits. It was certainly no normal church on the Latin pattern. Francesco Suriano observed in the late fifteenth century that it was kept locked, and opened by its Muslim custodian three times a year for Latin pilgrims and once (from Good Friday to Easter) for local Christians. Pilgrims complained of the substantial dues they had to pay for entrance. It seems that the established practice was for them to be allowed three stays in the church, on each occasion being locked in overnight.[29] These nights in the church gave the opportunity for individual devotions that extended beyond the immediate visits to sites under the friars' supervision, as Felix Fabri described: 'the greater part of the pilgrims were wandering about all the aforesaid holy places as each one pleased, passing hither and thither as the spirit of prayer moved them; for a pilgrim may enter the Holy Sepulchre, ascend Mount Calvary, or descend into the chapel of the invention of the cross, and other places as often as he pleases.' Not that everybody was devout all the time. Fabri comments that on the first stay, the pilgrims were making their confessions in preparation for communion; during the second, they were preparing to receive knighthood. On the third, however, the less zealous—who, alas, were the majority—would sleep, or eat and drink wine to excess, talking in a self-glorifying way and chatting in the chapels.

The similarities between some of these accounts are partly explained by literary borrowing, but they were produced even more by participation in the same experiences. Writers put their own spin on the visits. Felix Fabri, as we have seen already, described in his own way what was happening, and Pietro Casola quite often added comments about the existing appearance of the holy places—for example, the piece of stone that had fallen from the cupola above the Holy Sepulchre, which the Muslim authorities would not allow to be repaired. Pero Tafur is plainly describing his own experiences

---

[29] *Pietro Casola*, 258, 274.

and sometimes misunderstands what was going on. He saw the ministering clergy being released from the church when it was unlocked, and wrongly concluded that they had spent a whole year there; and, having encountered knights who were living in the friars' house, he thought that ten or twelve were permanently resident.[30]

The topography of the holy places was marked out by indulgences. Forgiveness of sins and remission of penance had been offered to Jerusalem pilgrims, and notably to crusaders, since the twelfth century, but the attachment of large indulgences to particular places was relatively new. The Fourth Lateran Council had complained in canon 62 about the 'indiscreet and excessive indulgences' that some bishops granted, and that had the effect of undermining the penitential system. Indulgences should not exceed forty days, and this moderate practice largely prevailed during the thirteenth century. In contrast, indulgences were a central feature of the new Holy Land pilgrimage of the fourteenth century. Their theological validity rested on the doctrine of the treasury of merits, which was confirmed by the bull *Unigenitus* (1343). They had already appeared in abundance in the Holy Land. James of Verona (1335) began his work with a long list, headed 'In the name of the Lord. These are the pilgrimages and indulgences of the Holy Land. Note that wherever a cross is marked here, there are indulgences from punishment and guilt (*a pena et a culpa*) for all true penitents who have confessed and are contrite. In other places where there is no cross, the indulgences there are for seven years and seven Lents.' Niccolò of Poggibonsi (1346) mentioned in his foreword that 'the reader will find here all the indulgences in order, and the dimensions and measures of the holy places'. He recorded twenty-six full and ninety-two part indulgences. They did not replace personal devotion at the shrines, but they were a major additional attraction to pilgrims, especially in those places where there was little left for the devout visitor to see. The learned Francesco Suriano (1481 onwards) actually took them as the title for his visitors' guide: 'Here begins the little treatise on the indulgences of the Holy Land'.[31] A lot of the pilgrims thought that these pardons had been granted by 'Pope St Sylvester at the petition of St Helena, the mother of the Emperor Constantine, and have always been confirmed and multiplied from then onwards by many supreme pontiffs'.

---

[30] *Pero Tafur*, 55–7.
[31] V. Castagna (ed.), *Pellegrinaggio ai Luoghi Santi: Liber Peregrinationis di Jacopo da Verona* (Verona, 1990), 203; *Niccolò of Poggibonsi*, 1; *Francesco Suriano*, 19.

In reality, the system emerged with the establishment of the friars on Mount Sion, and it continued for a long time. The Franciscans at Jerusalem were still dispensing indulgences in the seventeenth century. The Protestant George Sandys (1610) joked that 'for omitting Pater Nosters and Ave Marias wee lost many yeeres Indulgences . . . and contented ourselves with an Historicall Relation'.[32]

The operation of indulgences depended on confession and penitence for sins. We hear of the friar Francesco Trivulzio, accompanying a party of pilgrims 'exhorting the company to prepare their consciences well, if they wished to gain the indulgences and the merit of that pilgrimage'.[33] There is a paradox about this desire to collect pardons. There are few explanations in our sources about the motive for collecting so many. One would have thought that one plenary indulgence would have been enough for anybody, but that is a general problem in late-medieval religion. There was assuredly a desire to secure spiritual rewards for family, friends, and patrons, but that is only occasionally mentioned in the accounts. It has been suggested that the prominence of indulgences marks a sharp change in the character of devotion: 'One can see how the stress is shifted in a subtle way. The Gospel, from now on, is less meditated than moralized. The pilgrim's gaze is not so much fixed on the contemplation of the Lord as turned in towards himself.'[34] There was certainly a change in the pattern of piety, but I do not think that this contrast between contemplating the Lord and reflecting on oneself accurately describes it. Devotion to the image of the crucified Jesus was closely linked with sorrow for sin. It would be more correct to say that there was a shift from a triumphalist religion to one of sorrowful devotion to the passion—a change that reflected the position of humiliation the pilgrims felt in the Holy Land from the loss of Acre onwards. It was related also to a changed attitude to the ceremonies in the church of the Holy Sepulchre. Not only had the splendid liturgies of the twelfth century been abolished, but since 1238 the Latins had condemned as a forgery the great ceremony on Easter Eve in which the holy fire miraculously descended upon the Sepulchre and illuminated the lights there. Francesco Suriano described the vast crowds of Eastern Christians who attended, but added that 'the fire does not descend in truth (and in the opinion of us friars), although

---

[32] *Mariano da Siena*, 79–80; *Purchas his Pilgrims* (Glasgow, 1905), viii. 186.
[33] *Pietro Casola*, 221.
[34] C. Deluz, 'Prier à Jérusalem', *La Prière au Moyen Age* (Paris, 1981), 189–210.

all the nations except us friars feign this falsehood to be true'. The effect of this scepticism was to alienate further Latin devotion from that of the native Christians, who called Easter Eve *Id el Nar*, the feast of fire, and to reduce the celebratory element in their presence at the Holy Sepulchre. Ricoldo of Monte Croce (1288 onwards) had remembered how the pilgrims joined in the Easter sequence: 'each one cried so loudly, *Surrexit Christus spes mea, precedet nos in Galilea*, that the noise and tumult spread outside the church among the Saracens.' For Margery Kempe (1413) the Sepulchre was a place to sorrow for the death of Christ rather than to rejoice in his resurrection: 'When this creature with her fellowship came to the grave where our Lord was buried, anon, as she entered the holy place, she fell down with her candle in her hand, as if she would have died for sorrow, and later she rose up against with great weeping and sobbing, as though she had seen our Lord buried before her.'[35]

Few of these pilgrimage narratives are systematic accounts of the nature of the Holy Land; still rarer are attempts to write its history. They are narratives of a journey, frequently in diary format. Thomas Brygg (1392) and Guylforde (1506) are good examples of writers who carried this journal format throughout their whole pilgrimage. Even those whose works are more discursive noted on wax tablets events and scenes as they took place, and then wrote them up. Felix Fabri tells us that 'I never passed one single day while I was on my travels without writing some notes, not even when I was at sea, in storms, or in the Holy Land; and in the desert I have frequently written as I sat on an ass or a camel.'[36] Their declared purpose in writing was often to assist other travellers: 'since one dares to undertake more easily and with less fear things about which one has some certainty or knowledge . . . I wanted to tell them about the places, dangers and other adventures.' Alternatively, they might write, not for those who were going, but for those who could not go: 'the reason why I troubled myself about this is: firstly, many who have a great desire to visit the holy places, poverty impedes; and others abandon it, for the too great fatigue, and others again for want of a permission which must be had from the pope.'[37]

---

[35] *Francesco Suriano*, 48; R. Kappler (ed. and tr.), *Pérégrination en Terre Sainte et Proche Orient: Riccold da Monte Croce* (Paris, 1997), W. Butler-Bowdon (tr.), *The Book of Margery Kempe (1436)* (London, 1936), 111.

[36] *Felix Fabri*, PPTS 7–8, 56.

[37] *Saincte Cyté de Jérusalem*, cited J. Richard. 'Les Relations de pèlerinages au Moyen Age et les motivations de leurs auteurs', *Wallfahrt*, 145–6; *Niccolò of Poggibonsi*, 10.

On the whole, though, people did not feel they had to explain why they were writing. The desire to know about the Holy Land was self-evident. The brothers at Jerusalem were often asked for information by their guests. Accordingly, those who had spent a long time in the East naturally felt well placed to instruct their readers. The parish priest Ludolf of Suchem (1336–41), or perhaps a later editor, was inclined to be superior on the subject: 'Many people write at exceedingly great length about the countries of Outremer and about the state and condition of the Holy Land and its provinces, when they have only passed through them once. Now, I have lived in those parts for an unbroken space of five years.'[38] There were a lot of readers who used Burchard of Mount Sion (1283), and subsequently Francesco Suriano (1480 and later). Resident authors of that kind did not rely only on what they saw themselves: Ludolf tells us that he took information also from 'ancient books of history and . . . from the lips of truthful men'. Other authors did not aim at wide circulation, but wrote to keep a record for their family and friends as a remembrance of the glory of their noble deeds. Sebald Rieter (1479) used and annotated a guidebook that he received from his father, of the same name (1464). Francesco Suriano wrote at the request of his sister, Sixta, and her community of Poor Clares at S. Lucia in Foligno. The composition of his various drafts covered a period of some forty years, and although Francesco was hugely experienced about conditions in the East, the account was shaped primarily as a sentimental pilgrimage to the Holy Sepulchre, composed in the Venetian dialect. It is a literary equivalent of the 'holy mounts', *sacri monti*, which were beginning to emerge from the experience of the Jerusalem friars at precisely this time. The advent of printing naturally made it easier for writers to address a wide public and spread the awareness of the Holy Sepulchre within the culture of the West. The account of Bernard of Breydenbach, Felix Fabri's companion on the journey of 1483–4, was published in 1486, and by 1522 it had been printed twelve times in five different languages.

Almost all accounts are narratives of a journey to the Holy Sepulchre. Beyond this central feature, writers could extend their work in a number of directions. It will perhaps be helpful to take three examples composed in the course of a generation, chosen not because they exercised a lot of influence on contemporaries (two of

[38] A. Stewart (tr.), *Ludolf von Suchem* (PPTS 1895), 1.

them certainly did not), but because they illustrate the variety of approach that could shape these works.

Mr William Wey journeyed to Compostella in 1456, and then to Jerusalem in 1458 and 1462. He was a Fellow of Eton, and subsequently an Augustinian canon of Edington in Wiltshire. His *Itineraries* are contained in a nicely written volume, once owned by Edington and now to be found in the Bodleian Library at Oxford. They are essentially a file of practical advice to pilgrims, poorly organized and with a good deal of repetition. Some pages are in Latin, some in English, and they include reference lists that note the rates of currency exchange and provide a basic English–Greek vocabulary. Practical advice is given about negotiating a contract for the voyage at Venice: you should choose a place in the galley 'in the overest stage; for in the lawyst under, hyt is ys ryght smolderyng, hote and stynkynge'. There is a doggerel summary of the trip, giving advice about suitable behaviour and the availability of indulgences:

> And, when wee be passyd that place,
> We schal se Jerusalem in short space.
> Then knele we downe upon our kne,
> When we that holy cyte see;
> For to all that thydyr come
> Is yeve and graunt ful remyssioun.

It would be kind to think that the poem was a sort of mnemonic, incorporated by Wey, rather than the product of his own literary talent. On other pages he included a brief outline of a twelve-day programme for the Holy Land visit, and elsewhere a list of reasons for making the journey. The modern historian may turn to such a section with interest, but it is rough and repetitious, and is perhaps designed as an aide-memoire for preachers. It is however notable for the inclusion of Birgitta of Sweden as an authority. A more substantial element is a list of the 'holy places in the stations at Jerusalem', forming what is essentially an outline of the *via dolorosa* of Jesus, in twenty-two stops. Wey has been credited with being the first author to speak of the 'stations' of the cross or the passion. This is perhaps literally true, but the term 'station' was a normal one to use for a stopping-place in a procession, and its appearance should not be counted as an indication of a change in perception. Wey's writing seems to have been used by only one later writer, but it has a real importance as an attempt to collect material that would be of practical use to the traveller.

It is made more significant by William Wey's will for the monastery at Edington, which left goods 'to the chapel made to the lyknes of the sepulkyr of our Lorde at Jerusalem'. There are minor ruins of a chapel, long since demolished, which may have been the one. He left curtains of blue buckram, and 'a clothe stayned with the tempyl of Jerusalem, the Mounte of Olyvete, and Bethleem'. The 'tempyl' was probably the church of the Holy Sepulchre, which was often so described. There was also a crucifix from Jerusalem, and a reliquary box containing stones from various holy places, including Calvary and the Sepulchre. A number of 'bordes' contained the measures of the Sepulchre and other places, and paintings (seemingly) of the chapel of Calvary and the church of Bethlehem. There was also a large map, presumably the one now in the Bodleian Library, designed—since its length is seven feet—rather for display and devotion than for practical planning. We do not know whether other pilgrims provided for similar decorations for chapels of the Holy Sepulchre, but as a description of the arrangements planned by the donor, this is unique.[39]

Our second writer is very different. Anselm Adorno was a member of a family whose association with the crusades dated back to the Tunis expedition of 1270. It was originally from Genoa, but long established as one of the propertied houses of Bruges. He travelled to Jerusalem in 1471, and his account reflects the attitudes of the great city-based aristocracy. Anselm was an artistic and literary patron.[40] There is a complication in that the narrative of the pilgrimage was actually written by his son Jean, who had travelled with him, and had studied canon law at Pavia, and after the journey entered the service of the papal curia, ending as prebendary of Lille in Flanders. There is no reliable way of distinguishing the contributions of father and son to the history. The *Itinerary* (the title is modern) was not widely circulated at the time, and survives in only two manuscripts.

Anselm was in the service of the court of Burgundy, a centre of interest in devotion to Jerusalem and crusade planning, and he began with one of the greatest declarations of internationalism to be found in this literature:

Some people rather foolishly suppose . . . that there is no other country than the one where they were born. Some again, although they know that other

[39] B. Bandinel (ed.), *The Itinerasies of William Wey* (London, 1856), 9, 19, 21–5, xxviii.

[40] *Anselm Adorno*, 17.

countries exist, are like a mother who with unmeasured affection always says that her children are the most beautiful, and they say that their own land is like shining day compared with the gloominess of night.[41]

He continued with a long list of the great men of the past who had explored the world: Socrates, he said, regarded himself as a citizen of the world: *mundanus sum.* Unlike those earlier Burgundian travellers, Lannoy (1403, 1421, and 1446) and de la Brocquière (1433), his text showed no interest in crusading or in warfare with the Turks, apart from one indirect expression of hope that the church of the Holy Sepulchre might return to Christian hands. One might suspect that Anselm's knightly and Burgundian interests were omitted by Jean, but this would be a pure assumption, and the *Itinerary* was dedicated to King James III of Scotland rather than to the Burgundian court.

Anselm's travel was enterprising and observant. He declined the Venice route and sailed from Genoa. Perhaps his family history disposed him to do so. He was interested in the structure of government at Tunis, and in other aspects of Islamic culture: he provides, for example, an explanation of Arabic script. The description of holy places does not contain much information about indulgences, and focuses on devotion towards the historical Jesus. 'There is at Jerusalem a great church which is called after the Holy Sepulchre, the holy of holies where the world was placed or created, containing many holy places of the Lord's passion.' He observed that 'it would be more devilish than human not to be moved to an inward flow of devotion in such holy places, where the Lord and creator of earth, heaven and everything, as an unblemished lamb, shed his most sacred blood for us his creatures'. In a more discursive way than many of these writers he reflected on the temptations of the world and noted that 'contempt of the world is the way of salvation'.[42] One has the impression of a cultivated humanism influenced by the Brethren of the Common Life in Anselm's native Netherlands. Jean Adorno noted how when they set off 'they mounted their horses in their chapel of Jerusalem at Bruges, where they had confessed and communicated. That chapel had been founded and built by his predecessors and enlarged by him and by me and our family.'[43] In this respect, the Adorno narrative is unique: we still have the church which the family built on their extensive property off Pepper Street.

---

[41] Ibid. 26.   [42] Ibid. 258–62, 424–6.
[43] Ibid. 432. For the Adorno church at Bruges, see inset 'The Jerusalem Church at Bruges' in Ch. 10 below.

Felix Schmidt, or Felix Fabri as he is more commonly known, was a Dominican friar from Ulm in southern Germany. He travelled twice to the Holy Land. The journey of 1480 was a frustrating and difficult experience. The Ottoman Turks were besieging Rhodes, and the Venetians warned intending pilgrims against travel in the Eastern Mediterranean. Many turned back, and those who continued could spend only nine days in Palestine. Felix was left with an ambition to return, and he did so in more fortunate circumstances in 1483, when he included a visit to Mount Sinai and returned through Cairo. His social status was unremarkable: effectively, he was chaplain and companion to a small group of German lords, but he wrote what most people would regard as the supreme book of the Jerusalem pilgrimage, including details of shipboard life and descriptions of pilgrim attitudes and travels, encompassed in a huge and learned volume that he called enticingly his *Evagatorium* or Wanderings.

Part of the pleasure in reading Fabri lies in the variety of attitudes to pilgrimage that he expressed. He truly delighted in the experience: 'for my own part, I never have been happier in any place in the world than in Jerusalem, and I have spent exceedingly pleasant hours and days there.' More surprisingly, he presented us with an early example of the European love affair with the desert:

Something is always happening to fill a man with admiration, either of the strange aspect of the mountains, the colour of the earth and rocks, the numberless kinds of pebbles, or the exceeding rugged, barren and waste nature of the country, all of which things delight the inquiring mind. I confess that, for my own part, I felt more pleasure in the barren wilderness than I ever did in the rich and fertile land of Egypt, with all its attractive beauty.

He quotes in his dedication at the beginning of the work the view of Jerome that the visitor to Judaea will understand the Scriptures better; the original conviction that the purpose of pilgrimage was the search for biblical truth is intact here. Alongside such utterances we find the reservations that, throughout the history of the church, had been expressed about pilgrimage:

Good and simple Christians believe that if they were at the places where the Lord Jesus wrought the work of our redemption they would derive much devotion from them; but I say to these men of a truth that meditation about these places, and listening to descriptions of them, is more efficacious than the actual seeing and kissing of them . . . I have no doubt of this, that were there ten good Christians in my cell at Ulm, who had a desire to see the Holy

Land and the places sacred to the Lord Jesus, I could rouse their devotion and stir up their souls more deeply by my talk about those places than if they were actually lying bowed to the earth in the holy places themselves.[44]

Felix displays a similar range of attitudes in his approach to 'the treasure most precious to all Christians, the Sepulchre of our Lord', which was in his mind the goal of his pilgrimage:

Come then with joy and praise; look upon the place where the Lord was laid, and behold the end of your pilgrimage . . . As on Mount Calvary we pitied our Lord Christ, and shed tears, so here we rejoiced with our redeemer and offered to him sweet tears of joy and lively songs . . . The life of Christ is to me a rule by which to live; his death is my redemption from death.

He was concerned to understand all the holy places historically. About Calvary, he recorded correctly that it is

not called a mount in Scripture, but it is only common talk which speaks of it as a mount, since in truth it is not a mount, but a rock or crag . . . The place Calvary means the entire site of the church [an allusion to the original meaning of 'Golgotha']. The rock of Calvary supports the cross alone.

Similarly with the Sepulchre: the Lord's Sepulchre, he says, was originally like the old tombs that can be seen all over the place in the East. 'It cannot possibly now be like what it then was, because of the church which has been built above it . . . No part of the ground has remained like that described by the evangelists.' In a radical spirit, he regrets that the reconstruction had ever taken place: 'I would that no church had ever been built there, for then we should more clearly have understood the meaning of the Gospels, where they tell of the Lord's passion and resurrection.' Probably, he reckoned, the site would never have been changed had it not already been devastated by the Emperor Hadrian. He realized that one could no longer be sure what remained from the original, but this issue, which one might suppose was the 64,000-dollar question for a pilgrim, left him untroubled:

Whether the cave as it stands at the present day be the true and entire monument of Christ, or whether a part of it be there, or whether none of it be there, matters very little one way or the other, because the main fact connected with the place remains there . . . that is that this was the place of the most holy burial and resurrection of Christ.[45]

[44] *Felix Fabri*, PPTS 7–8. 1–2 (introduction); 9–10. 399–400, 512, 60.
[45] Ibid. 7–8. 379–81, 366–7; 9–10. 266; 7–8. 415.

Felix's keen observation makes his book distinctive, and it is strengthened by his enormous learning. He read widely before starting his second journey, and his knowledge of the literature, while it does not become oppressive, emerges on many pages. He used the account of Burchard of Mount Sion, 'which is in the library of the Dominicans at Ulm'. From the more distant past, he quoted from Arculf and Bernard the monk. Although he knew the Holy Sepulchre well from his visits there, he preferred to use the description 'which a respectable man named John Tucher, a citizen of Nuremberg, has written in the German tongue' because in 1479 Tucher had been in a position to make a particularly minute examination. Felix was not devoid of critical instinct, but in the end he preferred to present his readers with the perceptions which he had drawn from his authorities without a rigorous attempt to achieve conformity.

The commitment of Felix Fabri to the Holy Land did not efface his sense of belonging to his native city. Indeed, as with so many of the travellers, it seems to have deepened it. Pierre Monnet has pointed out that it is rare for fifteenth-century writers to want to stay in the East or to die at the Holy Sepulchre, as earlier pilgrims certainly did, and they began to include in their narratives descriptions of their return. When he saw the Holy Sepulchre, Felix remembered the sepulchre arranged on Good Friday in the parish church at Ulm, and he followed his book of the pilgrimage with a *Description of Germany, Suabia and the City of Ulm*. For him, a living chord linked the Holy Sepulchre with the city where he lived.[46]

CENTRE AND CIRCUMFERENCE

Many of the works we have considered so far were focused on Jerusalem. The conviction that it was the centre of the world remained intact. In 1533, long after European ships had reached India and America, Greffin Affagart noted the 'little rondeau engraved in a slab of marble on the floor' which recorded that it was 'the middle of the world', and an inscription with the old familiar text of Psalm 74: 12, 'working salvation in the midst of the earth'.[47] More poetically, Bernard of Breydenbach (1483) spoke of Jerusalem as *oriens mundi*, by which he perhaps meant 'the source of the world'. There were

[46] P. Monnet, 'Ville réelle et ville idéale à la fin du Moyen Age: une géographie au prisme des témoignages autobiographiques allemands', *Annales HSS*, 56 (2001), 591–621.
[47] *Affagart*, 65–6.

other accounts that associated a visit to Jerusalem with wider travels, and with a keen curiosity about unfamiliar topography, climate, customs, and animals. It is sometimes supposed that literature of this sort, which ranged widely beyond a specific devotion to the holy places, indicates the advent of the Renaissance.[48] Without any question writers were aware of the contrast between devotion and curiosity as motives for travel. Santo Brasca of Milan (1480) advised his readers

to make the journey solely with the intention of visiting, contemplating and adoring with great effusion of tears the most holy mysteries, in order that Jesus may graciously pardon his sins, and not with the intention of seeing the world or from ambition and pride to say, 'Been there! Seen that!'[49]

In reality, pilgrimage and travel stories had been combined more than a century previously. William of Boldensele (1334) was one of the first representatives of this new approach. Niccolò of Poggibonsi (1346) travelled widely in Egypt and the Middle East. The Spaniard Pero Tafur (1435–9) visited Egypt, contemplated a journey to India, and came back via Constantinople and Germany. Bertrandon de la Brocquière (1433) also made the perilous journey through the Ottoman dominions in Eastern dress. These examples of wide-ranging travel all antedate the middle of the fifteenth century.

The greatest travel book of the Middle Ages was written, so its author claimed, by an English knight, Sir John Mandeville, who left England in 1322, spent three decades in journeys to all the known world, and wrote his *Travels* about 1357. It seems more probable that a French writer, a knight or monk, adopted the invented personality of a fictitious Sir John Mandeville. The book was immensely influential. There are about 300 existing medieval manuscripts (about four times as many as for Marco Polo) and numerous printed editions, and it can be found, during the late Middle Ages, in ten languages.

The Book of Sir John Mandeville was not a single work. It is basically a combination of two major authors, William of Bodensele (for the Jerusalem pilgrimage) and Odoric of Pordenone (for the travels in Asia). Just as the original compiler rewrote and adapted his sources, so translators and copyists produced different versions in English,

---

[48] F. Tinguely, *Revue des Sciences Humaines*, 245 (1997), 51–65.
[49] *Pietro Casola*, introduction, 10.

French, and German.[50] There was no single programme behind this mass of writing, which incorporated a variety of opinion and imagination, was variously interpreted by its different editors, and pointed, Janus-like, at once to past and future. There is some truth in the view that it tended to displace Jerusalem from its centrality in geography and in culture, but this was not the intention. In the version closest to the original, the author called Jerusalem 'the best, the most virtuous and the most worthy (region) in the world; for it is the heart and the middle of all the land of the world'. Accordingly, the author maintained that every good Christian who could, should devote himself to the conquest of 'this inheritance, our land'.[51] The Mandeville literature held up a mirror to the people of the late Middle Ages that reflected their aspirations and fears of the mysteries of the holy places and of 'the East', which virtually meant the rest of the world.

The travel literature of the late Middle Ages combines a delight in wonders with a critical sense in a way that perplexes the modern reader. Legendary embellishments of the passion story were accepted: the meeting of Veronica and Jesus on the *via dolorosa*, which left the impression of his face on her towel, and the meeting of Jesus and his mother, when the Madonna was supposed to have wept and fainted. Parables were treated as if they had happened at a real place: the house of Dives was viewed without scepticism, as was the spot on the road to Jericho where the good Samaritan had performed his work of charity. The complex and elaborate story of the wood of the cross, tracing its history from the garden of Eden to Calvary and its discovery by Helena, was long familiar in the West, and the locations of the various episodes could be seen. There were historical legends which would have been difficult to fault without painstaking research, such as benefactions in the Holy Land by the Emperor Frederick Barbarossa, who in fact had died on the way, and those of Charlemagne, whose personal pilgrimage to Jerusalem was still accepted as a fact by Felix Fabri. The desire for relics was undiminished, and Fabri tells us how he was carrying with him jewels provided by wealthy friends who wanted him to touch holy

[50] On the German versions, where the difference is particularly marked, see K. Ridder, *Jean de Mandevilles 'Reisen': Studien zur Überlieferungsgeschichte der deutschen Übersetzung des Otto von Diemeringen* (Munich, 1991).

[51] I. M. Higgins, 'Defining the Earth's Centre in a Medieval "Multi-text": Jerusalem in *The Book of John Mandeville*', in S. Tomasch and S. Gilles (eds.), *Text and Territory: Geographical Imagination in the European Middle Ages* (Philadelphia, 1998), 29–53; B. Braude, 'Mandeville's Jews among Others', B. Le Beau and M. Mor (eds.), *Pilgrims and Travellers to the Holy Land* (New York, 1996), 133–58.

things with them. It is rare to encounter any story of a miracle-working relic, for the Holy Sepulchre was never significant as a healing shrine. Writers often fell to the temptation to provide wonders that would interest their readers. Even the sober Fabri admitted that he often mingled entertainment with information, and Arnold von Harff (1496), whose travels were undoubtedly extensive, added to them the claim to have been to India and Ethiopia, using material from the Mandeville literature.

At the same time, there was a spirit of criticism for which it is difficult to find earlier precedent. Descriptions of the Holy Sepulchre were coming closer to reality. Writers tried to instruct their readers by comparing the design of the church with ones they knew in the West. It was compared with the church of Münster in Westphalia (Ludolf of Suchem), with the Temple at London but much bigger (Guylforde, echoed by Torkington), with 'our church of S. Antony of Padua' (Capodilista), with St Mark's at Venice (Wey), with Santo Stefano, Bologna (Anthony de Reboldis, 1327/30), and with S. Maria Rotonda alias the Pantheon at Rome (Suriano, followed in the seventeenth century by Sandys and Lithgow—again with the proviso that it was bigger). These comparisons fell well short of being serious architectural descriptions. Some of them were motivated by local patriotism, and the Western churches mentioned were in most cases distinguished by their central design. But at least an attempt was being made to evoke some similarities.

By the final quarter of the fifteenth century, printing was encouraging the development of woodcuts; and the wish to portray the Holy Land played a significant part in improving the quality of representations. Several of the narratives from this period incorporated simple plans and sketches, but the decisive stage was the publication in 1486 of Bernard of Breydenbach's account of the 1483 journey. A rich and influential figure, who became dean of Mainz on his return, Breydenbach had taken with him the artist Erhard Reuwich of Utrecht to provide maps and drawings. Not all Reuwich's woodcuts were based on eyewitness observations: the shape of the pyramids, for example, was much too geometrical to be real. Other sketches were not naturalistic in a modern sense. His view of Jerusalem does appear to have been based on an observation made from a specific viewpoint, but it was integrated with a map of Palestine. Reuwich's drawing of the Holy Sepulchre isolates it from its setting beneath the great rotonda of the Anastasis, but it was very closely observed. At last, precise copies of the Sepulchre were coming back

fforma et dispositio dominici sepulchri

FIG 9.3 The 'form and disposition of the Lord's Sepulchre' shown in a wood-cut based on a drawing by Hans Reuwich in about 1483 and published in Breydenbach's description of his travels.

to Europe. Reuwich's work provided a source for both copies and inspiration to people such as Conrad of Grünemberg and Arnold von Harff, and some of his sketches were plagiarized in all sorts of contexts. When we find his pilgrim ship sailing unaltered into an edition of Columbus', *Voyages*, we are reminded not to believe too literally in what we see; but there was a new accuracy that could provide patterns for the architectural development of Western versions of the Holy Sepulchre.[52]

This artistic exactitude corresponded with precision in the awareness of the history of the Holy Sepulchre and its fabric. Felix Fabri's discussion of this was the most perceptive, but it was not the first example of such a precise approach. Even in 1336 Ludolf of Suchem had expressed doubts whether any of the alleged stones that had come from the Sepulchre were really authentic. There was also a new awareness of the inadequacy of accepted imagery. Affagart (1533) provided a careful description of what he saw, and criticized the way in which the resurrection was being shown in European churches: 'our painters are in error when they paint our Lord, at the time of his resurrection, rising from beneath a stone, showing him as having been buried.'[53] As this complaint shows, art was by no means always tied by the literal bands of history; but one of the forces shaping the art of the period was to be a more accurate representation of the holy places in the East.

[52] Ganz-Blättler, 300–8.
[53] Stewart, *Ludolf von Suchem*, 105; *Affagart*, 72.

IO

Sepulchres and Calvaries, 1291–1530

'A LONG WAY FROM JERUSALEM'

'There was a priest who preached the passion on Good Friday, so that many people wept. The foolish priest wanted to comfort them and said, "don't weep, dear child! It is now a good 1500 years since it happened . . . and it is a long way from Jerusalem to here." '[1] He was not the only priest to think that these were distant events in a distant place. Another was surprised at Margery Kempe's weeping before a statue of the dead Christ: 'Jhesu is ded long sithyn.' Her reply was that his death was fresh to her.[2] In this respect Margery was representative of late medieval spirituality, where the aim was 'to be the perfect imitator of Christ in intense sufferings, since it is more perfect to imitate Christ in sufferings than in actions'.

It has been suggested that the development of piety in the late Middle Ages, and more particularly in the sixteenth century, can be understood as a 'return to the sources'. There is some truth in this, but it must be stressed that the effort to create a link between the believer and the life of the historical Jesus involved an uncritical use of the biblical material, and can be argued to have distorted the original pattern of the Jerusalem events.[3] In any case, there was nothing new about associating the sufferings of Christ with those of his servants. The persecution of martyrs and confessors had always been seen as a re-enactment of the passion, and in later times sickness and other misfortunes would be offered to Christ. The sufferings advocated by late-medieval teachers were of a different kind. They

---

[1] B. Wachinger, 'Die Passion Christi und die Literatur', W. Haug and B. Wachinger (eds.), *Die Passion Christi in Literatur und Kunst des Spätmittelalters* (Tübingen, 1993), 1.

[2] S. Beckwith, *Christ's Body: Identity, Culture and Society in Late Medieval Writings* (London, 1993), 81.

[3] On the 'return to the sources', see the argument of D. Julia, 'Sanctuaires et lieux sacrés à l'époque moderne', *Lieux sacrés*, esp. 269–77.

arose from an imaginative participation in the agony of Christ on the cross, which could produce actual physical afflictions, from fasting or the experience of stigmata, as well as deep emotional distress. The passion of Christ was seen as immediately present to the believer:

> O to have been present,
> To have seen you hanging,
> To have wept for you, lamenting
> With the holy Virgin.
> I would have embraced you,
> Would have kissed your wounds,
> Would have been wholly reddened
> By your precious blood.[4]

The days when one great cross in the great church was enough for lay devotion were past: these images were designed to reach, if not every cottage, at least every parish church and urban dwelling.

To examine in detail the changes in late-medieval imagery would go beyond the limits of this book. The images were varied, and their development was cumulative, with the emergence of each new theme adding to the rainbow of possibilities. Ann Derbes has warned us against simplification, remarking that 'the visual culture of this period was far more fluid than it is often thought to be'. The most obvious change of all was the presentation of the crucifix so as to show the savage wounds inflicted on Jesus, and she points to about 1235–40 as the time when, in Italy, 'a full-scale transformation of traditional passion narratives took place'.[5] The body of Christ was represented as dead and deformed, and covered with innumerable wounds, as in Matthias Grünewald's crucifixion now at Basle (1500–8).[6] Features of the story were reinterpreted to emphasize atrocities. References to Christ wearing the crown of thorns scarcely go back beyond the twelfth century, and it was then usually understood as a symbol of kingship. In the thirteenth century, the pains of passion came to be linked with it (as at the Sainte-Chapelle), and finally it was presented as an act of atrocious and deliberate torture in the image on the Allendorfer altar of about 1415, now preserved at Eisenach.[7] The presentation of Mary was another thing that changed

[4] G. Constable, *Three Studies in Medieval Religious and Social Thought* (Cambridge, 1995), 218–28, esp. 228, 226.
[5] A. Derbes, *Picturing the Passion* (Cambridge, 1996), 158, 330.
[6] *Image of Christ*, 106, fig. 31.
[7] Möbius, *Passion*, fig. 55.

in the literature and art of the passion. Her part had previously been one of courage and stoicism, but in thirteenth-century meditation she played a larger role that underlined the depth of her sorrow. Its most famous poetic expression was the *Stabat mater dolorosa*, often ascribed to the Franciscan Jacopone da Todi, and visually Mary's part was enlarged by the addition to the Gospel narrative of a meeting with her son on the way to Calvary, accompanied by tears and fainting, the *Madonna dello spasimo* of counter-reformation devotion.

Public depictions of the passion now extended into very large-scale presentations, the 'populated Calvaries', which included every episode that history, piety, and legend might associate with the crucifixion. The motive was to assist meditation by including all the events on which devotion could be fixed while, once again, emphasizing the extent of the suffering. At the opposite extreme came the demand for head-and-shoulder portraits of the dead Christ on the cross, especially the one known as the image of pity or *imago pietatis*. The force of such images was strengthened by the belief that some of them were authentic pictures of Jesus. The 'original' of the *imago pietatis* had been seen on the altar by Pope Gregory I at mass, and he had supposedly had it painted in the church of Santa Croce at Rome.[8] A series of other cults followed, including the representations of the symbols of the passion or *arma Christi* and of the holy blood.

Art was designed to bring before the public the awareness of the events of the passion. Friar Michele da Carcano in a sermon in 1492 explained that 'images were introduced because people cannot retain in their memories what they hear, but they do remember if they see images'.[9] Accordingly, the reader was urged to imagine himself as present at the events, as the Blessed Virgin was at the crucifixion: 'Grant to me, who did not deserved to be present at these events in the body, that I may ponder them faithfully in my mind.'[10] For the late Middle Ages the passion story served as a master narrative in sequences of illustrations and in the massive meditations on the passion that were produced during the last two medieval centuries in Latin and in a range of vernacular languages.[11] This would suggest

[8] *Image of Christ*, nos. 58–60; H. Belting, *The Image and its Public in the Middle Ages* (New York, 1981), 28–33.

[9] Quoted M. Baxandall, *Painting and Experience in Fifteenth-Century Italy* (Oxford, 1972), 40.

[10] D. Despres, *Ghostly Sights* (Oklahoma, 1989), 31.

[11] T. Bestul, *Texts of the Passion* (Pennsylvania, 1996), 24.

that the personal devotions to Christ were firmly rooted in historical events, and it is true that some painters did depend fairly strictly on the text of the Gospels.[12] As a whole, however, the impression is misleading. The Gospels were enormously elaborated for purposes of devotion. The anonymous author of Pseudo-Bonaventure's *Meditations on the Life of Christ* about 1300 bluntly told his readers that 'the evangelists have not described everything'. He was happy to supplement the Gospels from a variety of sources. The 'suffering servant' prophecies of Isaiah were read as literal descriptions: Isaiah 50: 6, 'I gave . . . my cheeks to those who pulled out the beard,' became the source for one of the tortures in the passion. In this way the narratives added events which had no support in the Gospels. Time-honoured legends such as the healing of the spear-carrier Longinus from his blindness by the blood of Christ further enriched the scenario. Some of these events were historically possible. There could certainly have been a meeting of mother and son on the way to Golgotha, but now this was told of a weeping and fainting woman who is not described in the historical texts. Some of the most famous images had no historical foundation. The Veronica, a major object of devotion for pilgrims to Rome at least from the beginning of the thirteenth century, was slotted into the way to Calvary in a meeting that left the image of Christ on the cloth with which Veronica wiped his face. It was understood to be one of the authentic images of Christ: indeed, the name Veronica itself means 'true icon'. The Pietà, so significant in the Renaissance art of the West, in which the Virgin nurses her dead son, has no Gospel basis. The removal of the body from the cross, briefly mentioned by the evangelists, was built up artistically into a major theme.

It has been necessary to reflect on this concentration on the passion, because it inevitably had consequences for the contemporary attitude to the empty tomb. True, there were some powerful presentations of the resurrection: most famously of all, perhaps, the image by Piero della Francesca at San Sepolcro, where a vital Christ strides in victory out of his sarcophagus. (The date is uncertain, but must be in the middle years of the fifteenth century.) A century before, there had been a similarly powerful representation of the resurrection in the Holkham Bible Picture Book. Once again, Christ steps triumphantly out of his sarcophagus. This book then continues with

---

[12] B. Corley, *Conrad von Soest: Painter among Merchant Princes* (London, 1996).

the older theme of the visit of three women, who once again are seen coming to a decorated sarcophagus.[13] The existence of such images establishes the continued reality of devotion to the resurrection, but cannot conceal the extent to which this had been sidelined. It rarely appears as the culmination of sequences illustrating the passion. A manuscript of a fourteenth-century encyclopedia, the *Omne Bonum*, gives an impression of what was happening. A central image of the crucifixion was surrounded by thirty-six small panels of the Arms of Christ. At the bottom was the risen Christ in the empty tomb, but the imagery has been infected with that of the passion. Christ stands in a sarcophagus, identified by its three 'portholes' in a Gothicized form, with the wounds on his hands clearly displayed, and with the sun and moon (once traditional accompaniments of crucifixion pictures) in the upper corners.[14] Contemporaries had lost contact with the historical form of the Sepulchre, which was presented neither as the cave of the Gospels nor the existing edicule at Jerusalem. The departure was the more striking because more exact reproductions of the tomb were now arriving in the West.

The later Middle Ages had also lost contact with the earlier chapters of all the Gospels, which presented Jesus as teacher, preacher, and healer. In art, he was the sufferer; in literature, the passion occupied the centre of meditation. This spirituality differed greatly from (say) the dominance of liturgy in the early Middle Ages and the social Christianity of our own day, and it has been fiercely criticized by some scholars. Ewart Cousins has remarked that 'from a psychological point of view, the late medieval devotion to the passion of Christ is one of the most problematic phenomena in the history of Christian spirituality. It is also problematic from a doctrinal and spiritual point of view, for attraction to the suffering and death of Christ became so intense in some cases that Christians lost sight of the other aspects of the Christian mysteries.' David Aers has taken the same view: 'What happened was that it became possible to transform "Christ's humanity" into his tortured, bleeding body, and set up that body as the dominant figure of Christ in late medieval devotion.' His suffering, he argues, became isolated 'from the historical events which made it a suffering through and for

[13] W. O. Hassall, *The Holkham Bible Picture Book* (London, 1954), fo. 34ᵛ.
[14] K. Kamerick, *Popular Piety and Art in the Late Middle Ages: Image Worship and Idolatry in England, 1350–1500* (New York, 2002), 185–6, fig. 6.9.

others'.[15] The sense that Jesus was much more than a dying body did appear in John Wyclif, the Lollards, the Hussites, and other dissenting groups, but not much in the mainstream of Catholic devotion. The historical Jesus, the rabbi who taught and the preacher who demanded a new way of living, belonged to the piety of reformers whom authority was concerned to marginalize.

While late medieval piety was individual and affective, it was also woven into the structure of society. The very fact that many of the images had so wide an appeal tended to shape the thinking of social groups. Michael Camille warned us that 'the tendency to see late medieval devotional attitudes as intensely personal, expressive and increasingly private has resulted in our overlooking important links between the sacred and social'.[16] While donors had always demanded commemoration, the desire to participate in the memory of the historical events now introduced them into the heart of the image. A triptych by Robert Campin or 'the Master of Flémalle', now belonging to the Courtauld Institute, painted shortly after 1410, appears to show the sponsor as he completes his pilgrimage to the cross of Jesus. He stands in front of the cross in one wing of the triptych, looking towards the deposition, which is the theme of the main central panel; and on the further wing we see Jesus stepping out of his sarcophagus.[17] For all the emphasis on interior piety, artworks and narratives could also echo contemporary social and political conditions. Nicholas Love's *Mirror of the Blessed Life of Jesus Christ* was a version, prepared about 1410, of the Latin *Meditations on the Life of Christ*. It was in great demand, perhaps the most widely read book in fifteenth-century England. It took account of prevailing English interests, omitting a good deal of Continental material while introducing sections that were directed against Lollardy. Meditations also served as a vehicle for the circulation of hostility towards the Jews: far more than in material before 1150, such texts as that of Ludolph of Saxony strongly emphasized the fact that the persecutors of Christ were

[15] E. Cousins, 'The Humanity and the Passion of Christ', J. Raitt (ed.), *Christian Spirituality* (London, 1987), 375–91; D. Aers, 'The Humanity of Christ: Reflections on Orthodox Late Medieval Representations', D. Aers and L. Staley (eds.), *The Powers of the Holy* (Pennsylvania, 1996), 15–42.

[16] M. Camille, 'The Image and the Self', S. Kay and M. Rubin (eds.), *Framing Medieval Bodies* (Manchester, 1994), 77.

[17] M. Botvinnick, 'The Painting as Pilgrimage: Traces of a Subtext in the Work of Campin and his Contemporaries', *Art History*, 15 (1992), 1–18. A. Chatelet has denied the pilgrim reference in *Robert Campin: le Maître de Flemall* (Antwerp, 1996), no. 3, pp. 284–5.

Jewish. At times, though, a more amiable lesson was drawn. Margery Kempe, not normally responsive to conditions outside herself, saw the passion of Christ as embracing all human suffering: 'Sometimes, when she saw the crucifix, or if she saw a man with a wound . . . or if a man beat a child before her, or smote a horse or other beast with a whip, if she saw it or heard it, she thought she saw our Lord being beaten or wounded.'[18]

The Jerusalem pilgrimage came to provide a model for meditation. The *Zardino de Oration*, written in 1454 as advice to young girls, recommended them 'to fix the places and people in your mind—a city, for example, which will be the city of Jerusalem, taking for this purpose a city that is well known to you . . . You must shape in your mind some people well known to you, to represent for you the people involved in the passion.'[19] The advent of printing made it possible to provide for the reading public in general the means of meditating without even leaving their homes: a striking movement towards the privatization of devotion. An important example was *The Way which Our Lord Jesus followed from Pilate's House to Mount Calvary*, published at Antwerp in Dutch in 1499. More influential was the work of 'the priest Bethlehem', *A Devout Meditation on the Passion*, whose author claimed to know the Holy Land well, and who structured the work round the path to Calvary, with twenty-six stations or stops. It was first published at Antwerp in 1518, and many editions followed up to 1561. The most important classic was to be *The Devout Way to follow the Spiritual Pilgrimage* of the Carmelite Jan Paschius, who is said to have made the pilgrimage in 1527. This development predated the sixteenth-century decline in the Jerusalem pilgrimage, in which (as we shall see later) it may have been a significant factor.[20]

Pilgrimage to Jerusalem came to serve for understanding the spiritual life as a whole. The idea went back to Bernard of Clairvaux and long before him, and its most elaborate statement was in the trilogy by the French Cistercian, Guillaume de Deguileville, written in the years after 1330 and partly translated into English by Lydgate.[21] In about 1430 Peter of Merode explored the same idea in his

[18] W. Butler-Bowdon (tr.), *The Book of Margery Kempe* (London, 1936), 108.

[19] Baxandall, *Painting and Experience*, 45–6.

[20] H. Thurstan, *The Stations of the Cross* (London, 1906), ch. 5; W. Schneider, *Peregrinatio Hierosolymitana* (Münster, 1982), 226–9; B. A. J. Wasser, 'Die Peregrinatie van Iherusalem: Pelgrimsverslagen van Nederlandse Jerusalemgangers in die 15e, 16e, en 17e eeuw', *De Gulden Passer*, 69 (1991), 5–72.

[21] There is a good account by E. Faral, *Histoire littéraire de la France* 39 (Paris, 1952), 1–132, and a more favourable assessment by J. M. Keenan (see Bibliography).

FIG 10.1 In this painting, probably by Robert Campin, the unknown donor wears a travelling cloak and has his dog with him; the tortuous route he has followed can be seen behind, at the extreme left of the picture. The crucifixion (after the removal of the body of Christ) is behind him; his attention is fixed on the entombment in the main panel, and to our right we see Christ stepping out of his coffin.

Pilgerfahrt des träumenden Monchs (*Pilgrimage of the Dreaming Monk*). Later, friar Fabri, writing for a convent of nuns, contrasted a *ritter pilgrim*, or riding pilgrim, with a *Syon pilgrim*, who was on a spiritual quest, to the advantage of the latter. English spirituality was specially inclined to the notion of spiritual pilgrimage. Walter Hilton used the image of a pilgrim who wished to set out to Jerusalem, which 'be tokenyth contemplacyoun in parfyte love of God'. The presence of the idea in Chaucer's *Parson's Tale* confirms that it was widespread:

> And Jhesu, for his grace, wit me sende,
> To shewe yow the way, in this viage,
> Of thilke parfit glorious pilgrimage
> That highte Jerusalem celestial.

The hugely influential *Imitation of Christ* invited readers to think of themselves as pilgrims, and around 1400 Giovanni della Celle, an Augustinian hermit, wrote that 'this life is a pilgrimage . . . They are blessed who do not establish themselves in this world, but walk through it as pilgrims.'[22] This tradition expressed a different attitude to the humanity of Christ, which contrasts with the intense devotion to his suffering and which came to dominate fifteenth-century devotion, and is akin to Wyclif's vision of the Lord as teacher and reformer of morals, but without his reform programme. It was characteristic of the devotion of the period to use the language of pilgrimage, both in the literal sense and as a symbol of the journey of the soul to God. Yet even this language was concentrated most directly on the passion. The empty tomb had become a secondary centre for late-medieval spirituality.

SACRED SOCIETIES

Those who wished to commemorate their journeys to the Holy Sepulchre in the eleventh and twelfth centuries thought in terms of founding a monastery with a cult based on relics from the East. In the later Middle Ages the flow of new foundations had been reduced, and the link with the Holy Sepulchre was sustained by the creation of confraternities. The military orders, whose origin had been so closely associated with the Holy Sepulchre, now largely disappear from our subject. Their primary purpose had been the defence of the Holy

---

[22] The Prologue to the Parson's Tale, lines 48–51; E. Delaruelle, 'Le Pèlerinage intérieur au XVe siècle', *La Piété populaire au Moyen Age* (Turin, 1975), 555–61.

Land, and in that they had failed. They had to find a new function. The Teutonic Knights first established a headquarters at Venice, but long before 1300 they were concerned primarily with the conquest of pagan Prussia, which by the fourteenth century they had turned into an independent principality or *Ordenstaat* under their own control. The Templars were the primary victims of the new situation. During the two decades after the fall of Acre, they failed to define any new function of their own. The reasons for their suppression need not concern us here, beyond quoting Malcolm Barber's conclusion that it was 'a medieval tragedy in which society . . . crushed the life from an order which it had once been proud to raise up'. Its lands throughout Europe were either appropriated by royal authorities or transferred to the Hospitallers. The Hospital, or Order of St John, was protected by its commitment to medical and charitable functions. Its military activity was now shaped into naval resistance to Turkish expansion, and based on the island of Rhodes. The Order preserved in its forms of worship the memory of its origin at the Holy Sepulchre, but while its contribution to the defence of Christendom, first at Rhodes and then at Malta, was going to continue for centuries, it no longer had a very specific connection with the Holy Sepulchre.

The most noble of the fraternities that did possess a strong connection with Jerusalem, and the least formally organized, was the knightly Order of the Holy Sepulchre, whose influence among aristocratic pilgrims we have already encountered. It never became an order with a master, a rule, a governing authority, or corporate properties, but was a loose fellowship of people who had received the personal distinction of knighting at the Sepulchre. The ceremony first appeared in William of Boldensele (1334), who noted that 'I made two noble knights over the Sepulchre, clothing them with swords and observing other things which were accustomed to be done in making profession of the knightly order.' William's words may mean that the practice of knighting at the Holy Sepulchre was an established one, but I suspect that he means that the customary ceremonies of dubbing were being followed in this new context. Great nobles are recorded as travelling 'to visit the Holy Sepulchre and be knighted there', and Felix Fabri noted how the desire for knighthood and devotion to the Sepulchre were interwoven: 'I have often heard it said by knights that if the holy places were not in Jerusalem they never would cross the sea—no, not if they could obtain a hundred knighthoods there. But it is the holy places which move them to journey thither, wherefore this knighthood is more holy than any others.'[23] In the sixteenth century the friars themselves acquired the right to create knights, and charged a fee for the ceremony. In spite of the unstructured character of this order, if order it can be called, the members after their return home were important as publicists for the Holy Sepulchre.[24] It was only in the later sixteenth century, with the breakdown of the traditional pilgrimage, that attempts were made to bind the knights into a crusading order, and these proved unsuccessful.

The canons of the Holy Sepulchre were a different proposition. They had lost the shrine for whose service they existed. After 1187 they had to move to Acre, and although they returned to Jerusalem from 1229 to 1244 it proved impossible to restore the original liturgy, and their financial position there was insecure. The canons, however, had already acquired extensive estates, and a system of daughter houses, in the West. When Acre was lost, the prior of the Holy Sepulchre, now calling himself grand prior, fixed his residence at Perugia in central Italy. While in theory the grand prior exercised supreme authority, in practice he had insufficient means to control the regional priors such as those of Barletta, Messina, Barcelona, and Warwick. The canons as a whole had not lost all vitality. Their expansion continued, sustained by contacts with Jerusalem. About 1348, for example, Andrew of Antioch, treasurer of the order, established the important priory of Annecy. The Netherlands continued to be the site of new foundations during the fifteenth century. In 1431 Pope Martin V, at the request of Peter and James Adorno, approved the foundation at Bruges of a house 'for certain brothers of the Lord's Sepulchre, to whom Peter and James are attached with a special bond of devotion'. The pope said that he 'wished with intense desire to encourage this cult in our own days'. The Adorno family had a strong pilgrimage tradition that led them to a link with the canons of the Sepulchre, although the project to found a house was not in the event completed. The main body of canons survived until 1489, when Innocent VIII's bull *Cum solerti* transferred their properties to the order of St John to sustain the war against the Turks. It was impossible to apply this decision generally, and some of the

[23] *Felix Fabri*, PPTS 7–8. 612.

[24] Ganz-Blättler, 232–5; C. Nolte, 'Erlebnis und Erinnerung: Fürstliche Pilgerfahrten nach Jerusalem im 15ten Jahrhundert', *Fremdheit und Reisen*, 65–92; M. Letts (tr.), *The Pilgrimage of Arnold von Harff, Knight, 1496–9*, Hakluyt Soc. (London, 1946), ii. 94 p. 202.

houses continued far into the modern period as a reduced Order of the Holy Sepulchre.

The culture of the canons continued to maintain the memory of the Holy Sepulchre, where they still recognized responsibilities. The provost of Denkendorf in 1465 rehearsed the obligation to divide their revenues into three parts: to maintain the brethren, assist the poor, and 'pay a tribute to the Sultan of Babylon [Egypt] as a subsidy to the Holy Land for maintaining the divine offices'. They also maintained a cult of the Holy Sepulchre. When a new canal was being dug at Annecy in 1895, the remains of a monumental entombment were discovered. In the seventeenth century it had been in the conventual church of the Holy Sepulchre there, and although it is fragmentary, it was clearly a powerful composition in the tradition of large French entombment sculptures. Their liturgy, too, was concerned to preserve the memory of the Sepulchre. There are mentions of a number of service books from the Latin East, and a few survive, notably the important compilation at Barletta.

There is also a breviary from the Holy Sepulchre, copied in the fourteenth century, now in the Musée Condé at Chantilly, and a manuscript of uncertain origin containing a liturgy celebrating the crusaders' capture of Jerusalem, apparently designed to appeal to pilgrims. Another record of the twelfth-century ceremonies had been up-dated about 1300 for use in eastern Germany.[25] The 'domestic' liturgy of the Holy Sepulchre community was carefully followed at the new mother house at Perugia and the priories of the Sepulchre in the West, and formed the basis for the orders of service of the Templars, Hospitallers, and Carmelites. The maintenance of the usages of the twelfth-century Holy Sepulchre by canons in the West was a contrast with what was happening at Jerusalem, where the Franciscans on Mount Sion followed the Roman liturgy with the addition only of a few feasts of specifically Jerusalem origin. Liturgically the Holy Sepulchre was commemorated in the West more faithfully than it was in Jerusalem itself.

The witness at the houses of the canons was supplemented by the emergence of confraternities in major cities. There were undoubtedly brotherhoods of the Holy Sepulchre before the fourteenth century. The one at Cambridge has left us the twelfth-century 'round church'

---

[25] A. Linder, 'The Liturgy of the Liberation of Jerusalem', *Medieval Studies* 52 (1990), 110–31; A. Schönfelder, Die Prozessionen der Lateiner in Jerusalem zur Zeit der Kreuzzüge', *Historisches Jahrbuch*, 32 (1911), 578–97.

The Barletta Compilation

The most important record of the twelfth-century liturgy of the Church of the Holy Sepulchre is to be found in a manuscript that belonged to the priory of Barletta, one of the earliest and most important of the houses of the canons. The whole (more than 260 folios) is written in one thirteenth-century hand. It consists of a short chronicle and records of the liturgy observed at Jerusalem. The editor tells us that it consists of 'material excerpted from several books, according to the ancient custom of the institutions of the church of the Sepulchre of the Lord'. The ceremonies as they are described here could not have taken place at Jerusalem after 1187. There is no clear evidence of the date or purpose of the volume. The chronicle goes up to 1202, which is thus the starting-point. The composition of this collection was a serious and time-consuming project, and indicates the need to preserve a record of the ceremonies or make them available when the original books were no longer at hand. It is probable that the manuscript was written at Acre and then obtained by the canons at Barletta. The ceremonies could certainly not have been observed in their original form in a city of southern Italy. It is even questionable whether the volume was intended to provide a template for an adapted version based on the Barletta priory of the Holy Sepulchre: certainly the feast of 15 July, to celebrate the fall of the city, would have been an odd occasion in the circumstances of the fourteenth century.

C. Kohler, 'Un rituel et un bréviaire du S-Sépulcre de Jérusalem (XIIe–XIIIe siècle)', *ROL* 8 (1900–1), 383–500.

there, but little is known of its organization. We know more of those which appeared in the later Middle Ages. In the 1320s, under the sponsorship of Count Louis of Clermont, later Duke of Bourbon, there emerged a 'church, hospital and *confrarie* of the Holy Sepulchre of Jerusalem founded at Paris in the *Grant Rue* of St Denis'.[26] Its foundation was connected with the circles at court involved with crusading plans in the 1330s, and was close in time to the

[26] Charter of 10 July 1343, printed by B. Dansette, 'Les Pèlerins occidentaux du Moyen Age tardif', *Dei gesta per Francos*, 311–14.

establishment of the friars on Mount Sion. As one would expect, it observed a pilgrim cult. By 1340 there was a 'holy chapel of the Sepulchre' in the church; by the fifteenth century the annual gathering was on the 'solemn feast of the Staff'; and the records mention the special importance of the Palm Sunday procession. There was another confraternity at Paris with a chapel in the Cordelier church, which was on a more modest scale but which later tradition ascribed to St Louis.

The confraternities in the cities of Flanders and Holland were still influential in the sixteenth century. The brotherhood at Utrecht was founded to preserve 'an eternal recollection and memory of the holy places', and its pilgrims were recorded in a series of paintings by Jan van Scorel showing processions of members of the Utrecht and Haarlem confraternities, carrying palms of Jericho. The processions were proceeding towards a trompe-l'œuil of the Sepulchre at Jerusalem, painted with precision, which probably represents a model or picture actually on the altar of the guild chapel. Each brother was provided with a scroll bearing his arms, and details of his pilgrimage. Van Scorel notes of his own, 'I am John van Scorel, a painter, and canon of Utrecht.' Arent Willemsz, a barber of Delft who travelled in 1525, wrote of the Holy Sepulchre that 'without doubt this place is all-holy, for our salvation was perfected there'. The brothers' ceremonial infected the imagery of van Scorel's painting of Christ's solemn entry into Jerusalem, in which the Lord is shown as carrying a palm. Jan de Heuter, who accompanied van Scorel on pilgrimage, wrote a *Description of Jerusalem* on his return, although the work does not survive. The confraternities continued to be active after the time when writers were beginning to lament the decay of the pilgrimage: in 1544 Antonis Mor was still commemorating with a picture the pilgrimage of two canons of Utrecht. Reverence for the Holy Sepulchre, and active pilgrimage there, were features of the cultures of northwestern Europe well into the sixteenth century.

Cities, like the confraternities which were prominent in their lives, saw themselves as expressions of Jerusalem. The connections were inescapable: not only was Jerusalem the ideal city, but all major Western cities were the scenes of commemorative processions. Palm Sunday processions could now be realized much better in Augsburg or Siena (or almost anywhere else) than in Jerusalem itself: their Calvaries and Holy Sepulchres were available locally, and far more accessible than were those in Palestine even to those who went there on pilgrimage. Florence developed a particularly firm conviction of

FIG 10.2 Jan van Scorel's group portrait of the Haarlem brotherhood about 1530, with (beneath) inscriptions about each pilgrim.

its role as a new Jerusalem, and equipped itself with legends, and ceremonies that centred round the *scoppio del carro* on Easter morning. The statutes of 1339 mentioned the twelve gates, which echoed those of Jerusalem in *Revelation*, although the city actually had fifteen. The procession of the Magi was appropriated for the Medici family and their court in the fresco painted by Benozzo Gozzoli in 1459–60 for the chapel of their palace, and Giovanni di Rucellai shortly afterwards provided the city with a chapel of the Holy Sepulchre of its own. At the end of the century, supporters of Savonarola drew on the tradition of Joachite prophecy to present Florence as the New Jerusalem: 'arise, O new Jerusalem, all nations will conform to the religion of Florence!' Shortly afterwards, Botticelli painted a crucifixion that incorporated the city into the mysteries of the final Judgement: at Christ's left hand Florence is bathed in the sunlight of glory.[27]

Rome and Jerusalem both had claims to be the centre of the world. Innocent III in 1199 had applied to the Roman pontiff the crucial text, 'working salvation in the midst of the earth', and James of Vitry had distinguished between Jerusalem as head and mother of the faith, and Rome as head and mother of the faithful. In 1300 Boniface VIII issued a plenary indulgence for those visiting the shrines of the apostles to celebrate the first holy year. It attracted huge numbers of pilgrims and wide attention in the literature of the time. Boniface did not intend to dismiss the needs of Jerusalem through this innovation, and it was said that he deliberately resolved that the indulgence should only be available every century, so as not to distract from the power of crusade indulgences. The long absence of the papacy from Rome during its residence in Avignon posed in a sharp form the rivalry of the two capitals of Latin Christendom. Clement VI, who conceded the proclamation of another holy year for 1350, formally discussed the claims of the two cities: 'In Jerusalem Christ did signs and wonders. There he washed the feet of his disciples; there he suffered; there he shed his blood for our redemption and for the salvation of humanity. Therefore it seems that the pope should be

---

[27] D. Weinstein, 'The Myth of Florence', N. Rubinstein (ed.), *Florentine Studies* (London, 1968), 15–44; D. Finn and K. Clark, *The Florence Baptistery Doors* (London, 1980); M. Rossi and A. Rovetta, 'Indagini sullo spazio ecclesiale immagine della Gerusalemme celeste', M. L. Catti Perer (ed.), *'La dimora di Dio con gli uomini': immagini della Gerusalemme celeste dal III al XIV secolo* (Milan, 1983), 77–118; and C. Frugoni, *A Distant City: Images of Urban Experience in the Medieval World* (Princeton, 1991), 27–8. See also the inset 'Florence and the Scoppio del Carro', in Ch. 7, above.

present at (*visitare*) those places above all, and not Rome.' Since Clement had no intention of going to either city, the word *visitare* has a rather ambiguous meaning. He continued with the ancient argument that the Jews had rejected Christ and disgraced Jerusalem: 'Therefore it was ordained, not by human decree but by divine inspiration that the apostles should come to Rome, and that the special see of St Peter should be there, and that there the word of Christ should be universally preached.'[28] The renewal of Rome as a pilgrim centre in the last two centuries of the Middle Ages made it a formidable competitor to Jerusalem, because the same indulgences were more conveniently available there. As the English text *The Stacions of Rome* declared, 'if a man did but know the pardon to be had in Rome, he would not go to the Holy Land, for in Rome is pardon without end'.[29]

Not only confraternities and cities, but also kingdoms were seen as embodiments of the sacred in the West. The ambition to recover the Holy Sepulchre and to commemorate its saving power at home was important in the development of France as a holy nation already in the thirteenth century. The failure to organize expeditions to the Holy Land largely pushed the Sepulchre out of the heart of national thinking. Even so, there were great powers such as the court of Burgundy under Philip the Good where the holy places remained in the centre of politics and ideology, and other rulers claimed to be fighting holy wars, using crusading finance and terminology. Old Testament precedents were appropriated. Although Henry IV and Henry V both announced an intention to visit the Holy Sepulchre, the English war against France had little to do with Jerusalem. English propagandists felt on surer ground when they claimed to share a special call of God with Israel. Israel and England were joined in the chancellor's speech to Parliament in 1377 as chosen nations, and in 1416–17 the *Gesta Henrici Quinti* claimed that God 'had so marvelously deigned to receive his England and her people as his very own'.[30] The idea of a Christian ruler as a new David had been a theme of Charlemagne's ideology, but it is harder to find in earlier centuries

[28] G. Dickson, 'The Crowd at the Feet of Pope Boniface VIII: Pilgrimage, Crusade and the first Roman Jubilee', *JMH* 25 (1999), 279–307; and D. Wood, *Clement VI: The Pontificate and Ideas of an Avignon Pope* (Cambridge, 1989), 86–95.

[29] D. J. Birch, 'Selling the Saints: Competition among Pilgrimage Centres in the Twelfth Century', *Medieval History*, 2 (1992), 29–34.

[30] J. W. McKenna, 'How God became an Englishman', D. J. Guth and J. W. McKenna (eds.), *Tudor Rule and Revolution* (Cambridge, 1982), 25–53; Tyerman, *England*, 334–41.

the notion that a Christian kingdom was chosen to be a new Israel. Other national aspirations were more closely connected with Jerusalem. The Spanish kingdoms inherited Joachite speculations about a new David who would restore the citadel of Sion, an idea that lay behind the hope that the Spanish monarchy of the Renaissance would add to its triumphs in Granada and America the recovery of Jerusalem.

'THE EXACT DESIGN AND MEASUREMENT OF THE HOLY SEPULCHRE'

From the thirteenth century onwards, there had been fewer attempts to represent the Sepulchre in Western Europe. There was now a renewal of interest. Two reasons help to explain the emergence of these new devotions. One was the wide growth of lay piety. The huge expansion of the friars provided a militia for the instruction of the laity, and most notably of the population of the cities. The Franciscans, who enjoyed a Latin monopoly on Mount Sion and in the Church of the Holy Sepulchre, were well placed for expanding Jerusalem devotion in the West. There were new technical possibilities, too. Popular church art was expanding rapidly, vernacular manuscripts were increasingly available and were bought by the literate classes in the cities, and from about 1460 the possibilities of disseminating religious books and woodcuts were extended by the emergence of printing.

Guidebooks to the Holy Land, and versions of the Holy Sepulchre, had always been designed for people who could not go, as well as those who could. With the increasing popularity of devotion to the cross, the discrepancy between the small group of privileged people who could travel to the places of the passion and the multitudes of devotees was even more marked, and the demand for substitute pilgrimages was accordingly large. Another major constituent in the movement towards substitution was the large number of indulgences, which came to be attached to Jerusalem shrines in the West. It is cannot be a coincidence that new themes were flourishing in the West precisely when the Jerusalem pilgrimage was in serious difficulties in the sixteenth century, although it is more difficult to be sure which was cause and which effect.

Sometimes it is clear that substitutes were being provided for holy places no longer accessible. The most startling example was the shrine of Loreto, where a statue of the Virgin had been the object of pilgrimage. In the fifteenth century, the story developed that in 1296 the house of Mary herself had miraculously been transported from Nazareth by the hand of angels. The first full account of this remarkable event was given in a brief guide by the custodian of the shrine, Teramano, in the later fifteenth century, although it was only in 1507 that a pope for the first time acknowledged the legend, qualifying it with the words 'as the report is, and is piously believed'. The dissemination of relics could ambiguously be an inducement to go to Jerusalem and a substitute for the journey. The highly popular cult of the blood of Christ was based both on specimens allegedly brought from the East and others shed from a consecrated chalice. At Bimbach in Germany such a devotion, recorded in 1329, generated a veneration for the Holy Sepulchre, with gifts of property and the provision in the choir of a sevenfold cycle of the passion and resurrection. On the other hand journeys to holy blood shrines could offer a substitute for Jerusalem, by fulfilling all that a pilgrim might expect from the Sepulchre itself. The reforming Bishop Latimer is hardly an unbiased witness to the cult of the blood of Hailes, the abbey in Gloucestershire, which he was intent on suppressing: but he was probably accurate in saying that pilgrims there 'believe verily that it is the very blood that was in Christ's body, shed upon the Mount of Calvary for our salvation, and that the sight of it with their bodily eye doth certify them and put them out of doubt that they be in clean life, and in state of salvation without spot of sin'[31] Bernard Hamilton has drawn attention to the choice of substitutionary language to honour arrivals of relics, for example, when Pope Pius II welcomed the head of St Andrew from Patras: 'O you who journey to Jerusalem out of reverence for the Saviour, to see the places his feet have trod, behold the abode of the Holy Spirit . . . Here, here the spirit of God alighted [at Pentecost] . . . This mouth often spoke to Christ.' Perhaps, in truth, there is not much distinction between a substitute and a memorial. The dimensions of the Sistine Chapel were dictated by those of the Temple in the Old Testament during its building by Sixtus IV (1471–84). It has been suggested, indeed, that the ambitious rebuilding of the sacred places of Jerusalem by the Sultan Suleiman in the middle of the sixteenth century was in part a conscious response to the renewed attempts of

---

[31] J. Leinweber, 'Das Heilige Grab in der spätmittelalterliche Pfarrkirche zu Bimbach', *Archiv für mittelrheinische Kirchengeschichte*, 40 (1988), 67–71; G. W. Bernard, 'Vitality and Vulnerability in the Late Medieval Church', J. L. Watts (ed.), *The End of the Middle Ages* (Bridgend, 1998), 226.

the West to claim for itself the religious inheritance of the Holy City.[32]

The survival of Jerusalem models is poor, even in the later Middle Ages. Tremendous damage was worked by the Reformation and the Enlightenment, as well as baroque redecoration and the 'restorations' of the neo-Gothic nineteenth century. In England, almost all the 'Easter Sepulchres' have vanished, or have left only faint traces, and more ambitious projects were erased. The walls of the chapel of the Holy Sepulchre in Winchester cathedral were whitewashed, with in this case the paradoxical result that it has been possible to recover the paintings from the twelfth and thirteenth centuries. The decorations introduced by Mr William Wey at Edington are known only from the survival of his will, and a life-sized figure of the dead Christ, discovered in the fabric of the Mercers' Hall at London, looks as if it were originally part of a monumental entombment. If so, it is the only remains of such a monument in England.[33]

Nevertheless, the survivors are sufficient to allow us to note one of the new features of the representations: the demand for accuracy. For almost the first time one can on occasions use the word 'copy' without having to make qualifications. From about 1420 onwards, Western painting had acquired the capacity to provide an exact representation of its subject, a quality that is evident in the magnificent portraits characteristic of the Flemish school and of the Italian Renaissance. We need not concern ourselves here with the large question how and why that development took place, but, given that it had done so, it was natural for contemporaries to want to know what Jerusalem and the Holy Sepulchre 'really looked like', although it did not mean that all representations had to be literal ones.

Until about 1400, representations of Jerusalem almost all showed, as François Robin has said, 'a total denial of the problem'. In the tradition of illustrations provided to the French translation of William of Tyre's *History of Outremer*, Jerusalem appeared simply as a city, and in the favourite subject of Godfrey's prayer at the Holy Sepulchre, it was simply an altar-tomb, which contained 'no idea of the holy place'. The Limburg brothers, in the *Très Riches Heures*, showed

[32] B. Hamilton, 'The Ottomans, the Humanists, and the Holy House of Loreto', *Renaissance and Modern Studies*, 31 (1987), 12–13; E. Battisti, 'Il significato simbolico della Cappella Sistina', *Commentari*, 8 (1957), 96–104; M. Bernardini, 'Popular and Symbolic Iconographies', *Ottoman Jerusalem*, 95–102.
[33] J. Evans and N. Cook, 'A Statue of Christ from the Ruins of Mercers' Hall', *Archaeological Journal*, 111 (1954), 166–80.

Jerusalem in the Palm Sunday procession as a romanticized version of a French city, but with one building that is clearly the Anastasis rotunda. The drawing in which Jerome was shown at the Holy Sepulchre did make some attempt at portraying the church. These miniatures may have been completed by about 1415, but the date is uncertain. When we come to the *Egerton Hours* written in the 1430s, we find a more serious attempt at a genuine depiction. The church of the Holy Sepulchre and the Temple (that is, the Dome of the Rock) were represented, although with exotic details such as bulbous domes; and drawings of this type may be found in the subsequent generation, sometimes apparently a copy of the Egerton miniature.[34] An almost completely accurate version became widely available with the publication in 1486 of Reuwich's woodcuts in Breydenbach's book, which was mentioned in the previous chapter. Jan van Scorel's exact painting of the Holy Sepulchre in a guild portrait was presumably based on sketches made on his pilgrimage, as was his view from the Mount of Olives painted in 1526–7.[35]

Three shrines that are virtually intact give us a good insight into what was happening. They have in common a direct link with Jerusalem: either they were founded by pilgrims, or they were based on observations of craftsmen who had travelled to the holy places. Their design belongs to the third quarter of the fifteenth century. In other respects, they are different, memorials of diverse kinds, found in three areas of Europe. As it happens, the patrons all came from the patriciate or nobility of cities, but even so were a good deal different from each other: the aristocracy of Florence was used to commanding artists of a quality that could certainly not be matched by those of Görlitz.

Giovanni Rucellai's monument at Florence was a copy of the Holy Sepulchre, designed for a setting that already existed, based on information gathered in Jerusalem, but in fact created in a Renaissance style. It was essentially a memorial conceived by a great family.

The second example is a contrast. It did not originally contain an image of the Holy Sepulchre at all, but is a building designed by and

---

[34] F. Robin, 'Jérusalem dans la peinture franco-flamande (XIII–XVème siècle): abstractions, fantaisies et réalités', *Jérusalem, Rome*, 33–63; E. Pognon, *Les Très Riches Heures du Duc de Berry* (Chantilly, n.d.), 119; BL MS Egerton 1070 fo. 5.

[35] R. Pacciani, 'La "Gerusalemme" di San Vivaldo', in L. Vaccaro and F. Riccardi (eds.), *Sacri Monti* (Milan, 1992), 196–7; G. Gentile, 'Evocazione topografica', in Vaccaro and Riccardi (eds.), *Sacri Monti*, 91; Biddle, *Tomb of Christ*, figs. 32–9.

FIG 10.3 This copy with Renaissance decoration is attributed to Alberti, and is in the chapel of San Pancrazio in the Rucellai Palace at Florence.

The Sepulchre at San Pancrazio, Florence

This is perhaps the most handsome architectural representation of the Holy Sepulchre. Giovanni Rucellai, one of the richest men in Medici Florence, was the sponsor. He reported in a letter that 'I am glad to say that yesterday I finished organising the expedition to the Holy Land, where I have sent at my own expense two woodcarvers with an engineer and other workmen, so that they can obtain for me the exact design and measurement of the Holy Sepulchre of Our Lord Jesus Christ.' He decided that it should be located in a chapel in his local church of San Pancrazio. It was originally designed to be visible from the main body of the church, but the setting has been entirely transformed since 1808. According to Vasari, Giovanni committed the design to Leon Battista Alberti, whom he had employed for other projects. Alberti had never himself been to Jerusalem. In spite of the special expedition Rucellai sent to see the original, this is no exact copy, but a humanist, classicizing version. True, many of the special features were preserved, including the low doorway and the cupola; but its irregularities were adjusted into a simplified format, and although the proportions were reproduced, the exact measures were not. The 'finish' is thoroughly Renaissance in character, with rosettes and inscriptions of a classical taste, standardized by the new and improved technique of stencilling. The wording included the biblical, 'He is not here: behold the place where they laid him' (Mark 16: 6), and also an attribution which gives us the date of completion: 'Giovanni Rucellai ... had this shrine (*sacellum*) made in the likeness of the Jerusalem Sepulchre 1467.' A pilgrimage was established to the chapel for the moneylenders' guild and members of the Rucellai family, and in 1471 Pope Paul II granted an indulgence of seven years to those who visited it on Good Friday or Easter. A miniature wooden version of the shrine survives. It was certainly not the example brought back from Jerusalem, but is carefully finished with the details of Alberti's shrine. It is likely that it functioned as a reliquary, conceivably in the chapel of the Holy Sepulchre which we know stood on the Ponte Vecchio.

F. Borsi, *Leon Battista Alberti* (Oxford, 1975); G. Petrini, 'La capella del

Santo Sepolcro nella ex chiesa di S. Pancrazio in Firenze', F. Cardini (ed.), *Toscana e Terrasanta* (Florence, 1982), 339–43; H. A. Milton and V. M. Lampugnanti, *The Renaissance from Brunelleschi to Michelangelo: the Representation of Architecture* (London, 1994), no. 44; R. Taverner, 'Giovanni Rucellai e il suo complesso architettorio a Firenze', J. Rykwert and A. Engel (eds.), *Leon Battista Alberti* (Milan, 1994), 368–77; A. Grafton, *Leon Battista Alberti* (London, 2000).

for pilgrims, and full of Jerusalem references. It, too, came from the urban and international aristocracy, the Adorno family, but was conceived in a more communitarian spirit: it was combined with a hospital and almshouse, and (later at least) was the base for the city's confraternity of the Holy Sepulchre.

Our third example introduces us to a copy of the Holy Sepulchre chapel far more exact than that of Alberti. The inclination and capacity to produce 'true copies' had developed together. A second new feature which we find here was the incorporation of the Holy Sepulchre into a layout designed for popular pilgrimage, allowing worshippers to travel from the chapel of the holy cross to that of the anointing and finally to the Holy Sepulchre.

One could list many echoes of the Holy Sepulchre, less splendid than these: for example, in 1485 Pierre Odin, on his return from Jerusalem, constructed a model of Christ's Sepulchre near the cloister at Le Puy, as part of an ensemble recalling in fresco and sculpture the scenes of the passion.[36] A painting of the crucifixion designed for the high altar of the Schottenkirche at Vienna about 1470 included the scene of the deposition in the background. Its version of the Sepulchre was close to the original at Jerusalem, and even included a cut-away hill behind it to commemorate the way in which it was created in the fourth century.[37] Apart from these ambitious imitations of the Jerusalem Sepulchre, many medieval churches possessed sculptural versions designed for the Easter liturgy, which required the deposition of a crucifix, the eucharistic elements or, increasingly, a full-sized figure of the dead Christ. The physical presence of a figure of Christ became increasingly popular in the later Middle Ages, and

---

[36] A. Derbes, 'A Crusading Fresco Cycle at the Cathedral of Le Puy', *Art Bulletin*, 73/4 (1991), 561–76.

[37] J. Krüger, *Die Grabeskirche zu Jerusalem* (Regensburg, 2000), 36; E. Baum, *Katalog des Museums mittelalterlichen österreichischer Kunst* (Vienna, 1971), 96–8.

Ecclefia.
Hierofolymæ
BRUGENSIS.

Prætorium Familiæ Adorniorum.

FIG 10.4 The Jerusalem church at Bruges, completed by Anselm and John Adorno, who visited Jerusalem in 1470–1. The tower is a commemoration (not at all accurate) of the dome of the Anastasis at Jerusalem.

The Jerusalem Church at Bruges

That this church survives almost exactly in its fifteenth-century form is confirmed by views from 1562 and 1641. Pope Martin V in 1427 authorized at the request of Peter and James Adorno a chapel whose dedication is given as the passion of Christ and the Holy Sepulchre. This seems to have been the starting-point for the building of an impressive private church. Only four years later, Martin V gave permission for it to become the centre of a community of canons of the Holy Sepulchre, but the project was never implemented. In 1470, the will that Anselm Adorno made on his departure on pilgrimage appointed the 'chapel' as his burial-place, and after his death in 1483 his body was brought back from Scotland and buried in a joint tomb with his wife, which occupies a large space in the main body of the chapel. It is reasonable to suppose that the church was complete by that time. The design of the whole building is odd, with a choir on the north side, standing over a crypt and surmounted by a great tower. In spite of this, the intention to commemorate Jerusalem is not in doubt. The eight-sided tower must be a reference to the Anastasis, although it is in a sense inside out, since it is not surmounted by a dome and the octagon is outside the main church building, rather than inside as at Jerusalem. Pilgrimage references decorate the church. There is a large design showing a Calvary, which contains the signs of the passion, the crown of thorns, the skulls of Golgotha, the ladder, and tunic. Elsewhere, a Catherine wheel celebrates a pilgrimage to Sinai. The crypt forms a sort of ambulatory behind the main church, and now contains a relic of the wood of the cross. The original design did not include a version of the Holy Sepulchre itself, but about 1523 a copy, showing Christ in his sarcophagus, was added in a chapel off the ambulatory—a poor work artistically, and one that was designed for private devotion. By this time there was a fraternity of Jerusalem pilgrims based at the church. For the Adorno family as pilgrims, see Ch. 9 above.

FIG 10.5 This copper engraving of 1719 shows the fully developed site at Görlitz populated by the passion procession of Christ. In the centre distance is an accurate copy of the Holy Sepulchre (but here in the open air). The two-storey building to its right, with a spire, is a thematic version of Calvary.

Holy Cross, Görlitz

In the sixteenth century, this was the accepted name for the layout of three chapels built outside the city, the chapels of holy cross, the anointing, and the Holy Sepulchre. In the fourteenth century there was a cross on the site, which apparently marked a burial-place for unbaptized children. It is difficult to establish the progress of the buildings, but the decisive moment was the pilgrimage of the patrician Georg Emerich to the Holy Land in 1465, during which he was made a knight of the Holy Sepulchre. Emerich became the principal mover in the project, and it is probable that he himself funded the Holy Sepulchre chapel, while the larger holy cross chapel was directed by the city council. There are records of a number of donations during the 1480s, and we have mentions of pilgrims from Görlitz to Jerusalem in these years. In 1487 a 'parlourer of the holy cross' was mentioned as a witness, but the first certain date for the completion of the chapels is 1504. The Holy Sepulchre chapel is designed as a true model of the edicule at Jerusalem. Emerich had taken a 'craftsman' with him, who had perhaps made accurate sketches, and by the 1480s representations of this sort were undoubtedly available in Germany. There were certainly some differences: apart from anything else, the Görlitz model had to be weatherproof, since it was unprotected by a version of the Anastasis dome. But it is clearly as exact a copy as could be achieved. The holy cross chapel is not only larger, but wholly different in concept: it stands for Calvary, but is certainly not a copy. It is built on two storeys, and contains references to the events of the passion. The Adam chapel on the ground floor displays the rent which appeared in the veil of the Temple at the time of the death of Jesus. The upper storey contains the crucifixion, and below it a channel by which the blood of Christ could flow onto the tomb of Adam. There has been a good deal of discussion of the origins of this two-level design. It does seem, however, that the primary inspiration was a reproduction, in idealized form, of the two-level reality of Calvary as pilgrims to Jerusalem would see it. Subsequently the site was extended so as to provide for a complete processional way, which is illustrated in a copper engraving of 1719.

G. Dalman, 'Das Heilige Grab in Görlitz und sein Verhältnis zum Original in Jerusalem', *Neuer Lausitzisches Magazin*, 91 (1915), 198–244; E.-H. Lemper, 'Die Kapelle zum Heiligen Kreuz beim Heiligen Grab in Görlitz', *Fs. Wolf Schubert: Kunst des Mittelalters in Sachsen* (Weimar, 1967), 142–57; Möbius, *Passion*, 81–2, figs. 119–24. Gustaf Dalman proudly claimed that Emerich was one of his ancestors.

could take dramatic forms. In November 1547 Bishop Barlow of St David's 'shewed a picture of the resurrection of our Lord made with vices, which put out his legges of sepulchree and blessed with his hand, and turned his heade'. One need not suppose that the congregation thought its gestures were miraculous. It was not essential to have a stone monument, for an altar could be used, or a purpose-built wooden structure. The provision of a stone Sepulchre, however, was in increasing demand. Such monuments were often financed or maintained by a guild in the village. In 1389 the brothers and sisters of the guild of the resurrection at Chesterton (Cambridge) paid for a new Sepulchre, and in Northamptonshire we hear of such groups as the guild of the Lord's Sepulchre, the brotherhood of the Sepulchre, and the brotherhood of the resurrection. Such structures could be small and simple, but many contained statues relating to the resurrection, such as the guards, the women, and the angels; they were certainly not copies of the Jerusalem Sepulchre. Famous English examples are those in Lincoln cathedral, Hackington (Lincs.), and Patrington (Yorks), carved primarily between 1290 and 1350. Such monuments were usually to be found on the north wall of the chancel. They might take the form of an arched recess large enough to accommodate a life-sized effigy. An instruction for an elaborate structure at Yalding, Kent, in 1522 required 'a blynd arche to be made rising overe the same sepulture and the woodwork . . . to be made according to good wurmanship and afterward to be gilded with the resurrexion of our Lorde'.[38] As this implies, they were still being built right up to the Reformation. At Tarrant Hinton in Dorset there is the remnant of one in an Italian Renaissance style, marked with the initials of Thomas Weaver, who was rector from 1514 to 1536. This is another of the precarious survivals, since its remains were preserved at the replacement of the older chancel in 1874.[39]

[38] P. Sheingorm, *The Easter Sepulchre in England* (Kalamazoo, 1987), 36–7.
[39] J. Newman and N. Pevsner, *The Buildings of England: Dorset* (Harmondsworth, 1972), 417, fig. 43.

Not infrequently, the tomb of the local lord doubled as the Easter Sepulchre. This combination is probably a continuation of the ancient desire to be buried in a sanctified place, but we know that in the 1360s the bishop of Strasburg was dismayed to realize that the tomb he had prepared for himself was more splendid than the one that had been provided for the Lord: 'it should not be, that my grave is finer than God's.' Very few of these Easter Sepulchres remain intact in England, but in a medieval church one can often see the vestiges of the structure.

During the fifteenth century, the entombment of Christ emerged as a theme for popular devotion. The Gospels had given only a brief account of this event, and provided no evidence of the presence of the followers of Jesus, other than Joseph of Arimathea and Nicodemus. The apocryphal Gospel of Nicodemus, completed probably in the fifth century, elaborated this account, and entombments can be found from the tenth century in Byzantine manuscripts as part of resurrection sequences. An early example of its emergence as a sculptural representation in the West can be found at Strasburg about 1280, when it figured over the west door. In the fifteenth century, very large sculptural groups of the entombment, including Joseph, Nicodemus, Mary, John, the three women, and the guards (in defiance of historical probability) were created, especially in French churches. As early as 1395 Philip the Bold had a tapestry made of the entombment which was more than eighty metres long. Early examples of sculptural groups were at Langres, Freiburg in Switzerland (where the surviving group is dated—perhaps unreliably— 1423), and Mainvault in Belgium. They could not have been designed for the Easter liturgy, and in most cases were probably intended to stand behind an altar. Some at least were consciously designed to be the goal of pilgrimage. In 1443 Pope Felix V granted an indulgence to those visiting the monument at Bourg-en-Bresse, and said that it could replace the pilgrimage to Jerusalem. The link between this devotion and the Holy Sepulchre proper had become loose, although the Langres figures did incorporate stones from the Jerusalem Sepulchre as relics. The striking feature of this type of composition was that it treated the Sepulchre, not as a place of resurrection, but as the site of a burial. We noticed earlier that in pilgrimage accounts the Sepulchre could be reverenced as a place of weeping. It is interesting to observe, too, that depictions both of the entombment and the resurrection normally showed burial in a sarcophagus or coffin. One of the reasons for this was undoubtedly the contemporary drive

FIG 10.6 The entombment of Christ at Mainvault (Belgium), probably about 1400, is a good example of these late-medieval compositions, with their attendant figures. The body of Christ is shown with the Virgin Mary, Joseph of Arimathea, an angel, Mary Magdalen, St John, another of the holy women, Nicodemus, and two donors.

towards the Christianization of death: to see Christ entering and redeeming the coffin was a reassurance, at least to the rich who were able to afford this form of burial. It may be that this coffin-format was shaped also by the city plays, in which the emergence of Christ from a sarcophagus was an important feature. However this may be, we can find two different traditions existing side by side: the Jerusalem Sepulchre as it existed, and coffin/tombs that bore no similarity to it. The one thing we do not find is authentic history: attempts to portray the Sepulchre as it was described in the Gospels were very rare indeed.

STATIONS OF THE CROSS AND HOLY MOUNTAINS

A more striking change towards the end of the Middle Ages was the emergence of layouts designed for the faithful to walk through the Jerusalem mysteries, stopping for prayer before each picture or statue. Palm Sunday processions had been moving through the cities for centuries, but there is a difference: earlier processions, while being intended to attract the laity, were part of the liturgical offering of communities. These liturgical commemorations continued, especially in such orders as that of the canons of the Holy Sepulchre. To them were now added popular theme parks, within which the faithful could follow the history of Christ's death and resurrection. They appeared in the late fifteenth century. Normally guided tours were conducted by the resident clergy, very often friars, but the reflections upon the sacred mysteries would have been different from the liturgical character of the earlier processions.

From the time of Ricoldo (1288 onwards) Jerusalem pilgrims had spoken of 'the way by which Christ went up, carrying his cross'. There was still, however, nothing like the *via dolorosa* that the modern pilgrim finds there. Events were not followed in chronological sequence, and the standard programme started at the church of the Holy Sepulchre, calling at historical sites in an order of convenience. Additional locations were in the process of being identified: Marino Sanuto (1320) was the first to use the title *la Giudiziaria* for the Judgement Gate by which the Lord left the city on the way to Golgotha. The holy places known to fifteenth-century pilgrims differed from those which eventually were incorporated into the stations of the cross. This devotion was the result of a cross-current of influences from Jerusalem pilgrimage, biblical narrative, and the demands of Western piety. Much of the raw material necessarily came from the narratives of Jerusalem pilgrims, but the final selection was not made there. Herbert Thurston, in his still classic study, pointed out that, remarkably, 'the selection of the stations owes much more to the pious ingenuity of devotional writers in Europe than to the actual practice of Jerusalem itself'. The readiness of the friars to adopt Western schemes which contradicted their knowledge of the topography at Jerusalem is one of the curious features of the development.

In reference to Jerusalem itself, Mr William Wey (1458) had for the first time applied the word 'stations' to the progress of the pilgrims. By 1530 the Franciscan Antonio de Arada was using *estaciones* as a standard term, especially, but not only, for the holy places associated with the passion. Since he resided for a time with the friars on Mount Sion, it is likely that he is reflecting the style that they had by then accepted. In the West, representations of the Holy Sepulchre were beginning to be accompanied by shrines representing a sequence of mysteries. There are two early examples in the Iberian peninsula. Shortly after 1400, the Dominican Alvaro, having returned from the Holy Land, arranged his friary as a series of the mysteries of redemption. At Lorvao, near Coimbra, we hear of a holy lay sister who had vowed to go to the Holy Land. She made the pilgrimage by moving from altar to altar, recalling the mysteries, and was actually seen in a vision at Jerusalem. At Villingen bei Donäuschingen, a house of Clarisses, the abbess in the 1480s marked out the stations of the cross within the cloister walls, and secured an indulgence for the devotion from Pope Innocent VIII.[40]

In the years after 1465, Georg Emerich was designing Holy Cross, Görlitz, with a sequence of memorials of the passion and a precise copy of the shrine of the Holy Sepulchre. At Nuremberg, not far away, a series of stations was built by Adam Krafft for Martin Ketzel after his return from pilgrimage. There were eight stopping-places, each represented by a pillar that specified the distance from Pilate's house. A chronicler refers to the scheme, which seems to have been completed between 1472 and 1490, as the 'seven falls'. Louvain seems to have been laid out with pilgrimage stations after the return of Peter Sterckx from Jerusalem in 1505. At Seville the Casa de Pilatos, which was begun in 1481, originally incorporated reminiscences of the passion. On the return of Don Fadrique of Tarifa from Jerusalem in 1519 he reconstructed the building, creating a main

---

[40] Ganz-Blättler, 258–9.

gateway in Roman style—reminiscent, one supposes, of Pilate's
pretorium—with Jerusalem crosses, and outside it a series of stations
of the cross, which is still followed by the Good Friday procession.
Installations of this sort brought the Jerusalem events into the streets
of European cities in a new way. The purpose was to promote the
affective participation in the suffering of the Lord that was central to
late-medieval devotion. The strength of the system was its adapt-
ability: it provided a pattern that could be applied in a great variety of
places. One could follow the *via dolorosa* through the streets of a city,
up a hillside stage-managed as Mount Calvary, or around the walls
of a church. Once fully developed during the sixteenth century,
it became an almost universal Holy Week devotion for Catholics, a
template widely disseminated, whatever its difference from the
historical reality.

The theme park approach could show great variety. It produced,
principally in Italy, a number of elaborate layouts for pilgrims, which
have become known in the modern period as holy or sacred mountains, *sacri monti*. The two earliest installations were representations
of Jerusalem. It has been said that the design was that pilgrims
should 'follow, not the narrative of the Gospel story, but the
topographical layout'.[41]

The first ambitious design was that of Bernardino Caimi at Varallo
Sesia in Lombardy, begun in the 1480s. He was a friar who had twice
been warden of the house on Mount Sion. Not only did he know
Jerusalem very well, but he was possessed by a desire to bring a
precise grasp of its appearance to the faithful to assist them in visualizing the events. In his *Lent Book on the Articles of Faith* (*Quadragesi-
male de Articulis Fidei*) he connected the stories with their sites so as to
create a sort of theatre of the imagination: 'almost in the middle of
the court is now a rosemary bush, where the fire is said to have been;
and here Peter denied Christ.' His whole approach was shaped by
Ludovico Barbo's advice, 'imagine that you are present and pretend
to see'. This was the essence of Varallo. The aim was not to achieve
exact reproductions of the holy places, but to make the pilgrim present at the event, 'to isolate the original nucleus of the architectural
structure . . . extracting from it a sort of plaster-cast relic'.[42]

San Vivaldo, in Tuscany, had long been a hermit site. In 1499
or 1500 the Franciscans took it over, and soon (as the chronicler

[41] Neri, 134–6.
[42] On this paragraph, see Gentile, 'Evocazione topografica', 89–110.

Mariano da Firenze reports) they 'built most devout chapels and ora-tories like the places of the Holy City of Jerusalem, where are all the mysteries of the passion of the Lord'. The inspiration came from friar Thomas of Florence. He had a good knowledge of Jerusalem, and had been warden of the friars in Candia (Crete), but we do not actually know that he had travelled to the Holy Land. He must have known Francesco Suriano, who was warden of Mount Sion in 1493 and 1512, and was also resident in Tuscany. There are marked similarities between Varallo and San Vivaldo, but it is doubtful whether he had met Bernardino Caimi, and there is no record of a visit to Varallo.

The programme that shaped San Vivaldo was set out in a letter of Pope Leo X in 1516, where he spoke of the building of 'several small churches or chapels on the model of the places of Christ's humanity in the Holy Land, by brother Thomas of Florence, warden of the place and planner (*inventorem*)'. The pope mentioned how 'crowds of the faithful almost continuously visit, attracted out of devotion', and made it clear that the construction was still in progress. The pilgrim-age character was emphasized by the grant of abundant indulgences, seven years for each chapel commemorating a stage in the life of Christ, and one for other shrines. The similarity to the topography of Jerusalem was more evident than at Varallo: the physical geography of the site was not unlike that of the Holy City, with a natural gorge like the valley between the old city and the Mount of Olives. Only two of the holy places provided were outside Jerusalem: the church of the Nativity at Bethlehem and the Mount of Temptation. The version of the Holy Sepulchre was close to that in contemporary Jerusalem, although of different dimensions, and the chapels of Mount Sion and of Calvary echo the originals. The architectural style shows a ten-dency to Renaissance classicism, and, presumably from the very beginning, the holy places were designed to contain wall paintings and plaster figures that made the beholder present at an actual encounter with Christ. San Vivaldo was a model of Franciscan piety, of prayer founded on the imaginative representation of the events of the Passion, and of Jerusalem devotion. Here the faithful could see the sights, and earn the indulgences, that were so difficult of access in the East.

II

The End of the Pilgrimage,
1530–1630

In 1533, a noble from Maine in northern France, called Greffin Affagart, set sail from Venice for the Holy Land. He was painfully aware that the Jerusalem pilgrimage, which had endured in basically the same form for two centuries, was facing the prospect of collapse. It was to advocate its continuation that he wrote his account. He had been on the journey once already, and now was planning a long stay. Affagart was a man of conservative spirit, who was proud of being a knight of the Holy Sepulchre, and travelled with a Franciscan, Bonadventure Brochart. He lived with the friars on Mount Sion, and went on the established pilgrimage tours, while valuing the scholarship of his companion Bonadventure: 'without him I would not have properly understood all the mysteries as they had been fulfilled in the places to which we were taken'. For all that, he was conscious of being a participant in a declining institution: 'There used to be a great many people of high status, such as bishops, abbots, dukes, counts, barons and other people of substance, who paid for the ship, and thus poor people travelled more cheaply and easily.' Because there were now so few pilgrims, the regular service from Venice had collapsed: *le voyage a esté rompu*. People now went as best they might to Crete or Cyprus and landed at Beirut, but these arrangements were precarious, and if lords and princes do not return to their former devotion, he concluded, the pilgrimage was in danger of extinction: *le voyage est en péril d'estre perdu.*[1]

The decline was partly explained by the growing difficulties of the journey. Even in 1480, Felix Fabri had found it hard to complete his first voyage. In 1523, Ignatius of Loyola travelled by the traditional

---

[1] *Affagart*, esp. 1, 4, 62–4, 72–3, 20–1.

route, Venice to Cyprus to Jaffa, but many of his companions were deterred by the recent loss of Rhodes to the Turks. At Jerusalem, the Ottomans after their conquest in 1516 were showing themselves more oppressive to the friars on Mount Sion, whose provincial was horrified at Loyola's plan to stay to preach the Gospel in the Holy Land because of the damage it would do to his relations with the authorities. There was still a significant Christian presence among the population of Jerusalem. The first reliable figures that we possess, from 1525/6, show that there were 934 households, 616 being Muslim, 199 Jewish, and 119 Christian.[2] This latter element of over 10 per cent was much less supportive of the great pilgrimage than one might suppose. They were virtually all Eastern Christians, who were probably not sympathetic to the Latins, and whose access to the church of the Holy Sepulchre was subject to completely different rules. But the difficulty, in Affagart's eyes, did not arise from the problems of the journey or the situation at Jerusalem. On the contrary, he argued that the voyage was not as dangerous and expensive as people thought. The trouble was, he said, that 'since that wicked rascal Luther has been in power with his accomplices, and also Erasmus in his *Colloquies* and *Enchiridion* has attacked these journeys, many Christians have withdrawn and grown cold, especially the Flemings and Germans who used to be more devout in travelling than all the others'.[3]

He was right to be worried about the weight of criticism now being directed against pilgrimage. Erasmus had written to the doctors of the Sorbonne in 1526 that 'in the past men of proved religion held that it was no great matter to be at Jerusalem; and I do not think that Christianity would be any the worse if nobody went to Jerusalem, but they sought the footsteps of Christ in books, and devoted their efforts and expense to the relief of the poor'. For Luther, pilgrimage was associated with the scandals of indulgences and superstitious reverence for relics, and in his pamphlet on *The Misuse of the Mass* (1522) he produced a startling meditation on the grave of Christ:

When I was a child, I often heard in these lands a prophecy that the Emperor Frederick would deliver the Holy Sepulchre ... It seems to me that this prophecy has been fulfilled in this prince of ours, Frederick of Saxony. For

---

[2] K. R. Schaefer, 'Jerusalem in the Ayyubid and Mamluk Eras', D.Phil., New York, 1985, 227.
[3] *Affagart*, 20–1.

how else can we understand the Holy Sepulchre than as the Holy Scripture, in which the truth of Christ has been killed and buried and laid and so on by the papists? As for the tomb in which the Lord lay, which the Saracens now possess, God values it like all the cows in Switzerland.[4]

Affagart (or his adviser Brother Bonadventure) was aware of these attacks, and offered a thoughtful defence of the pilgrimage in terms that evoked the early centuries of the church:

Although going to Jerusalem is not a matter of absolute necessity, it is still very useful to Christianity . . . It is a sure confirmation and certification of faith to see the places where our holy Gospel law was founded and first established; there are little arrows of love; there is a spiritual consolation for those who go there at present, for they associate what they read in Holy Scripture with what they see with their eyes: because what we see moves us more than what we hear.[5]

This was the beginning, as Christine Gomez-Géraud has said, of 'a century which often put pilgrimage at the heart of its religious debates'.[6] Criticism by Protestants or humanists can be found in many parts of the Continent. Calvin, following Erasmus, observed with contempt that if all the fragments of the wood of the cross were joined together, one could build a large sailing-ship of them. In England, Hugh Latimer, bishop of Worcester, in a sermon of 1552, spoke dismissively of 'the popish pilgrimage, which we were wont to use in time past, in running hither and thither'. He wished to replace it with what 'may be called the Christian man's pilgrimage'. For him, the Sermon on the Mount constituted the eight steps of the true pilgrimage. The attempt to treat the beatitudes in this way is strained, but it is interesting that Latimer preserved the language of pilgrimage while making it an expression for spiritual progress instead of geographical travel. In Spain, Andrew of Loguna, in his *Viaje de Turquia*, elaborated the Erasmian position into an outright rejection of the very foundations of a knowledge of the Holy Land: 'what does it matter to me as a Christian whether something is two leagues away or three, or that Pilate and Caiaphas had their residences in the same street?' In any case, he added, 'people who go are not shown half of what they are promised', and what they do see may well be an impudent fraud. The publication in 1551 of Gregory of Nyssa's

---

[4] Gomez-Géraud, 72, 65; F. Behrend, 'Deutsche Pilgerreisen ins Heilige Land, 1300–1600', *Festschrift für Georg Leidinger* (Munich, 1930), 1–13.
[5] *Affagart*, 22.
[6] Gomez-Géraud, 13.

fourth-century criticism of pilgrimage, which was previously unknown to Latins, provided further ammunition for critics.[7]

The reflections of Affagart in 1533 leave us in no doubt that there
was already a crisis in the continuation of the great pilgrimage. It
looks as if there had been a sharp drop in numbers, starting a decade
earlier. While in 1519 190 pilgrims, of many nationalities, left Venice
in two ships, in 1522 there were only about forty, and in 1523 we are
given a figure of twenty-one.[8] The decline must reflect the problems
posed for travel by the Ottoman siege and conquest of Rhodes. It is
more difficult to be sure whether numbers briefly recovered, or
whether Affagart was reflecting on a decade of continued neglect.
While confraternities of the Holy Sepulchre continued to enjoy prestige into the 1540s, it is not clear that many journeys were being
made in the 1520s, let alone later, and Affagart certainly thought
that German and Flemish custom had been seriously reduced by
Protestant polemic. Some Catholic apologists long continued to
assert that the journey could be made without undue difficulty: 'I
decided to show that the business can be carried through much more
easily, and for much less money, than is supposed,' wrote John de
Blioul (Cologne, 1599). Some suggested that the voyage really was
still functioning: John Zuallart or Zulluardo, himself a Walloon,
wrote an influential guidebook in Italian, because 'it is the language
most commonly spoken on this most holy voyage'.[9] The popes continued to express an interest in the pilgrimage: when the Franciscans
were driven out of their house on Mount Sion in 1551, Julius III, an
active patron of the Jesuits, formed a project of establishing colleges
of the society in Cyprus, Constantinople, and Jerusalem. His bull of 6
October 1553 envisaged the collection of funds 'for the devout support of the poor of Christ flooding (*confluentium*) to the said holy
places'. The initiative folded, especially as the pope died just over a
year later. In practice, the Franciscans succeeded in obtaining a new
domicile, in a former Coptic convent, closer to the church of the Holy
Sepulchre. The loss of Cyprus to the Turks in 1571, however, made
still more remote the prospect of maintaining a regular pilgrim traffic

---

[7] Ibid. 61–150, 167.
[8] M. L. Favreau-Lilie, 'The German Empire and Palestine: German Pilgrimages to
Jerusalem between the Twelfth and the Sixteenth Centuries', *JMH* 21 (1995), 321–41.
[9] Gomez-Géraud, 337, 229.

from Venice, and the drive to assert the holiness of Jerusalem in the piety of Islam, undertaken ambitiously by the Sultan Suleiman, had deprived the Christians of some of their important remaining shrines.[10]

It is hardly surprising that, in spite of pious aspirations, anecdotal evidence suggests that few Latin pilgrims were travelling. In 1575, the learned German Lutheran Leonhard Rauwolf travelled with five unnamed companions, and in 1593 Nicolas de Hault recorded meeting fifteen pilgrims from the West, all of them arriving individually at Jerusalem. In 1604, Antoine Cestier from Marseilles counted fourteen French and Italian pilgrims at Easter, and in 1612 the Scot William Lithgow enumerated a very small pilgrim presence: there were six Germans ('noble gentlemen and good protestants') and four French, who had all come 'the neerest way from Venice' together with nine 'commercing Franks', mostly Venetians who were resident in Syria or Cyprus.

In the Iberian peninsula, Juan Ceverio de Vera had already noticed the impact of Oceanic travel on the Jerusalem journey. He wrote in 1596 of 'the small notice which they take of the journey to the Holy Land' in comparison with travel to America, which had now become commonplace. People speak of Jerusalem, he said, 'as if it were the other world'. This did not mean that the Holy Sepulchre had ceased to be a goal for Eastern Christians: William Lithgow said that there were about 6,000 people present at the holy fire ceremony on Easter eve, and Pietro della Valle (1614) also saw great crowds there.[11] But as far as Latin pilgrimage was concerned, all these descriptions simply confirm the comment made by Alcarotti at Novara in 1596: 'I wondered in my heart how that holy pilgrimage has now been reduced to oblivion, although it is so dear to God ... We have the clear evidence of a catholic doctor, that someone does not deserve to be called a Christian, who does not have this perfect knowledge, or at least wish to have it.'[12] The registers of the Holy Land Custody of the Franciscans indicate that only a few dozen pilgrims a year were visiting Jerusalem at this time.

[10] On the troubled history of the Franciscans at Mount Sion, see P. Cuneo, 'The Urban Structure and Physical Organisation', and Y. Natsheh, 'Catalogue of Buildings', *Ottoman Jerusalem*, 211–20, 659–64.
[11] Gomez-Géraud, 336.
[12] Giovanni Francesco Alcarotti, *Del Viaggio di Terrasanta* (Novara, 1596), 4ᵛ, correcting *noi* to *non*. Presumably the 'doctor' was Jerome, but it is hardly a fair statement of his views.

Most of the visitors around the end of the century observed the prominence of the Franciscans in the supervision of the holy places, in spite of problems they had encountered. The old set of pilgrimages and processions was seemingly still observed, but the pilgrims themselves sustained the old attitudes in only a weakened form. True, the Spanish composer Francisco Guerrero (1588–9) was deeply conservative: he recorded the local marvels without scepticism, including the river bed where David had picked up stones for his sling, and at his death in 1599 at the age of 71 he was planning a new pilgrimage. Leonhard Rauwolf, although Protestant, shared the traditional sentiments at the sight of Calvary and the Sepulchre: 'it cannot be otherwise, but that every true Christian that is upon the Mount of Calvary, and thinks there of the cross of Christ, and in the Sepulchre of the glorious resurrection, must find great passion within his breast'. On the other hand as a good Lutheran he dismissed as superstitious the veneration for indulgences that some of his companions showed. William Lithgow, too, felt 'a kinde of unwonted rejoycing' and sang Psalm 103 as he approached the city. He was, however, fiercely anti-papist, as a result of having suffered torture at Malaga during his earlier travels. He observed a strict neutrality about the authenticity of much that he was shown, ridiculed the Palm Sunday procession as 'an apish imitation of Christ', and recorded with unconcealed satisfaction the beating-up of the Father Guardian by the Turks. Pietro della Valle (1614) was a Neapolitan and a Catholic, and made use of the standard guidebooks, such as that of Zulluardo; but his approach was eccentric. He set out as the result of a broken love affair, carefully avoided being made a knight of the Holy Sepulchre, carried a staff wrought in gold designed to be left there, and wore a pilgrim's dress of his own devising. The holy fire ceremony had long been dismissed by the Latins as a fraud, but della Valle was specially venomous about the proceedings: 'I never saw a sight so ludicrous or so outrageous.' The Englishman George Sandys (1610) was cool about the devotions he observed, although he did say about Calvary that 'if one place bee more holy than another', it was the most venerable in the world. Sandys still held to the traditional 'crusading' attitude: 'O who can without sorrow, without indignation, behold the enemies of Christ to be lords of his Sepulchre?' His editor, Purchas, did not much care for this comment, and he supplied a footnote of greater theological correctness: 'as for the Sepulchre, he is risen, he is not there, and what then have his enemies, but what himself would not hold, and which could not hold him?'[13] The overall impression of many of these visits is that the late-medieval structures of the pilgrimage still survived at Jerusalem; that the holy places still had some compelling force in the eyes of visitors; but that their attitudes had become more independent, and more sceptical, than they had been in the great days of the past. At the two extremes were the conservatives who advocated the old values of the pilgrimage and the Protestants who dismissed the journey to Jerusalem as without any value at all.

THE SURVIVAL OF PILGRIMAGE LITERATURE

Against this pattern of decay, it is not surprising that we can observe a sharp fall in the demand for accounts of the Jerusalem journey. Christine Gomez-Géraud, in her magnificent survey of the literature, has noted that there were not many narratives printed in the first decade of the sixteenth century (that is, before the impact of Protestant criticism), and that by 1541–50 pilgrimage literature 'was virtually sentenced to complete disappearance'.[14] It seems logical that this decade, a few years after Affagart's pessimistic survey, should be a low point, but it is puzzling to discover that, although the number of travellers probably did not recover, there was from about 1570 a sharp rise in demand for accounts of the pilgrimage. Gomez-Géraud counts 208 editions of travel journals between 1458 and 1610, covering fifty-eight different voyages, the majority of them published towards the end of this period, and comments that 'we can be sure of one thing: even if the bands of pilgrims going to the Holy Sepulchre were far from equalling the numbers in medieval times, the great pilgrimage was enjoying renewed popularity at the end of the sixteenth and start of the seventeenth century'.[15] It is clear that there was a real public for these books, and the publication of so much in vernacular languages shows that demand extended well beyond narrow circles of scholarship.

---

[13] R. P. Calcraft, *Francisco Guerrero, El Viage de Hierusalem* (Seville, 1592), introduction and 95; H. H. Dannenfeldt, 'Leonhard Rauwolf: A Lutheran Pilgrim in Jerusalem', *Archiv für Reformationsgeschichte*, 55 (1964), 24, 28; W. Lithgow, *The totall Discourse of the Rare Adventures and Painefull Peregrinations* (Glasgow, 1906), 209, 218–19; *Pietro Casola*, 85; G. Sandys, *A Relation of a Journey begun A.D. 1610* (Glasgow, 1905), 184–5.

[14] Gomez-Géraud, 22, 199. Her study is based primarily on texts narrating pilgrimages actually made; the pattern would be different if statistics for guidebooks and other forms of pilgrim literature were included.

[15] Ibid. 240.

There would appear to be a number of elements in this revival of literature. Some was designed to encourage and assist those who went on the journey, but this was not the dominant feature of the publications as a whole. Much of the information it contained was enormously out of date. The popular *Voyage from Venice to the Holy Sepulchre* (*Viaggio da Venezia al Santo Sepolcro*) largely followed a text composed in the fourteenth century, and in the decade after 1561, of the seven editions published, only one concerned a journey made after 1537. Even more remarkably, the short account by the Swiss Ludwig Tschudi, who travelled in 1519, was published in 1606. In a century during which the eastern Mediterranean was changing a great deal, this shows a striking discontinuity between reading and reality.

There was a certainly a wide interest in travel literature as a whole. Printing now made it possible to present the reader with woodcuts of the architecture and geography, and successive editions of the *Viaggio* entertained its readers with pictures of camels, elephants, and other curiosities. Jerusalem remained a subject of real interest, even if people could not go, or did not want to go, and it was a topic about which Protestants as well as Catholics wanted to read. The account of Daniel Ecklin (1556), 'the first protestant pilgrim' appeared in no less than fourteen editions. The scale of German demand was illustrated by Feyerabend's massive German *Reyszbuch desz heyligen landes* of 1584, with its eighteen narratives of the Palestine pilgrimage. Almost all these books had a visit to the Holy Sepulchre as their centre, for most pilgrims, even more than in the past, included a visit to the Easter ceremonies as a key event in their journeys.

There was, however, a significant gap between the literature of the Jerusalem pilgrimage and that of the oceanic voyages. The explanation for this can be found in both theology and geography. Germany and Italy had only a limited interest in what was happening across the Atlantic. England, being both Protestant and increasingly involved in oceanic exploration, illustrates the movement away from older ways of writing. Richard Hakluyt, when he prepared the first edition of *The Principall Navigations* (1589), was aware of standing on the brink of a new age of geographical knowledge. He recorded how, when he was a young man, his cousin 'began to instruct my ignorance, by shewing me the division of the earth into three parts after the old account, and then according to the latter and better distribution into more'. He was conscious, too, that until very recently the English had not been prominent in exploration, and that they were despised 'for their sluggish security, and continuall neglect of the like attempts'. *The Principall Navigations* stood between the old and new geographies. It presented English exploration as being rooted in the former world of pilgrimage: 'I find that the oldest travels as well of the ancient Britons, as of the English, were ordinarie to Judea which is in Asia, termed by them the Holy Land, principally for devotions' sake according to the time'. The collection began with records of early travels to Palestine, from the time of 'Helena the Empress, daughter of Coelus king of Britain' and Constantine, and it continued with some brief accounts of English crusaders. Hakluyt did not include any of the English pilgrimage narratives, which one suspects had been lost to view by this time. The bulk of the first section came from Mandeville, in the abbreviated Latin or 'vulgate' version. Curiously, it was the only Latin material that Hakluyt did not provide with a translation. It is worth remembering that Mandeville's work contained information of genuine geographical value, for it was based on genuine and extensive travel, even if the author was in fact not the traveller. In the second edition of 1598–1600, Hakluyt omitted Mandeville without apology or explanation. He substituted some other early accounts of travel to the same regions, but the collection no longer began with them. The emphasis on exploration was shifting from its original roots in the Holy Land to the increasingly successful oceanic voyages.

SPIRITUAL PILGRIMAGE

Under the impact of Counter-Reformation piety, the elaborate planning of layouts that gave a sense of history and locality to the events of the life of Christ developed rapidly in the West. They perhaps were not consciously designed to replace pilgrimage to the Holy Land, but this was their effect. They often took the form of the 'sacred mountains', whose origins we considered in the previous chapter, and which were deliberately designed for the pilgrim. Some were devoted to themes other than the Jerusalem pilgrimage, such as the life of the Virgin Mary or of St Francis, but predominantly they were centred on the events of the passion and the resurrection. With the wide availability of techniques of representation, such as fresco and especially terracotta, they embodied scenes with which the peasant imagination could identify. Geneviève Bresc-Bautier describes this type of development as 'a real Disneyland'. When Samuel Butler visited Varese around 1830 he offered a balanced account of the

work, mainly sixteenth- and seventeenth-century, that he found
there:

> The Virgin had a real washing-stand, with a basin and jug, and a piece of
> real soap . . . There was everything else that Messrs Heal and Co. would send
> for the furnishing of a lady's bedroom . . . The object is to bring the scene as
> vividly as possible before people who have not had the opportunity of being
> able to realize it themselves through travel or general cultivation of the
> imaginative faculties.[16]

More widespread than these ambitious compositions were straightforward Calvaries, hills or streets designed to enable the faithful to
follow defined steps of the way of the cross. These were extremely
common in Catholic countries, and could be of monumental size: the
Calvary at Mont Valérien in the suburbs of Paris, planned in the
years after 1633 by Hubert Charpentier, who had already established
an order of the priests of Calvary, became a centre for the devotion of
the royal court and the people of Paris.[17]

At Bologna, the 'Jerusalem' tradition, already well established, was
further developed. Santo Stefano had now become known as the _sette
chiese_ (although there were really only six at most). The buildings,
which had progressively been filled with memorials of the passion
and resurrection, contained not only the twelfth-century representation of the Sepulchre, but the bowl in which Pilate had washed his
hands and a wooden emblem of the cockerel of Peter's denial. The
Celestinian fathers, to whom the site now belonged, produced a series
of devotional guides to the church. Francesco Patricelli, who wrote
the fullest and most informative of them in 1575, gave his work the
title, _The Chronicle of the mysterious and devout church and abbey of S.
Stefano of Bologna, anciently called Jerusalem_. In 1637, Antonio Casale
chose a more emphatic title: _New Jerusalem, called the sacred basilica of
Santo Stefano at Bologna_.

They were meant as books of devotion for pilgrims. Patricelli says
his book was planned 'to be of help to devout souls', and that visitors
came from far away: 'to enter such a church is like entering a paradise, and it presents a vision of great majesty, and wonderful holiness. For this reason all sorts of people, from the region and from
afar, come often to visit this holy place'. One major concern was
to make sure that readers knew about the indulgences that were

---

[16] G. Bresc-Bautier, 'Le imitazioni del Santo Sepolcro', _Crociate_, 250; S. Butler, _Alps
and Sanctuaries_ (London, 1931), 249–50.
[17] S. Schama, _Landscape and Memory_ (London, 1995), 440–2.

available. In 1566 Jacomo Ortono, vicar-general of the Celestine order, wrote a work for Bologna called *Treasury or brief Summary of Indulgences*, but no copy of this now seems to survive, and Patricelli preserves copies of a grant of Celestine I in the 420s (spuriously, obviously) and one of Sixtus IV in 1476. Antonio Casale in 1637 commended the visits because of the difficulty of visiting the Holy Land—the first time that Bologna was specifically recommended for this reason. Donato Pullieni expressed his admiration for the churches in 1600: 'I have seen some plans faithfully made of the Holy Sepulchre, which is very similar to our church, even in the minutest details, to an extent which has amazed me—and also Signor Vizani, who made a wooden copy of it.' Patricelli's description of the Holy Sepulchre at Jerusalem as 'mysteriously representative of all the places in which were enacted the mysteries of the passion of our Lord' was based on the Bologna version, which incorporated symbols of Calvary into the structure of the tomb. In addition to these more general considerations, we must notice a strong Bolognese patriotism in this literary tradition. Patricelli ended his book with a sonnet addressed to *tutti Bolognesi cari*, and with a Latin prayer to form a link between Jerusalem and Bologna, between pilgrimage and *campanilismo*: 'Almighty and eternal God, the builder and keeper of the city of Jerusalem above, be the builder and guardian of this our city.'

Devotional books were not necessarily designed to accompany an actual pilgrimage to a site in the West. They could be designed for a purely imaginative journey. The classic work was the *Spiritual Pilgrimage* of Jan Pascha, Carmelite prior of Mechlin in the Low Countries, which was re-edited by Peter Calentyn and published at Louvain in 1563. It covered a year's meditations, allocating a day to each stage of a journey to the Holy Land. Such publications were often equipped with pictures: Simon Schama has drawn attention to the remarkable 'pop-up' book of 1612, like a modern children's illustrated volume, with which Jacopo Lingozzo introduced readers to the scenes of the passion of Christ and Francis at La Verna.[18] They could also be privileged by indulgences. It was now possible to make the Jerusalem journey without walking outside one's house.

In spite of the obvious contrasts between Protestant and Catholic attitudes to relics and pilgrimage, there is an underlying similarity. Bernard Hamilton has argued that 'Protestant and Catholic attitudes . . . were . . . mirror images of each other, for both were more

---

[18] Ibid. 437–9.

concerned with the cultivation of interior piety than with the performance of external acts of devotion.'[19] He is right in thinking that
the evolution of Catholic spirituality was moving away from the
Jerusalem pilgrimage, at once by offering the same indulgences for
imaginative travel and by offering an entirely inward interpretation
of pilgrimage, which saw the journey to Jerusalem as a journey to
the presence of God. This was the teaching of Bernardino of Laredo,
in his *Ascent to Mount Sion* of 1535: 'this temporal Jerusalem denotes
for us the eternal and sovereign city for which God created us'—an
idea central to Counter-Reformation piety in such writers as Teresa
of Avila.[20] At the same time, the Protestant movement away from
pilgrimage was much more decisive, and was rooted in the very
nature of the reformers' theology. The contrast has been expressed
compellingly by Euan Cameron:

> There was a fundamental difference between the Protestant concept of
> 'holiness' and its Catholic counterpart, which has its roots in the basic
> teachings of the Reformation about God's work. For Protestants, God
> always exercised his power directly . . . For Catholicism . . . God's power was
> often, even ordinarily, delegated: to holy church, to holy people, into holy
> things.[21]

The point can be incisively illustrated from Zwingli's 25th article:
'time and place are subject to the Christian man and not man to
them; therefore those who bind themselves to time and place deprive
a Christian of his freedom.' For Protestant writers pilgrimage had
ceased to exist except as the journey of the Christian through life.

There is a curious disjunction between the two cultures in the
poem, *The Passionate Man's Pilgrimage*. Its author used the familiar
trappings of the pilgrim to strengthen himself against the imminent
threat of execution. Seventeenth-century report was that it was written by Sir Walter Ralegh under sentence of death in 1603. Catholic
imagery from Ralegh would certainly be unexpected, but whatever
its authorship the poem forms a missing link in the evolution of the
ideal of spiritual pilgrimage:

> Give me my scallop-shell of quiet,
> My staff of faith to walk upon,
> My scrip of joy, immortal diet,
> My bottle of salvation,

[19] B. Hamilton, 'Loreto', *Renaissance and Modern Studies*, 31 (1987), 12, 15.
[20] E. A. Peers, *The Ascent to Mount Sion* (New York, 1951), 66.
[21] E. Cameron, 'For Reasoned Faith or Embattled Creed?', *TRHS* 6 (8) (1998), 175.

> My gown of glory, hope's true gage,
> And thus I'll take my pilgrimage.[22]

The great classic of spiritual pilgrimage, John Bunyan's *Pilgrim's Progress*, was published in 1678. As Neil Keeble has shown, it is the culmination of a considerable tradition of such thinking in England, although Bunyan had read little outside the Scriptures, and its detailed imagery must have come from his own creativity. John Milton rather than Bunyan offered the final critique of pilgrimage. In his thinking, the visit to the Holy Sepulchre, which had once been the heart of the Jerusalem journey, now presented itself as particularly futile. The Gospel question, 'Why do you seek the living among the dead?' (Luke 24: 5) had become the decisive argument against any further visit to the tomb:

> Eremites and friars
> White, black and grey, with all their trumpery,
> Here pilgrims roam that strayed so far to seek
> In Golgotha him dead, who lives in heaven.

Conversely, all history had become a pilgrimage. *Paradise Lost* ended with the image of Adam and Eve making their way out of the garden:

> The world was all before them, where to choose
> Their place of rest, and providence their guide:
> They hand in hand with wandering steps and slow
> Through Eden took their solitary way.[23]

The pilgrim ideal had some interesting successors. It spilled out into the Grand Tour. Visits to Italy combined Catholic devotion with art patronage, the one hiding behind the other. In their art tour of 1613–14 the earl and countess of Arundel, themselves Roman Catholics, were accompanied by a party that included not only Inigo Jones, but some outstanding Recusants, including Tobie Matthew, who was priested at Rome. Protestant monarchs connived at this pretence: the journey of Nicholas Lanier in 1625, to buy pictures for Charles I, was disguised as a pilgrimage for the Holy Year, so as not to 'enhance the prices'.[24] More significant was the secularization of

---

[22] G. Hammond (ed.), *Sir Walter Ralegh: Selected Writings* (Manchester, 1984), 53–5, 284–5.

[23] *Paradise Lost*, III. ll. 474–80, 489–93; and N. H. Keeble, ' "To be a Pilgrim": Constructing the Protestant Life in Early Modern England', *Pilgrimage: The English Experience*, 238–56.

[24] E. Chaney, *The Evolution of the Grand Tour* (London, 1998), ch. 8.

the word: a 'pilgrimage' came to be simply a journey, usually a journey of importance and dignity. About 1600 *The Pilgrimage to Parnas-*
sus used the term of a journey of scholars. In 1625 *Purchas his*
Pilgrims was published as a successor to Hakluyt, now without any
reference to the Jerusalem journeys created by the devotion of past
ages. The wheel had come full circle. *Peregrinus* had originated as a
word for a traveller. To Purchas, a pilgrim was an explorer of the
world.

KINGLY POWERS AND THE END OF THE CRUSADES

We saw in Chapter 9 that the discoveries in the New World were
regarded by Columbus and the crown of Aragon as containing the
promise of the recovery of the Holy Sepulchre. Even the threatening advance of the Turks into eastern Europe did not prevent
propagandists from setting their eyes on the liberation of the Sepulchre. An anonymous treatise of 1518, written perhaps by a
Franciscan, advocated a general crusade to destroy the Turkish
empire and Islam and to restore the tomb of Christ into the hands
of the faithful. Although it was written before the fall of Belgrade,
it remained influential, and was repeatedly republished, for
example in 1522, 1532, 1541, and 1542. Johann Haselberg in
1530 indulged in a fantastic vision of a crusade to be led by
the Emperor Charles V for the recovery of Constantinople and the
Sepulchre and the creation of Christian order throughout the
world. The intensely traditional character of the thought of such
treatises is evident in the sermon of Matthias Kretz on *the Cam-*
paign against the Turks in 1532. In stressing the need for territorial
governments to provide forms of prayer to aid the devotion of
ordinary people, he referred back to the mandates of Innocent III
requiring a monthly procession and the recitation of Psalm 79 at
mass; his theory of martyrdom was that held by twelfth-century
writers; and he added an epilogue on 'those Christian princes and
lords who in earlier times went on crusades to the Holy Land and
against the Turk' beginning (he said) from Charlemagne onwards.
Even some Lutheran writers were ready to refer to precedents set
during the crusades. Johannes Brenz in 1537 reminded his readers
that 'for more than a hundred years our laudable emperors of old
waged praiseworthy and Christian wars at Jerusalem to weaken
the Saracens . . . These Christian wars are highly praised by St
Bernard, who rightly calls them holy and justified warfare (*sanctam*

et tutam militiam).'[25] The possibility of the recovery of the Sepulchre of Christ remained alive for a long time in the contemporary imagination. The German peasant rebellion of 1513 included the liberation of Jerusalem among its objectives, and the Spanish rebels of 1522–3 thought that their leader was destined to recover Jerusalem. When Charles V won his great victory against the French at Pavia in 1525, his secretary Valdés saw it as a miracle, which would allow the emperor 'to confront the Turks and Moors in their own land. Thus . . . he will restore the empire of Constantinople and the holy dwelling of Jerusalem.'[26] After the great victory of Lepanto over the Turkish fleet in September 1571, Marc-Antoine Muret preached at Rome that the time had come to deliver Jerusalem; and he was a humanist, and not at all a dyed-in-the-wool conservative.

Apart from specific mentions of the Holy Sepulchre as an objective, the forms of crusading remained part of the discourse of political and social life. In Hungary in 1514, the proclamation of a crusade against the Turks proved to be a trigger for an attempt at social revolution. The rebels marched under the sign of the cross, and described themselves as *crucesignati* and as a blessed people, *benedicta gens*. They claimed to have received indulgences—indeed, that indulgences were hereditary, perhaps a distortion of the idea that they could be used for the benefit of the departed. In the West, where the war against the infidel had been more incorporated into the political language of royal houses and the aristocracy, such radical developments were unlikely, but in England in 1536 the Pilgrimage of Grace marched under the signs of the five wounds of Christ, its participants saw themselves as 'Christ's soldiers', and a song promised them 'sins released and endless joy when they are dead'. The Pilgrimage of Grace was at its core an aristocratic reaction to the religious innovations of the government of Henry VIII, but it was also a popular rising, in which there appeared 'a very simple poor man' who called himself Lord Poverty or Captain Poverty. The northern rebels in 1569 were attacked because 'they do beare the image of the cross paynted in a ragge against those that have the crosse of Christ painted in their hearts'—a good Protestant sentiment.[27] The Spanish armada of 1588, which sailed under a banner blessed in the cathedral at Lisbon

---

[25] J. W. Bohnstedt, 'The Infidel Scourge of God', *Transactions of the American Philosophical Society*, NS 58 (9) (1968), 35–49.

[26] N. Housley, 'Holy Land or Holy Lands?', SCH 36 (2000), 244; N. Housley, '*Pro Deo et patria mori*', P. Contamine (ed.), *Guerre et concurrence* (Paris, 1998), 296.

[27] Tyerman, *England*, 364.

and was strengthened by the promise of indulgences, can perhaps be regarded as the last major crusading enterprise launched in the West. There were whispers of the old ideas even in the seventeenth century. It appears that the Treaty of Westphalia in 1648 caused some alarm at Istanbul, out of fear that European unity would threaten the traditional enemy, the Turks. Even in 1670 Leibnitz could suggest a Franco-German war against Turkey, but the French secretary of state recalled the discussion to modern reality: 'I have nothing against the plan of a holy war, but such plans since the days of St Louis have ceased to be the fashion.' Crusades now seemed to be a far-away historical enterprise.[28]

There were, in any case, powerful elements in sixteenth-century thought that were undermining the old attachment to the Sepulchre of Christ and the desire to recover it for Christendom. One was the sheer implausibility of successful military action at Jerusalem. It was a very long time since a Christian army had been active there. The recovery of Jerusalem increasingly belonged to the world of prophecy. Eschatological expectations were certainly not dead, but in major churches and kingdoms they were regarded with increasing suspicion, and were confined to dissident groups. Meanwhile, Catholic devotion was being directed into spiritual paths that largely replaced the former great pilgrimage. Protestant criticism, as we have seen, was more radical. As Christopher Tyerman has pointed out, the new theology 'condemned the whole paraphernalia of crusading penance, indulgence, and temporal privileges. In few places was the Reformation more clearly an instrument of change than in this rejection of one of the most inbred and characteristic institutions of the Christian West.'[29] It was an open question for some Protestants whether Catholics or Turks were the greater menace to the faith. Joachim Greff in 1541 reported them as saying, 'if you ask me, it is far better to live under the Turk than under some papist tyrant'. Protestants were certainly worried about the Turkish menace, and sometimes rejoiced in the victories of Catholic powers. They also showed a sympathetic interest in the story of the crusades. Tasso's *Gerusalemme Liberata* was written in 1580 in the climate of the Counter-Reformation and under the influence of the victory at Lepanto, but it was soon translated into English. The notable Anglican historian Thomas Fuller subsequently wrote a *History of the Holy War* (1639).

[28] W. Zander, *Israel and the Holy Places of Christendom* (London, 1971), 25.
[29] Tyerman, *England*, 348.

The magistrates of Haarlem in the Netherlands were glad to celebrate the supposed triumphs of their ancestors in the storming of
Damietta in 1219: in 1611 they commissioned a painting of the subject; in 1630 two tapestries were made. There was a procession in
which children carried replicas of ships and the towers, and two
plays. Such distant glories could serve to unite a religiously divided
community.[30] On the other hand, Protestantism opposed all the traditional forms of crusading, and was inevitably suspicious of the leadership of Catholic princes. At first (although he later changed his
view) Luther was apparently opposed to all military resistance to the
Turks: 'to fight against the Turks is to oppose the judgement God
visits upon our iniquities through them.'[31] Although the circumstances of the writing of the great choral *Ein feste Burg ist unser Gott*
are unclear, it may well express Luther's confidence in the power of
God, rather than of man, to resist the Turkish menace.

Belief in the special calling of medieval kings had come to be
based, in large part, on their commitment to the recovery of the
Sepulchre of Christ. This was particularly true of France. In the eyes
of sixteenth-century contemporaries, the reputation of the most
Christian king was sadly damaged by the alliance between Francis I
and the Turks, but his policy had a precedent of sorts in the success
of the kings of Naples in the fourteenth century in securing, by
negotiation, the establishment of a house of friars at Jerusalem.
There was some discussion between Francis I and the sultan about
Christian rights at Jerusalem, but the first major treaty (or Capitulations) in 1536 contained little about religion and nothing about the
holy places. In some sense the document did point forward to the
future, for later Capitulations were to provide the framework within
which Western powers would seek guarantees for the freedom to visit
the Sepulchre and for the safety of the holy places: but those developments lay far ahead. With the strong pressure to make Rome the
centre of Catholic Christianity, the idea grew that the city was 'the
site of the new Jerusalem and the new Temple . . . the providential
capital of the eternal empire of Christian piety', as Giles of Viterbo
presented it. Its calling still included, in his thinking, the duty of
mounting a crusade to recover the old Jerusalem: a task to which he
urgently drew the attention of Pope Julius II (1503–13).[32] By the

[30] P. Biesboer, *Schidlerijen voor het stadhuis van Haarlem* (Haarlem, 1983), 32–64. I
am grateful to Dr Alastair Duke for this reference.
[31] Bohnstedt, 'Infidel Scourge', 12.
[32] Housley, 'Holy Land or Holy Lands?', 245.

beginning of the next century, this connection with Jerusalem in Judaea was being forgotten. The rebuilding of the Lateran by Clement VIII (1592–1605) was full of references to the early church, to the Temple and Anastasis at Jerusalem, and to the relics of the passion, and seemed to embody the presence at Rome of the spiritual power which long ago had belonged to Jerusalem.[33]

Rome, of course, was a special case. The assertion of its authority as the realization of Jerusalem was in large part an answer to the disruption of Catholic Christendom, which had freed radical thinkers to seek to create the city on earth through the coming of the kingdom of God. The most startling attempt was the establishment of the community of the saints at Münster in 1533–5. Far more sober was the special calling that brought the Puritan settlers to Massachusetts in 1630, in obedience to the command, 'Thou shouldst be a special people, an onely people, none like thee in all the earth.'[34] Soon afterwards, attempts were made in England during the Commonwealth and Protectorate to create a new Israel. But by now we are far from the pattern of medieval aspiration. These movements had virtually no interest in the Sepulchre of Christ as a place, and some of them were indifferent to the fate of the historical Jerusalem.

The geographical expansion of Christendom also invited new lands to create new legends of sanctity, since they could not claim long service to the Holy Sepulchre, as France or Spain or Germany could plausibly do. In the emerging power of Sweden, both Catholics and Protestants gloried in the ancient civilization of the Goths, celebrated in Olaus's *History of all the Kings of the Goths and Swedes* in 1554. Latin America to some extent inherited the Iberian sense of special vocation: there are strong crusading elements in its legends and institutions, even including the name of a currency, the *cruzada*. One might even speculate whether the failure of North America to assimilate its Spanish population is in some way linked with the distant conviction contained within their culture that they, too, are a special people. Mexico, however, early developed its own sacred topography on the basis of a combination of Catholic ideas with Aztec memories: the Virgin of Guadalupe appeared to an Amerindian in 1531, at a site already honoured before the Spanish conquest. In most of this, the Holy Sepulchre could have little place.

It is a matter of dispute among historians what continuity may be

---

[33] J. Freiberg, *The Lateran in 1600* (Cambridge, 1995), esp. 142.
[34] J. Oldfield, 'City on a Hill', SCH 36 (2000), 299–301.

discerned between the crusades, and therefore the Western interest in the Holy Sepulchre, and colonialism, the European expansion into new worlds. French historians were fond of describing the crusading states loosely as colonies, *les colonies franques de Syrie*. The view was argued by Joshua Prawer in his book, *The Latin Kingdom of Jerusalem*, with its significant subtitle, *European Colonialism in the Middle Ages* (1972). More recently, Robert Bartlett commented that the colonizers of America came from a world that was already familiar with colonization.[35] Discussion over the past thirty years has revealed the difficulties involved in describing Jerusalem as a colony. It is true that, immediately after the First Crusade, Guibert of Nogent did speak of the 'new colonies of holy Christendom', *sanctae Christianitatis novae coloniae*.[36] Yet the word is really a modern and not a medieval one, and has a variety of meanings. In the great age of imperialism it meant primarily a distant territory whose government was controlled by the metropolitan country, a status which does not accurately describe that of the kingdom of Jerusalem. 'Colony' may also mean a settlement within a foreign population, which may be marked by deliberate isolation from the native culture: for Prawer, *apartheid* was an important distinguishing mark of a colonial society, but it is arguable how far he was right in seeing this as characteristic of the kingdom of Jerusalem. It must be remembered, too, that there were other regions where Europeans could learn lessons in colonizing, such as Spain, the Baltic, and the Germanic East; some, but not all, of which had strong crusade connections. Like 'feudalism' a favourite historians' term that has now fallen on evil days, 'colonialism' is a very imprecise way of describing the expansion of Europe before the great oceanic voyages.

Yet there were undoubtedly continuities. The Latin states in Syria were dependent on the West for its sympathy and for financial and military aid in crises, and even for the regulation of political affairs. Their designation as overseas, *Outremer*, carries a hint of this dependency. The Italian communities in Acre and the other trading cities had close ties with Venice, Pisa, and Genoa, which exercised an even more direct control over Mediterranean islands from 1204 onwards: they provided some sort of precedent for the settlement of the Azores and the Canaries. There were economic continuities:

---

[35] R. Bartlett, *The Making of Europe* (London, 1993), 314.
[36] Guibert, *Gesta Dei per Francos*, vii. 25 (RHC Occ. iv. 245).

sugar plantations linked the coastal plain of crusader Palestine, the islands occupied by Italian cities in the Mediterranean, and the early modern island colonies. The spice trade connects the Venetians at Alexandria and Acre with their successors and rivals, the Portuguese, in the ports of India. There were spiritual continuities, too: the friars in America followed principles of missionary policy formulated by Gregory IX and Innocent IV for their predecessors in Asia and Morocco, and exploration was inspired by the search for Prester John. When the Portuguese arrived at Calicut, they explained that they had come 'for spices and for Christians'. There remained, in the minds of Columbus and others, the hope of a providential deliverance that would bring a new world order. The eschatological prospect that Jerusalem would be returned to the Christians was for some a remote and barely living expectation, but for others an ever-present hope.

There were also massive discontinuities, ways in which the emerging modern world was quite unlike the culture of the societies that preceded it. Crusader Jerusalem was not a colony, but a pilgrim society, established by and administered for pilgrims. The search for the holy places had been central to the creation of Christian Palestine from the fourth century onwards. Even under Muslim rule Jerusalem remained an aspiration for pilgrims from the West, and in the closing centuries of the Middle Ages, when the prospect of a military recovery had become distant, there was a sort of 'pilgrim exception' at Jerusalem, a small community on Mount Sion that catered for continued pilgrimage. Jerusalem was not a lost possession at the extremities of the earth. It was not a Newfoundland. On the contrary, for medieval people, the Holy Sepulchre was the centre of the world, the providential place where 'God worked salvation in the midst of the earth.'

Within the traditional bounds of Western Europe, the power that most obviously continued the Catholic interest in the Holy Sepulchre was that of the Medici grand dukes of Tuscany. Their capital, Florence, had a strong traditional link with the Sepulchre, and their aspirations were grand indeed. In 1588 Duke Ferdinand commissioned from the sculptor Giambologna a series of splendid reliefs that were to celebrate the raising of the cross, crucifixion, deposition, burial, and resurrection—a typical statement of Counter-Reformation piety. They were designed for the stone of anointing near the Sepulchre, but Greek opposition prevented this, and, long after, they were given their present, and more obscure, place within the church.[37] The idea of a superlative memorial chapel or *capella dei principi* to equal that of any royal family was conceived by the first grand duke, Cosimo, who died in 1574. The foundation stone was actually consecrated on 5 August 1604. Its pretentiousnesss was remarkable, and has been unkindly described as leaving 'an unpleasant after-taste of cancerous bric-à-brac that grew and grew', and it has not been finished to this day. In the early seventeenth century Dukes Ferdinand and Cosimo II embarked upon an ambitious Mediterranean policy, developing Livorno into a great port, attempting to suppress Turkish piracy and working for the liberation of the Sepulchre. Their policy was to negotiate with political opponents of the sultan, and in 1613 Emir Fakhreddin, having lost his political base in Syria, took refuge at Florence. The story circulated that the ambition of the grand dukes was to bring the Holy Sepulchre, stone by stone, to Florence, and that the *capella dei principi* was designed to house it. That was certainly not its primary intention: the design and the dates both exclude the possibility. The story of the removal, however, was not mere fantasy. It seems that Cosimo II's adviser, Bernardino Vecchietti, a knight of the Holy Sepulchre, proposed in the course of discussions with Fakhreddin that if the building could not be secured for Christian possession in Jerusalem, it should be physically transported. He even suggested some of the practical measures that might be required. Not the least step was ever taken to realize this project.[38]

Its arrival at Florence would have provided a satisfying end to this study, which has been so much concerned with the desire of medieval Christendom to make available to Latin devotion its power and its presence; but it was not to be. The Sepulchre of Christ remained physically at the heart of Jerusalem, and for centuries it was largely ignored. The extent of the indifference was remarkable. There was virtually no notice taken in Western Europe when in October 1808 a fire destroyed a great part of the surroundings of the Sepulchre, and when it was rebuilt in its present striking format, which a nineteenth-century explorer described as looking like a steam engine, but which more strictly may be described as Turkish baroque, it was under Greek auspices.[39] As it happened, in the next generation a new surge of interest began in the Christian West towards the history and antiquities of the Holy Land. But that is another story.

[37] J. Krüger, *Die Grabeskirche zu Jerusalem* (Regensburg, 2000), 200–1.
[38] Neri, 88–93; D. Facaros and M. Pauls, *Tuscany, Umbria* (London, 1990), 132–3.
[39] Krüger, *Grabeskirche*, 11–12.

Bibliography

The bibliography for specific topics will be found at the foot of the appropriate inset in the main text.

GENERAL

History and Theology of Jerusalem

ARMSTRONG, K., *A History of Jerusalem: One City, Three Faiths* (London, 1996).

HUMMEL, T. and others (eds.), *Patterns of the Past, Prospects for the Future: The Christian Heritage in the Holy Land* (London, 1999).

JOIN-LAMBERT, M., *Jerusalem* (London, 1958).

KÜHNEL, B. (ed.), *The Real and Ideal Jerusalem in Jewish, Christian and Islamic Art*. Jewish Art, 23/4 (1997/8).

PETERS, F. E., *Jerusalem: the Holy City . . . from the Days of Abraham to the Beginnings of Modern Times* (Princeton, 1985).

POORTHUIS, M., and SAFRAI, C. (eds.), *The Centrality of Jerusalem: Historical Perspectives* (Kampen, 1996).

PURVIS, J. D., *Jerusalem, the Holy City: A Bibliography* (New York, 1988–91).

ROSOVSKY, N. (ed.), *City of the Great King: Jerusalem from David to the Present* (Cambridge, Mass., 1996).

SWANSON, R. N. (ed.), *The Holy Land, Holy Lands and Christian History*, SCH 36 (2000).

VINCENT, H., and ABEL, F.-M., *Jérusalem: recherches de topographie, d'archéologie et d'histoire*, 2 vols. (Paris, 1912–26).

Church of Holy Sepulchre

Akten des XII Internationalen Kongresses für Christliche Archäologie, *Bonn 1991*, Jahrbuch für Antike und Christentum, Suppl. 20 (Münster, 1995–7).

ARNULF, A., *Mittelalterliche Beschreibungen der Grabeskirche in Jerusalem* (Stuttgart, 1997).

CORBO, V. C., *Il santo sepolcro di Gerusalemme*, 3 vols. (Jerusalem, 1981–2).

COÜASNON, C., *The Church of the Holy Sepulchre in Jerusalem* (London, 1974).

FREEMAN-GRENVILLE, G. S. P., 'The Basilica of the Holy Sepulchre, Jerusalem: History and Future', *Journal of the Royal Asiatic Society* (1987), 187–207.

—— *The Basilica of the Holy Sepulchre in Jerusalem* (Jerusalem, about 1997).

HARVEY, W., *The Church of the Holy Sepulchre, Jerusalem: Structural Survey* (London, 1935).

Kötting, B., 'Die Tradition der Grabkirche', K. Schmid and J. Wollasch (eds.), *Memoria: der geschichtliche Zeugenswert des liturgischen Gedenkens im Mittelalter* (Munich, 1984), 69–79.

Krüger, J., *Die Grabeskirche zu Jerusalem: Geschichte, Gestalt, Bedeutung* (Regensburg, 2000).

Levine, L. I., (ed.), *Jerusalem: Its Sanctity and Centrality to Judaism, Christianity and Islam* (New York, 1998).

Ousterhout, R., 'Architecture as Relic and the Construction of Sanctity: The Stones of the Holy Sepulchre', *Journal of the Society of Architectural Historians*, 62 (2003), 4–23.

Piccirillo, M., *The Holy Land of the Crusaders*, http://198.62.75.1/www1/ofm/crus/CRUoAA.html, accessed 5 May 2004.

Zander, W., *Israel and the Holy Places of Christendom* (London, 1971).

Holy Sepulchre (Tomb of Christ)

Biddle, M., 'Jerusalem: The Tomb of Christ', *Current Archaeology*, 11 (1991), 107–12.

—— *The Tomb of Christ* (Stroud, 1999).

Wilkinson, J., 'The Tomb of Christ: An Outline of its Structural History', *Levant*, 4 (1972), 83–97.

Pilgrimage

Campbell, M. B., *The Witness and the Other World: Exotic European Travel Writing, 400–1600* (Ithaca, 1988).

Eade, J., and Sallnow, M. (eds.), *Contesting the Sacred: The Anthropology of Christian Pilgrimage* (London, 1991).

Graboïs, A., *Le Pèlerin occidental en Terre Sainte au Moyen-Age* (Brussels, 1998).

Le Beau, B., and Mor, M. (eds.), *Pilgrims and Travellers to the Holy Land* (New York, 1996).

Richard, J., *Les Récits de voyages et de pèlerinages* (Turnhout, 1981).

Sargent-Baur, B. N. (ed.), *Journeys towards God: Pilgrimage and Crusade* (Kalamazoo, 1992).

Stopford, J. (ed.), *Pilgrimage Explored* (Woodbridge, 1999).

Turner, V. W. and E., *Image and Pilgrimage in Christian Culture* (Oxford, 1978).

Vauchez, A., *Lieux sacrés, lieux de culte, sanctuaires*, Collection de l'école française, 273 (Rome, 2000).

Architectural Copies of the Holy Sepulchre and Round Churches

Kötzsche, L., 'Das Heilige Grab in Jerusalem und seine Nachfolger', *Akten XII*, 272–90.

KRAUTHEIMER, R., 'Introduction to an Iconography of Medieval Architecture', *JWCI* 5 (1942), 1–33.

NERI, D., *Il Santo Sepolcro riprodotto in Occidente* (Jerusalem, 1971) [It should be noted that the work was written long before the date of publication.]

UNTERMANN, M., *Der Zentralbau im Mittelalter: Form, Funktion, Verbreitung* (Darmstadt, 1989).

INTRODUCTION

On Memory and Image

CARRUTHERS, M., *The Craft of Thought: Meditation, Rhetoric and the Making of Images, 400–1200* (Cambridge, 1998).

FREEDBERG, D., *The Power of Images: Studies in the History and Theory of Response* (Chicago, 1989).

HALBWACHS, M., *On Collective Memory* (repr. Chicago, 1992).

LE GOFF, J., *History and Memory* (New York, 1992).

SCHAMA, S., *Landscape and Memory* (London, 1995).

SCHMITT, J.-C., *Le Corps des images: essais sur la culture visuelle au Moyen-Age* (Paris, 2002).

I. BEGINNINGS, TO 325

BAGATTI, B., *The Church from the Gentiles in Palestine* (Jerusalem, 1971).

—— *The Church from the Circumcision: History and Archaeology of the Judaeo-Christians* (Jerusalem, 1971).

—— and TESTA, E., *Il Golgota e la croce: ricerche storico—archeologiche* (Jerusalem, 1978).

BAHAT, D., 'Does the Holy Sepulchre Church Mark the Burial of Jesus?', *Biblical Archaeology Review*, 12 (3) (1986), 26–45.

BRANDON, S. S. F., *The Fall of Jerusalem and the Christian Church* (London, 1951).

GASTON, L. H., *'No Stone on Another': Studies in the Significance of the Fall of Jerusalem in the Synoptic Gospels* (Leiden, 1970).

GRANT, M., *The Jews in the Roman World* (London, 1973).

HALL, S. G. (ed.), *Melito of Sardis: On Pascha* (Oxford, 1979).

HUNT, E. D., 'Were There Christian Pilgrims before Constantine?', J. Stopford (ed.), *Pilgrimage Explored* (Woodbridge, 1999), 25–40.

JEREMIAS, J., *Golgotha* (Leipzig, 1926).

—— *Heiligengräber in Jesu Umwelt* (Göttingen, 1958).

KENYON, K. M., *The Bible and Recent Archaeology* (London, 1978), ch. 6.

MARGALIT, S., 'Aelia Capitolina', *Judaica*, 45 (1989), 45–56.

NIBLEY, H., 'Christian Envy of the Temple', *Jewish Quarterly Review*, 50 (1959–60), 97–125, 229–40.

SIMON, M., *St Stephen and the Hellenists in the Primitive Church* (London, 1958).

TAYLOR, J. E., *Christians and the Holy Places: The Myth of Jewish-Christian Origins* (Oxford, 1993).

—— 'Golgotha: A Reconsideration of the Evidence for the Sites of Jesus' Crucifixion and Burial', *New Testament Studies*, 44 (1998), 180–233.

THIEDE, C. P., *The Heritage of the First Christians* (Oxford, 1992), ch. 17.

WALKER, P. W. L., *The Weekend that Changed the World: The Mystery of Jerusalem's Empty Tomb* (London, 1999).

WILKINSON, J., *The Jerusalem Jesus Knew* (London, 1978).

—— 'Jewish Holy Places and the Origins of Christian Pilgrimage', *Blessings of Pilgrimage*, 41–53.

—— 'The Inscription on the Jerusalem Ship Drawing', *PEQ* 127 (1995), 159–60 [listing abundant earlier discussions].

2. CONSEQUENCES OF CONSTANTINE, 325–350

BARNES, T. D., *Constantine and Eusebius* (Cambridge, Mass., 1981).

BORGEHAMMAR, S., *How the Holy Cross was Found* (Stockholm, 1991).

BRENK, B., 'Der Kultort, seine Zugänglichkeit und seine Besucher', *Akten XII*, 69–122.

CAMERON, A., and HALL, S. G. (eds. and trs.), *Eusebius:* Life of Constantine (Oxford, 1999).

DRAKE, H. A., *In Praise of Constantine: Eusebius' Tricennial Orations* (London, 1975).

—— 'Eusebius on the True Cross', *JEH* 36 (1985), 1–22.

—— 'What Eusebius Knew: The Genesis of the *Vita Constantini*', *Classical Philology*, 83 (1988), 20–38.

—— *Constantine and the Bishops: The Politics of Intolerance* (London, 2000).

GIBSON, S., and TAYLOR, J. E., *Beneath the Church of the Holy Sepulchre, Jerusalem* (London, 1994).

HEIM, F., *La Théologie de la victoire de Constantin à Théodose* (Paris, 1992).

HUNT, E. D., 'Constantine and Jerusalem', *JEH* 48 (1997), 405–24.

KEE, A., *Constantine versus Christ: The Triumph of Ideology* (London, 1982).

KRAUTHEIMER, R., 'The Constantinian Basilica', *DOP* 21 (1967), 117–40.

LAVAS, G. P., 'The Rock of Calvary: Uncovering Christ's Crucifixion Site', *Real and Ideal Jerusalem*, 147–50.

LAVAS, G. P., and MITROPOULOS, T., 'Golgotha, Jerusalem: die Aufdeckung der Kreuzigungstelle Christi', *Akten XII*, 964–8.

MURPHY-O'CONNOR, J., 'Restoration and Discovery: Bringing to Light the Original Holy Sepulchre Church', *Patterns of the Past*, 69–84.

RENAUT, L., 'La Croix des quatres premiers siècles', *Supplice*, 12–22.

THIEDE, C. P., and D'ANCONA, M., *The Quest for the True Cross* (London, 2000).

TOLOTTI, F., 'Il S. Sepolcro di Gerusalemme e le coeve basiliche di Roma',

Mitteilungen des Deutschen Archäologischen Instituts, Römische Abteilung, 93 (1986), 471–512.

WALKER, P. W. L., 'Eusebius, Cyril and the Holy Places', *Studia Patristica,* 20 (1989), 306–14.

—— *Holy City, Holy Places?* (Oxford, 1990).

WARD-PERKINS, J. B., 'Constantine and the Origins of the Christian Basilica', *Papers of the British School at Rome,* 22 (1954), 69–90.

WARMINGTON, B. H., 'Did Constantine Have "Religious Advisers"?', *Studia Patristica,* 19 (1989), 117–29.

3. DISSEMINATION

ALBERT, J.-P., *Odeurs de sainteté: la mythologie chrétienne des aromates* (Paris, 1990).

AVI-YONAH, M., *The Madaba Mosaic Map* (Jerusalem, 1954).

BAGATTI, B., 'Eulogie Palestinensi', *Orientalia Christiana Periodica,* 15 (1949), 126–66.

BALDOVIN, J. F., *The Urban Character of Christian Worship: The Origins, Development and Meaning of Stational Liturgy* (Rome, 1987).

—— *Liturgy in Ancient Jerusalem* (Nottingham, 1989).

BARAG, D., 'Glass Pilgrim Vessels from Jerusalem', *Journal of Glass Studies,* 12 (1970), 35–63, and 13 (1971), 45–63.

—— and WILKINSON, J., 'The Monza-Bobbio Flasks and the Holy Sepulchre', *Levant,* 6 (1974), 179–87.

BAUMSTARK, A., *Comparative Liturgy* (London, 1958).

BINNS, J., *Ascetics and Ambassadors of Christ: The Monasteries of Palestine, 314–631* (Oxford, 1994).

BOWMAN, G., ' "Mapping History's Redemption": Eschatology and Topography in the *Itinerarium Burdigalense*', Levine, 163–87.

BREDERO, A. H., 'Jérusalem dans l'Occident médiéval', *Mélanges offerts à R. Crozet* (Poitiers, 1966), i. 259–71.

BROWN, P., *The Cult of the Saints: Its Rise and Function in Latin Christianity* (London, 1981).

CANUTI, G., 'Mosaici di Giordania con raffigurazioni di città: itinerari di pellegrinaggio?, *Akten XII,* 617–29.

CHITTY, D. J., *The Desert a City,* new edn. (Crestwood, 1995).

CLARK, E. A. (tr.), Gerontius: *The Life of Melania the Younger* (New York, 1984).

CROOK, J., *The Architectural Setting of the Cult of Saints in the Early Christian West, c.300–1200* (Oxford, 2000).

DAVIES, J. G., *Holy Week: A Short History* (London, 1963).

DIX, G., *The Shape of the Liturgy* (London, 1945).

DONNER, H., *The Mosaic Map of Madaba: An Introductory Guide* (Kampen, 1992).

DOUGLASS, L., 'A New Look at the *Itinerarium Burdigalense*', *Journal of Early Christian Studies*, 4 (1996), 313–33.

ELSNER, J., *Imperial Rome and Christian Triumph: The Art of the Roman Empire, 100–450* (Oxford, 1998).

FAVREAU, R. (ed.), *Le Supplice et la gloire: la croix en Poitou* (Poitiers, 2000).

FINNEY, P. C., *The Invisible God: The Earliest Christians on Art* (Oxford, 1994).

FLUSIN, B., 'Remarques sur les lieux saints de Jérusalem à l'époque byzantine', *Lieux sacrés*, 119–32.

FRANK, G., 'Pilgrim's Experience and Theological Challenge: Two Patristic Views', *Akten XII*, 787–91.

—— *The Memory of the Eyes: Pilgrims to Living Saints in Christian Late Antiquity* (London, 2000).

FRENCH, D. R., 'Journey to the Centre of the Earth: Medieval and Renaissance Pilgrimages to Mount Calvary', *Journeys towards God*, 45–81.

—— 'Mapping Sacred Centres: Pilgrimage and the Creation of Christian Topographies in Roman Palestine', *Akten XII*, 792–7.

FREND, W. H. C., *The Archaeology of Early Christianity: A History* (London, 1996).

GATTI PERER, M. L. (ed.), *La dimora di Dio con gli uomini: immagini della Gerusalemme celeste dal III al XIV secolo* (Milan, 1983).

GEYER, P., WEBER, R., and others (eds.), *Itineraria et alia geographica*, CCSL 175–6 (1965).

GORCE, D. (ed.), *Gerontius: Vie de Ste Mélanie*, SC 90 (1962).

GRABAR, A., *Ampoules de Terre Sainte* (Paris, 1958).

—— 'La Fresque des saintes femmes au tombeau à Doura', *L'Art de la fin de l'Antiquité et du Moyen Age*, 3 vols. (Paris, 1968), 517–28.

GUDEA, N., 'Kreuzförmige Zeichen auf Gegenstände des täglichen Gebrauchs aus vorkonstantinischer Zeit', *Akten XII*, 833–48.

HAHN, C., '*Loca Sancta* Souvenirs', *Blessings of Pilgrimage*, 85–96.

HIRSCHFELD, Y., *The Judaean Desert Monasteries in the Byzantine Period* (New Haven, 1992).

HUNT, E. D., *Holy Land Pilgrimage in the Later Roman Empire, 312–460* (Oxford, 1982).

—— *The Itinerary of Egeria*, SCH, 36 (2000), 34–54.

JENSEN, R. M., *Understanding Early Christian Art* (New York, 2000).

KARTSONIS, A. D., *Anastasis: The Making of an Image* (Princeton, 1986).

KÖTTING, B., 'Gregor von Nyssas Wallfahrtskritik', *Studia Patristica*, 5 (1962), 360–7.

LECLERCQ, H., 'Croix et crucifix', *Dictionnaire d'Archéologie Chrétienne et de Liturgie* (1914), iii. pt. 2, 3045–144.

LIMOR, O., 'Reading Sacred Space: Egeria, Paula and the Christian Holy Land', *De Sion*, 1–15.

LOERKE, W., ' "Real Presence" in Early Christian Art', T. G. Verdon (ed.), *Monasticism and the Arts* (Syracuse, 1984), 29–51.

McCAULEY, L. P., and STEPHENSON, A. A., *The Works of St Cyril of Jerusalem*, 2 vols. (Washington, DC, 1969–70).

MacCORMACK, S., '*Loca Sancta*: the Organization of Sacred Topography in Late Antiquity', *Blessings of Pilgrimage*, 8–40.

MARAVAL, P. (ed.), *Egérie: Journal de Voyage*, SC 296 (1982).

—— *Lieux saints et pèlerinages d'Orient* (Paris, 1985).

—— (ed.), *Lettres: Grégoire de Nysse*, SC 363 (1990).

—— *Récits des premiers pèlerins chrétiens au Proche-Orient (IVe–VIe s.)* (Paris, 1996).

MATTHEWS, J. F., *Western Aristocracies and Imperial Court, 365–425* (Oxford, 1975).

MÖBIUS, H., *Passion und Auferstehung* (Vienna, 1978), ch. 1.

MORIARTY, R., ' "Secular Men and Women": Egeria's Lay Congregation in Jerusalem', R. N. Swanson (ed.), *The Holy Land, Holy Lands*, SCH 36 (2000), 55–66.

OUSTERHOUT, R. (ed.), *The Blessings of Pilgrimage* (Urbana, 1990).

PARENTE, F., *La conoscenza della terra santa come esperienza religiosa dell'occidente cristiano dal IV secolo alle crociate*, Centro Italiano di studi sull'alto medioevo (Spoleto) 29(1) (1983), 231–326.

PATRICH, J., *Sabas, Leader of Palestinian Monasticism* (Washington, 1995).

PEREGRINATIO EGERIAE: Convegno Internazionale, Arezzo (Arezzo, n.d.).

PICCIRILLO, M., and ALLIATA, E. (eds.), *The Madaba Map Centenary* (Jerusalem, 1999).

PIÉDAGNEL, A., Cyril of Jerusalem, *Catachèses mystagogiques*, SC 126 (2) (1966).

POCKNEE, C. E., *Cross and Crucifix in Christian Worship and Devotion* (London, 1962).

RENOUX, A. (ed.), *Le codex arménien Jérusalem 121* (Turnhout, 1971).

SAFRAI, Z., *The Missing Century: Palestine in the Fifth Century* (Louvain, 1998).

SIVAN, H., 'Pilgrimage, Monasticism and the Emergence of Christian Palestine in the Fourth Century', *Blessings of Pilgrimage*, 54–64.

SMITH, J. Z., *To Take Place: Toward Theory in Ritual* (Chicago, 1987).

SULZBERGER, M., 'Le Symbole de la croix et les monogrammes de Jésus chez les premiers chrétiens', *Byzantion*, 2 (1925), 337–448.

TAFT, R. E., 'Historicism Revisited', in his *Beyond East and West* (Washington, 1984), 15–30.

TALLEY, T. J., *The Origins of the Liturgical Year*, 2nd edn. (Collegeville, 1991).

TONGEREN, L. VAN, 'A Sign of Resurrection on Good Friday: The Role of the People in the Good Friday Liturgy until c. 1000 AD and the Meaning of the Cross', C. Caspers and M. Schneiders, *Contributions towards a History of the Role of the People . . . to H. Wegman* (Kampen, 1990), 101–19.

—— *Exaltation of the Cross: Towards the Origins of the Feast of the Cross* (Sterling, Va., 2000).

VAUCHEZ, A. (ed.), *Lieux sacrés, lieux de culte, sanctuaires: approches termi-*

nologiques, méthodologiques, historiques et monographiques, Coll. de l'école française de Rome, 273 (Rome, 2000).

WEINGARTEN, S., 'Was the Pilgrim from Bordeaux a Woman?', *Journal of Early Christian Studies*, 7 (1999), 381–400.

WEITZMANN, K., '*Loca Sancta* and the Representational Arts of Palestine', *DOP* 28 (1974), 31–55.

—— *Age of Spirituality: Late Antique and Early Christian Art*, Catalogue of Exhibition of Metropolitan Museum of Art (New York, 1980).

WILKEN, R. L., *The Land Called Holy: Jerusalem in Christian History and Thought* (London, 1992).

WILKINSON, J., *Egeria's Travels*, 3rd edn. (Warminster, 1999).

—— *Jerusalem Pilgrims before the Crusades*, 2nd edn. (Warminster, 2002).

4. THE FRANKISH KINGDOMS AND THE CAROLINGIANS, 600–1000

ALEXANDER, P. J., 'The Diffusion of Byzantine Apocalypses in the Medieval West', A. Williams (ed.), *Prophecy and Millenarianism: Essays in Honour of Marjorie Reeves* (Harlow, 1980), 53–106.

AVRIL, F., and GABORIT, J.-R., 'L'*Itinerarium Bernardi Monachi* et les pèlerinages d'Italie du Sud', *Mélanges, École Française de Rome*, 79 (1967), 269–98.

BÄRSCH, J., *Die Feier des Osterfestkreises im Stift Essen* (Münster, 1997).

BAUERREISS, R., Sepulcrum Domini: *Studien zur Entstehung der christlichen Wallfahrt auf deutschen Boden* (Munich, 1936).

BAYNES, N. H., 'The Restoration of the Cross at Jerusalem', *EHR* 27 (1912), 287–99.

BERGER, B.-D., *Le Drame liturgique de Pâques: liturgie et théâtre* (Paris, 1976).

BIEBERSTEIN, K., 'Der Gesandtenaustauch zwischen Karl dem Grossen und Harun ar-Rasid, und seine Bedeutung für die Kirchen Jerusalems', *Zs. des Deutschen Palästina-Vereins*, 109 (1993), 151–73.

BORGOLTE, M., *Der Gesandtenaustauch der Karolinger mit den Abbasiden und mit den Patriarchen von Jerusalem* (Munich, 1976).

BULLOUGH, D. A., *Carolingian Renewal* (Manchester, 1991).

CHAZELLE, C. M., *The Crucified God in the Carolingian Era: Theology and the Art of Christ's Passion* (Cambridge, 2001).

CORBIN, S., *La Déposition liturgique du Christ au Vendredi Saint* (Paris, 1960).

DALMAN, G., *Das Grab Christi in Deutschland* (Leipzig, 1922).

Dimensioni Drammatiche della Liturgia Medioevale: Atti del I Convegno de Studio, Viterbo, 1976 (Rome, 1977).

FRAIPONT, I. (ed.), *Bede, De Locis Sanctis*, CCSL 175 (1965), 249–80.

FRIED, J., 'Endzeiterwartung um die Jahrtausendwende', *Deutsches Archiv*, 45 (1989), 381–473.

FROLOW, A., 'La Vraie Croix et les expéditions d'Héraclius en Perse', *Revue des Études Byzantines*, 11 (1953), 88–105.

FROLOW, A., *La Relique de la vraie croix* (Paris, 1961).

—— *Les Reliquaires de la vraie croix* (Paris, 1965).

GIL, M., *A History of Palestine, 634–1099* (Cambridge, 1992).

GOUGUENHEIM, S., 'Adson, la reine et l'Antichrist', P. Corbet and others (eds.), *Les Moines du Der, 673–1790* (Langres, 2000), 135–46.

GRABAR, O., *The Shape of the Holy: Early Islamic Jerusalem* (Princeton, 1996).

GRABOÏS, A., 'Charlemagne, Rome et Jérusalem', *Revue Belge de Philologie et d'Histoire*, 59 (1981), 792–809.

GRÄF, H. J., *Palmenweihe und Palmenprozession* (Kaldenkirchen, 1959).

GUTH, K., 'Heiligenlandfahrt in frühislamischer Zeit: Willibald von Eichstätt zum Gedenken', *Recherches de Théologie Ancienne et Médiévale*, 56 (1989), 5–18.

HARDISON, O. B., *Christian Rite and Christian Drama in the Middle Ages* (Westport, 1983).

HAUSSHERR, R., *Der tote Christus am Kreuz: zur Ikonographie des Gerokreuzes* (Bonn, 1963).

HEITZ, C., *Recherches sur les rapports entre architecture et liturgie à l'époque carolingienne* (Paris, 1963).

—— *L'Architecture religieuse carolingienne: les formes et leurs fonctions* (Paris, 1980).

HENDERSON, G., *Style and Civilization: Early Medieval* (Harmondsworth, 1972), ch. 6.

LOUTH, A., 'Palestine under the Arabs, 650–750: The Crucible of Byzantine Orthodoxy', R. N. Swanson, *The Holy Land, Holy Lands*, SCH 36 (2000), 67–77.

McGINN, B., *Visions of the End: Apocalyptic Traditions in the Middle Ages*, 2nd edn. (New York, 1998).

McKITTERICK, R., *The Frankish Church and the Carolingian Reforms, 789–895* (London, 1977).

MAYR-HARTING, H., 'Artists and Patrons', *New Cambridge Medieval History* (1999), iii. 212–30.

MAZOUER, C., 'Les Indications de mise en scène dans les drames liturgiques de Pâques', *CCM* 23 (1980), 361–8.

MEEHAN, D. (ed.), *Adomnan, De Locis Sanctis* (Dublin, 1983).

MÖHRING, H., 'Karl der Grosse und die Endkaiser-Weissagung: der Sieger über den Islam kommt aus dem Westen', *Montjoie*, 1–19.

NELSON, J. L., 'Rulers and Government', *New Cambridge Medieval History* (1999), iii. 95–129.

O'LOUGHLIN, T., 'Adomnan and Arculf: The Case of an Expert Witness', *The Journal of Medieval Latin*, 7 (1997), 127–46.

—— 'Palestine in the Aftermath of the Arab Conquest: The Earliest Latin Account', R. N. Swanson, *The Holy Land, Holy Lands*, SCH 36 (2000), 78–89.

PETERS, F. E., *The Distant Shrine: The Islamic Centuries in Jerusalem* (New York, 1993).

PILLE, U., 'Die Pilgerreise des Heiligen Willibalds', H.-W. Goetz and F. Sauerwein (eds.), *Volkskultur und Elitenkultur im frühen Mittelalter* (Krems, 1997), 59–79.

PRAWER, J., and BEN-SHAMAI, H. (eds.), *The History of Jerusalem: The Early Muslim Period, 638–1099* (New York, 1996); esp. J. Prawer, 'Christian Attitudes towards Jerusalem in the Early Middle Ages', 311–48.

RAW, B. C., *Anglo-Saxon Crucifixion Iconography and the Art of the Monastic Revival* (Cambridge, 1990).

RUNCIMAN, S., 'The Pilgrims of Christ', *A History of the Crusades* (Harmondsworth, 1951), i. ch. 3.

—— 'The Pilgrimages to Palestine before 1095', M. W. Baldwin (ed.), *A History of the Crusades*, 2nd edn. (Madison, 1969), i. 68–80.

SANSTERRE, J. M., 'Les Moines "grecs" et la politique de l'église romaine', *Mémoires de l'académie royale de Belgique*, Classe des Lettres, 66 (1) (Brussels, 1983), 17–21, 115–17.

SCHICK, R., *The Christian Communities of Palestine from Byzantine to Islamic Rule* (Princeton, 1995).

SCHMID, K., 'Aachen und Jerusalem', in K. Hauck (ed.), *Das Einhardkreuz* (Göttingen, 1974), 122–42.

THOBY, P., *Le Crucifix des origines au concile de Trente* (Nantes, 1959/1963).

VERHELST, D. (ed.), Adso Dervensis, *De ortu et tempore Antichristi*, CCCM 45 (1976).

VOGEL, C., *Medieval Liturgy: An Introduction to the Sources* (Washington, 1986).

WILKINSON, *Pilgrims*, 167–206, 216–30 (Adomnan, Bede); 233–51 (Willibald); 260–9 (Bernard).

YOUNG, K., *The Drama of the Medieval Church*, 2 vols. (London, 1962).

5. TOWARDS THE FIRST CRUSADE

BALARD, M. (ed.), *Autour de la première croisade* (Paris, 1996).

—— and others (eds.), *Dei gesta per Francos: Études à J. Richard* (Aldershot, 2001).

BARBER, M., *The Two Cities: Medieval Europe, 1050–1320* (London, 1992).

BECKER, A., *Papst Urban II* (Stuttgart, 1988), ii.

BIANQUIS, T., *Damas et la Syrie sous la domination Fatimide*, 2 vols. (Damascus, 1986–9).

BIDDLE, M., *The Tomb of Christ* (Stroud, 1999), ch. 4.

BLAKE, E. O., and MORRIS, C., 'A Hermit goes to War: Peter and the Origins of the First Crusade', W. J. Shiels (ed.), *Monks, Hermits and the Ascetic Tradition*, SCH 22 (1985), 79–108.

BLOCH, M., *Feudal Society* (London, 1962).

BOUSQUET, J., 'La Fondation de Villeneuve d'Aveyron (1053), et l'expansion de l'abbaye de Moissac en Rouergue', *Moissac et l'occident au XIe siècle* (Toulouse, 1964).

BULL, M., *Knightly Piety and the Lay Response to the First Crusade, c.970–c.1130* (Oxford, 1993).

CANARD, M., 'La Destruction de l'église de la résurrection par le calife Hakim et l'histoire de la descente du feu sacré', *Byzantion*, 35 (1965), 16–43.

CARDINI, F., *Il pellegrinaggio: una dimensione della vita medievale* (Rome, 1996).

CHAZAN, R., '1007–13: Initial Crisis for Northern European Jewry', *Proceedings of the American Academy for Jewish Research*, 38–9 (1970–1).

CIGHAAR, K., and others (eds.), *East and West in the Crusader States* (Louvain, 1996).

Le Concile de Clermont de 1095 et l'appel à la croisade, École Française (Rome, 1997).

CONTAMINE, P., *La Guerre au moyen âge* (Paris, 1980).

CORBET, P., 'L'Autel portatif de la comtesse Gertrude de Brunswick (vers 1040)', *Cahiers de Civilisation Médiévale*, 34 (1991), 97–120.

COWDREY, H. E. J., *The Cluniacs and the Gregorian Reform* (Oxford, 1970).

—— 'Cluny and the First Crusade', *RB* 83 (1973).

—— 'Pope Gregory VII's "Crusading" Plan of 1074', *Outremer*, 27–40.

—— 'Canon Law and the First Crusade', *Horns of Hattin*, 41–8.

—— 'Pope Urban II and the Idea of Crusade', *Studi Medievali*, 3(36) (1995), 721–42.

—— 'The Reform Papacy and the Origin of the Crusades', *Concile de Clermont*, 65–83.

—— *Pope Gregory VII, 1073–85* (Oxford, 1998)

DELARUELLE, E., 'The Crusading Idea in Cluniac Literature', N. Hunt (ed.), *Cluniac Monasticism in the Central Middle Ages* (London, 1971), 191–212.

EBERSOLT, J., *Orient et Occident: recherches sur les influences byzantines et orientales en France avant et pendant les croisades*, 2nd edn. (Paris, 1954).

ERDMANN, C., *The Origin of the Idea of Crusade* (Princeton, 1977).

ESS, J., VAN, *Chiliastische Erwartungen und die Versuchung der Göttlichkeit: der Kalif al-Hakim* (Heidelberg, 1977).

FLORI, J., 'Réforme, reconquista, croisade: l'idée de reconquête dans la correspondence pontifical d'Alexandre II à Urban II', *Cahiers de Civilisation Médiévale*, 40 (1997), 317–35.

—— *Pierre l'ermite et la première croisade* (Paris, 1999).

FRANCE, J. (ed.), *Rodulfi Glabri Historiarum Libri Quinti* (Oxford, 1989).

—— *Victory in the East: A Military History of the First Crusade* (Cambridge, 1994).

—— 'The Destruction of Jerusalem and the First Crusade', *JEH* 47 (1996), 1–17.

—— 'Les Origines de la première croisade: un nouvel examen', *Autour de la Ic*, 43–56.

—— 'Le Rôle de Jérusalem dans la piété du XIe siècle', M. Balard and A. Ducellier (eds.), *Le Partage du monde: échanges et colonisation dans la Méditerranée médiévale* (Paris, 1998), 151–61.

—— and ZAJAC, W. G. (eds.), *The Crusades and their Sources: Essays Presented to Bernard Hamilton* (Aldershot, 1998).

GABRIELI, F., *Arab Historians of the Crusades*, tr. E. J. Costello (Berkeley, Calif., 1969).

GILCHRIST, J., 'The Erdmann Thesis and the Canon Law 1083–1141', *Crusade and Settlement*, 37–45.

GRABOÏS, A., 'Anglo-Norman England and the Holy Land', *Anglo-Norman Studies*, 7 (1984), 132–41.

HAGENMEYER, H., *Peter der Eremite* (Leipzig, 1879).

HAMILTON, B., 'The Way to Rome and Jerusalem: Pilgrim Routes from France and Germany at the Time of the Crusades', *Santiago, Roma, Jerusalén* (Santiago, 1999), 135–44.

HASKINS, C. H., 'A Canterbury Monk at Constantinople c.1090', *EHR* 25 (1910), 293–5.

HILLENBRAND, C., *The Crusades: Islamic Perspectives* (Edinburgh, 1999).

HOFFMANN, H., *Gottesfriede und Treuga Dei*, MGH SS, 20 (1964).

JORANSON, E., 'The Great German Pilgrimage of 1064–5', L. J. Paetow (ed.), *The Crusades and other Historical Essays to D. C. Munro* (New York, repr. 1968), 3–43.

KEDAR, B. Z. (ed.), *The Horns of Hattin* (Jerusalem, 1992).

LABANDE, E.-R., '*Ad limina*: le pèlerin médiéval au terme de sa démarche', P. Gallais and Y-J. Riou (eds.), *Mélanges offerts à R. Crozet* (Poitiers, 1966), i. 283–91.

LANDES, R., *Relics, Apocalypse and the Deceits of History: Adhemar of Chabannes* (Cambridge, Mass., 1995).

—— 'The Massacre of 1010: On the Origins of Popular Anti-Jewish Violence in Western Europe', J. Cohen (ed.), *From Witness to Witchcraft: Jews and Judaism in Medieval Christian Thought* (Wiesbaden, 1996), 79–112.

McROBERTS, D., 'Scottish Pilgrims to the Holy Land', *Innes Review*, 20 (1969), 80–106.

MAETZKE, A. M. (ed.), *Il Volto Santo di Sansepolcro* (Milan, 1994).

MAYER, H. E., *The Crusades*, 2nd edn. (Oxford, 1988).

MORRIS, C., 'Memorials of the Holy Places and Blessings from the East', R. N. Swanson, *The Holy Land, Holy Lands*, SCH 36 (2000), 90–109.

OUSTERHOUT, R., 'Rebuilding the Temple: Constantine Monomachus and the Holy Sepulchre', *Journal of the Society of Architectural Historians*, 48 (1989), 66–78.

PÉQUIGNOT, C., 'L'Église de Villeneuve d'Aveyron: une église bâtie à l'image du Saint Sépulcre', *Les Cahiers de St-Michel de Cuxa*, 26 (1995), 147–53.

PHILLIPS, J. (ed.), *The First Crusade: Origins and Impact* (Manchester, 1997).

PIUSSI, S., 'Il Santo Sepolcro di Aquileia', *Antichità altoadriatiche*, 12 (1977), 511–59.

RIANT, P., *Expéditions et pèlerinages des Scandinaves en Terre Sainte* (Paris, 1865).

RILEY-SMITH, J., *The First Crusade and the Idea of Crusading* (London, 1986).
—— *The Crusades: A Short History* (London, 1987).
—— J. (ed.), *The Oxford Illustrated History of the Crusades* (Oxford, 1995).
—— *The First Crusaders, 1095–1131* (Cambridge, 1997).
—— RILEY-SMITH, L. and J., *The Crusades: Idea and Reality, 1095–1274* (London, 1981).
RINGEL, I. H., '*Ipse transfert regna et mutat tempora*: Beobachtungen zur Herkunft von Dan. 2:21 bei Urban II', in *Deus qui mutat tempora: Fs. für Alfons Becker* (Sigmaringen, 1987), 137–56.
ROBINSON, I. S., 'Gregory VII and the Soldiers of Christ', *History*, 58 (1973), 169–92.
RÖHRICHT, R., *Die Deutschen im Heiligen Lande* (Innsbrück, 1894).
SCHILLER, G., *Iconography of Christian Art: The Passion of Jesus Christ* (London, 1972).
SCHULZE, U., 'Ezzolied', *Lexikon des Mittelalters*, iv. 198–9.
SIVAN, E., *L'Islam et la croisade* (Paris, 1968).
SMAIL, R. C., *Crusading Warfare*, 2nd edn. with bibliography by C. J. Marshall (Cambridge, 1994).
SOUTHERN, R. W., *The Making of the Middle Ages* (London, 1953).
SUMPTION, J., *Pilgrimage: An Image of Medieval Religion* (London, 1975).
WEBB, D., *Pilgrims and Pilgrimage in the Medieval West* (London, 1999).

6. LATIN JERUSALEM

BARBER, M., *The New Knighthood: a History of the Order of the Temple* (Cambridge, 1994).
—— (ed.), *The Military Orders*, 2 vols. (Aldershot, 1994–8).
BAUMGÄRTNER, I., 'Die Wahrnehmung Jerusalems auf mittelalterlichen Weltkarten', *JerKonflikte*, 271–334.
BERRY, V. G., 'Peter the Venerable and the Crusades', G. Constable and J. Kritzeck (eds.), *Petrus Venerabilis, 1156–1956* (Rome, 1956), 141–62.
BOAS, A. J., *Crusader Archaeology: The Material Culture of the Latin East* (London, 1999).
—— *Jerusalem in the Time of the Crusades* (London, 2001).
BOEREN, P. C. (ed.), *Rorgo Fretellus de Nazareth et sa description de la Terre Sainte* (Amsterdam, 1980).
BRESC-BAUTIER, G. (ed.) *Le Cartulaire du chapitre du S-Sépulchre de Jérusalem* (Paris, 1984).
CERRINI, S., 'Le Fondateur de l'ordre du Temple à ses frères: Hugues de Payns et le *Sermo Christi militibus*', *Dei gesta per Francos*, 99–110.
COLE, P. J., *The Preaching of the Crusades to the Holy Land, 1095–1270* (Cambridge, Mass., 1991).
CONSTABLE, G., 'The Second Crusade as Seen by Contemporaries', *Traditio*, 9 (1953), 213–79.

—— 'Opposition to Pilgrimage in the Middle Ages', *Studia Gratiana*, 19 (1976), 125–46.

—— (ed.), 'Petri Venerabilis Sermones Tres', *RB* 64 (1954), 224–54.

—— 'The Place of the Crusader in Medieval Society', *Viator*, 29 (1998).

DONDI, C., 'The Liturgy of the Holy Sepulchre (XII–XVI Century)', Ph.D., London, 2000, 377–403.

EDBURY, P. W. (ed.), *Crusade and Settlement* (Cardiff, 1985).

EDGINGTON, S. B., 'The Hospital of St John in Jerusalem', Z. Amar and others (eds.), *Medicine in Jerusalem throughout the Ages* (Tel Aviv, 1999), pp. ix–xxv.

—— 'Holy Land, Holy Lance: Religious Ideas in the *Chanson d'Antioche*', R. N. Swanson, *The Holy Land, Holy Lands*, SCH 36 (2000), 142–53.

ELM, [C.] K., 'Die Eroberung Jerusalems im Jahre 1099', *JerKonflikte*, 31–54.

—— 'La liturgia della chiesa latina di Gerusalemme all'epoca delle crociate', *Crociate*, 243–51.

—— 'St Pelagius in Denkendorf', K. Elm and others (eds.), *Landesgeschichte und Geistesgeschichte: Fs. für O. Herding* (Stuttgart, 1977), 80–130.

—— 'Kanoniker und Ritter vom Heiligen Grab', J. Fleckenstein and M. Hellmann, *Die geistlichen Ritterorden Europas*, VuF 26 (1980), 141–69.

—— 'Die *vita canonica* des regulierten Chorherren vom Heiligen Grab in Jerusalem', M. Derwich (ed.), *La Vie quotidienne des moines et chanoines réguliers au moyen âge et temps modernes* (Wrocław, 1995), 181–92.

—— 'L'Ordre des chanoines réguliers du S- Sépulchre de Jérusalem', *Helvetia Sacra*, 4 (Basle, 1996), 137–96.

EMERY, P.-Y. (ed.), *Bernard de Clairvaux, Éloge de la Nouvelle Chevalerie*, SC 367 (1990).

FAVREAU, M. L., 'Zur Pilgerfahrt des Grafen Rudolf von Pfullendorf 1180', *Zs. für die Geschichte des Oberrheins*, 123 (1975), 31–45.

FLECKENSTEIN, J., and HELLMANN, M., *Die geistlichen Ritterorden Europas*, VuF, 26 (1980).

FOLDA, J. (ed.), *Crusader Art in the Twelfth Century*, British Archaeological Reports, International Series, 152 (1982).

—— 'Art in the Latin East', *Oxford Illustrated History* of the Crusades (Oxford, 1995), 141–59.

—— *The Art of the Crusaders in the Holy Land, 1098–1187* (Cambridge, 1995).

FRIEDMAN, Y., 'The City of the King of Kings: Jerusalem in the Crusader Period', *Centrality*, 190–216.

GERVERS, M. (ed.), *The Second Crusade and the Cistercians* (New York, 1992).

GOSS, V. P. (ed.) *The Meeting of Two Worlds: Cultural Exchanges between East and West during the Period of the Crusades* (Kalamazoo, 1986).

GRABOÏS, A., 'Le Pèlerin occidental en Terre Sainte à l'époque des croisades et ses réalités: la relation de pèlerinage de Jean de Wurtzbourg', *Études de Civilisation Médiévale: mélanges offerts à E.-R. Labande* (Poitiers, 1974), 367–76.

—— 'The Crusade of King Louis VII: A Reconsideration', *Crusade and Settlement*, 94–104.

—— 'Louis VII pèlerin', *Revue d'Histoire de l'Église de France*, 74 (1988), 5–22.

—— 'La Fondation de l'abbaye du *Templum Domini* et la légende du Temple de Jérusalem au XIIe siècle', *Autour de la 1c*, 231–7.

HAMILTON, B., 'Rebuilding Zion: the Holy Places of Jerusalem in the Twelfth Century', D. Baker (ed.), *Renaissance and Renewal in Christian History*, SCH 14 (1977), 105–16.

—— *The Latin Church in the Crusader States: The Secular Church* (London, 1980).

—— 'The Impact of Crusader Jerusalem on Western Christendom', *Catholic Historical Review*, 80 (1994), 695–713.

HIESTAND, R. (ed.), *Papsturkunden für Templer und Johanniter* (Göttingen, 1972–84), i–ii.

—— 'Die Anfänge der Johanniter', and M. Melville, 'Les Débuts de l'Ordre du Temple', J. Fleckenstein and Hellmann, *Die geistlichen Ritterorden Europas*, VuF 26 (1980), 23–80.

—— 'Kardinalbischof Matthäus von Albano, das Konzil von Troyes und die Entstehung des Templerordens', *Zs. für Kirchengeschichte*, 99 (1988), 295–325.

—— 'Un centre intellectuel en Syrie du Nord?', *Moyen-Âge* 100 (1994), 7–36.

HOCH, M., 'The Price of Failure: The Second Crusade as a Turning-point in the History of the Latin East?', J. Phillips and M. Hoch (eds.), *The Second Crusade: Scope and Consequences* (Manchester, 2001).

HOUSLEY, N., 'Jerusalem and the Development of the Crusade Idea, 1099–1128', *Horns of Hattin*, 27–40.

JASPERT, N., *Stift und Stadt . . . Santa Eulàlia, Barcelona* (Berlin, 1996).

—— ' "Pro nobis qui pro vobis oramus, orate": die Kathedralkapitel von Compostella und Jerusalem in der ersten Hälfte des 12 Jahrhunderts', *Santiago, Roma, Jerusalén* (Santiago, 1999), 187–212.

JOTISCHKY, A., 'History and Memory as Factors in Greek Orthodox Pilgrimage to the Holy Land under Crusader Rule', R. N. Swanson, *The Holy Land, Holy Lands*, SCH 36 (2000), 110–22.

KATZIR, Y., 'The Conquests of Jerusalem 1099 and 1187: Historical Memory and Religious Typology', *Meeting of Two Worlds* (1986), 103–13.

KEDAR, B. Z. (ed.), *Outremer: Studies in the History of the Crusading Kingdom of Jerusalem Presented to Joshua Prawer* (Jerusalem, 1982).

—— (ed.), 'The *Tractatus de locis et statu sancte terre ierosolomitane*', *Crusades and Sources*, 111–33.

KENAAN-KEDAR, N., 'Symbolic Meaning in Crusader Architecture: The Twelfth-Century Dome of the Holy Sepulchre Church in Jerusalem', *Cahiers Archéologiques*, 34 (1986), 109–17.

KÜHNEL, B., 'L'arte crociata tra Oriente e Occidente', *Crociate*, 341–53

LABANDE, E. R., 'Recherches sur les pèlerins dans l'Europe des XIe et XIIe siècles', *CCM* 1 (1958), 159–69, 339–47.

—— 'Pellegrini o crociati? Mentalità e comportamenti a Gerusalemme nel secolo XII', *Aevum*, 54 (1980), 217–30.

McGINN, B., '*Iter Sancti Sepulchri*: The Piety of the First Crusaders', R. E. Sullivan and others (eds.), *Essays on Medieval Civilization* (Austin, Tex., 1978), 33–71.

MAIER, C. T., 'Crisis, Liturgy and the Crusade in the Twelfth and Thirteenth Centuries', *JEH* 48 (1997), 628–57.

MENACHE, S., *The* Vox Dei: *Communication in the Middle Ages* (Oxford, 1990).

MILLER, T. S., 'The Knights of St John and Hospitals of the Latin West', *Speculum*, 53 (1978), 709–33.

MORRIS, C., 'Propaganda for War: the Dissemination of the Crusading Ideal in the Twelfth Century', W. J. Shiels (ed.), *The Church and War*, SCH 20 (1983), 79–101.

—— 'Picturing the Crusades', *Crusades and Sources*, 195–216.

—— and ROBERTS, P. (eds.), *Pilgrimage: The English Experience from Becket to Bunyan* (Cambridge, 2002).

NICHOLSON, H., *Templars, Hospitallers and Teutonic Knights: Images of the Military Orders, 1128–1291* (Leicester, 1993).

OWST, G. R., *Literature and Pulpit in Medieval England* (Cambridge, 1933).

PRINGLE, D., 'The Planning of some Pilgrimage Churches in Crusader Palestine', *World Archaeology*, 18 (1989), 341–62.

—— *The Churches of the Crusader Kingdom of Jerusalem: A Corpus*, 2 vols. (Cambridge, 1993–8).

RILEY-SMITH, J., *The Knights of St John in Jerusalem and Cyprus, c.1050–1310* (London, 1967).

—— 'Peace Never Established: The Case of the Kingdom of Jerusalem', *TRHS* 5 (28) (1978), 87–102.

—— 'Crusading as an Act of Love', *History*, 65 (1980), 177–92.

ROUTLEDGE, M., 'Songs', *Oxford Illustrated History of the Crusades* (Oxford, 1995), 91–111, 403.

ROWE, J. G., 'Alexander III and the Jerusalem Crusade', *Crusaders and Muslims*, 112–32.

SAUER, C., '*Theodericus, Libellus de Locis Sanctis*: Architekturbeschreibungen eines Pilgers', G. Kerscher (ed.), *Hagiographie und Kunst* (Berlin, 1993), 213–39.

SAVAGE, H. L., 'Pilgrimages and Pilgrims' Shrines in Palestine and Syria after 1095', H. W. Hazard (ed.), *A History of the Crusades* (Wisconsin, 1977), iv. 36–68.

SELWOOD, D. E., '*Quidam autem dubitaverunt:* The Saint, the Sinner, the Temple and a Possible Chronology', *Autour de la* 1c, 221–37.

SMAIL, R. C., 'Relations between Latin Syria and the West, 1149–87', *TRHS* 5 (19) (1969), 1–20.

UPTON-WARD, J. M., (tr.), *The Rule of the Templars* (Woodbridge, 1992).

WILKINSON, J., and others (eds.), *Jerusalem Pilgrimage, 1099–1185*, Hakluyt Society (London, 1988), ser. 2. 167. Translations of all major twelfth-century narratives.

7. CHRISTENDOM REFASHIONED

ANDREA, A. J., and RACHLIN, P. I., 'Holy War, Holy Relics, Holy Theft: The Anonymous of Soissons' *De Terra Iherosolimitana*', *Historical Reflections/ Reflexions Historiques*, 18 (1992), 147–75.

BASCHET, J., 'Inventivité et sérialité des images médiévales', *Annales HSS*, 51 (1996), 93–133.

BRESC-BAUTIER, M., 'Les Imitations du S. Sépulcre de Jérusalem (IX–XVe siècles): archéologie d'une dévotion', *Revue d'Histoire de la Spiritualité*, 50 (1974), 319–42.

CAMILLE, M., *The Gothic Idol: Ideology and Image-Making in Medieval Art* (Cambridge, 1989).

CROZET, R., 'Nouvelles remarques sur les cavaliers sculptés de Constantin aux XIe et XIIe siècles', *CCM* I (1958), 27–36.

DENNY, D., 'A Romanesque Fresco in Auxerre Cathedral', *Gesta*, 25 (1986), 197–202.

DERBES, A., 'A Crusading Fresco Cycle at the Cathedral of Le Puy', *Art Bulletin*, 73 (4) (1991), 561–76.

—— 'The Frescoes of Schwarzrheindorf, Arnold of Wied and the Second Crusade', M. Gervers, *The Second Crusade and the Cistercians* (New York, 1992), 141–54.

DUGGAN, L. G., 'Was Art Really the "Book of the Illiterate"?', *Word and Image*, 5 (1989), 227–51.

DURAND, J., 'Reliquie e reliquiari depredati in Oriente e a Bisanzio al tempo delle crociate', *Crociate*, 378–89.

ENAUD, R., 'Peintures rurales découvertes dans une dépendance de la cathédrale du Puy-en-Velay', *Monuments Historiques*, 14 (4) (1968), 30–76.

FAVREAU, R., 'Du triomphe de la mort aux suffrances de la passion', *Supplice*, 72–82.

GERISH, D., 'The True Cross and the Kings of Jerusalem', *Journal of the Haskins Society*, 8 (1996), 137–55.

HAMILTON, B., *The Leper King and his Heirs: Baldwin IV and the Crusader Kingdom of Jerusalem* (Cambridge, 2000).

JASPERT, N., 'Vergegenwärtigungen Jerusalems in Architektur und Reliquienkult', *JerKonflikte*, 219–70.

JUNGMANN, J. A., *The Mass of the Roman Rite*, 2 vols. (New York, 1951–5).

KATZENELLENBOGEN, A., *Allegories of the Virtues and Vices in Medieval Art* (London, 1939).

KOHLER, C., 'Un rituel et un bréviaire du S.-Sépulcre de Jérusalem', *Archives de l'Orient Latin*, 8 (1900–1), 383–500.

LAARHOVEN, J. VAN, 'Chrétienté et croisade', *Cristianesimo nella Storia*, 6 (1985), 27–43.

LE GOFF, J., *Medieval Civilization*, tr. J. Barrow (Oxford, 1988).

LEJEUNE, R., and STIENNON, J., *The Legend of Roland in the Middle Ages*, 2 vols. (London, 1971).

LIGATO, G., 'The Political Meanings of the Relic of the Holy Cross among the Crusaders and in the Latin Kingdom of Jerusalem: An Example of 1185', *Autour de la 1c*, 315–30.

LINDER, A., 'The Liturgy of the Liberation of Jerusalem', *Mediaeval Studies*, 52 (1990), 110–31.

LUKKEN, G., 'Les Transformations du rôle liturgique du peuple: la contribution de la sémiotique a l'histoire de la liturgie', *Omnes Circumadstantes*, 15–30.

MEURER, H., 'Zu den Staurotheken der Kreuzfahrer', *Zs. für Kunstgeschichte*, 48 (1985), 65–76.

MOULIN, C., 'Les Églises et chapelles Sainte-Croix en France', *Revue d'Histoire de l'Église de France*, 62 (1976), 349–60.

MURRAY, A. V., ' "Mighty against the enemies of Christ": The Relic of the True Cross in the Armies of the Kingdom of Jerusalem', *Crusades and Sources*, 217–38.

NORMAN, J. S., *Metamorphoses of an Allegory: The Iconography of the Psychomachia in Medieval Art* (New York, 1988).

PHILLIPS, J., *Defenders of the Holy Land: Relations between the Latin East and the West, 1119–87* (Oxford, 1996).

PIVA, P., 'Die "Kopien" der Grabeskirche im romanischen Abendland', R. Cassanelli (ed.), *Die Zeit der Kreuzzüge: Geschichte und Kunst* (Stuttgart, 2000), 97–119, 290–3.

RIANT, P., 'Des dépouilles religieuses enlevées à Constantinople au XIIIe siècle par les Latins', *Mémoires de la Société Nationale des Antiquaires de France*, 26 (1875), 1–214.

—— *Exuviae sacrae Constantinopolitanae* 3 vols. (Geneva, 1877–1904).

SCHMITT, J.-C., 'La Culture de l'*imago*', *Annales HSS*, 51 (1996), 3–36.

SCHÖNFELDER, A., 'Die Prozessionen der Lateiner in Jerusalem zur Zeit der Kreuzzüge', *Historisches Jahrbuch*, 32 (1911), 578–97.

SEIDEL, L., 'Holy Warriors: The Romanesque Rider and the Fight against Islam', T. P. Murphy (ed.), *The Holy War* (Columbus, Ohio, 1976), 33–54.

—— *Songs of Glory: The Romanesque Façades of Aquitaine* (Chicago, 1981).

TABAA, Y., 'Monuments with a Message: Propagation of Jihad under Nur al-Din', *Meeting of Two Worlds*, 223–40

8. FAILURE AND ENDEAVOUR, 1187–1291

BEAUNE, C., 'Les Sanctuaires royaux', P. Nora (ed.), *Les Lieux de mémoire, ii. La Nation* (Paris, 1986), 57–87.

—— *The Birth of an Ideology: Myths and Symbols of Nation in Late-Medieval France* (Berkeley, 1991).

BIRCH, J., 'James of Vitry and the Ideology of Pilgrimage', *Pilgrimage Explored*, 79–93.

BOLTON, B., 'Message, Celebration, Offering: The Place of Twelfth- and

Thirteenth-Century Liturgical Drama as "Missionary Theatre" ', R. N. Swanson (ed.), *Continuity and Change in Christian Worship*, SCH 35 (1999), 89–103.

COLE, P., and others, 'Application of Theology to Current Affairs: Memorial Sermons on the Dead of Mansurah and on Innocent IV', *Historical Review*, 63 (1990), 227–47.

CONNELL, C. W., 'Pro- and Anti-Crusade Propaganda: An Overview', P. W. Cummins and others (eds.), *Literary and Historical Perspectives of the Middle Ages* (Morgantown, 1982), 208–20.

DANIEL, E. R., *The Franciscan Conception of Mission in the High Middle Ages* (Kentucky, 1975).

DARDANO, M., 'Un itinerario dugentesco per la Terra Santa', *Studi Medievali*, 3 (7) (1966), 154–96.

DICHTER, B., *The Orders and Churches of Crusader Acre* (Acre, 1979).

DONDAINE, A., 'Ricoldiana', *Archivum Fratrum Praedicatorum*, 37 (1967), 119–79.

EVANGELISTI, P., *Fidenzio da Padova e la letteratura crociata-missionaria minorita* (Bologna, 1998).

FAVREAU-LILIE, M.-L., 'Durchreisende und Zuwanderer: zur Rolle der Italiener in den Kreuzfahrerstaaten', H. E. Mayer (ed.), *Die Kreuzfahrerstaaten als multikulturelle Gesellschaft* (Munich, 1997), 206–17.

GRABOÏS, A., 'Christian Pilgrims in the Thirteenth Century and the Latin Kingdom of Jerusalem: Burchard of Mount Sion', *Outremer*, 285–96.

—— 'Les Pèlerins occidentaux en Terre Sainte et Acre: d'Accon des croisés à St-Jean-d'Acre', *Studi Medievali*, 3 (24) (1983), 247–64.

—— 'Terre Sainte et Orient latin vus par Willebrand d'Oldenbourg', *Dei gesta per Francos*, 261–8.

HOUSLEY, N., *The Italian Crusades* (Oxford, 1982).

JACOBY, D., 'Pilgrimage in Crusader Acre: The *Pardouns d'Acre*', *De Sion*, 105–17.

JORDAN, W. C., *Louis IX and the Challenge of the Crusade* (Princeton, 1979).

KAPPLER, R., 'L'Autre et le prochain dans la *Pérégrination* de Ricold de Monte Croce', I. Zinguer (ed.), *Miroirs de l'altérité et voyages au Proche-orient* (Geneva, 1991), 163–72.

KEDAR B. Z., 'The Passenger List of a Crusader Ship, 1250: Towards the History of the Popular Element on the Seventh Crusade', *Studi Medievali*, 3 (13) (1972), 267–79.

—— *Crusade and Mission* (Princeton, 1984).

LINDER, A., '*Deus venerunt gentes*: Psalm 78 (79) in the Liturgical Commemoration of the Destruction of Latin Jerusalem', A. Bat-Sheva and others (eds.), *Medieval Studies in Honour of Avrom Saltman* (Jerusalem, 1995), 145–71.

—— 'The Loss of Christian Jerusalem in Late Medieval Liturgy', Levine, 393–407.

LITTLE, D., 'Jerusalem under the Ayyubids and Mamluks, 1197–1516', K. J. Asali, *Jerusalem in History*, new edn. (London, 1997).

LONGÈRE, J., 'Deux sermons de Jacques de Vitry *Ad peregrinos*', P. A. Sigal (ed.), *L'Image du pèlerin* (Gramat, 1994), 93–103.

LUPPRIAN, K. E., *Die Beziehungen der Päpste zu islamischen und mongolischen Herrschern* (Rome, 1981).

MAIER, C. T., *Preaching the Crusades: Mendicant Friars and the Cross in the Thirteenth Century* (Cambridge, 1994).

—— *Crusading Propaganda and Ideology: Model Sermons for the Preaching of the Cross* (Cambridge, 2000).

MICHELANT, H., and RAYNAUD, G. (eds.), *Pèlerinages et pardouns d'Acre: Itinéraires à Jérusalem et descriptions de la Terre Sainte* (Geneva, 1882), 227–36.

MONNERET DE VILLARD, U., *Il libro della Peregrinazione . . . di frate Ricoldo da Montecroce* (Rome, 1948).

MULDOON, J., *Popes, Lawyers and Infidels* (Liverpool, 1979).

O'CARROLL, E., *A Thirteenth-Century Preacher's Handbook: Studies in Ms Laud Misc 511* (Toronto, 1997).

PURCELL, M., 'Changing Views of Crusade in the Thirteenth Century', *Journal of Religious History*, 7 (1972), 3–19.

RACHEWILTZ, I. DE, *Papal Envoys to the Great Khan* (London, 1971).

ROSEN-AYALON, M., 'Between Cairo and Damascus: Rural Life and Urban Economics in the Holy Land', T. E. Levy (ed.), *The Archaeology of Society in the Holy Land* (London, 1995), ch. 30.

SCHAEFER, K. R., 'Jerusalem in the Ayyubid and Mamluk Eras', Ph.D. thesis, New York, 1985.

SIBERRY, E., *Criticism of Crusading, 1095–1274* (Oxford, 1985).

STEWART, A. (tr.), Burchard of Mount Sion, PPTS 12 (London, 1896).

STRAYER, J. R., 'France: the Holy Land, the Chosen People, and the Most Christian King', in his *Medieval Statecraft and the Perspectives of History* (Cambridge, Mass., 1971), 300–14.

THROOP, P. A., *Criticism of the Crusade* (repr. Philadelphia, 1975).

THURRE, D., 'I reliquiari al tempo delle crociate da Urbino II a san Luigi', *Crociate*, 362–7.

WEISS, D. H., *Art and Crusade in the Age of St Louis* (Cambridge, 1998).

9. THE 'GREAT PILGRIMAGE' OF THE LATE MIDDLE AGES, 1291–1530

ANDERSON, A., *St Birgitta and the Holy Land* (Stockholm, 1973).

BANDINEL, B. (ed.), *The Itineraries of William Wey* (London, 1856).

BELLORINI, T., and HOADE, E. (trans.), *Fra Niccolò of Poggibonsi, A Voyage Beyond the Seas* (Jerusalem, 1945).

—— (trs.), *Francesco Suriano, Treatise on the Holy Land* (Jerusalem, 1949).

BREFELD, J., *A Guidebook for the Jerusalem Pilgrimage in the Late Middle Ages* (Hilversum, 1994).

CACHEY, T. J. (ed. and tr.), *Petrarch's Guide to the Holy Land* (Indiana, 2002).

CROUZET-PAVAN, E., 'Récits, images et mythes: Venise dans l'*Iter Hierosolymitana*', *Mélanges de l'École Française de Rome*, 96 (1984), 489–535.

DANSETTE, B., 'Les Pèlerinages occidentaux en Terre Sainte: une pratique de la Devotion Moderne à la fin du Moyen Age?', *Archivum Francescanum Historicum*, 72 (1979), 106–33, 330–428.

DELUZ, C., *Le Livre de Jehan de Mandeville: une 'géographie' au XIVe siècle* (Louvain, 1988).

ELLIS, H. (ed.), *The Pylgrymage of Sir Richard Guylforde to the Holy Land, 1506* (London, 1851).

FLINT, V. I. J., 'Christopher Columbus and the Friars', L. Smith and others (eds.), *Intellectual Life in the Middle Ages: Essays Presented to Margaret Gibson* (London, 1992), 295–310.

GANZ-BLÄTTLER, U., *Andacht und Abenteuer: Berichte europäischer Jerusalem- und Santiago-Pilger, 1320–1530* (Tübingen, 1990).

GECK, E. (ed.), *Bernhard von Breydenbach: die Reise ins Heilige Land* (Wiesbaden, 1961).

HEERS, J., and GROER, G. DE (eds.), *Itinéraire d'Anselme Adorne en Terre Sainte, 1470–1* (Paris, 1978).

HIGGINS, I. M., *Writing East: The 'Travels' of Sir John Mandeville* (Philadelphia, 1997).

HONEMANN, V., 'Der Bericht der Hans Rot über seine Pilgerfahrt ins Heilige Land im Jahre 1440', Huschenbert, 306–26.

HOUSLEY, N., *The Later Crusades* (Oxford, 1992).

HOWARD, D. R., *Writers and Pilgrims: Medieval Pilgrimage Narratives and their Posterity* (London, 1980).

HUSCHENBETT, D., 'Die Literatur der deutschen Pilgerreisen nach Jerusalem im späten Mittelalter', *Deutsche Vierteljahresschrift*, 59 (1985), 29–46.

—— 'Die volksprachigen Berichte von Pilgerreisen nach Palästina im spätem Mittelalter', R. Jansen-Sieben (ed.), *Artes Mechanicae en Europe médiévale* (Brussels, 1989), 51–71.

LETTS, M. (tr.), *Pero Tafur: Travels and Adventures, 1435–9* (London, 1926).

—— (tr.), *The Diary of Jörg von Ehingen, 1454* (London, 1929).

—— (tr.), *The Pilgrimage of Arnold von Harff, Knight, 1496–9*, Hakluyt Soc., 2 (94) (London, 1946).

—— *Sir John Mandeville: The Man and his Book* (London, 1949).

LOFTIE, W. J. (ed.), *The Oldest Diarie of Englysshe Travel . . . the Pilgrimage of Sir Richard Torrington to Jerusalem in 1517* (London, 1884).

MILTON, G., *The Riddle and the Knight: In Search of Sir John Mandeville* (London, 1996).

MITCHELL, R. J., *The Spring Voyage* (London, 1964).

MORRIS, B., *St Birgitta of Sweden* (Woodbridge, 1999).

MORRIS, C., 'Pilgrimage to Jerusalem in the Late Middle Ages', *Pilgrimage: The English Experience*, 141–63.

NEWETT, M. M. (tr.), *Canon Pietro Casola's Pilgrimage to Jerusalem in the Year 1494* (Manchester, 1907).

PIRILLO, P. (ed.), *Mariano da Siena: Viaggio fatto al Santo Sepolcro* (Pisa, 1996).

PRESCOTT, H. F. M., *Once to Sinai: The Further Pilgrimage of Friar Felix Fabri* (London, 1957).

SCHEFER, C. (ed.), *Le Voyage d'Outremer de Jean Thenaud* (Paris, 1884).

SCHEIN, S., '*Gesta Dei per Mongolos* 1300: The Genesis of a non-Event', *EHR* 94 (1979), 805–19.

SCHNEIDER, W., *Peregrinatio Hierosolymitana* (Münster, 1982).

SEYMOUR, M. C., 'Sir John Mandeville', in his *Authors of the Middle Ages* (Aldershot, 1994).

STEWART, A. (tr.), *The Wanderings of Felix Fabri*, PPTS 7–10 (London, 1887–97).

——(tr.), *Ludolph von Suchem: Description of the Holy Land, written in 1350*, PPTS (London, 1895).

TINGUELY, F., 'Janus en Terre Sainte: la figure du pèlerin curieux à la Renaissance', *Revue des Sciences Humaines*, 245 (1997), 51–65.

TZANAKI, R., *Mandeville's Medieval Audiences* (Aldershot, 2003)

WATTS, P. M., 'Prophecy and Discovery: On the Spiritual Origins of Christopher Columbus's "Enterprise of the Indies" ', *American Historical Review*, 90 (1985), 73–102.

10. SEPULCHRES AND CALVARIES, 1291–1530

AERS, D., and STALEY, L. (eds.), *The Powers of the Holy: Religion, Politics and Gender in Late Medieval English Culture* (Pennsylvania, 1966).

ALLIATA, E., and KASWALDER, P., 'La settima stazione della Via Crucis e le mura di Gerusalemme', *Studium Biblicum Francescanum*, 45 (1995), 217–46.

ATKINSON, C. W., *Mystic and Pilgrim: the Book and the World of Margery Kempe* (London, 1983).

BANGS, J. D., *Cornelis Engebrechtsz's Leiden: Studies in Cultural History* (Assen, 1979).

BAXANDALL, M., *Painting and Experience in Fifteenth-Century Italy* (Oxford, 1972).

BELTING, H., *The Image and its Public in the Middle Ages* (New York, 1981).

BESTUL, T., *Texts of the Passion: Latin Devotional Literature and Medieval Society* (Pennsylvania, 1996).

BEYER, V., *La Sculpture Strasbourgeoise au XIVs* (Strasburg, 1955), 27–40.

BOURDIER, F. (ed.), *La Sculpture en Savoie au XVe siècle et la mise en tombeau d'Annecy*, Annesci 21 (1978).

BUTLER, S., *Alps and Sanctuaries of Piedmont and the Canton Ticino* (London, 1881).

BUX, N., *Codici Liturgici Latini di Terra Santa* (Jerusalem, 1990), enlivened by a notable English translation.

CARDINI, F., and VANNINI, G. (eds.), *San Vivaldo in Valdelsa: religiosità e società in Valdelsa nel basso medioevo* (Valdelsa, 1980).

CARSLEY, C. A., 'Devotion to the Holy Name: Later Medieval Piety in England', *Princeton University Library Chronicle*, 53 (1992), 156–72.

COUSINS, E., 'The Humanity and the Passion of Christ', J. Raitt, *Christian Spirituality* (London, 1987), 375–91.

DANSETTE, B., 'Les Pèlerins occidentaux du Moyen Age tardif au retour de la Terre Sainte: confréries du S-Sépulcre et paumiers parisiens', *Dei gesta per Francos*, 301–14.

DERBES, A., *Picturing the Passion in Late Medieval Italy* (Cambridge, 1996).

DESPRES, D., *Ghostly Sights: Visual Meditation in Late Medieval Literature* (Oklahoma, 1989).

DUFFY, E., *The Stripping of the Altars: Traditional Religion in England, 1400–1580* (London, 1992).

ELM, K. (ed.), *Quellen zur Geschichte des Ordens vom Heiligen Grabe in Nordwest-europa aus deutschen und niederländischen Archiven, 1191–1603* (Brussels, 1976).

—— 'Kanoniker und Ritter vom Heiligen Grab', J. Fleckenstein and M. Hellmann (eds.), *Die geistlichen Ritterorden Europas*, VuF 26 (1980), 141–69.

FINALDI, G. (ed.), *The Image of Christ* (London, 2000).

FORSYTH, W. H., *The Entombment of Christ: French Sculptures of the Fifteenth and Sixteenth Centuries* (Cambridge, Mass., 1970).

GENSINI, S. (ed.), *La Gerusalemme di San Vivaldo e i sacri monti in Europa* (Pisa, 1989).

GOODMAN, A., *Margery Kempe and Her World* (London, 2002).

HAMILTON, B., 'The Ottomans, the Humanists and the Holy House of Loreto', *Renaissance and Modern Studies*, 31 (1987), 1–19.

HIRSCH, J. C., 'Christ's Blood', *The Boundaries of Faith* (Leiden 1996), 91–110.

HOOD, W., 'The *Sacro Monte* of Varallo: Renaissance Art and Popular Religion', T. G. Verdon (ed.), *Monasticism and the Arts* (Syracuse, 1984).

KENNAN, J. M., 'The Cistercian Pilgrimage to Jerusalem in Guillaume de Deguilville's *Pèlerinage de la vie humaine*', J. R. Sommerfeldt (ed.), *Studies in Medieval Cistercian History*, 2 (Michigan, 1976), 166–85.

KIECKHEFER, R., 'Major Currents in Late Medieval Devotion', J. Raitt, *Christian Spirituality* (London, 1987), 75–108.

KUBLER, G., 'Sacred Mountains in Europe and America', T. G. Verdon and J. Henderson (eds.), *Christianity and the Renaissance: Image and Religious Imagination in the Quattrocento* (Syracuse, 1990), 413–41.

Kunst voor de Beeldenstorm, 2 vols. (The Hague, 1986), i. 35–8, ii. 185.

McKENNA, J. W., 'How God became an Englishman', D. J. Guth and J. W. McKenna (eds.), *Tudor Rule and Revolution: Essays for G. R. Elton from his American Friends* (Cambridge, 1982), 25–53.

MARROW, J. H., *Passion Iconography in North European Art of the Late Middle Ages and Early Renaissance* (Courtrai, 1979).

Merback, M. B., *The Thief, the Cross and the Wheel* (London, 1999).

Meyere, J. A. L. de, *Jan van Scorel, 1495–1562* (Utrecht, 1981).

Raitt, J., *Christian Spirituality: High Middle Ages and Reformation* (London, 1987).

Robin, F., 'Jérusalem dans la peinture franco-flamande (XIII-XVème siècle): abstractions, fantaisies et réalités', *Jérusalem, Rome*, 33–63.

Ross, E. M., *The Grief of God: Images of the Suffering Jesus in Late Medieval England* (Oxford, 1997).

Roth, E., *Der Volkreiche Kalvarienberg in Literatur und Bildkunst des Spätmittelalters*, 2nd edn. (Berlin, 1967).

Sheingorn, P., *The Easter Sepulchre in England* (Kalamazoo, 1987).

Strayer, J. R., 'France: the Holy Land, the Chosen People and the Most Christian King', J. K. Rabb and J. E. Siegel, *Action and Conviction in Early Modern Europe* (Cambridge, Mass: 1971), 3–16.

Thurston, H., *The Stations of the Cross* (London, 1906).

Vaccaro, L., and Riccardi, F. (eds.), *Sacri Monti: devozione, arte e cultura della controriforma* (Milan, 1992).

Van Os, H., *The Art of Devotion in the Late Middle Ages in Europe, 1300–1500* (London, 1994).

Vincent, N., *The Holy Blood: King Henry III and the Westminster Blood Relic* (Cambridge, 2001).

Wachinger, B., 'Die Passion Christi und die Literatur', W. Haug and B. Wachinger (eds.), *Die Passion Christi in Literatur und Kunst des Spätmittelalters* (Tübingen, 1993), 1–20.

Wasser, B. A. J., 'Die peregrinatie van Iherusalem: Pelgrimsverslagen van Nederlandse Jerusalemgangers in de 15e, 16e, en 17 eeuw', *De Gulden Passer*, 69 (1991), 5–72.

Wenzel, S., 'The Pilgrimage of Life as a Late Medieval Genre', *Medieval Studies*, 35 (1973), 370–88.

Wharton, E., *Italian Backgrounds* (London, 1928).

Wogan-Browne, J., and others (eds.), *Medieval Women . . . in Late Medieval Britain: Essays for F. Riddy* (Turnhout, 2000).

Woodall, J., 'Painted Immortality: Portraits of Jerusalem Pilgrims by Antonis Mor and Jan van Scorel', *Jahrbuch des Berliner Museums*, 31 (1989), 149–63.

Ziegler, J. E., *Sculpture of Compassion: the Pietà and the Beguines in the Southern Low Countries, 1300–1600.* (Brussels, 1992).

11. THE END OF THE PILGRIMAGE, 1530–1630

Balard, M. (ed.), *État et colonisation au Moyen Âge et à la Renaissance* (Lyons, 1989).

Blunt, W., *Pietro's Pilgrimage [Pietro della Valle]* (London, 1953).

Bohnstedt, J. W., 'The Infidel Scourge of God: The Turkish Menace as Seen

408 *Bibliography*

by German Pamphleteers of the Reformation', *Transactions of the American Philosophical Society*, NS 58 (9) (1968).

BUSH, M., 'The Pilgrimage of Grace and the Pilgrim Tradition of Holy War', *Pilgrimage: The English Experience*, 178–98.

CALCRAFT, R. P. (ed.), *Francisco Guerrero, El Viage de Hierusalem (Seville, 1592)* (Exeter, 1984).

CAMERON, E., 'For Reasoned Faith or Embattled Creed? Religion for the People in Early Modern Europe', *TRHS* 6 (8) (1998), 165–87.

CARAMAN, P., *Ignatius Loyola* (London, 1990).

CHANEY, E., *The Evolution of the Grand Tour* (London, 1998).

CHAVANON, J., (ed.), *Relation de Terre Sainte (1533–4) par Greffin Affagart* (Paris, 1902).

CONSTABLE, G., 'The Crusading Kingdom of Jerusalem—the first European Colonial Society: A Symposium', *Horns of Hattin*, 341–66.

DANNENFELDT, H. H., 'Leonhard Rauwolf: a Lutheran Pilgrim in Jerusalem', *Archiv für Reformationsgeschichte*, 55 (1964), 18–36.

FINLAY, M. I., 'Colonies—an Attempt at Typology', *TRHS*, 5 (26) (1976), 167–88.

FREIBERG, J., *The Lateran in 1600* (Cambridge, 1995).

GANSS, G. E. (ed.), *Ignatius of Loyola* (New York, 1991).

GOLDBERG, G., '*Peregrinatio, quam vocant Romana*: Miscellanea zu Stellvertreterstätten römischer Hauptkirchen', *Wallfahrt*, 346–51.

GOMEZ-GÉRAUD, M.-C., *Le Crépuscule du Grand Voyage: les récits des pèlerins à Jérusalem, 1458–1612* (Paris, 1999).

GREENBLATT, S., '*Marvelous Possessions'*: The Wonder of the New World* (Oxford, 1991).

HAKLUYT, R., *The Principall Navigations, Voiages and Discoveries of the English Nation* (London, 1589: facsimile edn. Cambridge, 1965).

HOUSLEY, N., 'Crusading as Social Revolt: The Hungarian Peasant Uprising of 1514', *JEH* 49 (1998), 1–18.

—— 'Holy Land or Holy Lands? Palestine and the Catholic West in the Late Middle Ages and Renaissance', R. N. Swanson, *The Holy Land, Holy Lands* SCH 36 (2000), 228–49.

KEEBLE, N. H., ' "To be a Pilgrim": Constructing the Protestant Life in Early Modern England', *Pilgrimage: The English Experience*, 238–56.

LITHGOW, W., *The totall Discourse of the Rare Adventures and Painefull Peregrinations* (Glasgow, 1906).

LAFAYE, J., *Quetzacoatl and Guadalupe: The Formation of Mexican National Consciousness, 1531–1813* (Chicago, 1976).

LAZZERI, Z., 'I santuari di Terrasanta e la famiglia dei Medici', *Archivum Franciscanum Historicum*, 15 (1922), 207–11.

MARAVAL, P., 'Une querelle sur les pèlerinages autour d'un text patristique', *Revue d'Histoire et de Philosophie Religieuses*, 66 (1986), 131–41.

OLDFIELD, J. R., 'City on a Hill: American Exceptionalism and the Elect Nation R. N. Swanson, *The Holy Land Holy Lands*, SCH 36 (2000), 299–318.

PICCIRILLO, M., 'In the Service of the Holy Sepulchre: The Documentary Work of Three Franciscans of the 16th and 17th Centuries', *Patterns of the Past*, 167–78.

PRAWER, J., *The Latin Kingdom of Jerusalem: European Colonialism in the Middle Ages* (London, 1972), ch. 18.

—— 'The Roots of Medieval Colonialism', *Meeting of Two Worlds*, 23–38.

PURCHAS, S. (ed.), *Hakluytus Posthumus, or Purchas his Pilgrims, by Samuel Purchas*, Hakluyt Society (repr. Glasgow, 1905).

SANDYS, G., *A Relation of a Journey begun A.D. 1610* (S. Purchas (ed.), *Purchas his Pilgrims* (Glasgow, 1905), viii. 88–248).

TORRÒ, J., 'Jérusalem ou Valence: la première colonie d'Occident', *Annales HSS*, 55 (2000), 983–1008.

VAUGHAN, D. M., *Europe and the Turk, 1350–1700* (Liverpool, 1954).

VERLINDEN, C., 'De la colonisation médiévale italienne au Levant à l'expansion ibérique en Afrique', *Bulletin de l'Institut Historique belge de Rome*, 53–4 (1983–4), 99–121.

YERASIMOS, S., 'Voyageurs européens en Palestine ottomane, 1517–1600', *Revue d'Études Palestiniennes*, 11 (1984).

ZANZI, L., *Sacri monti e dintorni: studi sulla cultura religiosa e artistica della Controriforma* (Milan, 1992).

Biblical Index

General Index